Boy From Pocatello

TITLES BY ALAN NICHOLS*

The Historical & Technical Sciences for Discovery of the Secret Tomb of Emperor Chinggis Qa'an (2022)

The Hunted & The Hunter: The Search for the Secret Tomb of Chinggis Qa'an (2021)

Brothers at War: Two American Brothers in World War I as Volunteers in the French Army (2021)

Curriculum Guide for the Arts: Master Plan for Curriculum … San Francisco Public Schools, ed. (2010)

Travels with Annie [Short Stories] (2005)

Adventures in Time [Poems] (2000)

Journey — A Bicycle Odyssey Through Central Asia (1991)

San Quentin — Inside the Walls (1991)

To Climb a Sacred Mountain [Travel] (1976)

Water for California (2 vols.) (1965)

San Francisco Commuter [Poems] (1962)

FLAG EXPEDITIONS

XINGGIANG / TIBET MOUNTAIN BIKE EXPEDITION …
May-July 1986 (56 YEARS OLD)

CENTRAL ASIA BIKE EXPEDITION … Turkmenistan / Uzbekistan / Tajikistan / Turkestan / Kazakhstan … *June-July 1993* (63 YEARS OLD)

JOURNEY II CYCLING THE SILK WEB … *July 1998* (68 YEARS OLD)

GANGKHAR PUENSUM II … Bhutan's Sacred Mountain …
September 2001 (72 YEARS OLD)

CYCLING THE SILK WEB … Iran / Turkey …
March 25 - June 2, 2004 (74 YEARS OLD)

CYCLING THE SILK WEB … Zian / China / Kashgar / Xingiang …
April 10 - May 25, 2005 (75 YEARS OLD)

KANG RINPOCHE / LAKE MANASARAOVAR / PILGRIMAGES EXPEDITION …
Sept 28 - November 2, 2007 (77 YEARS OLD)

PILGRIMAGE TO MONGOLIA … Sacred Mountains, Chinggis Qa'an, Roy Chapman Andrews – all God's of their Times …
May 22 - July 1, 2010 (80 YEARS OLD)

DEAD MEN TELL TALES: THE TOMB OF CHINGGIS QA'AN … Inner Mongolia, Ninjsia … *September 15 - October 12, 2012* (82 YEARS OLD)

SURVIVAL AND DEATH … Prairie Flora on the Missouri Riveri …
July 26–August 2, 2013 (83 YEARS OLD)

CARDIAC ARRHYTHMIA AT ALTITUDE . . . *2018* (88 YEARS OLD)

* For a complete list see *Author Publications and Explorations,* pg. 661.

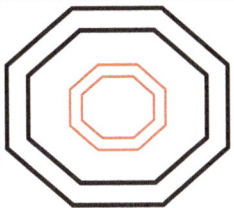 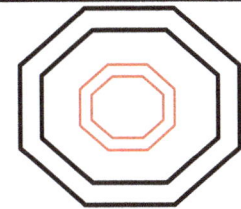

Boy From Pocatello

Alan Nichols
GRADUATE, Pocatello High School
BACHELOR OF ARTS, Political Science, Stanford University
DOCTOR OF JURISPRUDENCE, Stanford University Law School
DOCTOR OF SCIENCE. University of California/CCPM (Hon.)

REGENT PRESS
San Francisco, California
2025

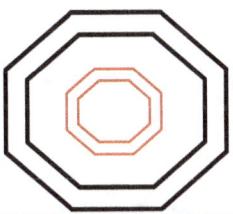 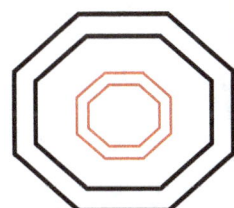

Copyright © 2025 by Alan Nichols

[Hardcover]
ISBN 13: 978-1-58790-680-0
ISBN 10: 1-58790-680-5

[Softcover]
ISBN 13: 978-1-58790-681-7
ISBN 10: 1-58790-681-3

[E-Book]
ISBN 13: 978-1-58790-682-4
ISBN 10: 1-58790-682-1

Library of Congress Control Number: 2025034202

All rights reserved under International and Pan-American Copyright Conventions. No part of this book may be used or reproduced in any manner whatsoever without the written permission of Regent Press, except in the case of brief quotations embodied in critical articles and reviews.

FRONT COVER: The author and his favorite Tibetan horse (which are small and tough) on his journey out of Lhasa, Tibet's capital. (That's why he has his best Tibetan smile.) The Dalai Lama's former historic home Potola, from which he fled when the PLA (Chinese so called People's Liberation Army) invaded and occupied Tibet, is behind the mountain range behind him.

PHOTO CREDITS: All images are from the author's private collection, other private collections or from stock photo sources and public domain sites on the internet. Every attempt has been made to confirm copyright clearance. Please address any issues to Regent Press.

Manufactured in the United States of America
REGENT PRESS
www.regentpress.net
regentpress@mindspring.com
San Francisco, California

BOY FROM POCATELLO
IS DEDICATED

TO MY FATHER,
JOHN R. NICHOLS, PH.D., STANFORD

AND MY FATHER'S BROTHER, MY UNCLE
ALAN H. NICHOLS, B.A., STANFORD

BOTH WAR HEROES AND MEN OF SERVICE
TO THEIR BELOVED FAMILY,
THEIR NATION, AND THEIR WORLD,
LOCALLY AND GLOBALLY.
THANK YOU BOTH.

LOVE.
ALAN,
YOUR SON
YOUR NEPHEW

Contents

PART I
It's A Long Way To (or From) Pocatello

[1930-1935] Palo Alto Seedling / 3

Letter to my Uncle / 10

[1935-1941] Jack... King of the "Neigyhood" / 16

[1935-1940] Honey Trips / 23

[1938-1946] Fallen Leaf Paradise / 26

[1940s] The Spirit World / 31

[1942-1945] "Pokey" to Pocatello / 34

[1944] A Latin Disaster... NYC / 37

[1944] Back To Honey's / 40

[1945] "Home Body" Returns / 42

[1944-1946] Psyche Talk / 52

[1947-1948] Academia in the Hills of Idaho State University / 56

[1939-1949] Jobs... Jobs... Jobs / 59

[1951-1953] Stanford University / 64

[1952-1954] The Korean War / 68

[1954-1990] Stanford Law... Another SF Lawyer / 72

Prioritas – Femitas / 80

"Nihonjin Desu Ka" / Japan / Happiness / 88

Dalai Lama Go Home / 92

PART II
To Climb a Sacred Mountain (... and Listen)

HOLY MOUNTAIN JOURNEYS / 107

THE PILGRIM'S TRAILHEAD / 108

PILGRIMS PLANNING AROUND THE WORLD GUIDE / 115

SACRED MOUNT LASSEN ... CALIFORNIA / 131
The Violent, Mysterious Totem

PART III
Sacred Mountains ... Founders, Spirits, Religions

SONGS & PSALMS OF THE MOUNTAIN GURU / 169

SACRED MOUNTAIN SPIRITS AND GURUS / 185

MOUNTAINS AS SACRED SPACES / 193

SACRED MOUNTAINS:

KAILASH ... TIBET / 197
Worship on a High Circle

OLYMPUS ... GREECE / 209
The Home Throne of Zeus

FUJI-SAN ... JAPAN / 233
The Way of All Pilgrims

OMINE-SAN ... JAPAN / 253
The Ascent to Buddhahood

SINAI ... EGYPT / 275
In Moses' Footsteps

ARUNACHALA ... INDIA / 299
Who Am I?

THE FIVE TAO SACRED MOUNTAINS OF CHINA / 325

TAI-SHAN / 331

HENG-SHAN (NORTH) / 333

SONG-SHAN / 335

HENG-SHAN (SOUTH) / 337

HUA-SHAN / 341

MOUNTAIN X / 353
Cannot Be Revealed

TABOR . . . ISRAEL / 363
Voices From the Mountains

HIRA . . . SAUDI ARABIA / 381
Allah's Desert High Points

FOUNDERS / 387
Buddha . . . Moses . . . Muhammad . . . Jesus

PART IV
MIGHTY HIMALAYA
CAVE MYTH AND SACRED PEAKS

SACRED MOUNTAINS:

EVEREST . . . NEPAL, CHINA, TIBET / 409
Elevation Doesn't Raise Holiness . . . Necessarily

MAKALU . . . NEPAL / 419
Snowbound Spirits

KANGCHENJUNGA . . . NEPAL, INDIA / 427
Cave Rock Hermit Paradise

GANGKHAR PUENSUM . . . BHUTAN / 435
The Three Unifiers

SACRED MOUNTAINS CAN BE ANYWHERE

SACRED MOUNTAINS:

BEN NEVIS ... SCOTLAND / 445
Spirit Like Mountains Has An Easy Way and a Hard Way

DAMAVAND ... IRAN / 453
Wrong Interpretations Become Pleasant Surprises

KARISIMBI ... UGANDA, AFRICA / 461
Gorilla Eyes

KILIMANJARO AND MERU ... AFRICA / 469
*A Black and White History of
Sacred Mount Kilamanjaro, Africa's Highest Mountain*

MATTERHORN ... SWITZERLAND / 479
Go Back and Save Your Life

TAN-TAN ... MOROCCO / 487
*From the Mountains of Western Sahara
to the Depths of the Atlantic*

CHIRRIPÓ ... COSTA RICA / 495
A Miracle Can of Chicken Noodle Soup

VICTORIA PEAK ... BELIZE / 511
A Coconut Miracle

MOUNT ATHOS ... AEGEAN SEA / 519
The Mountain of Monks ... Aegean Sea

PART VI
THE AMERICAS

SACRED MOUNTAINS:

DENALI ... ALASKA / 547
Yahoo and His New Wife ... Form The Great White

WHITNEY ... CALIFORNIA / 555
Home of the Great Spirit of the Sierra

JUNIPERO SERRA ... CALIFORNIA / 561
To Be A Saint

RAINIER . . . WASHINGTON / 571
*From Destruction Comes
Sacred Mount Rainier*

SHASTA . . . CALIFORNIA / 581
Success Brings Joy; Failure Brings Wisdom

HALEAKALA . . . MAUI / 589
Under One Sun

WAI'ALE'ALE . . . KAUAI / 609
*Water, Water Everywhere
Sacred Mount Wai'ale'ale*

SAN JACINTO . . . CALIFORNIA / 617
*Mother Nature's Walking Range . . .
Sacred Mount San Jacinto*

DAVIDSON . . . SAN FRANCISCO / 629
A Small Hill With A Big Heart

MONADNOCK . . . NEW HAMPSHIRE / 637
*Sacred Mountain Beauty . . .
The Mountain That Stands Alone*

ENDNOTES

AFTERWARD: THE PAINTER PEI DU / 646
FROM IMAGINATION COMES REALITY / 648
THE SEVENTH AVENUE GANG / 649
THANK YOU / 650
BIBLIOGRAPHY / 653
ALAN NICHOLS PUBLICATIONS & EXPLORATIONS / 663
THE JAIL HOUSE LAWYER WAS A GRAND JUROR / 672
SILK WEB GENES / 674
CYCLING THE SILK WEB & CLIMBERS / 675

Pocotello, Idaho. Early 1940s.

Part I

It's A Long Way To (Or From) Pocatello

1930-1935
Palo Alto Seedling

Family seeds thrive in the redwoods

Born under the Palo Alto redwoods

I was born not "under a star" but under the quiet, majestic redwoods in a California Bay Area town, "Palo Alto" ("large tree" in Spanish), in a hospital that no longer exists. That space now holds a small public park. Why there rather that at Stanford University Hospital which is much larger and better known? In those days the medical school's Stanford Hospital was in San Francisco. In fact, as a young boy I used that hospital for minor aches and problems. Anyway, now at age 95, the birth hospital doesn't mean much!

Years earlier, my mother Shirley was born in Palo Alto, and my father, a long-term Palo Alto resident, was born a few years earlier in New York City. My mother always praises her children, my sister Isabel (aka Nicky) and me, as well as most other people she knew. My father, Jack, in those days, administered large institutions — educational, administrative, private, public, international, federal, and local.

Still alive anyway with love for the family

I remember my mother and father with continuing love and admiration. The same applies to my three children: Sharon and Alan, Jr. (with my wife Lolita); and Shan (with my wife Joanne); my grandchildren, Brooke (Sharon's child); Call, Max, and Tucker (Alan Jr. and Jen's children); Joanna, Maxine, Grace and Charlie (my son Shan and his wife Lindsey's children).

I began writing this tome from "an old people's home" known today as "senior living." *Boy From Pocatello* is my last of over 30 publications of fiction, non-fiction, poetry, politics,

Psyche issues of a scattered family

law, and exploration. It is difficult to get everyone together since we are a scattered family living in Dallas, Texas; San Francisco, California; New York City, New York; Seattle, Washington; Oklahoma City, Oklahoma; and Greenbrae, California, as well as some other places. It doesn't require a Dr. Jung or a Dr. Freud or a karma expert to analyze my psychological issues, having a family spread all over the country while I write.

A "Stanford" Family Record

Palo Alto is a town built around and for Stanford University and the University Hospital on the Stanford campus. My mother and father, my uncle and aunt, my cousins Jean and Nina, as well as my grandmother "Honey" Charles (my mother's mother), and my great-grandmother, Anna Peck, are graduates of Stanford. My father earned a Doctorate in Education at Stanford in the 1930s. He became a school administrator, first at a nearby public school district in Santa Cruz, California, and then (at least in my five-year-old consciousness) the Superintendent of Education in Lancaster, a southern Californian desert town.

Father's career

The little I remember about Lancaster includes my obsession with jumping off the back stairs behind the kitchen and visiting my beloved caregiver, "Jackie," with long hair and large breasts. She lived down the street from us in Lancaster.

"Jackie"

I also remember riding with my sister in the back seat of our Dodge car, bathed in the first clear light of the rising desert sun. At 5 years old, I feel the thrill of exploration during a three-day auto trip from Lancaster, California, to Pocatello, Idaho. My Dad took over as President and Executive Director of Idaho State College, which later, thanks to many Pocatellans and Dad's stewardship, became Idaho State University.

My Mom, my sister Nicky (four years older), and I lived as nomads, following my father to his various U.S. Navy assignments during World War II, until my sister left for a special opportunity that allowed during World War II high school seniors to attend college without finishing high school. As a token of appreciation for my father, I began my freshman year at Idaho State University and afterward transferred to Stanford.

Pre-five-year-old travel

Travel and exploration are an important part of my history, especially as I age. This is perhaps because of these early family travel experiences starting in the 1930s, especially our family three-day drives from Lancaster, California, to Pocatello, Idaho. These early adventures are obviously a precursor and inspiration to the worldwide "Mountain" traveling I pursued for the rest of my life and the importance that I place on education, writing, family, history, athletics and religion. These trips are a big part of who I am (or was).

Who I am

While I don't remember many details of my first four years of life in Palo Alto, I do know that period included having loving and supportive parents, Shirley and Jack. They were a highly compatible couple and a vital part of my existence. During my first five years, we lived with my grandmother next to Stanford.

Parents

Much of our family life included outdoor picnics and, in my case, tagging along with my Dad on his fishing or hunting trips in Idaho or with my Mom, Dad, and their friends on Sunday excursions in the hills around Pocatello.

Outdoors

In those early years, I met my very old great-grandmother Anna Peck. She may have been the famous woman Mountaineer who we discovered in records 85 years later at the Explorers Club world headquarters in New York City when I was President.

Great grandmother,

My grandfather Allen Watson Charles, my grandmother Honey's husband, graduated from Stanford Law, as did Honey herself. He was a Palo Alto judge, attorney, and a member of the Stanford Law School faculty.

Hometown

While driving to San Francisco with Honey and some friends as passengers, there was a collision with a Southern Pacific Railroad train while they were crossing the tracks. Before the crash, my grandfather helped the others escape but was still in the car and killed when the train smashed into it.

Although Honey had a Stanford degree, she had no way to support her family without Allen. Realizing the situation, the California Supreme Court held a hearing where they examined Honey for her knowledge of the law pursuant to the California Constitution at that time and determined that she was eligible to qualify as a court-appointed lawyer. That way she could support her family as a temporary judge and attorney, particularly for estate law.

Life became very difficult for her, but she persevered in taking care of my mother and my uncle so that later, they were able to graduate from Stanford, and my uncle was also from the Stanford Law School.

Honey, 10 years later, remarried a Stanford economics professor, Eliot Jones, PhD. Their life became very enjoyable. They also often welcomed visits from the Nichols family from Idaho. My mother Shirley made sure our family visited Honey on many occasions. In fact, on several occasions, I lived with Honey and Eliot, particularly during vacation times while I was at Stanford. During those times, both in high school and while at Stanford, Honey very generously loaned me her 1929 Buick coupe, complete with shades that made some of my dates very interesting.

I never met or knew my grandfather, who was Honey's husband. But he was a great person by reputation and also built our cabin at Fallen Leaf Lake for the whole family for generations. Sometimes, those who we miss, like me and my grandfather, are lifetime and unforgettable losses.

After a three-day drive from Lancaster over the Sierra Nevada Mountains, we arrived in Pocatello, Idaho, where Dad was hired to be the president of Idaho State College (later Idaho State University). I always feel that my own acceptance and good treatment in Pocatello is due to people's respect for my father. Pocatello would be my home for the next fourteen years. We moved into a small brick home on Seventh Avenue, directly across the street from the huge green grass campus expanse of Idaho State. It's only about a block across this field to my dad's office as College President. Our family lived in an older three-story building previously owned by a rich Idaho sheep herder. I am assigned a second-story bedroom at the top of the stairs with my own bathroom. Our new home is part of my boyhood, "neigyghood" as we called it, and our "Seventh Avenue Gang."

Uncle Alan, My true hero

My first act coming home is to hang my Uncle Alan's war medals on the wall. I know that I am named after him. He was a hero volunteer fighter pilot in World War I. He flew a French Spad fighter for the French Army Air Corp. I never actually knew him of course, but I am left with his foreigners' version of *Croix-de-Guerre,* one of France's highest honors, and other awards for his bravery. Being a World War I fighter pilot was a dangerous job. There was a twenty-five percent mortality of pilots while in training! Later, my uncle died from a 'dog fight' over Germany with a German fighter.

Even at five years old, I showed my enduring love and support for my Uncle Alan by displaying his picture and awards on my own bedroom dresser. They are still on my wall at age 95.

Love in abstentia

Despite my never knowing my Uncle Alan or my grandfather, we are close, literally and figuratively.

A French Spad in World War I.

My hero Uncle and namesake Alan Hammond Nichols.

Tanks being moved to the front, after America joins World War I. Dad, as a member of the U.S. Tank Corp, was under the command of Colonel George Patton of World War II fame.

My hero Father John Ralph (Jack) Nichols.

Letter to my Uncle

San Francisco, CA
Fall, 1992
Alan H. Nichols
Memorial de l'Escadrille Lafayette
Villeneuve – l 'Etang
Paris, France

Your Nephew

Dear Alan,

I'm your nephew. Your brother Jack, my dad, named me after you. I have spent a lifetime in your memory … trying to live up to it. Never wondering, until now, if my struggles are communicated in some esoteric way to you. Tonight it is raining. I just finished re-reading your letters to your dad, my grandfather. Your parents, then your brother Jack, and later your sister Dorothy, kept them. They're all here, every one, along with the pictures Cliff Kimber sent back. All in their original envelopes, the Croix de Guerre with two palms, your accounts statements from Morgan, Harjes, your writing tablet, the flag that flew over your grave. The paper is fresh and crisp, the ink has not faded, you could have written them yesterday. Your brother Jack, my father, gave them all to me over thirty years ago. My wife, Nancy (your editor), had me go through them, and her work has brought you to life again. As long as I can remember, your picture, your Certificate of Award of the *Croix de Guerre* have been in my room. As a child, when I felt alone, I thought of you, a hero. Somehow I wanted to make up for your life with my own. I still do, all these years later.

Our family deaths

Doc music and drama critic

Jack with American Tank Corp under famous Colonel Patrton

Jack marries my mom, Shirley

Dad becomes grape farmer

Your death seemed to take the life out of the family. Your sister, Helen, died a young woman, of an illness, a few years after you. Your mom and dad were never the same. They died a few years after Helen.

That left only Jack and Dot. Dot also became ill and left Stanford before graduating. She later became a drama and music critic for the Palo Alto Times. She also wrote for some other newspapers and became a recognized expert on Shakespeare. She never married, and died in 1990 at age 87, much liked and honored in her old age.

Dot and Jack never talked about you. Now that they are both dead, I kick myself for not asking.

Immediately after your death, Jack joined the American Tank Corps under Colonel George Patton, who later became very famous in the next World War II. Jack lived through the horrors of the ground war in its last death throes on the battlefields of France. The war you died in came to be known as World War I.

Upon his return, Jack married Shirley Charles, that shy, slight girl who lived around the comer from your old home on Webster Street in Palo Alto, the daughter of a judge and Professor of Law at Stanford. They had two children, me and my sister, Nicky (her name is really Isabel, but she doesn't like to be called that), also a Stanford graduate.

Shaken by your death and the slaughter of the war, Jack wanted something totally different and decided on farming. He graduated from Oregon State Agricultural College and began farming grapes in the San Jocquin Valley just in time for the great depression in farming in the 1920's. He taught school to earn a living and found he enjoyed it. He returned

Medal awarded to Alan Hammond Nichols by the French government.
1914-1918
Escadrille Lafayette Internationale Des Aviateurs
To Commemorate Your Supreme Sacrifice / Alan Hammond Nichols / 2 June 1918
The World Must Remain At Peace / The Silver Wings of Peace Harmon Trophy

University President

U.S. Commissioner of Indian Affairs

to Stanford for his Ph.D., and became a school administrator just like his dad, Walter. He was President of two universities, advisor to General MacArthur during the occupation of Japan after World War II, United States Commissioner of Indian Affairs, and United States Assistant Secretary of the Interior. That "broad engaging smile" you talked of in your letters from Paris stayed with Jack throughout his whole life. You would have been very proud of your little brother. I am.

Alan in Korean War

Much later, after graduating from Stanford, I volunteered to serve in something known as a "police action" the Korean War. I was a 1st Lieutenant in the U.S. Army — just what you wanted to be, but I didn't know that then.

Dad dies playing basketball while 70

While working with the Near East Foundation, which provided technical assistance to African nations, Jack died at age 70, in New York City, where he was born. Mom returned to Palo Alto and died there in 1991 at age 90. There's another Alan H. Nichols, my son. He graduated from Stanford too, and has three sons of his own.

Your death from 'dogfight'

With your verve you would probably still be alive today if you hadn't been hit in a dog fight over Germany. I'll bet that even in your nineties, you would have remained friendly, thoughtful and introspective. You probably would still enjoy walks, thinking about the future, and find adventure.

While reincarnation as a literal fact is no closer to being proven today than it was in 1918, somehow in my own consciousness I feel, no, I know, you are part of me.

My Uncle Alan's Certificate of Service in the Lafayette Flying Corps.

I was born in a hospital that is now a park in Palo Alto some years after you died in the operating room of that hospital at the Front in France. We're both interested in new ideas, open to new things, iconoclasts, independent, and love the outdoors. So much of my outlook parallels yours – somewhat puritanical, full of energy, adventurous, and impatient with delays and inactions. I can't help but wonder how much Jack unconsciously molded me after you.

You wrote of wanderlust. That spirit stayed with Jack and with me. Dad's careers took him all over the United States (I followed along, with reluctance, through seven different high schools as a teenager), Japan, the Near East, Europe and Africa. And how I would have loved sharing with you my travels all over the world.

My heart brightens every time I read of your love for California. I once walked from our cabin at Fallen Leaf, near Lake Tahoe, to your beloved Yosemite and I spend time every year in the North Sierras driving cattle. In pure exuberance I ran a 100 plus mile race from Tahoe to Auburn. I know your mountains, wild flowers, meadows and forests. For it is there, like you, I find solace, mystery, reawakening, inspiration and ecstasy.

I hiked higher than Uncle Alan flew in WWI

Once I hiked on a pilgrimage in Tibet higher than you ever flew – over 19,000 feet! I have felt that wonder of excitement of being among the clouds, albeit afoot and not in a cockpit.

You are part of me

What you would have become was always so much a part of me as a boy and as a man. All my life I have wanted to accomplish what I had dreamed were your goals, even though I didn't know what they were. The living can still become what the dead wanted to be. The few months before your death you struggled with what to do with your life. I have spent a lifetime doing the same.

Always together

You did make a difference, in Jack, in me, and maybe in your grand-nephew Alan jr. I have come to love you as a symbol of all things that can be, and in that way we have always been together.

Lots of love,
Alan

1935-1941
King of the "Neigyhood"

Nothing is more important to any boy than his tribe — physically, emotionally, socially, spiritually

The Seventh Avenue Gang

My Seventh Avenue neighborhood in Pocatello provides extraordinary and never-ending opportunities for me to be a part of the "Seventh Avenue Gang"! I make important and permanent friends, play all the sports, and do many exciting things that young boys dream up to enjoy. For instance, on very hot Idaho summer days, one of our parents would drive the whole gang, or most of us, to go swimming at American Falls, Indian Springs, Lava Hot Springs, and other public hot pools near Pocatello.

Swimming expeditions

Outdoors

Sometimes chaperoned by a parent, mostly on our own, our boyhood gang adventures often include long hikes, mountain picnics, bike rides, sports on "our" squatter's lot, and just being together in the neighborhood, mostly outdoors. We live in the sun, in the rain, and even in the ubiquitous winter snow-storms. Together, we build snow tunnels in the winter and occupy caves in the vacant lot between Durwood's and my homes in the summer.

Constantly together... Summer, Winter

Gang Sports

Most of our 7th Avenue Gang live on 7th Avenue. We are loyal, constant companions. We play sports in their season — football, basketball, wrestling, track, boxing, and when we are older, tennis. We are usually outdoors except when it's raining or snowing hard, and on those occasions, we get together at one of our houses to play board games, especially Monopoly.

Gang walks to Washington Elementary School

Our gang walks to school together almost every weekday, rain, snow, or shine. I left my house first, walked down the alley, passed our neighborhood "sports" lot to Durwood's house, and shouted, "Durwood"! He joined me, and from there, we picked up the other gang members, "Johnny" and "Toby" across 7th Avenue, "Jack" on the corner, and "Bill" who lived on 8th Avenue. "Byron," who lived on 5th Avenue, met us on the way. Sometimes, we also called for Jim, who lived on 10th Avenue almost straight across the street from our school. We go as a group to our destination, Pocatello's Washington Elementary School on 10th Avenue.

Night games

Occupying private lot next door for our sports projects

During the day, and sometimes early evening with light from my and Durwood's next-door homes, we played our favorite sports — football, basketball, baseball, and even track on the lot between Durwood Fry's and my home. I don't know who actually owned the lot in those days, but no one ever objected to our Gang taking it over. We even dug a huge cave, trenches, tunnels, and other interesting cave structures. By the time we were in 6th grade, someone had built a home on our gang lot, so we found alternatives on the campus.

We had our own October Halloween trick-or-treat adventures around town. One is to stop cars going up and down 7th Ave by piling fall leaves across the road at night. They look like piles of rocks. Drivers react to our shouts from behind the trees, "Look out for the rocks," by slamming on their breaks. Usually, they laugh about it since things are going slowly anyway. We always eliminate the leaf piles before going to bed so the police wouldn't get wise to us.

The Davis boys, Robert and Toby, live on Seventh Avenue across the street in a small red brick home. Their father is a railroad engineer for the Union Pacific Railroad. They are a large Roman Catholic family and often argue religion with other gang members with different religious opinions, mostly

Protestant. Once a year, in the summer, the Davis boys and their dad made homemade root beer and real beer in their basement. The root beer was sweet and delicious, and each of us probably drank enough to drown.

Our parents pursued different careers. My Dad was the President of Idaho State, well-known and well-liked in town. Under my father's direction and inspiration, Idaho State advanced from a "Junior College" to a "University" during his tenure (1934-1946). The tree and grass-covered campus consisted of many buildings, including athletic facilities, a school of pharmacy, a library, a theater, dorms, cafeterias, and other structures which are typically part of most college institutions.

Two of our "Gang's" parents are medical physicians. Johnny lived across from me in a small, gray stucco house, and Jack resided with his large family down 7th Avenue about half a block. Jack's dad was a very popular and a successful general physician. He often treated my boyhood ailments. Dr. Newton, who lived on a ranch outside of Pocatello, was the University's head doctor and also treated some of my illnesses and injuries.

Jack, King of the Neighyhood."

Once, when we were all very young, maybe five or six years old, Jack painted a sign for himself, nailed it to a stick, and showed it to our whole 7th Avenue gang. It read: "Jack, King of the Neigyhood." It made me a little jealous as I always wanted to be the gang leader, the captain, the best known of my friends in school and otherwise. But I didn't have the skills to make my own sign.

The Sahlberg boys, Don and Tom, also lived across 7th Avenue from my house with their parents. Their father was one of the town's well-known electricians and owned an electrical shop downtown.

John, the other John (we called him Johnny), was also a doctor's son. He was a little younger than me and lived across the street. Years later, to my surprise and pain, he married

Jerry Anne, who I had thought and hoped was my girlfriend. Johnny and I are also the founders of the 7th Avenue Smoking Club, headquartered in an old shack in my home's backyard.

Byron Jones is one of my constant personal friends even though he does not technically qualify to be a member of the Seventh Avenue gang because he lives on 5th, not 7th, across the alley from Pocatello's best bakery. It always smells especially well and reminds me I'm hungry when I'm visiting Byron's home. His father, Dr. Victor Jones, is a respected Professor of Biology at Idaho State and one of my father's special and gifted hunting and fishing friends.

Sunday Smoking Club

Although the meetings of our local smoking club are secret, they are usually held before anyone is awake on Sunday mornings, but someone must have "squealed." After less than five weeks of holding our Smoking Club meetings, while I am at my Washington Elementary School, a huge truck comes into our backyard and removes our whole backyard clubhouse and all our illicit club "artifacts" ... tobacco, fireworks, and used golf balls from Pocatello's only golf course. We feel too guilty to object! I never said anything about this to my parents, who obviously didn't want to harbor 6 and 7-year-old smokers.

Durwood Fry lives next door to me on the other side of the 'gang' lot. Our bedrooms are on our respective home's second floors. We string an electrical wire across "our" vacant football and sports lot, and this becomes a confidential nighttime communications center for all the neighborhood Gang bedrooms.

Durwood's father owns and manages Pocatello's only Dodge car Agency and regularly sells a car to my parents. While I am on a nationwide exploration with my Dad during World War II, as I explain a bit later, almost all of my fellow neighborhood Gang members, when they were teenagers, drove heavy Dodge car-carrier trucks from Detroit, Michigan, where they were manufactured about 1,725 miles to Fry's Pocatello, Idaho Agency. I was impressed by my friend's ability and experience doing heavy and tough driving, and I personally regret missing that experience.

Johnson Avenue Home

For several years, our family lived in the middle of the neighborhood on 7th Avenue. Then, my father sold our home there and bought a lot four blocks away on 11th Avenue at the edge of town. He hired a contractor to build a two-story home in the foothills adjoining the Idaho State Aeronautics Education Depot. He added a sleeping porch to our new home with beds and usually open windows, even in the winter, on the grounds that the fresh air is "good for us." We also had beds for each of us inside our respective bedrooms.

During the construction of the new family home, we moved across town to a large yellow home next to Pocatello's Portneuf River. A steel bridge there crossed the river.

Johnson Avenue Sledding

I miss the lively closeness of our neighborhood "gang" and "our" vacant lot, but our gang seemed to be weakening anyway as we each pursued our own interests. Even so, I often ride my bike or walk across town from Johnson Avenue to 7th Avenue. The bridge next door to our Johnson Street house was about one and a half miles away from Seventh Avenue, but after our move to the 11th Avenue home, it's less than half a mile to our 7th Avenue stomping grounds.

The steep street on the opposite side of the river turned out to be a glorious place for gang sledding during Pocatello's snow-filled and frozen winters. The thrill of sledding precipitous Johnson Street from the hill to the bridge, with enough momentum to cross the river bridge, brought our "Gang" back together for a while.

None of us ever missed the bridge and plunged into the deep and fast-flowing Portneuf River. I don't think anyone who took the plunge would have survived.

Above: Washington Elementary school that the Seventh Avenue Gang attended.
Below: Colonial Hall where the author had a basement room when attending Idaho State University.
Following Page: A few of the Seventh Avenue gang's 1930's "Homes on the Range" that are still standing

Alan's House 1

Alan's House 2

Alan's House 3

Jack's "King of the Neigyhood" house

Pinkerton's Dance Studio

Durward's House

Tom's and Don's House

1935-1941
Honey Trips

The Family drives biannually from Pocatello to Palo Alto to see my grandmother — a 2360 mile round trip

Mom and Honey

President Hoover

Mom, a resident's wife

Trips over the Sierras

My mother Shirley is very close to her mother who we all call "Honey." She lives across the road from the Stanford golf course. With her husband (now deceased) Honey enjoys a lifetime of connection to the Stanford University, and is a personal friend of ex-president and Mrs. Hoover, who made Palo Alto their home for some time. Honey is the first of several generations of our family, starting in the late 1800's, who either graduated from Stanford, taught there, or at least significantly supported it.

My mom Shirley is a very modern woman and a graduate of Stanford. She is well versed in her college cultural and social roles and the vast, often unrecognized, duties of a University President's wife — social, political, supportive — especially self required by her strong partnership with Dad.

While I'm a young boy our family, with my mom and dad taking turns driving, visit "Honey", mom's mother, at least twice a year — at Christmas and in the summer. In those days it was usually a 3-day trip from Pocatello to Honey's older but comfortable shingled house with two garages on four acres in the countryside. It is a long tiring drive and sometimes we would stop and rest for a few days at the family cabin at Fallen Lake, which is six miles from the southern end of Lake Tahoe, not far from Donner Pass over the Sierra-Nevada Mountain Range in California. My sister Nicky and I always ride in the back seat. All too often we fight, orally and now and then even physically. To make it easier for all of us we often eat dinner and rest in motels along the way for one or two evenings during our car trip to Honey's or our return to Pocatello. I become addicted to chocolate milkshakes and cheddar cheese sandwiches as a special treat at lunches. The trips are long, boring and anxiety producing, especially for me and my sister.

The Last fight!

After three days on the road during one of these trips, Nicky and I are tired, upset and fighting about something I no longer remember. We are shouting at each other and even hitting. It is our last fight. Nicky puts down her seat and says, "This is terrible, I will never fight again with you." My immediate thought is that this gives me an opportunity to carry on and "win." But this incident did end our fights against each other for all time. From that event in the 1930s we never fight again, orally or physically.

Nicky leaves

To my regret, Nicky died at 94 years of age in Boise, Idaho June 9, 2021. I miss her. I didn't have the sense to spend more time with her and her husband Perry while I had the chance. She married Perry Swisher, a newspaperman from a family of 12 children living close to Pocatello. They lived most of her married adult life in Pocatello and Boise. Perry, always active politically, held an important position as President of the Idaho Power Commission and leader of the Idaho Senate.

Nickey's husband became President of the Idaho Power Commission

When I think about my sister and brother-in-law I realize how much I admire them and like to be with them. I always seem too busy pursuing other things for the long journey to Boise by car.

I personally love the idea of living in Pocatello and still remember every night from my corner second floor bedroom listening to the Union Pacific trains as they whistle their way through our town, carrying freight and passengers between the east and west coasts and points in between.

The memories and love I have for Nicky are vivid to my mind. I love Idaho and especially Pocatello. My sister did too.

Years later I return to live with Honey for almost a year.

1938-1946
Fallen Leaf Paradise

A Gift from my Grandfather Allen

100 years at Fallen Leaf

For over 100 years, our family has enjoyed a cabin built on U.S. Forest Service Land at Fallen Leaf Lake, about six miles from the southern end of Lake Tahoe in California. That cabin was badly burnt in a major forest fire in 2021. It has been restored by my son Alan Jr. and other family members to be usable, at least for now. This cabin was originally built by my parents and grandparents for all the family to enjoy camping nearby, hiking the surrounding mountains and trails, and swimming in the lakes as well as Fallen Leaf. Over the years, thirteen other cabins have been built on the same "Stanford Hill" on sites originally leased by Stanford professors from the U.S. Forest Service. We all placed our cabins on the hill above and adjoining Fallen Leaf Lake itself. Today, the western lakefront is owned by the Stanford Alumni Association, who bought the campsite over 25 years ago. Trails are built from our cabin down to the Stanford Camp on Fallen Leaf Lake, Alpine Springs, and other nearby mountains, lakes, and ridges.

Peaks and Lakes

I still remember and will never lose my fond feelings for those lakes and areas above our cabin — Grass Lake, Lucille Lake, Thousand Island Lake, Pyramid Lake, Tahoe Creek, Pyramid Peak and Lake, Tallac Peak and Lake, and Angora Peak and Lake. These trails, peaks and lakes are still a part of our family, and especially part of my own joys over my lifetime.

Fallen Leaf
Painting courtesy of the Lake Tahoe Historical Society from
A Lake and its People (1850-1950) by Janet Kaidantzis

Thousand Island Lakes

Food

Once, while I am camping with a friend at Thousand Island Lakes at the base of Pyramid Peak, we overstay our plans and run out of food. Neither of us want to leave, so we flip a coin to decide who would hike back the five miles and return to the cabin for more supplies. I lost the flip yet enjoyed hiking the ten or twelve-mile round-trip journey on the rugged, steep, rocky trail from our camp back to our Fallen Leaf cabin. I picked up food and hiked back so we could camp for a few days longer at Thousand Island Lakes.

Cabin Head Quarters

Our cabin was a headquarters and a source of happiness for me as a young boy and young man. Even though we live in Idaho, we spend almost two weeks a year in California with our family and, at times, with other Charles family members, also descendants of Honey, particularly my Aunt Caroline, Uncle Allen and cousins Jean and Nini.

Cabin Sharing

Members of the Charles and Nichols families have shared the Fallen Leaf cabin for as many years as I can remember. We all recognize the obligation to help maintain the cabin and keep it clean and usable for everyone. My aunt Caroline also works out an excellent schedule, allowing our growing families to share Fallen Leaf along with Honey and Eliot,

Who gets Fallen Leaf

my step-grandfather, my sister and her husband. Since July and August are usually the best weather at Fallen Leaf, we swap those months each year. The family who resides at the cabin in July one year will have it in August the next year.

Each branch of the family decides the expenses and time allocation for each family member. We all cooperate. Everyone helps with maintenance, taxes, and improvements. We are thoughtful and kind, and each family member happily shares the pleasures and obligations of life at Fallen Leaf.

My Dream

I often dream of living at Fallen Leaf for an entire year — winter, spring, summer and fall, but have yet to carry out my hope. I never seem to have enough time. Trout fishing has always been an important activity for me, but isn't as joyful as cross-country hiking, swimming, exploring, climbing mountains and cross-country skiing.

Trips to Myers Grocery Store

There is a realization that even after there are 13 cabins at Fallen Leaf's "Stanford Hill" are built, there are no stores for milk or other necessary fresh provisions. One of the old cabin stories my parents tell is that, before the lakefront store was built and the roads to the Lake completed, one of the thirteen cabin owners would volunteer each week to hike, usually with a horse or donkey in tow, from the Stanford camp into Myers, a small town five or six miles away over a high ridge, for the supplies for everyone, particularly to pick up milk in large milk cans to strap on to the mule. Now, the Fallen Leaf store is at the south end of the lake, less than half a mile from our cabin, much higher on the ridge.

Educators

In the early days, most of the Fallen Leaf residents who were connected with and worked at Stanford spent the whole summer at Fallen Leaf since the teaching duties at Stanford lasted only nine months. This leaves three months to enjoy the lake and the surrounding wilderness. Much of the communal life includes evening get-togethers at one of the cabins to discuss and debate academic and current news.

Boating and swimming

One of the special pleasures for all our family was to rent canoes, kayaks, or row-boats from the store and to row to the far eastern end of Fallen Lake, five or six miles away.

At times, especially when young, we swam across the lake and back, totaling three or four miles. The water seems freezing at first, but after a while becomes tolerable. The southeast end of Fallen Leaf provides a chance for tourists and visiting fishermen to camp, fish, boat, and hike. The number of trout

Grandfather's fishing spot

that once teemed in the stream off Fallen Leaf is now vastly

Grandfather's fishing spot

diminished. My grandfather, a founder of the Stanford Hill community, often fished along the shore where once was a fisherman's Lodge, which burnt down before my time. Today, people mostly fish for Rainbow trout near the Stanford Camp at the northwest end of the lake. The Stanford camp is an integral part of the lake with its own boat docks, sand beach, lodge, and many rooms for alumni.

Stanford buys camp

Over the years, there has been a significant, but not intrusive, development of summer homes and access roads on both the north and southwest sides of the lake. The small paved roads down both sides of the lake enable residents and hikers to drive from their homes to trail parking and hiking for available peaks, lakes, and Mountains around the area.

The Stanford Alumni Association took over the lodge at Fallen Leaf and has been especially generous with us neighbors. They share their beach, dining hall, boating, and some special events with residents. Once, while I was alone at the cabin, Stanford employed me as they had a policy of providing working opportunities to local residents.

One of our special events was to hike high in the Mountains above the Stanford cabins, take off all of our clothes, and swim in the freezing lake water which seemed to warm up after such a "frozen" beginning.

Episcopal Church

Not far from the Stanford camp and our cabin is a small Episcopal church with services in the summer, which I attend regularly when there. I also attend some special church events and even a few weddings. This Episcopal chapel down the hill from our cabin is an important part of my personal spiritual life at Fallen Leaf, as is my Episcopal Church in Pocatello and other homes.

1940's
The Spirit World

Spiritual path

For me, my spirit is and always has been directly related to Nature on account of my interests, participation in my church, love, companionship, mountains, music, and family. I am always interested in matters of "Spirit." Spirit is a major aspect of my life. Maybe some long past relative carried a similar interest, but not my parents. We, as a family, seldom attended Church together. Weather permitting, Mom, Dad, a few of their or my friends, and I enjoyed picnics, walks, and hikes on summer Sundays at Fallen Leaf Lake or my cattle ranch in Northern California.

My friend, and part of the 7th Avenue Gang, Byron Jones, also encouraged me to participate in a small Trinity Episcopal Church downtown across the road from Pocatello High School. I don't remember the full name of Father Asboe, the priest at the time at this Episcopal Church. I liked him and he included me in Church activities. In the course of my participation, I became emotionally involved in all the Bible stories, and was introduced to biblical philosophy and ways to apply Christian attitudes and beliefs to various aspects of my life. My interest in Christ's message is strong but also competitive. As time passed, I became more interested in all religions and spiritual awareness rather than a one-sided, denominational life.

Choir boy

As a boy and teenager, I was an altar boy and choir boy. I owned, and still own, a lot of religious and spiritual literature and carry an almost obsessive interest in religious matters. Later, I became involved both as an attorney and "believer" in the organization, and development, of religious activities in Episcopal, Christian Science, Buddhist, Hindu,

Religions

31

even Taoism and Eckankar (where my friend Darwin Gross was the "Master").

Over 70 years studying Sacred Mountains

For over 70 years, I focused on the discovery, exploration, and study of the Sacred Mountains of the world. Some of that has become part of this book.

Pocatello, the town of my youth, is a largely Mormon LDS (Latter Day Saints) town. I am impressed with the strong Mormon family closeness but their message never became an inherent part of my involvement.

Jesus Connection

By the time I was in high school, I felt a strong personal relationship with Jesus Christ. I attended churches and absorbed varied views of religion, but didn't pay much attention to the denomination. For example, I communicated with the spiritual Christ in a Roman Catholic church on Van Ness Avenue in San Francisco. When we were traveling around America with my father during World War II, I often attended a local church, cathedral, or some spiritual organization.

Law and Religions

I also spent many years doing legal and other work for Eckankar, the Episcopal Church, and Christian Science, including articles and books. I closely observed and even took part in spiritual sects in my travels in Africa, Japan, the U.S., India, China, Mongolia, South America, and Europe. I traveled along the "Silk Road" countries (11 nations) and bicycled from Istanbul, Turkey to Xian, China, a former capital of China.

A Musical Aside

Classical music

My Dad particularly enjoyed classical music, which was almost always turned on the radio or recording when he was home. Mozart, Beethoven, and Strauss broadcasted from our radio on the afternoon of the Japanese attack on Pearl Harbor in 1941.

His interest in music was an opportunity for me. When I was about seven years old he told me that he would be asking

Instruments

Dr. Gardner, the head of the music department at Idaho State in Pocatello, and pay him to teach me any musical instrument I picked. I first chose the saxophone but, after a month or so of lessons, found that I didn't like it.

Trumpet

Dad was persistent in his encouragement. The trumpet was a better choice for me. It turned out to be an extraordinary chance for me to play both in Pocatello and bands in various high schools and even dance bands throughout the United States during our family travels. It was a delight to make friends, play with fellow students, and to be a part of a group with mutual interests. It assuaged the difficulties of arriving at each school knowing no one.

Breakfast and the classics

A friend knew that I liked classical music and often asked what I'd like to hear while having breakfast. I enjoy nutritious breakfasts accompanied by Beethoven, Mozart, Vivaldi, Strauss, Tchaikovsky, Brahms, Chopin, and other famous classical, especially symphonic, composers. While I no longer play the trumpets regularly, I hope to start again if possible. Playing a musical instrument is supposed to be a good activity to raise "cognitive activity." So is my enjoyment of these classical music composers.

1942-1945
"Pokey" to Pocatello

The joy of returning "home" is directly proportionate to the neighborhood and the members of your "gang"

World War II begins

Early morning Sunday, December 7, 1941, I started a hike alone in the foothills behind our 11th Avenue home on the eastern side of Pocatello adjoining the University airport.

On my return home in the late afternoon, I looked down from the adjoining foothill onto our backyard and was sure something was wrong. Dad, Mom, and my sister Nicky were not talking but seriously and quietly listening to the radio. I couldn't hear it but I ran down the hill to our backyard. My Dad told me Japanese fleet aircraft attacked the American Navy ships in Pearl Harbor, inflicting serious damage, killing thousands of Americans, and sinking many, mostly anchored ships of the American fleet in Honolulu. Dad said this will be the beginning of World War II.

Lt. Commander Dad joins the Navy for WWII

My father (who during World War I was a volunteer ambulance driver for the French army and then a tank driver for the American Army when the United States entered the war) joined the US Navy in World War II as a Lt. Commander (later a Commander). He was tasked with creating Naval Colleges and courses in prominent U.S. Universities for Naval Officers to expedite their education, mostly relating to the sciences.

The whole family follows Dad to Seattle, Washington

Soon after World War II began, I left Pocatello's Franklin Jr. High. My sister Nicky left Pocatello High School. Our whole family followed Dad to his multiple assignments beginning with the University of Washington in Seattle. I was admitted to a Seattle Junior High and spent most of my time

Dad ordered to Washington, DC Headquarters

We live in the woods

Junior High

Hawaiian Home in the Woods

B B War

Dance band

playing at a city sports development center. I still remember being fascinated with the sawdust furnaces at home and school.

By summer, Dad was transferred to the Naval War Department in Washington, D.C. My Dad and Mom found us a home in the woods a few miles outside of Falls Church, Virginia, a suburb of Washington D.C. I transferred to a Falls Church Junior High School. The education itself was pretty weak but the teachers were kind. Thanks to my playing football for the school and trumpet in a small dance band, I was able to have a little, much-needed, social life.

While living in Virginia, the house Dad found for us was a Hawaiian-style home on Lemon Road, deep in the Virginia woods. It was quite a long daily bike ride to and from my school in Falls Church, Virginia. Not only was my new home built in this strange Hawaiian architectural style, but it was buried in a thick dark growth of Virginia pines. There were only one or two Virginian kids nearby around my age. They were a little strange. They introduced me to one of their favorite pastimes.

We ran through the woods hiding behind trees trying to shoot each other with our BB guns. The only real danger was to get shot in the eye. In any event, the thought of being shot in the eye made me a little nervous, but we all agreed to shoot low to avoid the chance of being shot in the eye.

I also was asked to join a real dance band in Falls Church although my prior trumpet experience was with marching and concert bands. That was interesting since dance bands are a very different genre, especially for trumpets. There wasn't much time for socializing since I attended band practices by bike and went back home the same way to our Virginia home in the woods.

One of my teachers at Falls Church Jr. High talked to my mother and invited me to live with her when my father had been ordered to set up an accelerated Naval school at Columbia University in New York City. My mother told me that my 7th grade teacher in the local Junior High School likes "the new boy from Pocatello." Since her sons were in the Pacific theater of war fighting the Japanese she had plenty of room in her house in Falls Church near the school. She said she also needed some company.

When my Mom asked if I'd be interested, I told her that I appreciated the generosity and invitation, but sadly declined. I felt it was apparent that Mom and Dad did not want me with them in New York, especially since my sister would be leaving the family to take up her chances for early admission college courses. Educational facilities were desperate for students since almost all the available men in America were part of the U.S. armed forces. She went first to Idaho State, where my Dad was on leave as President, and then transferred to Stanford where she graduated with a special degree, enabling her to provide nursing and science health services to mostly polio-stricken children. She later returned to Pocatello to teach elementary school, while my Mom and Dad with me were still on the move.

1944
A Latin Disaster . . . New York City

Sometimes Disasters Create Saints

New York City

    I joined my parents in our new apartment in New York City near Columbia University on Riverside Drive and Morningside Heights. We had a beautiful view of the Hudson River from our apartment's large roof. My Dad was assigned to an office near 104th Street. I transferred from my junior high school in Falls Church, Virginia, and enrolled for the remainder of my freshman year in a liberal "experimental" and admired modern high school, Lincoln High, managed by Columbia University's School of Education, a famous well-respected institution.

Columbia University

    As usual, I also found a job. I'd been working at my gardening business in Pocatello. In New York City I found work at a small cleaner in the Morningside Heights neighborhood to deliver and pick up laundry and dry cleaning. When it rained or snowed or was too windy, I discovered that I could deliver and pick up the clothes using underground passages found everywhere in connected basements of large buildings. It was a little dark and I was always fearful of robbery or even assault in the dark underground passageways.

New York City Clean Up

    This was a difficult time for me. The other students were stand-offish. There were no team sports to sign up for an activity. There were no important activities for me to participate in.

Other students

    It also turned out I was transferring from an academically undemanding school in Falls Church to a very modern and advanced school in New York. I was far behind in my academic courses, especially in the hard courses like Latin, and was on the psychological edge of failure. In those days Latin was required for admission to any good college.

Columbia Latin failure

Grades were not even awarded in this "open," non-traditional school in any course except Latin. The strict old "traditional" Latin teacher gave me an "F" in her course. I was used to A's. I was brokenhearted to be doing so poorly, concerned that any failure in Latin was a symptom that I would fail in life and not gain admission to any college.

I hid my sadness at school, but when I was left by myself, I cried all the way home from school, climbing up from Lincoln High to our apartment while cursing Morningside Heights and walking down toward the Hudson River. Luckily my Dad was taking a nap there when I arrived at our apartment. At his request, I told him why I was so sad. He was an experienced educator, but seemed very unsympathetic and said, "Come on let's take a nap, and then we'll talk about it."

Dad prescription: a nap and advice

When we did talk, it was a shock to me. He said unsympathetically, "You received 'F's because you aren't doing the work." And I told him, "I can't do the work because the vocabulary doesn't mean anything to me, and I'm not prepared on account of the elementary level of Latin taught at my prior Virginia school." He said that if I wanted to avoid F's, I must discuss this with my teacher. I was not in the mood to talk or even listen to Dad's advice. I was still overwhelmed and took a nap myself. Our talk about this was over. It was Friday.

Crying and napping for failure

I didn't return to classes until Monday. This was a very low point for me. Throughout my career, I always tried to be a top achiever, worked hard, and was very ambitious… I am failing. To receive the lowest grade from probably the best Latin teacher in New York — for me that was a true disaster. And my own Dad seemed neither sympathetic nor empathetic.

Next Monday Latin teacher speaks to me

But the next Monday at school, the Latin teacher took me aside, "Listen I know how upset you are from the bad grades I gave you. First, I want to say that you deserve it. You don't deserve anything more. Secondly, I understand why. You're not dumb. You attended an inferior school in Virginia, of all places, and are trying to keep up with the serious and sophisticated studies here. You've actually done OK in everything here at Lincoln, except Latin."

Latin teacher's offer

Then she said, "I'll do one thing for you. At noontime, four noons a week, I will meet with you and teach you Latin as it should be." I was so grateful I cried again. Thereafter, I went to her office every single day, sometimes even more than four times a week. I took my sack lunch and she taught me this difficult subject. Strangely, I couldn't remember what grade I finally received in that course at the end of the year. But it was at least a 'B', which was a major accomplishment for me, and I was proud. My gratitude for this teacher was overwhelming. She gave so much, not just her lunch period but of herself to help an individual messed up kid for six months, four days a week. She fits my concept of a true angel, dedicated, and wonderful.

Result

Speaking of women, Amy was a fellow student at Lincoln High in NYC. She was a very nice person. She became my friend and we dated a few times. I spoke of her at greater length in the later chapter on women in my life. That covered our joy on our Broadway experience with Amy's father's birthday present tickets to "Oklahoma."

Our family left New York not long after, so I never saw Amy again. But I often dreamt of her and never lost my fond attraction.

1944
Back To Honey's

There is no place like home if it's Honey's

Orders to Monterey Language Institute

While we were in New York, Dad was ordered by the Navy to Monterey, California to attend the Armed Forces Language Institute. He was already proficient in German, Spanish, and French . . . English too of course. He was also knowledgeable about American Indian tribes from his special relations with the Black Foot, Chumash, and other mid-western tribes. It was close to the end of the war in the Pacific and obvious that the U.S. Navy was training him to be a part of the American forces' occupation of Japan. The Navy wanted him to play a prominent role in support of General Douglas MacArthur, head of the U.S. forces occupying Japan after World War II, especially as related to "reforming" Japanese public education.

Transfer to Sequoia High School in California

For the family, it meant another move. Dad went back to Monterey and I transferred to Sequoia High School in Redwood City, California. My Mom and I lived with my grandmother Honey at her home. Afterward, my mother traveled to Monterey to live with Dad off base but near the Monterey Language Institute.

Daily 30 mile high school bike commute

I biked about fifteen or sixteen miles back and forth between Sequoia High and Honey's home every day. Sequoia was a huge high school and a hard place to adjust and make friends. It was too late in the season to go out for football but I was allowed to try out as a recruit with the basketball team. I also tried out for wrestling but didn't make either team.

Thank you, Joyce

I was fortunate while there to meet, Joyce, a fellow student and a nice person who lived in Redwood City near the high school. She was good-looking, sociable friendly, and kind. She was not rich and didn't have a chauffeur to pick me up at Honey's or anything like that. Sometimes I borrowed Honey's 1929 Buick Coupe "Petite," a family car recognized by the whole family by Honey's name for her. It became a dating car with Joyce. It was a coupe with pulldown window shades and a perfect place to kiss Joyce goodnight after a date.

Honey's 1929 dating coupe

I lived so far from high school; Honey's home was in the countryside so it was hard to meet people. Joyce organized some nice parties with her friends. I was grateful to her for sharing her school friends with me, a stranger "from Pocatello" no less. Her friendship assuaged but didn't eliminate my strong feelings of loneliness.

Assuaging my loneliness

1945
"Home-Body" Returns

My return to Pocatello is a glorious development. I discover Heroes are returned homebodies, Cowards have nothing to come home for.

General MacArthur requisitions Dad to help with occupation of Japan

While I was at Sequoia High School in Redwood City, California, Dad joined General Douglas MacArthur as an education advisor to the general and the army occupation team in Japan. This was what Dad trained for at the Monterey Language Institute. He fulfilled his duty to change the Japanese education system by introducing principles of American education such as the role of governance, local boards of education with principals as administrators, and the introduction of English into the curriculum. Additional goals included the elimination of some of the Japanese aggressive, warlike precepts such as terminating the emperor's role of inspiring the Japanese army, air force, and navy and honoring the Japanese kamikaze suicide fighters. These precepts had been taught in Japanese schools before and during World War II.

Mother and I to Honey's

My Mother was not allowed to join my father in Japan so she went to live with me and her Mother (my Grandmother "Honey") in her home. My Mother Shirley was extraordinarily well-traveled and ready to live in Japan if and when allowed. She took the bed that I was using in one of the bedrooms rather than sleeping downstairs where I moved.

Before Dad left for Japan my Mom and Dad, realizing the difficult times I was experiencing with these years of traveling, changing homes so many times, and feeling the isolation bitterly, asked me if I would like to return to Pocatello while Dad was in Japan. My reply was a positive, ecstatic YES! I was overjoyed by the idea.

Return to Pocatello? YES!

The first week I returned to Pocatello, my mother arranged for me to stay with one of her long-time friends' children, Ralph and Bernice Comstock, whom I knew and liked. Their home was on 10th Avenue, only a block from our family home on 11th Avenue.

7th Ave. Gang

I couldn't wait to see all the many people that I knew, especially the "Seventh Avenue Gang." I was a bit shocked to see how High School, Aging, Dating, and Working changed all of us. The new look was a shock to me. I really didn't have a close gang of friends anymore. We were all so busy with our respective lives that there wasn't much of the old spirit left, except for my special friends like Jack and Byron.

Losing Jerry Ann

In the first week of my return, an important priority for me was to look up my old and, as I see it, my first "girlfriend" Jerry Anne, and visit her during her lunch break at the moving company down by the railroad tracks, where she worked. During our conversation, she told me that she was not my girlfriend as I assumed. After leaving Pocatello in 1941 with my dad, I admittedly did not communicate much, if at all with her, my alleged "girlfriend." She, in the meantime, found a "boyfriend," Johnny. He was part of the Seventh Avenue Gang and once was a neighbor across the street from my own 7th Avenue family home. She told me frankly that she couldn't reestablish our relationship (and obviously didn't really want to).

It was disappointing. We seemed close when I left with my family and when my Dad joined the Navy, and I assumed that she would wait for my return. Her position was understandable but still a source of distress for me and apparently

1946-1947 High School Yearbook, Pocatello High School, Idaho

ALAN NICHOLS

TOP ROW: Coach "Chick" Atkinson, F. Chase, A. Nichols, W. Farnes, D. Cotant, G. Sato. BOTTOM ROW: L. Satterfield, D. Fry, J. Roberts, E. Dahlstrom, P. Sainsbury, W. Leach, B. Jones, Mgr. H. Steffens.

At the Idaho State Basketball Tournament Nichols, Fry, Roberts and Jones are part of the "7th Avenue Gang" and originally learned basketball on the 7th Avenue Gang John Roberts basket behind his home on 7th Avenue. The basket was attached to the garage and the "floor" was the paved car entrance to the garage.

P.S. We won every game except the last one at Boise High School.

Alan Nichols Forward*

ALAN NICHOLS

Laws for the P&H Limited come up frequently. When they do, these members of the department consider them: Jay Hawkes, Dick Petit, Roger Kerr, Virgil Camp, Gary Paxman, Harold Paige, Durwood Fry,* Bill Brydon,* Ruth Bilyeu, Alan Nichols,* Norma Monroe, Phyllis Rinker, Joe Sato. Miss Hoffman, Clive Barratt. Julia Hatch.

Senior Hi-Y passengers confer: Keith Gill, vice-pres.; Bob Pew, pres.; "Babe" Caccia, adviser; Bryon Jones,* treasurer; Don Hawkley, secretary; and Alan Nichols, chaplin.* They are talking over plans for the Older Boys' Conference.

*Members of the 7th Avenue Gang

even to her mother who was always very kind to me.

Nevertheless, I enrolled at Pocatello High School for my last year of high school. I was a member of the Pokey High basketball team and reclaimed old friendships, especially with Byron, Jack, Durward, and George. (Our Pokey High theme song begins "We're loyal to you Pokey High / We're the red and the blue Pokey High…".)

Intramural sports

That year, we had a good basketball team and won our bracket of teams in the final state tournaments. A team from Boise, Idaho won their bracket. The championship playoff was to be held in our Pocatello High School between Pokey and Boise. Before the game, the crowd was very noisy with special songs of encouragement, supporting me and our team. Unfortunately, I didn't play well enough afterward to deserve their cheers.

While I was traveling with my family for about three years, most of the neighborhood gang became full-blown professional heavy-duty truckers. They were hired to drive trucks full of new cars which were in great demand after WWII. Their route was from Detroit, Michigan to Durward's father's Dodge Agency in Pocatello, about 1,736 miles, sometimes in winter snow or rainstorms over the Rocky Mountains. By the time I returned home, they were all experienced drivers but I was never allowed to do such driving myself.

Driving heavy duty trucks over 1736 miles

Although I had experiences, adventures, and jobs in many places while traveling all over the U.S., my accomplishments, to me, seem minor in comparison to driving a huge truck. Yet, when I returned, Johnny, Byron, and Jackie told me that they were inspired by the things that I did on my own while following Dad on his Navy assignments. Jack asked numerous questions about the Saturday field trips I took alone by bus from Falls Church, Virginia to many museum adventures

Mutual admiration

Favorite Washington, DC Museum

in Washington, D.C. They seemed most impressed with my lunch every Saturday at an art museum surrounded by South Sea Islander art. I explained that it was very warm and comfortable in that museum; much more comfortable than the cold winter outside there in Washington D.C. I obviously enjoyed myself, even though on Saturdays, I had to get up early in the cold to catch the bus. I often napped afterward in the warm and humid corner of this favorite art gallery.

My friends appreciated that I survived as an outsider in several high schools, made new friends (OK socially), and did well in sports and academics. I also joined a marching band, thanks to my years of trumpet and band experiences.

Dad went to Japan with General McArthur. My mother returned to Pocatello from her sojourn with her mother Honey. Meantime my sister graduated from Idaho State College and continued her education at Stanford. Dad was due to return to Pocatello from his last post in Japan, to continue his job as President of Idaho State University.

High School graduation

It was June 1947 and I was about to graduate from Pocatello High School. It was a sad moment when Mom told me, a couple of months before graduation, that Dad would not be able to get back home for my graduation. That made me very sad but I still went through my graduation ceremonies at Pocatello High with my classmates, Mother, my Aunt Dorothy (Dad's sister) and my sister in the audience, but not Dad.

Pokey High Graduation

All my strong feelings of loneliness were revived just to know that my Dad couldn't attend my high school graduation. I felt abused, ignored, and disturbed, fearful that I didn't mean enough to him compared to General MacArthur, U.S. Foreign policy, and maybe his ego. I didn't feel a real celebration of my graduation, only sorrow, that my Dad wasn't there. At the end of the graduation, I was standing in the middle of

Sorry Dad can't attend my graduation

the auditorium stage with friends and fellow graduates. Each of us had received our Pocatello High School Graduation Certificate.

Transfer from emotional disaster to high point of my life.

At that point, from the corner of my eye, I saw Dad, in his U.S. Naval Commander uniform walking down the aisle with a huge smile on his face. My aching feeling disappeared. From an emotional disaster, this became a high point in my life. Dad, who survived two world wars serving our country, joined me for my important event. After the ceremony was finished, I walked calmly down the aisle. My Dad and I both smiled and hugged. My fellow graduates and the crowd at the auditorium of Pocatello High School passionately cheered for Dad. It was a joyful example of our whole country's happiness that World War II was over and that millions in the military and their families survived and were now together.

Cheers for Dad

I was so proud of my dad. He was kind, considerate, an important educator and teacher, an OK hunter and fisherman, and was well-liked by the Idaho State and New Mexico University communities, their students, teachers, and staff.

After his return from the war, my dad returned to continue his work as President of Idaho State and then, after my first year there, he became President of New Mexico A&M, a scientifically advanced school in Las Cruces, New Mexico. He also became very knowledgeable and active in supporting the many American Indian tribes in our part of the country like the Blackfeet, whose tribal reservation was close to Pocatello and other tribes. After completing his Presidency of New Mexico A & M President Truman nominated him, and the U.S. Senate confirmed his appointment, as The Commissioner of the United States Bureau of Indian Affairs which controlled Indian rights and tribal activity throughout the United States.

Two years later, Dad and Mom were reading the morning

Washington Post in their Washington D.C. apartment only to find that he was discharged as Indian Commissioner, without any discussion or notice, and "booted" upstairs to be the Assistant Secretary of the Interior, in charge of all U.S. possessions in the Pacific Ocean, the scene of many bitter battles with the Japanese Army and Navy in World War II. Dad became head of Civilian Civil Defense, which was a major federal effort because of the Russian threat and the development of atomic warfare. Dad died in New York City. He was playing basketball at 70 years old on a cold afternoon in Central Park. He was taken to the hospital. Mom called me so I flew to New York in time to say goodbye.

My mother and father enjoyed their lives together, and are still together in a joint grave at a cemetery south of their home near Stanford in Palo Alto, California. I am sure that they continue to be kind and loving with each other.

1944-1946
Psyche Talk

To better understand our mind and brain, mental process and activities, and our own psychology, answering important inquiries is more helpful than talking

Maybe it was the travel and the impermanence of everything while living all over the country during World War II. Maybe it was my inability to marry Jerry, my alleged but ignored first girlfriend. Maybe it was the disintegration of my beloved 7th Avenue neighborhood gang. Maybe it was my fear that I wouldn't graduate from Stanford as the fourth generation of my family to do so. Or maybe something else.

Psychiatric help

In any case, my mother and my sister concurred with Dr. Herbert Lehman, a psychiatrist, and traditional psychoanalyst, who recommended psychiatric help for me. He and they concluded that I showed signs of instability or depression, and suggested two meetings a week rather than the usual once-a-week treatment. I was opposed and said so. From classes in high school, independent psychiatry, my psychology studies, and reading on my own, I've learned about the incapacitating potential of depression. I told my family and Dr. Lehman that I didn't think that my psychiatric situation was serious enough, that treatment would be unlikely to help me, and that I had no real respect for the questionable process and ideas of usual psychotherapy. But my mother, whom I respected greatly, convinced me that I did need help and that I should see Dr. Lehman, whose office was across the street from Pokey High, more than once a week. For her,

Dr. Lehman

Once a week sessions

and because she was an extremely bright, wise, and a loving woman, I did sessions once a week for a while and it seemed to slightly improve my emotional life and attitude.

Psychoanalysis

Dr. Lehman's office

Sometimes my mother drove me to or from my appointments. I also began a study of psychiatric treatments and psychoanalysis on my own. The more I read, the more I concluded that this could be most interesting and possibly useful for me. One day when my mother picked me up at high school and drove me to Dr. Lehman's office for an appointment, I said that I still don't think once or even twice a week's psychiatric interaction was enough to be worth the high cost of the effort, but that three or four days a week in psychoanalysis might be a real opportunity emotionally. Lehman's office was close to my high school. Whenever I walked to school or rode my bike, it gave me time to think about the subjects and the process of my psychoanalysis. Several years later in a particularly difficult situation, long after Dr. Lehman confirmed that his work with me was as much as he could do and complimented me for my improved understanding, I asked him to come and help out on my new situation. He did, and I was shocked by how much older he seemed. It must be a hard life's work. That was confirmed in some writings of Freud and Jung.

Dr. Lehman revisited later

3 years Psychoanalysis helpful

My psychoanalytical experience took about three years, beginning with four sessions a week and gradually reducing to two. Gradually, I learned to deal with all the challenges and changes due to our moving with Dad during the war. I came to appreciate my mother's resiliency but also her weeping about how hard it was for them to travel so much, packing, unpacking, and settling in our new homes.

In retrospect, I enjoyed the sessions with Dr. Lehman, in spite of the times I cried or was deeply depressed. I came to appreciate their value to my psyche and came to better understand the concepts of analytic psychological reflection.

In fact, for many years my reaction to this development was "Thank Goodness."

My parents were not rich and I was not aware or even asked them how they handled this expensive treatment. This became highly "relevant" in my mother's last days many years later.

My special mother — wise, educated, and socially important — died in the year 2000. I took care that, as she wanted, she joined Dad for the rest of eternity in the same tomb in a cemetery not far from Palo Alto and Stanford.

My father Jack Nichols's during his term as Dean at Idaho State University

The Administration Building at Idaho State University under construction.

1947-1948 Academia in the Hills of Idaho State University (I.S.U.)

7th Avenue Gang to College

After high school, most of the "Seventh Avenue Gang" left for their respective colleges. Jack went to Stanford as an undergraduate and then followed his Dad to medical school (and later became a physician at Ohio State University in a show of support for his Dad). George, Bill, Durward and Johnny went to Idaho State University I.S.U. I returned home, and my Dad resumed his position as President of I.S.U. after returning from Japan. I decided to stay at Idaho State University rather than follow the family tradition of applying to Stanford. I received nothing special because I was the President's son, and my Dad seemed to go out of his way to remove any appearance of favoritism towards me.

I attend ISU

No Nepotism

Because all the servicemen were returning from World War II, the universities and colleges, including I.S.U., were jammed with students. I was assigned to a basement space, not even a real room, in Colonial Hall (still standing), already overcrowded. My father and mother were too busy with a burgeoning I.S.U. to be involved with me, even though they lived only five or six blocks from my dorm. Probably to make sure that I took part in college student life, unfortunately for me. I almost never received any invitations for meals or weekends at "home."

Basement room at Colonial Hall

Life Ski Era

I found escape in the joy of experiencing a new sport in my first year of college: skiing! Many small ski runs began to operate in the Mountains surrounding Pocatello. I lacked the

"Nichols Hall" to honor the author's father John R. Nichols, Ph.D., 13 years as President of Idaho State University

Alan Nichols, age 94, revisiting the campus of Idaho State College that due to his father Jack Nichols' stewardship as President (1934-1946) became Idaho State University.

balance to be a good skier, but I kept at it and continued later. Before I transferred to Stanford, a friend, who was also a student, and I set up a ski repair business for students, waxing, painting, and even repairing skis. My basement space in my dorm room for our "ski business operations" became an efficient and operational advantage for our business.

Ski work for students

Later, at Stanford, I worked to become a better skier, but in my opinion, I never became "good" in spite of skiing almost every weekend at Idaho State and often at Stanford. My weekend trips to the snow involved long drives to the Mountains of Idaho, Northern California, including Mount Shasta, Squaw Peak, Donner Summit, Southern Tahoe, Kingswood, Mount Lassen, Baldy, Yosemite, and others. We ate at the cheap, sweet, and salty bargain places along the way.

Stanford

Driving to ski slopes

Usually, I went with friends in their cars. Sometimes, I drove with my friend Jack from the Seventh Avenue Gang. During vacations when he used to go back to Pocatello I would take care of his car. I was more than happy to do that. One Christmas vacation he lent me his car for a skiing trip where I found a job in Yosemite National Park working in the Ansel Adams (the famous photographer) art store. Throughout many years of skiing and some snowshoeing, the business I operated with a friend, repairing and renting skis and snowshoes, paid for all these ski trips and equipment.

Jack's car

Ski Business supports skiing

I have a lifetime interest in sports, but skiing does not have the team sports opportunities that football, basketball, baseball, and such provide. I could improve in many other types of individual sports – bicycling, tennis, volleyball, hiking, and, even now, at 95 years of age, pedal-assisted cycling. I still have no talent in mechanical bicycle repair, but I am indefatigable about cycling all over the world, including Asia, South America, China, Japan, Hawaii, Turkey, Greece, and Mongolia for example.

Cycling, tennis, hiking

1939-1949
Jobs ... Jobs ... Jobs

It was summer, and I was again looking for a job in Pocatello. It was too late to recreate my usual gardening business, which I had operated for several years. I took care of many big gardens, weeding, watering, mowing, and shoveling snow from their walks in the winter.

Someone told me I should apply at I.S.U. for a job collecting garbage. It didn't even occur to me to see if my Dad, as the College President, might help me or at least offer some suggestions. But he was very much against nepotism, especially using his position to favor a family member. His attitude may have come originally from his own father, my grandfather Walter Hammond Nichols, a prolific author of boys' books such as The Measure of the Boy, Trust the Boy, A Morgan Rifleman, and others, all published by Macmillan. He was also the principal of Palo Alto high school, Superintendent of Schools in Palo Alto, and a part-time School of Education professor at Stanford.

Garbage "management"

I applied to Idaho State for an open position of collecting garbage and was hired. My boss, a fellow worker and driver of our garbage dump truck, was a rough character with a bottle of whiskey hidden under his seat from which he often imbibed in quick sips.

At each stop, I used to leave the truck and carry a large metal collection can into the dorm or other building and empty the building's cans into the large can I was carrying. The boss, experienced and older, pretty much used to sit in the truck and complain about my work. One afternoon, while picking up garbage on the top floor of a women's dormitory, I noticed two half bottles of wine in their trash and saved them, knowing my driver would be interested. I brought them down separately for him. His eyes lightened up, and he took a large swig from one of the bottles. Suddenly, his face turned red, and he yelled, "It's piss." We both laughed all the way to the dump.

Forest Service

I also got temporary summer jobs with the U.S. Forest Service, especially around Tahoe and some of the areas around Pocatello.

Working in the desert

I later joined my parents in New Mexico, where Dad was the President of New Mexico A&M (now New Mexico State). Without his help, I found a job as a low-level worker with a Navy team testing the new US Navy Aerobee rocket at its White Sands Desert base outside Las Cruces, New Mexico near White Sands National Park. Based on my experience, it was a well-paying job and interested me on both the military and scientific levels, even though I was just a laborer in a research lab.

Near the last two weeks of my summer job, before going back to school, our whole Navy Rocket Research Team was in the desert, working on the rocket guidance system. The desert was very hot where we were. I was directed to hoist the rocket up and down many times by a pulley system to test the experimental guidance equipment installation. The last time, I lost control of the rope since the rope was wet with my sweat. It slipped through my hands; the rocket collapsed, breaking and damaging all the loosely attached rocket gear being tested. The team I worked with over two months was so discouraged and disgusted that they never talked to me again.

Rope slips

Test rocket collapses

Lab crew shuns me

I'm admitted to Stanford

Thereafter, each day at the lab, the crew captain would give me my assignment, but no one else would even speak to me. Luckily for me, it is the end of the season. While on the job, I applied to transfer to Stanford and was admitted for my sophomore year. It would soon be time for me to leave for Stanford. Thank goodness. I'm on my way to following our family's Stanford tradition as an undergraduate sophomore and assigned to a large student facility in Menlo Park, a small town adjoining Palo Alto.

When I arrived at Stanford, I again experienced difficulty

obtaining a good job. My girlfriend Dorothy's mother, worked for the California Employment Commission and found me a summer job as a peach machine mechanic with a major California canned fruit company, the huge Del Monte Corporation in Oakland across the Bay. I earned good money by doing the job well in spite of my general mechanical incompetence and lack of experience. I helped keep the peach machines operating and was appreciated by most of the women machine operators. The other male mechanics intentionally sabotaged the machines to make these women operators miserable and lose credit with their supervisors.

I've always appreciated anyone who helped me find work: a janitorial staffing job in a community center in Seattle Washington; military work at White Sands, New Mexico; snow removal in Idaho; delivering newspapers in Pocatello; delivering clothes in New York City; band work in New York and California; summer labor jobs with the U.S. Forest Service and contractor. But I wanted to be a lawyer and hoped at least for a permanent opportunity in a good law firm.

WHO KILLED JANE STANFORD*
By Richard White (History)

"In 1885 Jane and Leland Stanford co-founded a University to honor their recently deceased young son. After her husband's death in 1893, Jane Stanford, a devoted spiritualist who expected the university to inculcate her values, steered Stanford into eccentricity and public controversy for more than a decade.

In 1905 she was allegedly murdered while in Hawaii. According to the Honolulu coroner's jury, Jane dies from strychnine poisoning. With her vast fortune the University's lifeline, the Stanford president and his allies quickly sought to foreclose challenges to her bequests by constructing a story of death by natural causes. The cover-up gained traction in the murky labyrinths of power, wealth, and corruption of Gilded Age San Francisco. The murderer "walked."

Deftly sifting the scattered evidence and conflicting stories of suspects and witnesses, Richard White gives us the first full account of Jane Stanford's murder and its cover-up. Against a backdrop of the city's machine politics, rogue policing, tong wars, and heated newspaper rivalries, White's search for the murderer draws us into Jane Stanford's imperious household and the academic enmities of the university.

*From *Who Killed Jane Stanford?: A Gilded Age Tale of Murder, Deceit, Spirits and the Birth of a University* (2022) published by W. W. Norton.

Arch at the main quad Stanford University.

1951-1953
Stanford University

My grandmother Honey lived close to the Stanford campus and was very generous when I visited about loaning me her car, "Petite," a 1929 Buick two-seater roadster, while I was a student there. It had shades and was big enough to be enjoyable, especially with dates. This was very useful because, in my undergraduate consciousness, women became especially important.

Starting school as a Stanford sophomore, I was housed for some time in a former research army camp which Stanford used for overflow students in Menlo Park. Feeling a little ostracized there, I joined the Sigma Nu fraternity located away from the main campus atop a small beautiful hill. To fit in, I felt compelled to become rowdy like some of my "brothers."

I misled my brothers into thinking that I really liked alcohol, a major part of our fraternity celebrations. I competed on behalf of my fraternity in most of the intramural campus sports — track, football, baseball, basketball, tennis — and injured my knee as a quarterback in football. I spent a week in the Stanford hospital after surgery and a lifetime of nursing my left knee.

At our fraternity initiation, everyone drank too much beer and, under the excuse of being drunk, it was reported, accurately, that I walked down our fraternity lodge dining room table almost naked but shod. At the time of our noisy celebrations, I also blew my trumpet.

I tried out for basketball and boxing at Stanford in my sophomore year, but was not good enough and was "cut." I spent the rest of my Stanford time in intramural sports. Our fraternity also competed in water sports in the spring on Sears Lake on the Stanford campus.

Alan Nichols as an undergraduate at Stanford University.

I enjoyed playing quarterback for my Sigma Nu fraternity. But a lot of the participants were strong players with much experience. They hit hard, especially on the quarterback. The side hit to my left knee hurt me for life. It required two knee cartilage operations, the first at Stanford and the second after I graduated. It took several years to rehab my left knee. The bad knee eliminated any activity in team sports. I took up tennis, biking, and hiking. I never lost my passion for activity and sought different outlets with age.

I was very busy while at Stanford. I wanted to succeed academically and socially. I did have time to enjoy Stanford football and basketball games. I didn't have the talent or the time to be a part of the official Stanford sports band or symphony orchestra.

I am proud I was appointed and then elected Student Secretary General of the Stanford United Nations, a national student organization of the UN to encourage peacemaking.

A teacher suggested, based on his observations of me and his own knowledge and experiences of the movies, that I should contact some of his movie connections in Hollywood. I thought that this was unrealistic and never carried out his suggestion.

I was basically healthy while at Stanford but endured some short-term hospitalization for colds, flu, and injuries. I was always "involved" and also worked, especially at the law school library. I did well in my major, Political Science.

I was happy to do a "big favor" for my 7th Avenue Gang friend from Pocatello, Jack, by storing his car at my fraternity. I used his car, as agreed when he used to go home on vacation. To be honest, he was doing me a big favor by loaning me his car, especially during Christmas holiday events and for my summer jobs.

Admiral Nimitz, commander and Chief of all Pacific forces in World War II, who's daughter was also a member of the Stanford Institute of International Relations of which Alan Nichols (right) was President.

1952-1954
The Korean War

America defends South Korea

To my surprise, and probably that of several thousand other young men, the U.S. declared war against North Korea, and in 1953, Reserve Officers' Training Corp (ROTC) officers and enlisted men were inducted into the U.S. Army. Many young Americans eligible for the Korean War draft were leery about joining the army or reserves. They were aware of the high casualties in World War II (1939-1945). As American troops, we were surprised to be fighting a foreign war so soon after World War II. We sensed that our fathers and uncles had worn themselves out by the end of that major war. However, I personally felt a strong connection and motivation to support South Korea against the North Korean/ Chinese invasion.

WWI

WWII

"Brothers At War"

I wanted to live up to patriotic volunteers like my uncle and father who both initially served as ambulance drivers in the French Army during World War I. When the United States joined the war my father became a tank driver in the U.S. Army Tank Corp. His commanding officer was Colonel George Patten who later became a vital general in WWII as a leader of armored divisions in Africa and Europe. My uncle stayed as a fighter pilot in the French Air Force and died a hero after being wounded near the end of the war in a dog fight with a German fighter in the skies above Germany. He was able to return to France and land in a field, succumbing to his wounds the next day. I wrote a book of World War I stories about my father and uncle in France, *Brothers At War* (Regent Press, 2020).

I was too young to be drafted in World War II but that situation no longer applied and I looked forward to service in the United States Army in Korea. I joined the ROTC at Stanford and trained there as an officer and became a Second Lieutenant. I was ordered to Fort Lee near Maryland for military training and actually looked forward to the opportunity to fight rather than just talk about North Korea's (and later China's) invasion of South Korea.

Join ROTC at Stanford

Once in Japan, most American troops, including me, went by boat through the seaport Sasebo in southern Japan to the Korean port of Pusan on South Korea's west coast. Many of the specialized troops were flown to Japan by the American Air Forces.

Troop ship to Pusan Korea

Japan is one of my favorite nations and peoples. It was a key support area and citizenry for the war against North Korea. The Army granted leaves from duty in Korea to go to Japan for a few days off. One of my joyful experiences during the war in Korea was a "leave" in Japan.

U.S. transforms Japan

Our U.S. Army's assigned objective was to stop the invasions of North Korean, Chinese, and some Russian troops into South Korea. They pushed us all the way back almost to Pusan, Korea, a port facility in South Korea. U.S. forces experienced huge casualties, but nobody that I knew considered it a possibility that American forces would be defeated and leave Korea. We later held on to our section of Korea at the 29th parallel. This at least became a symbol of American determination.

Objective in Korea

I still clearly remember the individualized combat with North Korean units just outside and east of Pusan. I stumbled across a North Korean army spy who was alone. He ran away from me. I fired my 30-caliber pistol at him but missed. He fired back at me. Neither of us said anything. I was very conscious of the serious American death casualties we suffered, even though North Korea was a small country, undermanned

Individual fight with North Korean

ROTC — The Korean War

North Korean prisoners

and dependent on the PLA (Peoples Liberation Army) "volunteers" from China. The North Koreans, at one point, felt their tactics weren't going to work and that they were defeated. To our disgust, these prisoners ripped off the clothes the U.S. Army provided them. They took advantage of the American Army's indulgence of enemy prisoners.

By that time, our commanding General, Douglas MacArthur, became unpopular. I think that's why he lost his opportunity as planned to run successfully for the Presidency of the United States.

U.S. Army leaves the Korean battlefield

Finally, an agreement was reached. The fighting stopped. The U.S. Army forces withdraw. North and South Korea established an occupied border at the 39th parallel. It was clear to me that the U.S. lost the Korean War, at least temporarily. Even though "Our War" in Korea was lost, we learned much about our military, which was more political than military. Looking good to the politicians was maybe more important than winning the struggle. From the point of view of U.S.

Army morale, I believe that I was one of the few members of the South Korean force who saw the Army and the Korean War as "opportunities to serve"... that I most value. Over seventy years later, I still believe in and love my country.

Leave Korea

I still treasure some of my mementos, medals, emotions, and thoughts from my time in support of the Korean War. That war effort was still in my opinion, a credit to our country. We supported the South Korean's defense against invasion by North Korea (supported by China).

Korean War Treasures

When I first reached the war zone in Korea through Pusan, a South Korean east coast seaport, I was transferred and assigned as a United States Army Liaison Officer to South Korean infantry troops. I figured that was probably because of my United States 47th infantry Division experience and training. While serving, I finally lost my eyesight from infection, probably from all the mud. I also lost my hearing in my right ear from the extreme noise without ear protection, South Korean cannon, machine guns, and other weaponry fire. Since the war ended, I was shipped back by troopship to America, discharged, and referred to civilian doctors in San Francisco. Luckily, they cleared my eyes with antibiotics, not penicillin, and provided a broadcasting hearing aide in my right ear. Those problems were cleared up in time for my return to a second year of law school at Stanford, a little tougher and wiser. Although I was relieved from active duty, I joined an army reserve group on campus at the Hoover Institute.

Back to law school and U.S. Army reserve

I was not called again by the army, so I was able to proceed with my life as a student, then a lawyer and even a politician.

1954-1990
Stanford Law ... Another San Francisco Lawyer

*Law Schools turn out lawyers
in order to provide winners and losers*

Begin Life Again

I felt that I was starting over in my life, wondering what to do next. When I was six or seven, I worshiped an uncle whose picture still hung on my bedroom wall. He was my model, who gave me my name and taught me how to serve and how to perform. He attended Stanford and could have been a lawyer but died in WWI, "shot down" over Germany on January 23, 1918. My other uncle (my mother's brother) Allen Charles, Esq., was one of the leading partners of the Lillick, Geary, Wheat, Adams and Charles Law Firm on the 5th and 6th floors of the California Building on California Street in San Francisco. My Uncle Allen was a well-respected admiralty lawyer especially known for handling significant ship collisions and maritime matters.

"I didn't know how closely their lives would have been a part of my own. I only knew that law school at Stanford would be tough. I wanted to do my best and hoped that people would be proud of my generation of law graduates."

Stanford Law School

Library Job for Stanford

I started Stanford Law School and obtained a job at the Law Library. The Stanford faculty and leadership were outstanding, in my opinion. I became very personally interested in Indian law, water law, finance, and corporate organization.

Active job hunting

Thanks to excellent professors such as George Osborne and Dean Carl Spaeth, I did well (Phi Beta Kappa). Toward the end of my schooling, I actively pursued jobs. I considered many possibilities and answered many calls from law firms in Hawaii, Los Angeles, Seattle, New York, Chicago, and Salt Lake, and finally decided that my best chance of succeeding was to stay near home where I was familiar with the area, people, and businesses. Many of my professors agreed, but none of my family had much interest.

Indian Law / Black Feet

I wrote what was considered a key article in my senior year. It was about Native American Indian Water Rights. My father, Jack, became an important personage with the Black Feet (aka Black Foot) Indian tribe who lived on the Federal Indian Reservation, immediately outside Pocatello, Idaho. The Black Feet were a powerful tribe from Montana until they were forced into Indian reservations. With that history and with my dad's talent, I was still surprised when United States President Truman, a Democrat, appointed Dad the administrative head of all federal Indians. He was confirmed by the United States Senate as the U.S. Commissioner of Indian Affairs. He and my Mom moved to Washington, DC. to serve that cause while I was at Stanford.

Turn down Chicago Indian Law firm offer

I was offered significant employment as a new lawyer based on my knowledge of Indian rights and connections to practice Indian law in a large law firm specializing in Indian law in Chicago but I turned it down after much consideration. I decided to begin my real law life with the Lillick firm, where my Uncle Allen was a leading lawyer in San Francisco.

My Uncle Allen's law firm was well known internationally in admiralty law in the San Francisco office and business law in our Los Angeles office. They told me that they needed a good attorney. Most of the partners and associates seemed to like me. I realized that it's a waste of time to spend a lot of effort giving interviews and considering other law firms. The Lillick firm had a strong policy of unity and encouraged young lawyers from the Northern and Southern California offices to meet at least once a year at one of the offices. Their attitude and activities impressed me, so I was ready and willing to be hired.

Anti-nepotism policies

I knew about the firm's anti-nepotism policy and also that my uncle could not be involved while I was being recruited by his law partners. He was busy trying a huge ship collision case in France and had no time to be involved in hiring one or two new young lawyers, which, of course, included me.

Invitation to join Law Firm

I accepted the firm's offer to join. They apparently felt it was worth it, even though hiring me violated their nepotism prohibition. I agreed of course.

Search for a job is over

Once I accepted a job as an admiralty lawyer with the Lillick law firm, my search was over. My office was on a high floor (the 5th) of the California Street building in San Francisco, occupied mostly by admiralty and maritime law firms and individual lawyer offices.

Seniors Ira Lillick and Joe Geary's continued leadership

The success of the "Lillick Office," recognized as one of the best admiralty law firms in America, was based on the continued participation of Mr. Lillick and Mr. Geary, two founding leader-partners. Ira Lillick was kind enough to tell me about how the firm was organized. He was proud of his accomplishments and said, "The future for this firm is in the hands of the young lawyers here and in the Los Angeles office."

Lillick advice and importance of new, young lawyers LA Office more business

Every now and then, he provided us with opportunities to visit our Los Angeles office, which was more business-oriented. We met with the young lawyers there, and alternatively, young attorneys from the LA office visited our San Francisco offices.

My role and, apparently, the purpose for hiring me was to expand legal specialties like wills, trusts, subdivisions, and corporate and municipal organizations. No matter what other cases we worked on, each lawyer assigned also became involved in shipping and admiralty law matters. For me, it meant more and more responsibilities. Each attorney was provided an office with a desk, chair, light, files, typewriter, and a high-quality secretarial staff. One of the pleasant surprises was that I was assigned a skilled technician who, although not a lawyer, provided invaluable support. These people were usually friendly and knowledgeable in the legal areas in which we worked and were supportive of our efforts.

Lillick firm legal associates support

As I advanced with the firm, I was given maritime matters like ship collisions, maritime board meetings, and cargo disputes. I became interested in many types of law. When I found good opportunities, I took them gladly. The law provided me with an interesting well-paid opportunity. I enjoyed a continuing connection with Stanford Law School and my uncle. This was only the beginning.

Case assignments — ship collisions, water rights, U.S. Maritime Commission

The details of the supportive activities of the law firm were vital to me. The Lillick office included other knowledgeable, skilled, and competent attorneys, as well as many new lawyers. As was true in my case, young lawyers were assigned all kinds of cases with different legal requirements and with the support and advice of an older attorney in the firm. Since this was an admiralty law firm, many of my extra cases involved water rights, and maritime, shipping, and cargo laws that were considered specialties in admiralty law. My uncle was a well-known specialist in litigating ship collision situations. When two ships collide and result in the sinking of one or both, the legal issues are extensive, and the cases often take years to resolve.

Lillick firm legal associates support

I was assigned many cases involving the U.S. Maritime Commission, a leading regulatory federal government agency enforcing maritime laws and regulations in the United States. These kinds of cases almost always involved insurance questions because the sums were high; insurance companies were knowledgeable and participated regularly in their cases.

Briefs for senior attorneys and clients

The formation of shipping companies, shipping groups, and agreements involved significant fees, although the maritime law specialty seemed rather restricted. Along with senior members of the firm, including my uncle (Allan E. Charles) and another senior attorney in the office (Joseph J. Geary), I wrote legal briefs. They reviewed, advised, and revised them as they were being produced before submission to the Federal Maritime Board. (See, for example, docket number 790, Complainants Encinal Terminal et al. Verses Respondent Pacific Westbound Conference).

When I first began at Lillick's office, I had relatively minor cases, like my apple-trees-in-an-accident case. An office client ran off the road into an apple orchard. My job was to prepare the case for trial and research how apple trees should be valued for damage. After a few months, I took on a sensitive litigation involving the 1913 Municipal Bond Act. Now and then, I handled divorce cases and even unconventional criminal cases related to water regulation and activities.

Consistent with one of my interests as an editor of the Stanford Law Review, I prepared a new article, "Water Rights." A friend from many years and in Law School, Harold Rogers was very interested in my project. We worked out a way for us to share writing the 2-volume book *Water for California – Planning, Law, Practice, and Finance* to be published by a leading legal publishing house, Bancroft-Whitney. This book, in two volumes, includes water organization, water

2 volume "Water for California" with my friend Harold Rogers

development, and water rights, plus special tables, detailed analysis, water districts, private & mutual companies, and water finance. The project was long, difficult, and complicated. Volume One, which Harold mostly prepared became 669 pages. Volume Two, my work, was over 1000 pages. When you consider our law practices, families, and other activities, it was an overwhelming project. In my case, I also prepared some law review articles about various aspects of improving and impacting water rights and water finances in California.

Hal Dobbs

One of my admired fellow attorney associates, Hal Dobbs, a few years older than me, became interested in politics and served on the San Francisco Board of Supervisors. He ran cleanly but unsuccessfully for Mayor of San Francisco. He encouraged and showed me how to continue to be a productive lawyer in the firm and also to engage in political activity.

Hal lives in St. Francis Woods

Hal Dobbs lived in the beautiful tree and flower-filled Saint Francis Woods area of San Francisco in a huge home with his large family. (My home was nice, yet not as pretentious as Hal's house about six blocks from where I lived. Both were in beautiful areas in West San Francisco adjoining the Sunset district and included nearby hills for hiking and biking. Mount Davidson, "Holy Mountain" (described later), and Twin Peaks, another prominent recognized area of San Francisco, are just across a small valley from Forest Hills where I lived.

Holy Mountain

Like Hal Dobbs, who left the firm and became heavily involved in politics, I left the firm to form my own law firm after several years in order to pursue other interests including real estate development and local politics.

21st Assembly District Politics

We lived in the 21st Assembly voting district, and, after work one day, the first political meeting I attended was a district meeting. It was a gathering of Republicans, and we heard remarks by a local Assemblyman, John Busterud, who I later helped campaign successfully.

Friends and supporter of Assemblyman John Busterud

I supported his run as a State Senator and later as the California State Attorney. He later ran unsuccessfully for Mayor of San Francisco. He, his wife, and our family become close friends. Our regular District political meetings were conducted at the local headquarters on California Street in San Francisco.

Run for Congress against Nancy Pelosi

A large part of my attention, after my job and the family, became Republican politics. I ran, unsuccessfully, for Congress against Nancy Pelosi, a Democratic Congresswoman. She became a famous politician for whom I had little respect. After her reelection, she sent me a letter threatening a libel lawsuit if I did not deny and withdraw comments and critical remarks I made about her in my campaign. I replied in a letter to her that all my oral and written comments that I said about her were all true and I welcomed her attempting a lawsuit against me. In fact, I would boost me in my political career. I never heard from her again.

Campaign Manager Roles

I also become campaign manager for many Republicans, including excellent California state Senators, Governors and other outstanding Republican office holders. I led political committees supporting President Nixon, President Ford, several senators, both state and local, the San Francisco Mayor, and members of the San Francisco Board of Supervisors. Mayor Shelley, a labor leader and prominent Democrat, appointed me as head of the San Francisco School Board and I was elected after confirmation from the Board of Supervisors. I was credited as a hardworking, effective, and popular candidate. Politics gave me an opportunity to know my community and to serve as best I could.

Democratic "labor" mayor appoints me to San Francisco School Board

Politics to serve

In those days, Republicans dominated the Governorships, Mayors, State Senate, Congressional delegation, and many other positions. My involvement provided many

Change in California political atmosphere

speaking opportunities and chances to serve. Over time, the political atmosphere changed significantly. Republicans were always a minority in California but still elected by the voters, Republicans, Democrats, and independents.

I also became a member of several private clubs. One of them was an outstanding social support organization, with a beautiful wooded property along the Russian River we called The Grove.

"Prioritas – Femitas"

Making love sheds a lot of hate

First love, my mother Shirley

Naturally, the first woman I remember with love is my mother, Shirley Nichols. She gave birth to me at the Palo Alto Hospital on February 14, 1930. It was not just any February in 1930, but Valentine's Day! Maybe this explains my pleasure and appreciation of women. A key to my own birth is love... February 14, Valentine's Day.

Strong marital relations

More practically and considering my own history, I've decided some things: For one, I'm going to be honest and straightforward in this book about my four failed marriages, my relationships, and my strong interest in women.

First names only

Out of respect and in the interests of privacy, I will not use the last names of lovers and will not specifically identify my wives or girlfriends. I will use only their first names. The readers can understand of course, from my own lack of marital success (four out of four), that I have had difficulties in my life with wives. Many men experience such difficulties, including divorce and suffering. Women were crucial to my happiness and, one way or another, are more important as part of my joy than my anxieties throughout my life.

As I entered adolescence, the spirit of the Seventh Avenue Gang faded as our interests were overcome by girls and women. Our parents picked up on our attitude and required us to learn to dance at Pinkerton's Dance School, a business operating in our neighborhood. I acquired a strong attachment to and fascination with women. In spite of the female part of our culture that seems to me hell-bent on acquiring all the attributes of men, I believe most women are generally kind, helpful, supportive, and often eager to be enjoyable companions.

Affection has always been important to me. I never indulged in sexual consummation until the first night of my first marriage. For me, love can be more a powerful dream than an experience, probably because of my shyness and hesitancy or perhaps due to a sense of Mormon morality. Latter-Day Saint Mormonism was a prominent aspect of Pocatello culture, even though it was not my personal religion. I attended the Episcopalian Church, which was downtown near the high school. Although my mom and dad were not churchgoers, my "Gang" friend Byron encouraged me to attend with him and his mother. My lack of actual sexual intercourse until marriage probably explained my interest in pornography and a strong imagination.

Unrealistic dreams

My own first love interest was Jerry Ann. She lived with her mother in a small home on 10th Avenue. Her mother was a kind, pleasant teacher. Jerry was my first serious girlfriend. It wasn't until college that my formal evening dates with others in Pocatello began, usually on their respective front porches or at the movies.

Six different high schools

In high school, while traveling with my family during WWII, I enjoyed girlfriends in Falls Church, Virginia, Amy in New York City, and Joyce in Redwood City, California. I looked up Jerry Ann as soon as I returned to Pocatello while my dad was called to serve as the Education Advisor to General Douglas MacArthur during the U.S. occupation of Japan. One of my key dates at Stanford was Lolita, whom I later married at the Stanford Chapel and she became mother of my daughter Sharon and son Alan Jr.

As to my first love — Jerry Ann, lived on 10th Avenue in Pocatello. I never knew her father, but she had a talented brother who also attended Stanford. She was also blessed with a very kind mother, a Pocatello elementary school teacher.

Six different high schools

Jerry Ann and I were very responsive to each other's interests when we were young, around nine or ten years old. We went to the same school, Washington Elementary, on 11th Avenue in Pocatello. We cared for each other. For a while, we attended the same Episcopal church. So, when I left Pocatello to travel with my Dad and the family around America during World War II and attended six different high schools, I often dreamed of Jerry Ann. I was sure she was the woman that I would meet again, talk to again, and possibly even marry. My memory and hopes for a future with her often lessened my depressive and lonely feelings when not in Pocatello "paradise."

Marriage?

Marriage is important in Idaho, so for me and Jerry Ann it wasn't especially unrealistic. But we didn't communicate for years. I'm sure that's no way to establish or maintain a loving relationship.

When first return to Pocatello I visit Jerry Ann

While we were separated, I enjoyed kind, loving experiences with other women, but when I finally returned to Pocatello, the first thing I did, with significant love in my heart, was to arrange a lunch meeting with Jerry Ann near her job in the office of a moving company. I told her, "Jerry Ann, I've been thinking about you for all these years that I've been gone." In response, she said, "I too, but I assume all this time that you are traveling with your family and maybe will never return . . . no letters . . . no calls . . . nothing from you. So right here and now, I'm going with and planning to be engaged to another member of your old Seventh Avenue Gang — Johnny."

She thinks I'm never returning and is planning engagement to Johnny of the Seventh Avenue Gang

She's right but I miss her

Hearing that was a shock and a surprise, but the more I thought about what she said, the better I understood. I don't know if I could wait for years for someone without receiving any communication from them. So, we parted, and it is one of the most memorable regrets of my life. I never saw her again. I was told she did marry Johnny. I hope that she is still living and is happy.

I also had a "girlfriend" in the Fall's Church, Virginia school we both attended. I didn't see her much since she lived in a different town a few miles away, not safely reachable on my bike at night. She was more of an imagined girlfriend, more a dream than a reality, but I enjoyed knowing her at school.

After moving to New York City and being assigned to a Columbia University "guinea pig" experimental high school (Lincoln High School) in Harlem, I got to know Amy who also attended Lincoln High School. We were attracted to each other, and she invited me to her birthday party at her parents' fancy apartment on 5th Avenue. To my surprise, after a fine dinner and birthday song, her father gave us two tickets to the famous musical Oklahoma, which had been recently premiered on Broadway. It was a wonderful and exciting event in my life. We enjoyed ourselves immensely, and I took her for ice cream afterward at the famous Fifth Avenue Creamery. I smiled and hummed tunes from this fantastic production all the way home . . . "There's a bright golden haze on the meadow. "The corn is as high as an elephant's eye, and I think that it's growing right up to the sky . . . "

Amy birthday at "Oklahoma"

Soon after we returned back to California where my Dad was ordered to training in Monterey. My mom and I stayed with her mother, my grandmother, the family calls Honey. I bicycled ten or twelve miles every day, round-trip, from Honey's home to Sequoia High School in Redwood City. It was one of those huge modern high schools in California. I did well academically, but it was too late to join a sports team or the school band as the seasons were already beginning, and they didn't need another trumpet player. It was the only high school where I was not able to join the band and participate

Big commute from Honey's home to Sequoia High School

Joyce

Joyce

in a sports team. I felt "left out," but I got some good exercise on my bike, and I did meet Joyce.

My grandmother, Honey was generous and lent me her 2-seater 1929 Buick Coupe with pull-down shades. Joyce lived in Redwood City, and we enjoyed a few dates. I was thankful that I didn't have to pick her up on my bike!

Joyce parties

Joyce was pleased. I liked her. I was not in this high school long enough to establish long-term friends, yet thanks to her I was invited to some school parties. Sequoia wasn't so bad after all. While I was at Honey's home, while my parents were at the Naval Language School in Monterey where Dad was learning the Japanese language.

Dorothy

At Stanford, I was sure that I was going to marry a beautiful, affectionate Texas woman, Dorothy. I not only was very close to her, but was fond of her brother and her very pleasant mother.

Marriage

The subject here is women. It may have been a mistake that, although I very much dreamed about intimate relations, I was uncomfortable and avoided the temptation to indulge in sexual intercourse until my first marriage. I was "from the old school," as they say. My four marriages included Lolita, whom I married at the Stanford chapel; Joanne, twenty years later at the Yosemite Lodge; Nancy, at an Episcopal Church; and Becky, twenty years after that at the Fallen Leaf Lake chapel near Lake Tahoe.

Few women in my life but critical part of my life

Years later, when Becky and I were camping in a California state park in the Sierras on a trip to Death Valley, the camp director visited us several times and talked incessantly. He bragged about the length of his marriage, lasting over 21 years. I responded that I had been married for over fifty-five years. This was a shock to him until I explained that was because my marital longevity was not monogamous but multiple marriages! I added all my marriages up and enjoyed the memories of all those years and was willing to sincerely brag about them.

A few others

As I mentioned, my connection with women was limited in numbers but exceptionally important to me. We already mentioned Jerry Ann, Amy, Joyce, Dorothy, my wives, and a few others. Over time, from 1940-2023 (so far), my interest has always been aroused by women who were kind, thoughtful, loving, empathetic, outdoorsy, affectionate, and joyful. Dorthy, who I thought I would marry at one time, lived in a Stanford residence full of nice women, including Lolita, who later became my first wife.

Three or four women whom I do not marry also had prominent parts in my life, including a gorgeous high school sweetheart, who also lived on 11th avenue in Pocatello. We enjoyed our togetherness and friendship on her front porch. There were probably one or two more, including a Palm Springs friend, and Amy in New York City.

Marriage and Divorce

It surprised me how long I remembered these very special women. I consider myself lucky to have known them all and experienced great happiness, pleasure, and freedom. It's a surprise, considering the four women I did marry, that I didn't marry more. I can't remember why we each broke up. I think I was with Lolita for about twenty years and Becky told me we were together for twenty-one years. I don't remember all the things that went wrong in these marriages, but I do remember all the good things.

A red haired family friend

The vice president of Idaho State University, who took over when Dad left for Navy WWII duty, brought his family, including a very nice red-haired daughter. Our two families spent some time together on holidays and weekend picnics. Friends and family were confident that one day I would (or should) marry her, but that never happened. I'm embarrassed to report that she wasn't quite good-looking enough for my taste, although she was exceptionally kind. I think that she might have been an exceptional wife. I never saw her again after I left Pocatello a few months later.

Positives

On my journeys with my family over the whole country, my time in Japan, and my exploration of foreign places, I met women I liked and whose company I enjoyed.

Emphasizing positive aspects of my relationships with each one of my four wives, I became aware that each woman provided support, love, and enjoyment even though the divorces resulted in financial and emotional burdens and difficulties.

LOLITA

I met my first wife, Lolita, at Stanford. She was a wonderful mother to my children, son Alan and daughter Sharon. She was a very active, supportive, and sociable person who attracted people. She was interesting and enjoyable. She was a long-time president and leader of the San Francisco Opera Guild, a major social organization in San Francisco and helped me in my law business.

JOANNE

Joanne and I enjoyed raising our youngest son, Shan. She supported me with her skills and knowledge of the law and contributed to my law firm Nichols, Rogers, Doi, and, Chan. I started a law firm after I left the Lilick firm. She was most helpful with my legal writing career, including the two-volume, 1,600-page legal reference book "Water For California", which I wrote with my partner Hal Rogers and published by a leading law publishing firm, Bancroft and Whitney.

NANCY

Nancy was a truly "literary" wife who inspired me in my authorships in law, poetry, and exploration. She was also very helpful in my political career. She was most helpful when I became chairman of the San Francisco School Board, and campaigned against Congresswoman Nancy Pelosi. Her interest in books and authorship was a joy to me. Nancy is the only wife, as far as I know, who wrote a book criticizing me after our divorce.

BECKY

While all my wives were involved in my explorations, my last wife, Becky, was ready to travel anytime and anyplace, including enjoying the thousand miles of roads in the Middle East, and Tibet. Nothing was as special as our bicycle trip from San Diego's Pacific Ocean to St. Augustine's Atlantic Ocean and back.

Becky, a true traveler, was ready to support and join me in explorations to find the tomb of Genghis Khan, biking over the Himalayan Mountains from Urunchi, under Chinese control, and several trips circumambulating Kang Rimpoche in Tibet, the most admirable Sacred Mountain in the world.

Thank you all... Lolita, now deceased, Joanne, Nancy, and Becky. I bless you and thank you all for our lives together.

Love — Alan

"nihonjin desu ka"
Japan / Happiness

Japanese appreciation

Am I Japanese? No. I'm not Japanese. As a patriotic American in World War II, I used to hate them. But they're my favorite people now and I've been there many times. At heart, and in my old age, I often "feel" Japanese. Since the end of World War II, I've hiked and studied the country's impressive Sacred Mountains. It's difficult to remember all my experiences in Japan and my R&R (rest and recuperation) leaves there from service in the Korean War. Being in Japan was like a vacation in contrast to Korea, which was at times fearful, snowy, dangerous, and usually muddy!

Vacation from Korea

I spent a few days' leave in Japan from the war in Korea, absorbing and enjoying the cleanliness, landscaping, and natural unity before returning to face the Korean War.

In Japan, I enjoyed the company of a nice Japanese geisha woman and took her to lunch. Our conversation in English was a pleasant surprise. We enjoyed our time together but avoided any intimacy.

Japan supports U.S.

Mount Fuji-san

I remember many extraordinary expeditions before and after the Korean War exploring the Sacred Mountains of Japan. One of my first expeditions was to climb Mount Fuji-san along with thousands of Japanese during the short summer climbing season. At sunrise, we all shouted from the top and sides of the Mountain: "Kamikaze."

Gotemba hot tub and hot sand

I know of extraordinarily complex conditions at Mount Fuji since foreigners, including Americans, were not encouraged. I also made several trips to a Buddhist temple nearby in a town called Gotemba. I visited a Japanese temple to enjoy glorious hot tub bathing. The next few days we climbed a series of Sacred Mountains in that area.

Japan Sacred Mountains

Years later, I also climbed Sacred Mountains in Southern Japan. I came upon a beautiful Buddhist temple, and as I stood there admiring it, an upper window opened, and a Buddhist priest put his head out. "Can I help you?" he said in English. I replied, "Thank you." I told him that we enjoyed a Japanese hot sand burial that morning and felt his temple would be a grand visit but it was closed. He came down, opened the cargo door of his vehicle, invited us to get in, and offered to take us nearby to a Sacred Forest and Sacred Mountain. We joined him happily.

Buddhist Priest kindness

My attitude had already changed from hate for our enemy in WWII to admiration and gratitude now.

As I dream and think of Japan, several thoughts arise, including my admiration for my dad, who served Japan as General MacArthur's Education Advisor in the United States occupation of Japan after World War II. Also, I appreciated the kindness of the Buddhist Shinto priest who saw that I needed help and personally took me and Becky to beautiful places in his own car. I still remember several geishas who were not in the sex business but were beautiful, kind, and considerate. They often recited verses of poetry in English that were happy and worthwhile.

Love of Japanese Spirit

I loved and still love Japan, its people, its culture, and its holiness. I slept several nights in a temple in Kyoto, temples expressing the spirit of Buddhism in Japan. Before going into the Sacred Mountains, I found happiness in Kyoto, North and South Japan, Fuji-san, and even the islands nearby.

Happiness sites

The temple and the priests enhanced my outstanding and spiritual life in Japan. I recently read a book about death by Arnold Toynbee. He is the only one I found who does not seem to catch that spirit. American soldiers in the Korean War

Mystical spirit of Japanese women in Japan

were attracted to the Japanese people and their culture. Many of them married Japanese women. In my opinion, it was particularly because of the mystical spirit these women seemed to carry with them. That is a great part of the history of Japanese people…in all directions…in towns and temples.

I remember my night with the angels when the Japanese mountain police let me alone in my sleeping bag in the center core volcano atop Mount Fuji and allowed me to actually sleep all night next to the altar of an important temple in Kyoto.

Immersed in Japanese culture

It was a delight and a pleasure to immerse myself in the joyful quietness pervading the culture of Japan, which I experienced there on many occasions. One of my earliest experiences, my first summer there, was joining thousands of Japanese to climb Mount Fuji-san.

There were so many people at the top that there was no place to spend the night. There were not enough small lodges available for everyone, but I never refused an opportunity for an adventure in the spiritual worlds of Japan. I carried a couple of blankets and a sleeping bag to the top, pretending I didn't know any better. I hiked to the very bottom of the largest crater to set up my camp and experience slumber that I would always treasure. The Japanese left me alone, although I am sure it was some kind of violation of their regulations. I accepted the mountains' gift of a spiritual experience atop their most important Sacred Mountain Fuji-san. When the night disappeared, an inspiring, explosive, and holy sunrise appeared on the eastern slope. Hundreds of Japanese shouted "Kamikaze" as the sun rose. I stood with them on the summit and shouted along with them.

Japanese police overlook my camp site in one of the summit volcanos on top of Mt. Fugi-san

Left alone to sleep atop Fuji

"Kamikaze!"

Shortage of

I was fortunate enough to buy some food from one of the lodges, a blessing since I was very hungry and it was a long hike back down. I was also lucky to be alone descending the

Mountain at the bottom of the Fuji trail. No one bothered me. My walk down the Mountain by myself was in an ecstasy. Near the end of the trail, a Japanese man joined me and talked to me about Mount Fuji. He spoke perfect English. When we got near the exit, there were many restaurants, and he asked me if I would like to have breakfast as his guest.

Walking with policeman

That slightly aroused my suspicion about his objective, so I politely declined. Another Japanese hiking down the mountain soon after, also began a conversation in English with me after the first man excused himself to find water. The second Japanese hiker warned me that the first Japanese, who was walking with me much of the way, was a police agent and I should avoid him. So, I picked up another trail and took another exit without any problem and without interruption. It was a significant relief to be on Mount Fuji and not end up in jail for trespassing. When I got to the bottom, I knew, from prior experience, where the train station was, so I bought a ticket to return to Kyoto.

Escape from trail

This time Fuji-san contributed to my love for Japan and its people. The most beautiful, spiritual sleep I ever had was in the crater of that important Sacred Mountain. In fact, when I returned to Japan after being released from the Army on my way to America, I spent some extra time meditating and reflecting on Japan before taking the troop-ship home.

My being in Japan only confirms my love of exploration and appreciation of Japanese culture and spirit. It initiated my world biking and hiking explorations in China, India, Tibet, Mongolia, the Silk Road, and other parts of Asia, as well as America.

While many American troops were critical of their Korean War experience and the U.S. Army, I came away after my Japanese visit exhilarated, wiser, and particularly Happy.

Dalai Llama GO HOME!

I wish I were supernaturally strong so I could put right everything that is wrong

One of the saddest things in human experiences is to be misled. Where is the Dalai Lama now . . . Russia, Ukraine . . . and what does he have to say today (2024).

Visit to XIV Dalai Lama India HQ

I had the opportunity to meet the Dalai Lama. After explorations on the lower reaches of Makalu and Everest Base Camp with a companion, Dick Blum, and a visit to some Tibetan Temples in the nearby valley, we were able to hike out to a road where a car picked us up. We were then driven to Dharamsala, India. The government in exile of Tibet, including the XIV Dalai Lama, resided in Dharamsala, thanks to the generosity and bravery of the Prime Minister of India, Nehru. Tibet and India have been enemies in the past years, yet China was now threatening a military invasion of Tibet for allying with India. We were met and put up at the Dharamsala Government administrative quarters.

Dalai Lama "Audience"

The next morning, we met several others, mostly Tibetans of the Tibetan government in exile, and took part in an "audience" with the 14th Dalai Lama. He was a delightful host and a convincing supporter of his cause to save his Tibetan people from China's genocide. I still remember and am a little surprised that he didn't have a bad word for China or the Chinese, in spite of their destruction of Tibet, its people, and over 6,000 monasteries.

My fellow companion Dick and I each had a chance for an individual conversation with the Dalai Lama. We were

Dick Blum Leader

both much impressed. In fact, after that, Dick became a leader in supporting Tibet and, in particular, the Dalai Lama. Dick formed a Himalayan Institute to provide support for Tibetan activities. We also met a few important Tibetans dedicated to rescuing Tibet from its degradations and destruction, but in retrospect, I discovered that they were not supported by the Dalai Lama and, as a result, lost their positions.

Return Home

Shortly thereafter, we returned home to my life of explorations and my family, my San Francisco School Board duties as Chair of the Governing Board, and my political effort to support the Republican governor and an Idaho senatorial candidate. Dick went back to supporting his wife-to-be, United State Senator Diane Feinstein of California. Unfortunately, Dick is now deceased.

The reason for including Dalai Lama with Mount Everest as a Holy Mountain is because the Dalai Lama and Mount Everest were the most popular person and Mountain in the world at that time. Of course, Everest, as a Sacred Mountain, has thousands of years of fame, while a famous person is limited to a lifetime at best, perhaps with some historical extension. In my case, I was never strong or skilled enough to climb Everest.

Go Home, Now

I later strongly felt that, politically and personally, the Dalai Lama lacked the courage and wisdom to live up to his reputation. The Dalai Lama was a failure, at least for the Tibetan people. I and a few other friends picketed two of his speeches in California with a pamphlet saying, "Go Home, now." Instead of visiting America and Europe over and over again, he apparently thought selling his books and preserving his popular non-violence philosophy, all personal benefits, were appropriate while his countrymen remained suffering under the military occupation and control of the PLA (China's People Liberation Army).

The author with the 14th Dalai Lama

Details follow: see a copy of the brochures a few of us used to outline our point of view and distributed publicly as to the failure of the Dalai Lama to help the Tibetans still suffering in Tibet from the Chinese genocide.

Freedom Without Fighting for It

I also admired the 14th Dalai Lama tremendously, but I wondered whether anybody or any nation or people can obtain their freedom without actually fighting for it and being willing to give their own lives for their country. But it appears his moral message was more important to him than his Tibetan peoples' survival. He felt it was other people's duty, particularly, Europeans and apparently Americans, to fight and die for Tibetan survival.

At the same time, he was constantly telling the world that he will not support nor be a part of anybody killing anybody else, no matter what the cause or circumstances. The Tibetans have a long warrior history of fighting for their own causes themselves. They also worshipped and admired the Dalai Lama. So far, the Tibetans in Tibet had little hope for freedom.

Peace Delegations Ineffective

The Dalai Lama sent several peace delegations to negotiate with communist China. China ignored his toothless efforts. The Dalai Lama even felt it was inappropriate to call the Chinese his "enemies." The Chinese realized that the Dalai Lama's anti-violence philosophy carried no weight against them, in spite of the worldwide protests in favor of the Dalai Lama's spiritual and religious consistency.

Slowly but surely, I personally concluded that the Dalai Lama was psychologically unqualified. He was fearful and could not do anything personally to free his own people. Philosophically, he must have decided it was wiser to advance his own interests and ideas along with Tibetans who had managed to escape already from Tibet and China's violence against Tibetans still living and suffering under the military occupation of China. The Dalai Lama, as I saw it, was criticizing those Tibetans led by the Dalai Lama's own brother for struggling and fighting back against the Chinese.

Dalai Lama criticized Tibetan guerillas trying to free Tibet

Many claimed the Dalai Lama knew about the efforts of the Tibetan fighters but did nothing. When it became publicly known of the Tibetan Guerilla's Operation, his public reaction was to criticize those brave Tibetan warriors. Because of the Dalai Lama's publicly stated opposition to any violence by Tibetans, the fighters stopped their guerila warfare activities, some leaving and returning home, some making a last desperate effort against the Chinese and some more directly committing suicide. Some made one last raid against overwhelming Chinese forces and never returned. I believe those Tibetan guerillas were morally justified to fight for their own and their fellow Tibetan's freedom.

Tibetan guerillas give up

According to numerous news reports, the Chinese have never yet paid in a real way for the destruction of over 6,000 Tibetan monasteries, killing hundreds of thousands of Tibetans and demeaning Tibetans economically, environmentally, spiritually, and humanly.

Genocide

In fact, the United Nations' recognition of China's genocidal atrocities added a more specific definition of "genocide"… "population transfer" is a genocidal event whenever a government makes life impossible or barely survivable for the indigenous locals. China did just that and flooded Tibet with Chinese citizens protected and supported by China's armed forces. Busloads, truckloads, and trainloads of native Chinese civilians had forcefully taken over Tibet, including government administrations, property ownership, and development, economic activities, as well as public water infrastructure so essential for survival there.

UN: Population Transfer

I became so disillusioned with the Dalai Lama, who was once a personal hero to me, that on two occasions, I organized pickets against the Dalai Lama and advocated his return to Tibet to protect His own people and His nation. He apparently had little respect for what needed to be done if "His" people were ever to earn their own freedom without violence. In the meantime, at least the Dalai Lama's life continued happily, especially because of India's provision for his home and safety, along with some escaped Tibetans. Now, he still seems admired by millions of people worldwide and worshipped by his fellow Tibetans. He survived the genocide against his fellow citizens and led a protected life, thanks to India's generosity.

Picket Dalai Lama to "Go Home"

Unfortunately, once I became aware of what was going on, I also concluded from my own research that the Dalai Lama misrepresented the doctrine of Ahimsa (nonviolence). That doctrine accepts the concept that a person or a people fight and commit violence if necessary to save themselves against any genocidal effort to destroy them. Self-defense is a

Ahimsa misrepresented

moral justification for violence.

Under the guise of Ahimsa, the Dalai Lama did nothing about the failures of the several low-level teams of negotiators who took the time to supposedly negotiate a peace. It never happened, and China's representatives were almost all minor officials. The peace he claimed to want never happened. It was obvious to everyone involved.

The Panchen Lama, the second most significant Lama in Tibet, at first supported the Chinese with the Dalai Lama's approval, but the Panchen Lama then came to realize what a waste of time and effort that was and wrote a powerful story about the Chinese Communist Tibetan genocide in Tibet. It refers to the systematic, intentional denial of Tibetan civil rights, education, freedom, and employment.

Panchen Lama eliminated

The 14th Dalai Lama is extraordinarily popular worldwide. He was also an active author and official head of Tibetan Buddhism and the Tibetan government. He sacrificed the freedom of his people without any fight while he was dependent and still living on the compassion of the government of India.

The 14th Dalai Lama still lives. I still live. Billions around the world still live. Millions of Tibetan peers do not.

Who Lives Who Died

1959: His Holiness the Dalai Lama, Tenzin Gyatso, seated on his throne and wearing the gold peaked cap which is his crown, smiles while giving an audience in Lhasa, Tibet.

The historic Potala in LIhasa, Tibet, the home of the XIVth Dalai Lama until he escaped the PLA Chinese Army invasion and occupation of Tibet to Dharansala, India. The foreground lake has been replaced by the Chinese from a lake into a concrete Chinese PLA military drill ground.

STANFORD WELCOMES
THE FOURTEENTH DALAI LAMA

I am definitely happy.

The Dalai Lama's life is happy:

- Worshipped by his fellow Tibetans
- Enjoys world-wide media admiration
- Writes, publishes, and copyrights over 24 books, some best sellers
- Receives hundreds of honors and awards including the Nobel Peace Prize
- Lives happily and securely in comfort outside Tibet in India.
- Travels with his entourage in safety all over the world.
- Socializes at the highest international levels of jet-set society, arts, education, governments.

(All "quotations" in italics are from the Dalai Lama's own writings)

But now it's time to

GO HOME
TO TIBET

FOR 60 YEARS THE GENOCIDE CONTINUES

- 1.3M deaths from China's occupation. (By 1996, 173,000 while in jail.)
- China's Tibet genocide by population transfer continues in violation of Geneva Convention IV.
- 6,200 Tibetan monasteries destroyed.
- Children (including 6 year olds, women, monks, and nuns jailed, tortured, killed for loyalty to the Dalai Lama).
- Systematic, intentional denial by China of Tibetan civil rights, education, employment.
- China's railroad to Lhassa will complete the genocide as it has in Xinjiang, against the Uighurs and Inner Mongolia against Mongolians.

The abuse of monks and nuns has been going on since 1961. Atrocities are commonplace-crucifixion, vivisection, disemboweling, burning, beating to death, burning alive, dismemberment, hanging upside down, tearing out tongues, dragging to death behind horses, electric shock into orifices, especially womens', rape.

Tibet is like a giant prison camp.
Tibetans are drowning in a sea of Chinese.
The Tibetan people are being wiped out from the face of the Earth.

Now it's time to

GO HOME

FOR 60 YEARS, THE DALAI LAMA'S POLICIES HAVE FAILED

I have left no stone unturned.

Negotiation.
I am committed to negotiations. 1961-2005

Negotiation has failed, Oct. 25, 2004

China has refused to negotiate or even meet at any meaningful level.

I realized (in 1994) it would be impossible to negotiate with people who behave in this crude and criminal fashion.

Peace Plans.
The Dalai Lama's 5 Points, the Salzburg Proposal and innumerable plans over the years are ignored by China except as occasions for increased Chinese violence against Tibetans, e.g. the current Strike Hard campaign in Tibet.

Kowtowing to China.
- Every time I saw Mao, he inspired me again.
- I want to help the Chinese in any way I can.
- I advised Tibetan escapees to return to Tibet to help their country.
- Softening of Dalai Lama's Tibet Uprising Day speeches

World-wide Publicity Campaign: sells Dalai Lama books, earns admiration, royalties, VIP friends, awards for the Dalai Lama but does nothing for Tibetans in Tibet.

Ahimsa (non-violence) makes occupation easier for China and undermines Tibetans willing to fight for their freedom.

FOR 60 YEARS, THE DALAI LAMA DISTORTS AHIMSA (NON VIOLENCE)

I'm happy in exile.

- Ahimsa is not a psychosis or a suicide pact. Self defense and survival are part of the doctrine.
- Ahimsa is a personal moral commitment not a political statement or directive to others being subjected to violence and threats.
- Absentee ahimsa as practiced by the Dalai Lama is a hypocrisy. Unlike Mahatma Ghandi, Martin Luther King, and Suu Kyi, the Dalai Lama lives outside Tibet in comfort, safety, and honor while his Tibetans daily suffer Chinese threats, arrests, and atrocities.

"The Dalai Lama is always laughing. totally enjoys himself."
Professor Robert Thurman,
friend and co-author with the Dalai Lamai.

Now it's time to

GO HOME

WHAT CAN THE DALAI LAMA DO NOW?

- Return to Tibet to lead his people.
- Advocate a boycott of China-made goods.
- Advocate a boycott of the Beijing 2008 Olympics.
- Use his world-wide popularity, books, friends and admirers for Tibetans in Tibet.

I will go back to Tibet within 2 years. 1996.

My kata presentation (to his leaders in Lhassa) implies my intention to return.

What about dangers to the Dalai Lama upon his return?

I have no fear of death..

With a sincere and open heart there is no need to fear others.

My enemy is my best friend because he gives me the opportunity to learn from adversity.

Only the Dalai Lama can stop the holocaust. He must

GO HOME

WHAT CAN WE DO NOW?

It is not a time to pretend to just sound good.

If you confront your (enemies) rather than avoid them, you will be in a better position to deal with them.

Until China gives Tibetans freedom and human rights:
- Don't buy anything made in China
- Boycott companies who do business with China.
- Avoid travel and investments in China.
- Communicate to whomever you can, by all means available, your advocacy: friends, elected officials, the Tibetan Government in Exile, Chinese embassies and authorities, all media, the United Nations.

- Join the Alliance Against Chinese Genocide. Visit www.lovetibet.info.
- Contributions appreciated but are not tax-deductible. Not supported by any government agency.

It's time for the Dalai Lama to

GO HOME

PART II

To Climb A Sacred Mountain (. . . And Listen)

The recognition and practice of any spiritual path is not enough. The key to understanding the Sacred Mountain and the Sacred Mountain Guru is more to listen than anything else. There's more wisdom than gold, jewels, silver, oil, minerals, and even fresh air in them than all the hills put together.

Holy Mountain Journeys

The Way – A Pilgrimage

This is not so much a story about man's spiritual source or some universal teaching but about one person's journey. It is a case study, a pilgrimage to seek truth and wisdom in the religions of the world and its holy Mountains.

Religions . . . From God

Spiritual experiences do not negate formal religions. Their stories all stem from the same God or some sacred powers. There is much spirituality in Travel, Adventure, and Inspiration in this book of Sacred Mountains.

Today's Spirit . . . Paths

It is also a trip to the other planes of man's existence, conscious and unconscious. It is an experience of the major religions of today's world and a few ancient spiritual paths. It is a chance to feel and be part of human emotions on the astral and causal planes. It is a journey of the mind. It is a pilgrimage of effort, learning, joy, and growth in spirit.

The Spiritual Search

This section of "Boy from Pocatello is the story of one man's search for self-realization and, ultimately, God's realization of a unique path — on the Sacred Mountains of the world. It contains much truth, even more than the author is aware. The spiritual seeker, the adventurer, the inquirer, and the explorer will find much sacred knowledge here. Whether we know it or not, we all have our own searches in the physical world, life adventures, explorations, religions, meditation, awareness, enlightenment, spirit, and contemplation. As individual souls, we each are a co-worker with the highest spirit of human appellation, no matter what it's called.

The Pilgrim's Trailhead

I'm now 95 years old. It is joyous but hard to believe that my energy, strength and spirit are still with me. To climb a Sacred Mountain moved beyond a dream to an exploration.

The Spiritual Search

Like each of us, a Mountain stands alone. It is a symbol of powerful, true reality.

Maybe the mountain is in Idaho, on the leaves in an aspen forest, feeling both the warm sun and the chilly bite of fall. Or it could be in the jungles of the West Maui Mountains, searching for the lost King's Highway, the Old Missionary Trail. But by that time, the idea of my exploration flows from the unknown consciousness of my soul into conscious desire. It becomes as important as my family, my safety, or my security.

Searches for truth

Until I'm in my mid-thirties, I don't know how and where I am going. Searches for "Truth" mean little except for tests in school or after-dinner conversations. Its illusory pursuit is for philosophers and ministers and malcontents. No more. I, too, must know what is true — for me. And that's what I find on my round-the-world pilgrimage to the Sacred Mountains. This story shares the wisdom hidden in these holy wilderness peaks as I see it.

Who Are We

For three years, I researched, dreamed, and planned. There is a little history on the role of Mountains in religions, so I picked my Mountains to represent some major religions, ancient and current. Who are we? Where do we come from? Who or what or how shall we be?

What do we believe? How can we find the answers: Study? Meditate? Take drugs? Experiment? Contemplate? Find a guru? Meld with nature? Religions and philosophies, history, psychology, and medicine all map pathways to truth. But I am compelled to seek in the physical world, in nature's isolation, outside myself, knowing full well my answers lie within me.

A Sacred Mountain, for me, is a glimpse of my infinite, my reality, my core. It provides a peek through a crack in the door of unforgettable scenes. Obviously, what we are and have been is locked within the electrical and chemical parts of each of our own cells. But I am unable to unravel that knowledge by introspection alone. For me, as with millions before me, whether founders or followers, Mountains can be the outside force that triggers the spark of self-illumination. Travel, for which education is said to be a poor substitute, is a necessary part of my own "Pilgrim's Progress."

Mountains self illuminations

Some men climb Mountains because they are there. I climb for another reason. It's not happenstance that in the annals of religions, Mountainous areas set the stage for the critical events in the lives of spiritual leaders: for Jesus, Moses, Muhammed, Tao, Buddha, and many many others. Those who follow — monks, pilgrims, gurus, shamans, and me — find why.

Why climb spirit Mountains?

From my studies, I know/ about each religion and its Mountain or Mountains. Completely absorbed, perhaps self-hypnotized, on each peak, I become an American Indian, ancient Greek, Orthodox, Christian, Jew, Moslem, Hindu, Buddhist, Shugendo, Polynesian, or other specific spirit paths. Thus, I probe the source of the mystique surrounding the relationship between man and Mountain . . . and me.

Probing the Mountain mystique

Real Truth

The real truth is always personal, not abstract. Honest stories of personal physical, mental, emotional, and spiritual experiences are more enlightening to me than conceptualizations or "preaching." And more interesting! That is why this

Earth bound space voyage is an "I" book. That is why this earth-bound space voyage is three journeys: an adventure to climb awesome sacred summits of the world, a study of the wisdom of those Mountains, a history of the pains and exhilarations, and a search for the mysteries of these hallowed high places.

The Birth of A Sacred Mountain

Sacred Mountains made not born

How did I know where to go? The world is full of Mountains and hills. Thousands have religious significance. Many have none. A few have become universally recognized Sacred Mountains of this planet. Why? Probably because they are made sacred, not born. Only a few are chosen, whether by God or man, for their unique role. They are sacred because humans say so.

Sacred Mountain Sampler

The Sacred Circle Route

Here, I chose my Mountains because they represent the world's major religions, ancient and current. Each Mountain illustrates a different stage in history, for example:

Mount Lassen

Mount Lassen (Mountain of Nature) in California. A geologically active volcano in the continental United States. A tribal totem for four separate Indian tribes. A gigantic living memorial of what Stone Age and modern man consider Sacred.

Mount Olympus

Mount Olympus (Mountain of Gods) in Greece. The source of the spiritual power of the ancient Greeks, the seat of Zeus, and the home of the Gods. It is a symbol of an important early stage of all Western understanding.

Mount Athos

Mount Athos (Mountain of Priests). A mountain on the Athos peninsula of the Aegean Sea, with over twenty-five Eastern Orthodox Christian monasteries. "To be a monk."

Mts. Temptation, Tabor, Olive and Calvary

Mounts of Temptation, Tabor, Olives, and Calvary (Mountains of Love) in Israel. Christ's temptation, transfiguration, crucifixion, and resurrection on these Mountains. For me, it is a "Renewed empathetic realization of Jesus Christ."

Mount Sinai (Mountain of Miracles) in Israel's occupied desert. The sacred meeting place of God and Moses to Jews, Muslims, and Christians. "Awe, in Moses' footsteps."

Mount Arunachala (Mountain of Revelation) in Southern India. The Mountain Mirror of the Self. "The sacred source of all energy." A recognition for all of us: "Who am I?"

Mount Fuji-San (Mountain of Worshipers) in Japan. A Mountain that is a nation-spirit.

Mount Omine-San (Mountain of Worship) is deep in Japan's Central Alps. The epitome of a Mountain's role as a place of, and to, worship. "Spiritual progress and return from death."

Mount Haleakala (Mountain of Creation) in Maui, Hawaii. Here, the great Polynesian demi-God, Maui, like the mythological figures of most religions, captured the sun. "Experiencing our mysterious beginnings."

On these Mountains, men find Grey Fox, Pele, Brahman, the Enlightened One, Jehovah, Allah, Zeus, and God. Will they, these Gods, still be there? Will they communicate with me? How better to find out than to go where "Gods like these have existed on these Mountains, physical places between heaven and earth."

Sacred Mountain

The very act of planning and imagining Sacred Mountains stimulates new energies. I distill the essence of Polynesian, Indian, Greek, Islam, Hindu, Buddhist, Orthodox, Christian, Hebrew, Shinto, and Shugendo religions. Their ideas become a part of my own conscious and unconscious. The effort explodes into a fusion of insight before and after my pilgrimage begins!

Law case trial in Arizona — hard, pressuring and sleep disturbing

3am awakening

Dawn light

Message from spirit, Jesus, Mohammad, ahi, Buddha, Hindu, Maui, Athos, Zeus

I am trying a law case in Arizona, working very hard with little sleep, concentrating, and under heavy pressure. There is no room in my conscious mind for thoughts of religion or Mountains. I fall into bed about 3:00 a.m.

Suddenly, I awake. From my window, I see the early dawn light spread over the Arizona Desert. My dream is single flashes, the essence of the religions I know. I quickly arise and write down my revelations:

From Jesus: "The only human relationship without debilitating effect is love, the ultimate morality."

From Muhammad: "Man is not a spiritual vegetable or a God, but a man who accepts life and enjoys the world, its perfumed women, intercourse, fruit, power, success."

From the Yahi Tribe: "Separation from nature, its majesty, sacredness, mystery, beauty, as stone-age man knows it, is life for my soul as well as my body."

From Buddha: "The mind that meditates can find peace and truth and feel the cosmic energy."

From Hindu Scripture: "Look inward to find God in the self, Atman."

From Maui: "We are all one, from the same mysterious but single source known to us all if we could but rediscover it."

From Athos: To be a monk, an ascetic, is not to be ... at least for me."

From Zeus: "True religion lies at the human, not some supernatural, level."

Find my trail and God

Mohammad, Atman, Buddha, Jesus, Nature, Spirit

I. I climbed a Mountain in my mind to find my truth — my God and my belief.
   Knowing of the trail marked so well in words recorded in our age:
   Of Muhammad's life and Atman's soul, of Buddha's thought and Jesus' love and Nature spirits primitive.

Every cell	II.	And at the early first, you began your every cell can tell you how it was:
Heat and cold ... universal		The moisture, heat, and motion fused into creation. Driven from the womb, God's garden, growing, changing, moving, believing, along with the others, tested to the limit by the fire and flood, the heat and cold, the sickening and the sacrifice.
		We, the living — began — in our beginning — all the same.
Nature and Buddha ... unity	III.	Do not deny her from whom you came. Breathe her — touch — be her. Nature's been your mother o'er the eons and lives in every piece within you, beckoning to join you with her others — the sky and birds, the trees and rocks, the lakes and breeze, the sun and ground.
Thou art a man and God	IV.	Live not the life of a man like your image of a God for thou art a man and God.
Self / Jesus love		So, escape not to vegetables or rock but live enrobed in perfumes of the fruit, of life, of love. Shirk not from gain nor pleasure but take them in their measure and Be blessed that flesh will still respond.
Reach for Infinity	V.	To the essence of all self be true — To love in Jesus' name your Self, your friend and lover, child and wife, your neighbor even more and the ones you touch today.
I am my God	VI.	Plumb the mind — A treasure that seeks to meditate as Buddha spake: on cause and joy, pity, love and finally serenity reaching for the infinity stored within your soul.
Truth in me		
Who am I and why?	VII.	I, like those before me, am my God.
		Whether Joe or Jesus, Mac or Buddha, Jane or Nature, The Truth is in me. I am the truth.

Naught else do I know so well, nor do I need to know:
What are my thoughts? Who am I?
Why am I that I am?

My Journey Begins

You are never really prepared, only receptive to adventure. In any event, I am on my way to absorb some of the Sacred Mountains of the World.

June 27 – beginning

On June 27, my quest begins. It is a hard beginning. I choke back my tears. My stomach aches with anxiety about what might happen. Guilt permeates my thoughts for leaving my family, my law office partners, and my pressing duties as President of the Board of Education. At the International Airport, my young son's eyes filled with tears. Was he asking why I was abandoning him? My wife is still unreconciled to the journey after a year of warm discussion. Only my daughter Sharon seems to accept it and possibly approve. But we all understand.

There is no turning back!

Pilgrim's Planning Around the World Guide

The sacred Mountain will light your way and show who you are physically, mentally, emotionally at your highest levels no matter how dirty you may become

Before The First Step

The Usual Words of Advice

Whether you are climbing all the Mountains in one journey or several, here are some how-to or not-to-do-it hints.

Hiking map

Some basic pre-arrangements should be made: transportation to and lodging in the major cities and a way to get to the base of the Sacred Mountains you plan to visit. The alternatives are functions of time, money, and comfort. For air transportation and lodging, a travel agent can be helpful, but be sure your reservations are verified in writing. That note from your travel agent neighbor, "It's all taken care of," won't help in the inevitable competition for rooms at the only known and available (but over-booked) hotel in the city against a busload of well-heeled tourists and their leader, or threats and gratuities. For the key cities and the Sacred Mountains, you're as well off making your own arrangements.

Transports to lodgings

International services

Since international airlines vigorously promote round-the-world tickets, put them to work and take advantage of the many services they provide when planning the trip. There are special fares available and some side trips which can be included without extra charge. If you pick the right ticket agent (the good-looking one at the end of the line), maybe he/ she will take you to lunch, and you may end up with your own private stewardess/steward guide.

Airline services

Major airlines serve directly or indirectly all the "base camp" cities: San Francisco (Mount Lassen), Athens (Mount Olympus), Tel-Aviv/Jerusalem (Mts. Tabor and Sinai), Bombay or New Delhi, Tokyo (Mountains Fuji-san and Omine-san) and Honolulu (Haleakala). Local scheduled flights regularly connect Athens to Thessaloniki (Mount Athos), Bombay or New Delhi to Madras (Mount Arunachala), and Honolulu to Maui (Mount Haleakala) without the loss of much time. Buses and taxis to and from all of these airports to hotels are readily available. All flights should be booked in advance if travel is during the summer or holiday seasons. This precaution forces the traveler to keep to a basic schedule. This can be both a boon and a disadvantage.

Base city to Sacred Mountains

Sinai walk

Hitch-hiking

Rent a car

Once you are at the base city, there are innumerable ways to reach the Mountain areas. I try many of them except hitch-hiking or walking. In most cases, it takes over two weeks to walk, and in some (Sinai), it is virtually impossible. While hitch-hiking isn't very practical in India, Japan, and the Sinai, it might be worth a try in Maui, Greece, and Israel; but blame yourself if you end up at the bottom of somewhere other than the Mountain. All the major cities involved have local and international rent-a-car (and with a driver) agencies. To drive yourself, an international driver's license, easily obtained at an American Automobile Association office for a few dollars and three passport photos, is helpful. Reservations for rentals in advance in the summer is a good precaution in Greece and Israel

Trains and buses

Trains are reasonable modes of travel in Greece and India and a great way to go in Japan. Special tour buses run to Mount Fuji-san, Sinai, and Haleakala. Regular local buses, with stops at every village, demi-village, and no-village, operate in all the countries within hiking distance of these Sacred Mountain objectives.

Of course, Athos may be reached only by foot or by boat.

It's advisable to buy a current local map showing the roads. And when in doubt, ask lots of questions of the natives — many times! (A phrase book showing your destination on a map, pronouncing it correctly or gestures can be helpful). Specific recommendations (ground travel)

Boat

Maps and cross examinations

Ground travel

Mount Lassen (Western USA)

MOUNT LASSEN: Rent a car in San Francisco and drive about 235 miles to Redding, California, via the San Francisco Bay Bridge, Highway 80, and then Highway 5. From Redding, follow the Mount Lassen signs east on Highway 44 (skip the entrance to Mount Lassen Park) past "Subway Caves" and then turn off to the right on a rough road to "Butte Lake," trailhead for the ascent described here. Unless someone picks you up, you'll have to hike back. If you want to climb only the Mount Lassen summit itself, enter the Lassen National Park on Highway 36, head west from Highway 5 at Red Bluff, California, and park your car at the highest point on the road within the park. A well-marked trail begins there.

Hotels and Greek Tourist Office

MOUNT OLYMPUS: After your arrival in Athens, Greece, rent a car (the hotels and Greek tourist office have pamphlets in English on rates, types available, etc.) and drive about six or seven hours (400 Kilometers) to the village of Litochoro at the base of Mount Olympus. You can hire a guide there or go on your own. Unless you're a purist (masochist?) and want to "hike all the way," take the road to Prioni Falls as far as you can by car. The trail from there is obvious.

Rent a car to Litochoro, at base of Mount Olympus

MOUNT ATHOS: From Litochoro to Thessaloniki, it is about a two-hour drive (117 Kilometers) at most. From Thessaloniki, it's two to three hours on a secondary paved road to Tripiti, where you take a converted fishing boat to the Athos docks. Historically, this is as far as females of any species are allowed to travel due to Monks religious beliefs.

Drive to Tripoli for Mt Athos boat

Check schedules since there are a limited number of sailings. Get a boat ticket for Daphne, the port of immigration for Athos, and upon arrival, take the bus (less than an hour) to Karie, the capital of Athos, where you must obtain another permit (seven-day limit on Athos). From there, you can walk or catch another boat to Kasolyvia or another monastery to begin the ascent of the peak next morning. After returning to Daphne or Tripiti, turn in the car (there may be a pick-up charge) at the Thessaloniki airport and fly to Athens (Olympic Airways). Make reservations in advance since these flights are usually crowded, and you'll never out-elbow or out-shout the Greek standbys.

Mount Athos boat

Thessaloniki and Mount Athos

The roads and signs in Greece are excellent and easy to follow. There are some advantages to reversing the route by flying to Thessaloniki from Athens (after picking up a request for a permit from the U.S. Embassy in Athens), renting a car there, and going to Mount Athos before Mount Olympus.

MOUNTAINS OLIVES, CALVARY, AND TABOR: Rent a car at the Tel Aviv Airport and drive to Jerusalem. Stay there long enough to rest, make reservations for the trip to and from Mount Sinai, and visit Mount of Olives, Calvary and anywhere else you want in the Holy Land. There is an Israeli Tourist Office that will help you in Tel Aviv or Jerusalem.

Roads to Nazareth and Mount Tabor

Drive to Nazareth and Mount Tabor; it will take all day if you stop or take any side tours. The road up Mount Tabor is narrow, winding, and partly unpaved, but no problem, unless you find yourself in the middle of Israeli army maneuvers.

MOUNT SINAI: From Mount Tabor, drive to Tel Aviv via any route that looks interesting since all the main roads are good and well posted. Pick up your tour bus to St. Catherine's Monastery at the base of Mount Sinai. It will take the better part of two days. A small aircraft flight is now available from Tel

Mount Sinai / St. Catherine

Aviv to a hostel in the desert; a few miles by jeep or bus to St. Catherine's (an old monastery). Take a plane or tour bus back to Tel Aviv for the flight to Madras via Bombay or New Delhi.

Mount Arunachala and Madras

MOUNT ARUNACHALA: Roads in South India are well marked, but from Madras to the ashram at the town of Tiruvannamalai at the base of Arunachala (about 135 miles), it's better to leave the driving to someone else (a bus or hired private driver). Madras is a major city and provincial capital in India and the closest large city to Mount Arunachala. Buses can be fun and an excellent opportunity to "feel" the country and the people, but spend time in Madras finding out exactly which bus from which terminal to take, when it leaves, where you get your ticket, and when and where you have to transfer, if at all, or you'll "feel" a lot more villages and people than you anticipated. For the return trip, the Ashram at Sacred Mountain will help you board the direct bus for Madras or let you know if anyone is driving. Depending on the bus you take, the trip is from six to eight hours.

Mount Fuji-San by train

MOUNT FUJI-SAN: Take the train from Tokyo to Gotemba' (four to five hours). The Japanese Tourist Agency will help you plan it in English. You can stay in Gotemba or take a bus (two hours) or taxi (45 minutes) to Lake Kawaguchi. Reservations are advisable and can be made from Tokyo. From Lake Kawaguchi, buses run regularly to the Fifth Station trailhead on Fuji-san. If you have an extra day or two, and if you want to, you can begin the hike at Lake Kawaguchi at the base of Fugi-san. The trail begins at the Sengen Shrine there.

Lake Kawaguchi, Fifth Station and Fugi Trail head

Mt. Omine-San

MOUNT OMINE-SAN: Whichever trail you take down Fuji-san, (Sliding Sands is great fun), it can be a little complicated to get to Omine-san by train. A local train will take you where you pick up the National Railway train from Tokyo to Kyoto (JNR New Tokaido Line). That takes about three hours.

Kyoto to Yusungi

Mt. Delujawa — No Women

Shugendo history Special arrangements if hiking Shugendo

Car to Haleakala Mountain

Pass and permit for park service cabin inside volcano

One distinct trip ... or many

Travel timing: June, July, August

From Kyoto, you take a train with at least one transfer to Yusungi (four hours). From there, your best bet is a taxi (over one hour) to Dologawa, the village closest to Omine. There are many inns there in which to stay. You can walk (thirty minutes) or take a taxi to the trail beginning. The sign says "No Women" in Japanese, but for women liberationists (Buddhist style), there is a separate but almost equal hill to climb. Special arrangements are necessary if you want to participate as a Shugendo pilgrim.

MOUNT HALEAKALA: There are several flights a day from Honolulu to Maui. Rent a car at the Maui Airport and drive the thirty miles to the top of Haleakala (about 45 minutes), where the trail begins down into that volcano. You'll need advance reservations from the U.S. National Park Service to stay overnight in the cabins inside the volcano walls.

Where, When and Who

The first question to resolve is whether you wish to visit the peaks in one trip or many. To do it all together costs less, takes more concentrated time, gives a better feel for the similarities and contrasts of the Sacred Mountains in their different cultures, reduces distractions, requires more baggage, compromises weather considerations, makes planning more difficult, and is more exhausting. The total time available is important. An experienced world-traveling friend explained to me before I left, "It can't be done in forty days and nights." For such skeptics, the Appendix details how it is possible to do it anyway.

While some of the spirit of the adventure is lost, traveling to only one or a few of the Mountains together gives more flexibility as to the time of year to travel. June, July, and August are the only feasible months to climb all the Mountains in one trip. Otherwise, monsoons, cold, and snow will make the trip miserable and even impossible.

Individually, the optimum months are:

Best times to climb on Mountains included in this book

Mt. Lassen	August & early September
Mt. Olympus	July, August & September
Mt. Athos	Around Easter & early Fall
Mt. Tabor	Easter, Spring & Fall
Mt. Sinai	Spring & late Fall
Mt. Arunachala	October – December (especially November)
Mt. Fuji-San	July & August
Mt. Omine-San	Late Spring & early Fall
Mt. Haleakala	November & December

For the exploration report on each of these mountains, refer to the Table of Contents.

Go alone?

You decide

The final pre-planning question is whether to go alone. It is always safer to be with someone in the wilderness and more enjoyable traveling — assuming you get along well. It is a matter of taste. Or, depending on your companion, it can be a matter of love on a shared adventure. For me, being by myself is indispensable for appreciating and discovering the spiritual forces permeating the Mountainsides and summits. Whatever you do, it's vital to spend much of the time on the climb alone.

In Anticipation

When I left, only my planned schedule was set. The fare was "paid" in terms of credit card mythology. Though I had completed the basic research, my travel planning and Mountain information were only sketchy. My local travel agent gave up. Hilton had no "canned America" hotels at the final destinations.

Travel Agents

Travel plans

Request for advance permit

My letters requesting information and reservations were still floating around the world somewhere, unanswered. From Greece, though my checks were accepted, pleas for more information were ignored, and a request for an advance permit to visit Mount Athos was denied.

Preplanned

One agency withdrew after agreeing to handle the arrangements in Israel, advising me not to make the trip in light of the Six-Day War situation. By the time I left San Francisco, I still had not heard anything from India or Japan.

These deficiencies were serious since the timing was tight, with less than six weeks available. The plane schedules fix the critical parameters of time.

It was my first trip to most of these countries. The areas are little traveled by American tourists. The big problem was not hiking by myself but getting to the Sacred Mountains I wanted to visit. In between climbs and plane flights, I needed a hotel room to make local travel plans, clean up myself and my gear from the last Mountain, and get set practically and mentally for the next adventure. It was unsettling not to have reservations in the middle of the tourist season in many of these countries, particularly in Japan.

One thing is ever ready: my blood. There were some questions as to whether there was any blood left in me after all the shots and pills for yellow fever, smallpox, hepatitis, typhus, plague, typhoid, cholera, tetanus, malaria, and three types of polio. But these can be important for survival.

My last night at home was a flurry of eliminating "essentials." To keep to the time limits, I planned to take only what I could carry with me. Losing a single item on a Mountain or in a plane could ruin the whole trip. For a year, I made lists, bought and prepared equipment, planned menus, cutting, changing, adding. I put it all in one pile on that last evening, but it was too bulky and heavy. By the next morning, I had reduced my load to eighty-four pounds in two parts. My tent and sleeping bag were lashed to the pack frame, to be checked on the plane. The rest was hung on my belt and stuffed in coat pockets and backpack. There was barely enough room in my plane seat for all of this, not including me.

Nevertheless, this baggage is a pyramid of logic

Baggage to be carried

a. To avoid scattering gear all over the world on wrong airplanes, in storage lockers, hotels, and Mountain tops, everything must be carried in a pack up and down the Mountain.

On Sacred Mountains

Baggage

b. "Everything" means camera and recorder (including unipod, film, tapes), tent, all-weather (hot, cold, wet) clothing, twenty-four days of food, sleeping bag, medical kit (small drugstore), rescue kit, canteens, desk (introduction letters, tickets, passport, international driver's license, shot records, money, checks, pen, paper, maps), library (cut-up parts of books on survival, first-aid, Old and New Testament, Qur'an, Bhagavad Gita, Upanishads, Gospels of Buddha, Precepts of Shugendo and guide books), kitchen (gas stove, spoon, cup, knife and vitamins) and a spray can of mace (for human and animal defense departments).

Put under seat

c. It all needs to fit under my airplane seat and in the overhead rack for thousands of miles around the world.

To be carried

d. It must be carried over 5,300 feet straight up and down, not counting sideways distances.

Passport

e. My passport is for one person, "male," not "mule."

Mission Impossible

Logical Conclusion: "Mission Impossible." But it works.

Logic never applies to this trip, anyway. Oh yes, and take along my book To Climb A Sacred Mountain.

Weightless Baggage — My Sermon on The Mount

Take who you are to these Mountains

You take what you are to the Mountain. You hope that your body, emotions, and spirit, like the things in your pack, will be useful even though burdensome. Some may be a nuisance or worse, like a Mountain stove that explodes or an out-of-control fear of heights.

Loneliness. Exhaustion. Concentration. Exhilaration. Along the trail, all these illuminate the patterns of personality with which you begin. These unconscious patterns, like factory dyes, dictate the shape of the product: the hiker's actions, thoughts and emotions, goals, and beliefs. They are the emotional baggage. They repeat themselves, sometimes dangerously, in all kinds of terrain and situations. They affect the journey before it begins. To change, to be free, and to be open to new growth requires an awareness of these patterns and a will to be what you imagine on the Mountain.

Emotional baggage

Unconscious forces of the psyche affect Mountaineers in the wilderness in specific ways. For example, fear of failure, ridicule, and unmanliness can make it impossible to turn back or not go at all, no matter what the state of preparation or the problems anticipated. Sometimes, the result is called bravery, sometimes stupidity. The fact that others are against your journey can weaken or strengthen your determination to go. Penny-pinching often wastes tremendous energy when planning or traveling (buying inexpensive socks or avoiding excess baggage charges). Carrying physical exercise to exhaustion as a means of relieving pent-up emotions is a peril to hikers. A habit of arriving late in the work-a-day or social world, thus avoiding unstructured time and relationships, can carry over to the climb. This results in delaying or creating hardships for others, missing food drops, and even causing unnecessary search parties. Also, too much independence and an unwillingness to ask for help can often prove disastrous.

Mountain psychology

Late versus on time

Some never enjoy trip planning and its anticipations. But such activities are necessary: they serve to assure future success in reaching the summit and assuaging fears of injury, loss, failure. But they can be overdone. On the other hand, anxiety about a journey can displace your other worries; your concern about the success of a climbing project can require so much effort and time that you forget your other problems. "Being prepared" is good advice for an expedition. Too much "fearing

Planning too much and too little

the worst" is a serious emotional handicap. It is so often a neurotic insurance that all will go well. It gives, for example, full vent to hypochondria and carrying too much, like so many Boys Scout troops one sees on the trail staggering under huge packs. There's a limit to the shots you need and the necessary medicines to carry. Fear can ruin the joy of anticipating or going on an adventure or even prevent one from going at all.

Confident / self reliant

Any journey increases one's awareness of emotional patterns and awakens a new appreciation for the unconscious forces that bring serenity, joy, concern for others, and personality improvement rather than self-congratulation.

Anyone who attempts to follow this route will discover new confidence and courage, the ability to do whatever he or she wants. The pilgrim will find himself or herself physically fit, imaginative, creative, mentally alert, emotionally strong, intellectually open, and receptive. You will want to share what you find with others. Your growing self-reliance and your resources and fullness will increase your drive and will to succeed. Your objectives will change, and the new ones will assume more importance. That's part of the reward of a Sacred Mountain pilgrimage.

Sacred Mountains light your way

Find your way

The Sacred Mountains will light your full self, showing you the way. They will prove that you can be what you will on the physical, the mental, or the highest levels.

See the following pages comparing what was planned and what actually took place.

I purchased food for twenty-four days to be carried in my pack. It was to be supplemental with local food and restaurant meals wherever possible. The weight and bulk were so great I cut down to a planned eighteen days of packed food. Then the last night I eliminated most of those items and actually took the following:

Items Purchased to be Carried in Pack	Items Eliminated	Actually Taken In Pack
Salt and pepper	none	all
Special mountain multi-vitamin N capsules (50)	none	all
18 packages of snack packs (combination of raisins and different nuts and seeds)	16	2
18 candy packs (hard)	16	2
13 sesame seed bars	7	6
18 packs dried fruit—raisins, prunes and apricots	all	none
3 boxes crackers	all	none
36 packages of powder drink mix (mostly lemonade)	none	all
18 packages of beef jerky	12	6
16 packages of powdered fruit punch	8	8
2 packages oatmeal	none	all
12 packages of freeze-dried dinners (chicken, turkey, veal, lamb, beef stroganoff)	10	2
4 packages of dried applesauce	none	all
4 Packages of dried potatoes	3	1
4 packages of dried peaches	all	none
4 packages of dried fruit cocktail	all	none
4 packages of dried carrots	2	2
4 packages of dried peas	2	2
4 packages of dried milk shake mix	all	none
4 packages of dried omelet mix	all	none
8 packages of dried peanut butter mix	all	none

AIRLINE PLANNED ITINERARY

CITY	DEPARTURE DATE	DAY OF WEEK	LOCAL TIME	STAY (Days)	CARRIER	REMARKS
San Francisco	June 24	Wed.	05:00	3	car	Mt. Lassen
San Francisco	June 27	Sat.	07:00	-	TWA	
New York	June 27	Sat.	17:00	-	BOAC	
Athens	July 7	Tue.	14:45	10	TWA	Mt. Olympus Mt. Athos
Tel Aviv	July 17	Fri.	18:15	10	Air France	Mt. Tabor Olives, Sinai
New Delhi	July 18	Sat.	9:25	-	India Air	
Madras	July 24	Fri.	22:30	7	India Air	Mt. Arunachala
Calcutta	July 25	Sat.	06:30	-	India Air	
Tokyo	July 30	Thu.	21:30	6	JAL	Mt. Fuji-san and Omine-san
Honolulu	July 30	Thu.	11:00	-	Aloha Air	
Maui	Aug. 3	Mon.	08:40	4	Hawaiian Air	Mt. Haleakala
Honolulu	Aug. 3	Mon.	11:40		Pan Am	

*The guide on the following pages was written many years ago for the explorations at the time. The specific plans may or may not apply or be useful now given the changes in travel, politics, weather, etc.. In fact following the plans as well as my activities today could get you imprisoned, shot, or into some other serious danger. Of course you might say quite properly that even carrying out the plans at the time carried unavoidable similar risks.

ACTUAL ITINERARY
Forty Days Around the World

CITY	MOUNTAIN	DATE OF ARRIVAL	PERIOD OF STAY (Days)	CUMULATIVE DAYS
	Mt. Lassen	June 24	3	
San Francisco		June 27	1	4
London/Athens		June 28	1	5
	Mt. Olympus	June 29	4	9
Soloniki		July 2		
	Mt. Athos	July 3	4	13
Athens		July 7	1	14
Jerusalem	Mt. of Olives	July 8	1	15
	Mt. Tabor	July 9	1	16
Tel Aviv		July 10	1	17
	Mt. Sinai and Desert	July 11	4	21
Jerusalem		July 15	1	22
	The Wilderness	July 16	1	23
Tel Aviv/Bombay /Madras		July 17	1	24
	Mt. Arunachala	July 18	5	29
Madras/Calcutta		July 23	1	30
Tokyo		July 23		
	Mt. Fuji-San	July 24	4	34
Kyoto		July 28		
	Mt. Omine-san	July 28	3	37
Tokyo		July 30		
Honolulu and Maui		July 31	1	38
End	Mt. Haleakala	Aug. 2	2	40

Sacred Mount Lassen

People View-Point

If you're alone and seek the summit
On Sacred Mount Lassen's topmost chair of rock
The twilight golden trails
Will lead and take you there.
        . . . THE MOUNTAIN PATH*

Location:	California
Range:	Cascade Range
Elevation:	10,457 ft
Prominence:	5,230 ft
Coordinates:	40°29'17"N
	121°30'18"W
Spirit:	Historically Native American Tribes
	(Yahi, Yawa, Atsugiwi, Mountain Maidu)
Pilgrimage:	*The Violent, Mysterious Totem*

*Each *Song/Psalm* in the following pages (36 in all) references the source of inspiration in small caps and are not an exact quotation from that source. The inspirations are the book *Greek Lyrics* translated by Richard Lattimore and the Arunchala Ashram Magazine *The Mountain Path*. See bibliography. Some of the sources are anonymous and can be credited to a Holy Mountain Guru.

ANGEL VIEW-POINT

The Violent, Mysterious Totem

Stone Age Gods remind us of Nature's truths.
Like those on the twilight golden trail.

History Of Violence, A Sleeping Volcano

Violence, especially Nature's, fascinates me. That's a reason I begin my sacred journey at Mount Lassen in Northern California.

Esoterica: Myths, Mysteries, Imaginables

Lassen's geologic history is worthy of being considered and so dramatic and foreign to the thinking of geologists it constitutes a mystery, a possible myth, and certainly an imaginable even though we might not necessarily conceive that it is confirmed scientifically whether or not we know how or even understand it if we weren't a specialized geologist. Mount Lassen part of the Pacific Cascade Range produced one of the largest lava domes on earth creating a small but deep lake in one of Lassen's summits (after two hundred thousand years of activity and eruption). Scientists tell us that Mount Lassen erupted more than 400,000 times between 1914 and 1928 and was the only other volcanic eruption in Continental United States in the twentieth century.

Sacred Mount Lassen history reads like a myth, a mystery, and an imaginable . . . one of probably thousands of "scientific accomplishments", that to most if not all should be considered "esoterica."

Buried in the native Shaman's mind is the dim memory of tribal history, of fear, extraordinary, supernatural. It is the memory of the white-hot anger of Grey Fox that came from the Mountain as an awesome rumbling. Grey Fox had created the world and the tribe. He could destroy both. Only the Shaman might save the tribe from the horror, the violent shaking, the ground suddenly splitting open underfoot. Only his memory of the rites to be performed might keep the white-hot rock from crushing the tribe. But even he could not stop this wall of molten rock, crushing, crunching and burning everything in its way as it flows down the Mountain. In the clouds of gas, the rains of ashes, and the huge boulders hurtling through the air, the Indians knew that their world was blowing up. Wicuhirdiki, now Mount Lassen,[*1] spoke to them only in thunder and roars.

The Indian tribes who survived five-thousand years of periodic outbursts say little in their recorded myths of five hundred years of outbursts, the source of Lassen's violence. Why? At least one tribe attributed the shaking earth to an enraged "No-Sugi-Yauna" As a child No-Sugi-Yauna is very thirsty. One day a woman who has a baby boy offers him a drink from her large, beautiful breasts, but she is milk-less as she holds and suckles him. In his frustration, he eats her and shakes the world with his anger. Another tribal legend tells how the shaking earth makes new rock formations but is stopped by a very old woman whose hair is almost green. In the middle of the earthquake, she picks up a rock and pounds it on another rock while she sings. She prays for the world to stop shaking. She is answered and the shaking ceases, but not before many people die and those who live in canyons suffer from the rocks shaking down on them.

Geologists confirm the Indians' legends. Their dread of a powerful spirit that could shake the earth, Wicuhirdiki, one tribe's name for Mount Lassen, has a fierce history. It is born from the sides of the geologic giant Tehema, a 12,000 foot high stratovolcano whose cauldron of molten rock (magma) is over fifteen miles across. Like her strata-volcano sisters, Mount Shasta nearby, Mount Hood in Oregon, and Mount Ranier in

Washington, Mount Tehama grew from the out-pourings of a huge vent from the earth's core. This vent is periodically cleared by a tremendous explosion of gas which results in a spray of ash, cinders and volcanic bombs followed by a stiff, gray flow of molten lava.

Mt. Tehama explodes into Mt. Lassen

Approximately a million years ago, Tehama became the southern anchor of what is now the Cascade Mountain Range adjoining today's Sierra Nevada Range. Together they form a string of gigantic violent volcanoes known as the "Pacific Circle of Fire," whose explosive activities declined only in the last 20,000 years.*[2] Tehama's unusual explosiveness is its own destruction. As the core of the volcano blasted away, the walls weakened and collapsed into the cauldron. The northeast wall became Mount Lassen, one of the largest plug-type volcanoes in the world. The "plug" is one cubic mile and a million tons of boiling, cooling and cold lava. The flows from this type of volcano are stiff, pasty masses of gray mud and even white lava with a high silica content. Once the plug blows out, the eruptive action of such volcanoes is usually sluggish. The four distinct craters at Mount Lassen's summit testify to her unusually stormy and violent history.

Lassen's Wall

About 5,000 years ago, Lassen's wall rose "overnight" (geologically speaking); 2,500 feet in five years. Eruptions and changes continue to occur.

Largest plug volcano

At 4:30 p.m. on Sunday, May 22, 1915, a mushroom cloud over thirty thousand feet high appears above Lassen National Park.

The rise of Mount Lassen

Lassen peak with a volume of 0.6 cu miles (2.5 km) is one of the largest lava domes on Earth. From its former northern flank of now-eroded Mount Tehama about 27,000 years ago there were a series of eruptions over the course of a few years. The mountain has been significantly eroded by glaciers and is now covered in talus deposits.

Massive exlosion

Largest eruption in the United States

Lassen dormant not extinct

Cinder Cone

Violent peak effects religion

This explosive eruption at Lassen peak devastated nearby areas and spread volcanic ash as far as 280 miles (450 km) to the East; This dramatic explosion is the most powerful in a series of eruptions from 1914 to 1917. Lassen Peak and Mount Saint Helens in the Washington State Cascades, are the only two volcanoes in contiguous United States to erupt during the 20th Century.

Lassen Peak is now dormant meaning the volcano is inactive and has a functioning magna chamber under the ground still capable of eruptions.

In the Northeastern region of Lassen Volcano National Park, a Cinder Cone with an elevation of 700 feet (210 meters) rises above the surrounding area, and forms a symmetrical pyroclastic cone as is comprised of five basaltic lava flows.

Prior to 1914, Lassen Peak probably had at least one explosive eruption to create the summit crater 350 feet (110 meters) deep with a diameter of 1,000 feet (300 meters). Deposits from older mud flows can be traced specifically to the Lassen Dome and have been found in other areas (Hat Creek, Lost Creek, and the Eastern Devastated Areas).

Like their Indian forebears, the thousands of people who see the cloud are awe-struck. Ashes and cinders spew over northern California and as far as Reno, Nevada, 125 miles away. The first explosion spouts thousands of tons of hot rock (many over thirty tons each), snow and mud. The force in the hot magma core of Mount Lassen blows out the vents and fissures in the earth's crust. The source of this awesome heat power originating forty miles below ground level is still unknown. Atomic fission and fusion of uranium and thorium, the pull of gravity twenty-five miles below the surface (exceeding 130,000 pounds per square inch) and the earth's rock outer core all contribute to recent volcanic eruptions in the continental United States.

Will Lassen erupt again? The thought occurs to me driving from Redding, California, to the area around Mount Lassen. Lassen still hisses from its steam vents and is known to set off small earthquakes. No geologist considers Lassen an extinct volcano, only a "dormant" one. That was the label that Sunday morning in 1915!

Butte Lake speaks

In anticipation of my first Sacred Mountain, my stomach churns in apprehension. Is it wise to begin my quest on a volcano, to camp on the trigger of a natural atomic and hydrogen bomb? Instinctively, I know that any exploration of the sacred mysteries of the unknown would be flirting with dangerous forces, but why start here?

Come what may, my journey begins upon arrival about one o'clock in the morning at Butte Lake in a corner of Lassen National Park. I flop into my sleeping bag five feet from my car.

Up With The Atsugiwi

Foreboding exchanged for motion, beauty and human absorption

I wake before dawn to find myself on the soft, sandy floor of a lodgepole pine forest. I eat a little breakfast and begin to hike to Mount Lassen, using the same approach the Atsugiwi Indians used every spring for thousands of years. As always, once my pack was on and I took the first steps, I am excited, cheerful, expectant. My uneasy forebodings were assuaged by the exercise, Nature and this Sacred Mountain. The morning freshness permeates my psyche. The beauty, the wild life, absorbs me. It takes but a few of the huge old Jeffrey Pines to make the forest a cathedral for me. The pine-nut hunting squirrels chew cones that cover the cathedral's floor. The porous soil and dry summers make it difficult for new young trees to grow, so nothing interrupts the majestic gestures to the sky of the Jeffrey Pines.

Butte Lake becomes cold and dead quartz

As I follow the trail that skirts the edge of Butte Lake, I pass through a natural skeleton of the earth's crust, the

Fantastic Lava Beds

"Fantastic Lava Beds." These beds are miles of jagged basalt lava twisted into odd, black shapes offset by white gleaming bits of quartz now cold and dead except for the lichen which gives it a gray green scaly hue in the dawn light. This lava, which was once pasty, red-hot masses of molten rock, now shows its age and impotence.

Side hike to "Cinder Cone"

The walking is harder on the steep sandy volcanic ash whitened by diatoms (the remains of tiny microscopic plants). But I cannot resist taking, hard walking or not, an interesting side-trail. I detour on a seven-hundred-foot climb to the Cinder Cone, a cone of perfect symmetry resulting from successive eruptions of lava ash, cinders and pumice (lightly frothy lava full of gas bubbles before it cools), all of which were forced up through a vent in the earth's crust.

Volcanic bombs

Except for tourists' footsteps, the sides of the cone are smooth, as if raked daily by some giant gardener. Water, even when it falls from the heaviest rainfall, seeps into the porous cinders without eroding or running down the slopes or disturbing the surface. The base of this volcano is surrounded by large round rocks of glassy basalt called "volcanic bombs." These bombs were blown from the volcano's vent and rolled down the slope. The reward for my detour to Cinder Cone is a panorama of that end of the park, the lava beds, other dormant volcanoes, a multi-colored desert called the Painted Dunes, nearby lakes and, of course, Lassen Peak miles away. At the top of this crater, a patch of voluntary willows and western white pines are the only plant life to gain a foothold in the ash.

On my way back down, steam-like clouds form and hover atop Mount Lassen. It comforts me to know that such clouds are normal and not the first signs of an eruption, much as the Indians are comforted by knowing that such clouds are only smoke from Chief "Strong-Like-The-Tree." The story goes

Chief Strong-Like the-Tree traded chief-ship for maiden Dimple-in-the-cheek

that he gives up his chieftainship to woo a hard-to-get maiden, "Dimple-in-the-Cheek." When the Spirits, angry at the long courtship, abduct her, the Chief tracks her last footsteps past this cinder cone towards the Mountain. Knowing the situation, he furiously digs until he reaches the Council of Spirit Fathers. They are so impressed with his strength and devotion that all is forgiven. Dimple-in-the Cheek and the Chief marry and live happily forever inside this Sacred Mountain. The steam clouds over Mr. Lassen are the smoke of Strong-like-the-Trees' peace pipe at the Council Fire of the Spirits.

Strong-Like-The-Tree peace pipe at the Council Fire of the spirit

As each mile brings me closer, Mount Lassen grows larger; I pass Emigrant Lake, Nobles Emigrant Trail, Soap Lake, Badger Flat, Hat Creek and Hat Creek Lake in that order. The second night I camp at Summit Lake, about six-hundred feet higher and nineteen miles farther from my day's starting point. Although bounded on one side by a forest and on the other three sides by cars, yelling children, trailers, campfires, smog, rest rooms and all the other accoutrement of civilization, Summit Lake retains its blue serenity, reflecting Mount Lassen, at dusk, in its dark center pool.

Final two-and-a-half-mile ascent

The next morning, I take the five-and-a-half-mile trail from Summit Lake, via Cliff and Shadow Lakes, to the highway summit from about 6,700 feet to 8,500 feet. It is here that the final two-and-a-half-mile ascent to the peak begins.

Inspiration from sleep on the summit

I am glad to begin again. Many miles before, even at my first glimpse, this Mountain uplifts me. I am inspired. It's pure rock summit, its white side walls of snow fields and its size dominate even the clouds. The local Indians are inspired by an overwhelming presence of Mount Lassen. And so am I. Lassen is like the winds, moon, stars, sun and the earth itself. To the Indians, it is mysterious, too large to control or understand. But to me, and perhaps to those Indians, Lassen itself is Religion, God, Nature.

I say to my tape recorder: "I'm going to climb this Mountain, be part of it, feel Nature in me, and understand what the earth is. That valley below me, that pine, that range, is more real than my San Francisco office in the canyon of buildings on Montgomery Street in San Francisco." Only a quiet whisper of a light wind through the pines above me replies to my challenge.

Compare Montgomery street office to Mountains

Winds are of special significance to the Indians. They carry the souls of the dead. The stronger the wind, the further it carries the dead away from their homes and tribe. That's understood. Anyone can enjoy a soft warm breeze in a meadow, but a harsh wind on top of a peak can be hell. Winds can have emotional, even spiritual effects, when one is alone on a Mountain. They can irritate, anger, freshen, destroy or stimulate imagination and fear. They seem to come from nowhere, go nowhere. To anyone who lives or spends much time outdoors, they become an important aspect of life. They are the classical background music of the open country. They sing of the many moods Sacred Mountains can have. To the Indian, the wind, bird calls, the flow of a stream, and the trees, are all sacred. Religion and Nature are not separate, but integral parts of their lives.

Winds carry souls of the dead

Unity of nature and the wind

Thus, everything is invested with the unity I feel here on Lassen... more peaceful. I better understand the quality of my life when I feel such unity. I can experience the Native American's unity with Nature without the usual threatening superstitions and fears.

Indians unity

Going up the trail, I become sensitive to an anxious atmosphere. Big cumulus clouds, some white and puffy, others gray, but all potentially black, roam the horizon. A storm is brewing on the peak. It is my muscles, my heart, my purpose merging with the Mountain. To sleep on her summit will be to conquer not the Mountain but myself. And so, I trudge through

My muscles merging with the sacred Mountain

the woods in deep snow and slippery ice. Glimpses of the top most rocks and passing clouds beckon to their heights. I lie down under a stunted Juniper, out of the wind, on my first rest stop without even taking off my pack. Lake Manzanita and the entire park are spread out below. The cold breeze cools my overheated body, now purged of all impurities by my climbing effort, my sweat, the cold air, and the sun. I am light-headed from the thin oxygen. My body soaks up the last warmth of the day. But the rest is short lived. The chill and long shadows of late afternoon tell me to keep moving.

Body purged from keeping on the move

Above the lower snow fields, around a turn to the west on the trail, I see the clouds turning black. I must rest again. All is absolutely still. The cold sun is shining and the wind is gone. Not a sound, not a bird, not a person. I push on. Range after range of Mountains stretch ahead, each range becomes a lighter and lighter blue the further away it is. Shadows of clouds, ghost-like, creep over the woods, rocks and Mountains below.

Silent Mountain range shadows

Out of "nowhere" comes a young couple on the trail looking for a way to reach the highway. They offer to share their orange juice with me. I refuse, knowing they will need all the sustenance they have. They are poorly dressed, in light sweaters with tennis shoes. As I watch them descend down the trail out of sight, I feel very much more alone. It becomes important to me that they return safely. Their act of sharing offers a rare quality in civilized city life. But it is common among those who live close to Nature, even temporarily. But there is no time for these musings.

Young lightly dressed couple in trouble

I begin to race against the storm and darkness, climbing another thousand feet higher. I can see the pinnacle, almost taste it, three-fourths of a mile above me. But I am exhausted. It is now 7:20 p.m. I am less than half a mile from the top. Something about the Mountain keeps calling, challenging me

Race against storm and darkness

to keep going. Darkness comes in a swirling mist of falling snow. Just below the topmost peak in a small sandy crater is a spot to pitch my tent. I am unable to see or keep my hands from freezing as I set the pegs and ropes. The rain flap seems at first impossible. Once inside the tent, I bundle into my sleeping bag. The apple juice cocktail and half-cooked freeze-dried chicken tetrazzini cooked in melted snow make me comfortably full and warm, ready for sleep.

Pitch tent

Cooking

The storm clears momentarily. In the cold white moonlight, wisps of dark fog float directly across my crater. The wisps seemed like Indian spirits of the Mountain, restless, foreboding. I shudder.

Indian spirits

The gale and sleet resume their rage. I sleep only fitfully. Several times oxygen starvation wakes me. I gasp for air as if I'm running a long-distance race in my sleeping bag. What a place to have a heart attack! Only by drifting back to sleep do I relieve my creeping panic.

Oxygen starvation

During the night, someone or something shuffles outside the tent. It is impossible in this weather for an animal to survive. Is it a person or are rocks shifting with the changing temperatures? There are other sounds and noises I don't understand. Maybe it's the wind or a steam vent or Grey Fox, human destroyer and creator. I shove a knife into my sleeping bag, preparing to defend myself against an unknown assailant.

Knife defense against Mountain fears

Those strangers have many miles to go following the route I pointed out to them. Though I thought I was a twentieth century man unhampered by beliefs in demons and vengeful spirits, I still feel feared the power of the Holy Mountain. The same dangers familiar to all prior generations not so many centuries ago jeopardized my own life. I sensed how much the Indian must have feared this violent Mountain especially in such storms.

Gods in harsh environments . . . wind, cold, mystery, presence . . .

Man often believed that Gods live on Mountain peaks like this one. Man, usually practical, placed some of his Gods in environments where man does not and cannot live. Such places have no water, no fuel for a fire, no animals, trees or shrubs. Here the Mountain is windy, cold, uncomfortable. Primitive man must have concluded only a superhuman could live in such places. He knew something lived on a Mountain peak. During the night I heard it. I felt it. I feared it. It was as alive as I was.

Blanket of snow, fog covers crooked crags

In the freezing early dawn, the need to urinate forced me outside the tent. The raging storm was over. The entire Mountain was a blanket of snow; sharp cracked crags, like weird monsters, appeared and disappeared in moving patches of fog.

In bag, warm, soft, consciousness of dreams

With morning came the sun, renewal. Only the thought of breakfast forces me out of my bed, lazy, dozing. Thanks to the wonders of our civilization, I survived the Mountain where no Indian could live: clothes, tent, stove, sleeping bag and insulated ground pad comforted me. My breakfast of left-over chicken tetrazzini and applesauce is finished, the cup and spoon were scraped clean in the snow. I gloried in a warm place in the sun sheltered by a large golden rock. The warm sun brought thoughts back to my dreams of the night before. Consciousness of dreams was another side effect of living in the open for a period of time. The heights blurred the real and unreal.

Negative ions raise awareness Summit dreams

As many Mountaineers know, people's attitudes and personalities change at high altitudes. The concentration of negative ions particularly affects the brain cells so we seem to see more clearly inside ourselves. One of the important side effects of Mountains is more awareness, especially of dreams.

"I dream of a man and his children who stow away on a boat by hiding and sleeping in a linen closet behind a shelf.

The dream reflects the danger I feel, the cramped space of my tent and my desire to travel. When everyone else on the boat is asleep, the man and his children sneak out and walk around as if they were regular passengers. They need the exercise since they are cramped inside the closet. The cramps, the walking, the exercise were obvious left-overs from the "dream day" before. The need to "appear" like a regular passenger fits a personality pattern that was part of my "intangible baggage."

Miss Home: unconscious, censoring personal dream; participant not just observer

Although my journey is an escape, in part, from domestic trials, another dream confirmed what I knew was also true — I missed home already. In this dream my unconscious censoring devices allow me to be a participant rather than an observer of the action.

Again, the question: why am I here on this Mountain? Was Mountain climbing to be my occupation instead of law?

Polite and dramatic dream revelation in India and punishment for India presence!

In another dream there are many people and a man trying to be a lawyer. He is dressed poorly in ragged clothes. I am sure that he will never be a success. As I watch him: I wonder whether I am not in ragged clothes. Somehow, I remember his being mean or punishing me. Isn't this trip some kind of a physical punishment? In retrospect, this dream is a prelude to a dramatic revelation to come in India.

Pleasant day on summit Lassen Peak quite quiet, lovely, impersonal

By late morning the peak is warm, quiet, lonely, but hospitable, unlike its mood the previous night. I have a pleasant day photographing, rock climbing, exploring, but the cold reminds me it is time to leave. By the time I strike camp it is almost dusk.

Descent To Heaven

Soul experience

Going down the trail on Sacred Mount Lassen in the twilight is a perception of the soul. In one direction you see purple Mountains, a gray darkening sky, and night beginning. In the other direction, you see the contrasts of bright oranges, blues and silver in the sky. On the dark side there is a slight breeze, on the other, none. A special reddish light floods the whole Mountain. Straight above through an opening in the dark clouds, with a tint of silver, is a remaining light of daytime blue.

Special light

Highest "heads" in the west

At almost 9,000 feet on the first shoulder of the Mountain, I see two gas pumps. Impossible. Feet are the only means of transportation here. They turn out to be modern looking men's and women's toilets. Probably the highest "heads" in the West.*3

Golden light floods into me

The whole slope ahead is bathed in golden light. Even a "Please Keep On The Trail" sign appears to be a golden plaque. The golden light, the thrill of being, floods into me. The Eternal Hunting Ground. Nirvana. Paradise. The place of my ancestors. Though tired, I feel good, clean, fresh. I am descending into heaven.

Descending into heaven

Dead Juniper

The first tree, an almost dead Juniper, reaches out its branch arms to the golden trail. The smell of two pines adds incense to the pilgrimage. The sharp biting cold wind disappears. Soon I will be in complete darkness, tranquility. Is this how it will be when I return to the dark, the womb, the night, death? Is this the way to begin again?

Complete darkness . . . tranquility

Words from the Twilight Golden Trail erupt as if they were a volcano's vent to my inner core:

ALAN NICHOLS

Along the twilight golden trail I sing
Of death and birth, of cold and heat,
of love and hate, of comfort, pain.

On one side there is blackness.
The other has the blues
Where the sun will serve its course on
other lands
and faces, leaving us in blackness or maybe
with the moon . . .
On the twilight golden trail.

My soul feels full of nothing.
My heart feels full of awe.
My body feels the tiredness . . .
On the twilight golden trail.

There is no moon to grace me
since the cloud has covered sunset
and will surely cover moonrise . . .
On the twilight golden trail.

Car and firelights show below me
while I walk in dimming lightness
feeling but not seeing . . .
On the twilight golden trail.

The Mountains with their colors
and their cliffs all sharp and rocky
are fading into blackness
mere silhouettes against black
cloudness . . .
On the twilight golden trail.

BOY FROM POCATELLO

I think I see a light
and wonder, "Is it real?"
It must be from inside me.
So I find my way alone
in a peace and growing comfort,
in a flooding, glowing warmness
On the twilight golden trail...

There's still a streak of lightness
in the far-off eastern sky,
a pale reflection from the sun
and from the moon before my eye.
And there's a certain whiteness
on that high peak far ahead,
from its snow bank shines a glimmer
that refuses to be dead.
 though the night is fastly falling
On the twilight golden trail...

It is lonely, it is lovely,
as I think of being worldly
and of friends and others
who I wished could too be there
And I think of love that lingers
and mystifies the air...
On the twilight golden trail...

The blackness is all-covering,
from the west no lights remaining.
But the whitened stones and dust
still guide me
On the twilight golden trail...

A small animal darts away into the shadows. Two squirrels scamper in the forest. A bird flies up in front of me. Night-life wakens: the owl, fly catcher, woodchucks, the deer and a cougar. The light fades to black and the twilight golden trail fades into the night.

Twilight fades into the dark

In Ishi's Footsteps

The next morning, I determine to find the Yahi Indian centuries-old trail from the high slopes of Mount Lassen down to their winter home along Mill Creek. The Yahi Tribe has special significance, especially because of their last Indian survivor, Ishi ("I am a MAN").

Yahi History

For over 3,000 years, Mount Lassen has been the summer home and Sacred Mountain for four separate and distinct Indian groups — the Mountain Maidu, the Atsugiwi, the Yahi and the Yana. Numbering about 4,025 in 1775, by 1890 two of the tribes had been annihilated and the others reduced to their modern population of about 385, thanks mostly to Christian white man's diseases, violence and atrocities.

Summer home – Mountain Maidu Atsugiwi, Yahi, Yana

Christian diseases and atrocities attacked and decimated tribes

The ranchers thought that they wiped out the Yahi by 1868, but in 1871 a group of cowboys and ranchers in Tehama County find blood from a wounded steer. Using dogs to follow the steer's trail, they cornered some thirty Indians in a hillside cave. The self-appointed posse immediately opened fire to slaughter every Indian, including several children. These white settlers' "idea of mercy" was widely reported in the newspapers, noting that one of the sheep-herders couldn't bear to kill children with his .56 caliber rifle. "It tore them up so bad," he said. So, he used his .38 caliber revolver instead. That rock shelter is now known as Kingsley Cave in memory of this genocide.

Yahi slaughtered in Kingsley Cave

Early in the morning on August 29, 1911, a lone Indian

staggered into Oroville, a small town in northern California near Mount Lassen. This strange white man, emaciated, sick, exhausted, is thrown into jail like an animal. The "wild man" becomes front-page news. Luckily, some anthropologists recognize the possibility of studying a living stone-age Indian. At first, they are barely able to speak to him with common Maidu words. Later, they take him to a new home in San Francisco at the University of California Museum. This Indian calls himself "Ishi", meaning "I am a man" in the Yahi language. Ishi projects over 3,000 years of culture suddenly into the twentieth century. A few professors and, in a lesser way, thousands of museum visitors, glimpse the stone-age through Ishi's eyes.

Last Wild American Indian, Ishi (translated "I am a man")

His adaptability, warmth, and wisdom cast doubts on the superiority of man in our age. Electric lights, airplanes and automobiles don't impress him . . . merely "white man's magic". Tall buildings in downtown San Francisco are not as significant to him as the cliffs and crags at Mount Lassen.

White man magic.

On the other hand, he is amazed at the enormous crowds on the streets, never having seen more than twenty or thirty people in one place. To him, one of our more significant achievements is the water faucet.

Crowds, water faucet

His criticism of our society is pointed: excessive liberty was given to menstruating women and dogs (illness could come from playing with dogs and letting them lick your hands); men are sick as being "too much automobile;" more importantly, there are "too much coyote doctor" or evil spirits among these "civilized" white people.

Ishi's critique of our culture

So integrated within himself and nature, he has no separate "religion," but his friends' "Christianity" interests him. He asks many questions about "life after death" for Christians, yet there is no anxiety for his own immortality; his afterlife was assured as it was for all of his tribe. Anyway,

Ishi interested in our Christian religion

he doubts that the "White God" cares much about having Indians with him, nor does he expect that women are eligible for that God's heaven.

Crucifixion

He is deeply moved by a movie about Christ's last days at Jerusalem, the Passion Play. But he assumes from the crucifixion that Christ is a bad man, from his painful death on the cross. Perhaps Christ's refusal to save himself by stating the truth to a sympathetic Pontius Pilate is too unnatural to understand. Would there not be too much "coyote" in a man who tries to sell a message of love by self-destruction? Or maybe he couldn't absorb all 2,000 years of violent Christian history, with millions so willing to die (and kill) for "Him who died for us".

2000 years of Christian violence

Technique of stone age living, intelligent, honesty, natural wisdom

Ishi gives much more than he receives. He demonstrates the techniques of stone-age living: weapon making, shooting, carving, tracking, singing, dancing. Though shy and stoic, he is curious about everything. His intelligence is coupled with complete honesty, leavened with natural wisdom. His politeness and infectious good humor make it too easy to impose on his fading health. Personal cleanliness and conscientious industry make him ideal for his newly assigned task as a museum janitor.

Museum janitor job

One summer a few friends return with him to his tribal area along Mill Creek. They live and sing with Ishi like fellow tribesmen — with a human encyclopedia of stone-age culture as their guide. They react in amazement at his ability and character; a magnetic person, at one with himself and Nature, his two worlds and his friends.

Stone age culture guides

"I go, you stay"

Ishi faces death like life — simply, quietly. Dead at the museum one morning, he leaves a note to his friends, written in his recently acquired English. "I go. You stay."

Whenever I think of Ishi, I feel deeply, sadly. I feel the

loss of something, someone, who really matters. Ishi and his tribe, along with the Yana, Maidu and Atsugiwi, have the spirit of Lassen in their natures. They summered on the slopes, in their circular brush enclosures with several entrances but no roof. It was a welcome change to go from their winter diet of wild acorns and salmon to deer, trout, berries, herbs, pine nuts and onions in Spring. While the women worked with plant life, food and baskets and care for the young, the men did everything that related to animals: hunting, fishing, making tools and weapons.

The specialty of men and women

All four tribes had separate and distinct languages. Although the Mountain played an economic role in tribal life, it was not the prime source of gratification of their material needs. The Indians hunted deer and caught fish, but their main needs (acorns, salmon, obsidian and salt) were obtained elsewhere. They hunted deer with bows and arrows, spears, rocks and even knives. They were Mountain tribesmen, strong minded and wiry. Carrying nothing but his weapon and a pouch of acorns, an Indian might chase a deer for two or three days, never allowing it to settle down and eat, until it fell from exhaustion.

Hunting

Ishi and the tribe . . . the lost spirits

Their attitude about this Mountain could be compared, though much more intensely, to that of a modern family's relationship to their summer cabin in our culture. One which is in use all summer, every summer; a different family life from their usual experience — vacationing, carefree. It is a feeling I always have when I first arrive at a summer Mountain wilderness, especially when I've been there before. Everything is fresh: the sun, the cool air, even the rain.

Summer home

Like all people, Ishi and these tribes have special creation myths to explain man's beginning — the creation of the earth, moon, sun, sky by Grey Fox, the world flood, the presence of evil in the form of a devil (called Coyote), the

Creation Myth in moon, sun, sky, grey fox, coyote, devil

creation of man, and from him woman, the lost opportunity for immortal life and the discovery of fire.

The legends tell of the void before creation, the coming of Ko-do-yan-pe ("Earth-Namer" or "Creator," some of whose functions are later assumed by Grey Fox) 'who makes life easy, happy and deathless', and Coyote, who makes man suffer and die. In their struggle for supremacy, Creator is defeated and disappears to the east. But in the meantime, Creator and Coyote go over the world to create the rivers and Mountains.*4 Although there is no special reference to Mount Lassen, all of the Indians are sure that most of the Mountains are made by the evil Coyote, since the land is usually so steep, rocky and rough.

By November, at the latest, the cold winds and early snows forced them to their separate tribal areas at the lower levels along the tributaries of the Sacramento Valley. Ishi and his fellow Yahi tribesmen always traveled to their winter homes along upper Mill Creek.

I wondered, could I feel the presence of their spirits if I follow their route to the lower valleys?" I take a well-traveled trail to the "Bumpuss Hell" hot springs below Mount Lassen. On the way, the scene fills with a large family of browsing deer, squeaks of pikas, and calls and screeches of hawks, blue jays, swallows and an owl. Rocks turn and twist into a museum of glacial movement, volcanic cones and the broken off sides of great Mount Tehama in the distance. From one rock ledge I can see the Pacific Coast Range and the geologic meeting of the Cascade and Sierra Nevada Mountain ranges. The Creator, not Coyote, must have created this sight of splendor.

The sweet air becomes rotten with hydrogen sulphide and the sweet valley becomes a hell above ground. Geysers, volcanoes, clouds of sulfur gas rise from the earth, steam-vents hiss, roaring springs pressure-heated beyond the boiling

Ko-do-yan-pe "creator"

Mountain made by evil coyote

November migration

Mill Creek winter home

Bumpus Hell

Hydrogen sulfide Dangerous steaming

point, bleep-blopping mud pots. The ground is hot and rumbles. Chemicals and heat break the soil into its own essences, like a dirt rainbow: yellow sulfur, bright crystals, black, gold, red oxide irons, chalky white lime, brown and gray clays, even oranges and copper greens. Yet fascination draws me closer into the dangerous steam and caves. I gingerly step around bubbling potholes, trying to jump from rock to rock to avoid breaking through the brittle crust into a boiling pot. A wrong step means boiled human, in gray mud with a touch of iron and sulfur. First aid supplies left by the Park Rangers are more of a prominent warning than a solution for the sure burning death of falling into any boiling mud.

Potholes . . . first aid warnings

Finally, I take off my boots and rest at the outlet to the valley — a small murky stream bordered with green algae and, lower down, pink heather and moss. The chorus of hisses, gurgles, blops, and running water continues. My eyes smart from the sting of the gas clouds. I am still conscious of the rotten egg smell. My feet submerge in warm gray mud and give me the feeling that I am communicating with the very core of mother earth, violent, unapproachable, yet brings joy to my tired feet.

Sulphur Creek. Kings Creek. Then down Mill Creek. On my topographic map it looks like the only way to leave Lassen is in that direction. It must be the ancient Yahi route. All goes well at first — a smaller valley of steam vents and mud pots, so I hold my boots while I wade down Sulphur Creek in a steep, narrow defile and then into a meadow, a Shangri-la, with a horde of wild flowers — lupine, daisies, monkshood, and mustard, a lush green with grass and skunk cabbage up to my shoulders. Mother earth seems intending to prove the exquisite color and softness of her skin, to contrast with the pus and boils of Bumpuss Hell nearby. The beauty of

Warm, violent core of mother earth

this afternoon, and this paradise, and the wet spongy ground lifts my whole body making each step springy, like a weightless moon-walk. Even a deer threesome is unafraid here and lets me come within twenty feet before bouncing off. I am exultant, unaware of the obstacles downstream.

Moon walk

Deer calm

Further down Kings Creek grows to a river from its tributaries and clears the sludge of Sulfur Creek. The sides become cliffs, forcing me higher and higher along deer trails, through open forests and lawn-like meadows manicured by grazing animals.

Higher Trails

By five o'clock in the afternoon I am tiring. I lie down in a meadow and temporarily revive myself by dunking my whole head in a brook. My attempt to follow the zig-zag river contour to avoid the steep cliffs wears me out. It will be impossible to meet my planned car-pickup ride by 6pm at the highway, miles away.

Walk out but meeting impossible

According to my map there is a trail at Carson Meadow, but when I find the trail, it angles in the wrong direction. I push back cross-country towards the river only to find a roaring waterfall, twenty feet wide and fifty feet high, cascading through river boulders below by way of a narrow chute. Sheer reddish shale cliffs dominate both sides of the river. What a disappointment. Below the cliffs, the water tunnels through a huge snow bank. If I dare, I might try to rope down the cliffs to the top of the snow roof and cross over the river there. But the thin snow crust has already partially caved in. Or I can go through the tunnel in the water; the chances of drowning in that rush, with or without my heavy pack, would be significant.

Alone, now lost. To hesitate will mean being lost in the wilderness. Blocked by good sense or cowardice, I start to climb back up the cliff, hoping to find somewhere below the snow bank to get safely down to the river. Scrambling up the

Alone, lost on climbing trail

steep, loose shale cliffs above, grabbing bushes and rocks, I inch my pack up by hand. At some places, only by tremendous effort am I able to move fast enough to keep slightly ahead of the loose rock avalanching me downwards over the cliff to the river below.

Temporary Rest

Soaked in sweat, I struggle towards a lone pine tree. Here is a place to rest, and bushes to hold on to. It is also a good vantage point to find a more agreeable route to the river, then far below. But here is another impassable cliff. Dejected, I yell "Shit!" at the river below. I have to climb again, three hundred yards straight up. My pack and shaking legs keep me off-balance as I finally cross the top of the cliffs, high above the river.

"Shit!:

Seven pm. Worn out. Fall into clump of bushes

It is now seven o'clock; I was exhausted and the river is even further away. I know I should quit and make camp, but I decide to try to go down once more through a group of trees below me. Below the trees, a rock-slide upends me. Grabbing rocks and painful nettles, I finally slow myself down and maneuver into a clump of bushes. I pull myself and my pack together to decide what to do next. From these bushes a deer trail in a steep meadow clearly leads down to the river bed. I shout my relief. Once in the river bed, I look upstream and realize it has taken three hours, a grueling effort, to reach this point only three hundred yards below the bluff where I originally overlooked the snow bank and waterfall.

Three hours, grueling effort to go only three hundred yards down bluff

Dazed... trudging down

As I pick my way downstream around boulders, over boulders and under boulders, it becomes apparent that my map is out of date. Its "trails" and "roads" don't exist anymore. The cliffs and wide turns in the river force me to cross many times. I lose my balance on one crossing and a log rips open my leg. I am too tired to care or even sit down to bandage it. Finally, I give up trying to stay dry. I wade through the torrent, pack, boots and all, sometimes up to my neck. Every muscle aches, but all I can do is trudge, too dazed to stop or even to feel the cold, the wet clothes, the sloshing water in my boots.

About ten o'clock, I think I see a car's head lights. I backtrack uselessly upstream about a mile. I am getting confused. The white light of the moon reflects on the dirt roads ahead and make them look like highways. A wind in the trees, the gurgle of the streams, sounds like voices. Any hum becomes a car in the distance. The highway has to appear beyond the next turn, the next forest, the next meadow. By midnight, I am staggering in a trance. Too stiff and in pain even to rest, I become unaware of either sound or light. Almost by magic, my pack comes apart, the tent and sleeping bag dropping on the ground. An omen — a warning — stop and sleep. Sitting down, I hear a noise ... louder, louder. It is a car! One hundred and fifty yards in front of me, headlights appear and vanish. Civilization! A deserted highway. A sign, "Mill Creek"!

I try to catch a ride but only two cars pass, speeding up at the sight of a desperate, tired man hitchhiking, a hatchet hanging from his side, huge pack, hair standing on end, unshaven. A station wagon heading towards the park seems to slow down. It stops. I open the door and a park ranger says, "Are you Hammond?" I said "Yes. Hallelujah!" It was one a.m.

This wearing, even frightening adventure, reminds me that Nature requires respect as well as understanding and receptivity. To forget her danger, to deny her power is to court injury or even death. On the lower reaches of Mount Lassen, I was careless. To be alone with Nature, drink her beauty, know her wisdom, her mysteries, absorb her power, feel her peace, one must first learn to survive. The thought comes to me — maybe it is silly to climb up and down Mountains strapped to

Pack falls apart . . . omen . . . deserted highway, headlight . . . mill creek

Park ranger: "Are you Hammond" "Yes. Hallelujah"

A respect for nature

Pain with nature

heavy loads, playing Indian or pilgrim. Is it necessary amidst the comforts of our civilization to experience pain in order to become a part of the wilderness of Nature?

Logically no. But I always have . . . part of the time . . . like all other animals.

Mountain nature . . . religious reality

Are "Mountains" and "Nature" personal deifications or universal religious realities? Both are female, mother, lover. Mother Earth. Mother Nature. Climbing a Mountain, like love or sexual intercourse, raises, then purges physical and mental tension; concentrate, touch, smell, sight, one's whole self into moments of ecstasy like the climax on reaching the highest point and, if one becomes fully responsive, he or she leaves with a residue of personal warmth, of completeness.

Climbing distractions

When climbing, individual problems dissolve by some force or by the distractions of anxiety about the Mountain or the route of the climb, or by the effort to bring to use all physical resources. Simple desires for rest, for water, for a place (the top, a trail, a ledge) replace the complex changing goals of civilized life.

Senses awakening . . . cold spring water . . . New oxygen . . . wild flower perfume . . . brilliant color . . . bird cry . . . vivid dreams . . . easy elimination

All senses reawaken. The pleasurable taste of cold spring water. The touch of bark and leaves and dirt. The cooling invigoration of dunking feet and head into a stream. The freshness of newly made oxygen I feel entering a forest. The delicate perfume of the wildflower meadow. The visual thrill seeing the brilliant oranges, blacks, reds, purples and golds of sunset. The cheerful song of a lark or the terrorizing cry of a hawk. Sweat without stinking. Vivid dreams. Eliminate anywhere, eat anything, live only to survive.

Nature Dangerous

Yet, Nature has her dangers. Wrong steps or just careless ones can cause serious harm with scores of natural booby-traps. Heat prostration. Starvation. Frozen limbs. Festering sores. Loneliness. Poisons of dangerous animals, insects and plants.

Fears of such things create anxiety in me when I approach the Mountain, especially when alone; feelings, as old as man in Nature, for over five million years.

Extreme fatigue

Often, living with nature causes extreme fatigue. Perhaps it is only when all the human emotions and strength are used up and thus are unable to interfere with Nature, that one can find the spirit, God. The euphoria of exhaustion is the elimination of desire, leaving only the act of lying asleep on mother earth, necessary for fulfillment. When your body and mind have been ground into the dirt, into the rock, then you become a part of the Mountain, ready then to soar beyond the world, on the wind, through the panorama on a bed of wildflowers by a Mountain meadow cool as an alpine lake. The places of Mountains are wrested from the earth. They exist between the earth and infinity. Bigger than Nature's other creations, yet a part of them reach upwards into the cosmos. Mountains in their geologic struggle overcome the very crust of the earth itself. Man, harnesses much of the power of the earth's crust, renewing his victory by conquering the Mountain. This relationship of man and nature, symbolized and made real by the Mountain, is personal. It becomes sacred like God, or to an Indian, his Totem.

Euphoia of exhaustion and elimination of desire

The Mountain wrested from the earth and infinity

Sacred like a God or an Indian totem

Through Native American Eyes

I follow the Indian trails to the peak and back. The winds, the voices of the past, the spirits of this great Mountain take hold of me. From my physical experience, and backed by my study, the sacred mystery of Mount Lassen reveals itself to me. I understand how these Indians, my human ancestors, feel about Nature's violent volcano.

See Sacred Mount Lassen

Understanding

Hat Creek Indian mothers told their children this story: There was a "gorilla" with a human face. One night he stole a baby from his mother when her back was turned and hid in the lava tube caves near the Wicuhirdiki (Mount Lassen). The tribe chases him but did not catch him. They try to smoke him out by throwing burning sticks in the caves. That only makes the Mountain furious, and in its anger, it bellows smoke.

Hat Creek Indian mothers story of gorilla baby

The experts doubt the validity of this story. It might well have been a modem invention to keep Indian children from playing in the lava tube caves after dark.

Modern motivation to avoid lave caves

Why remember it at all? Because it is the only written myth of these Indian tribes which talks directly about the Mountain itself. Ishi reports no such stories of the Mountain. After searching the literature and talking to Indians and experts, I find the record is blank. Why? The puzzle bothers me. Somehow, I know the answer is important to my own search.

Rare story . . . not from Ishi

The generally accepted reason for this silence is that Lassen is not sacred or important to the local Indians as were the other Sacred Mountains of the Cascade and Sierra ranges, Mount Shasta, Mount Rainier, Mount Hood and Mount Whitney to the Indians of those areas. Furthermore, archaeologists, in spite of strenuous efforts, are apparently unable to find satisfactory remains of Indian occupation at Lassen similar to what they find at Indian summer camps on those other Mountains. Of course, the absence of physical evidence can be explained by the more recent volcanic eruptions of Lassen, but it does not explain why there is almost no reference to the Mountain in Indian myths and stories.

Mountains not sacred

No archaeological evidence

But I know from my own experience that Mountains have significance to all those in the tribe. Shamans, fathers and young boys go to the Mountains to seek power, the same power that I find. When boys attain manhood, they generally go there alone for several days to obtain skill and luck in deer hunting,

Mountain significant to all in the tribe

archery, fighting, Shaman-ism and other spiritually important experiences. After a boy makes his first animal kill, his father talks to him, blows smoke in his face and sends him to the Mountains for at least five days. When a child dies, the father goes to the Mountains for solace from their spirits. Youths preparing to be shamans, and thus to be important persons in the life of the tribe, are lectured by their fathers or uncles, and their nose septa are pierced. Then they would go alone, unclothed, into the Mountains for several days and nights. There they carry out the quests of swimming, securing bird feathers, smoking and cutting themselves. It is in the Mountains that from such quests they might fall into a trance, bleed from the nose or the mouth, and become the magical forces of a Shaman. Self-power. Self-reliance. Celebration. Enlightenment. Like the Indians, I find there was no better place to feel such spiritual accomplishments than on the Mountains.

These Indians associate the Mountain with a chance to avoid the summer heat of the valley and a time of plentiful food. It is a respite from the winter cold and hunger, from warfare and the vermin of their permanent village in the valley. They return to the Mountain every summer as ducks return north. It is not coincidental that these four tribes, who fight each other elsewhere, live in peace on Mount Lassen.

It is an elevated no-man's land. Not only are there four separate tribes, in contrast to the single tribe dominance around other Mountains in the Cascades and Sierras, but here they meet in small bands in nonviolent contact like herds of elk or deer.

These Indians are awestruck and believe natural things are sacred. To them that also means they fear them. They fear storms, thunder, bears and rattlesnakes. Special bear and rattle-snake shamans are powerful in many tribes. As is usual with fears, cause and effect is confused. For example, falling rocks or loud shouting in the Mountains cause rain, according to tradition.

Ghosts and spirits

They believe in ghosts and spirits. They are sure that such spirits affect their health, the weather, the future and can bring life or death. Some spirits are good and some are bad, but Indians fear and avoid them all. Mysticism and the supernatural pervade their whole culture, even their everyday activities.

Magic

They believe in magic. For example, the number five is magic and sacred to the Mountain Maidu Tribe.

Mountain was center of universe

Indians in the Lassen area think that their area is the center of the universe. There are few of the migration myths so common to other Indian tribes and most religions. Known as Wicuhirdiki by the Atsugiwi Hat Creek Indians, or Waganupa by the Yana, the Mountain (Lassen) is the biggest thing in these Indians' lives. They can't miss it, especially since all natural phenomena and every hill and valley are known in exact detail by every Indian. The Mountain's importance is indirectly admitted by the Mountain Maidu tribe. They speak of five directions: North, East, South, West and toward Wicuhirdiki.

Five directions included sacred wicuhirdiki

Mountain role creating spirituality... death

The final factual piece necessary to understand the Mountain's role in spirituality is that the most important things to an Indian are secret. Indians do not speak of the dead. Ishi never does or did. It is too dangerous. The places of the dead are feared and everything connected with the dead purified. 'Mentioning the name of a deceased person in the presence of his relatives is forbidden. The Atsugiwi made it a taboo to look back enroute to a funeral.

Totem and secrecy

Another personal and tribal secret is the Totem. Each young Indian selects his own totem: an eagle, bear, raccoon, frog, tree, etc. That personal Totem is a secret and the Indian models his life after the one he chooses. It is very dangerous if another person knows that Totem; with such knowledge he has power over the other. This is carried so far by Ishi that he will not even give his name to his friends, let alone reveal his individual Totem.

Research provides a hypothesis about Mount Lassen. From these basic facts, Mount Lassen is indeed a paramount Sacred Mountain, a center of the universe, at least to the four tribes in that area, important far beyond their material needs. The silence about it in mythology and ritual is explained either by concluding that it is completely insignificant or too significant.

Nature was religion – secret, tribal

The latter alternative becomes obvious. Nature is religion. Nature's creations are Totems in a Totem religion. Each person and each tribe merges its inner self with something specific in Nature. These most mysterious and sacred things of Nature are secret in such a personal religion, a secret religion and a tribal religion. My presence at Mount Lassen proves the hypothesis: Mount Lassen is a Sacred Mountain to the Indians there. It is a tribal Totem. But what is it to modern man?

Tribal totem on sacred Mountain

Harmonizing unconsciously on the sacred Mountain

Living on the Mountain makes me part of it. Harmonizing myself with Nature, I become more "Indian." My thoughts of the Indians' attitudes toward this Mountain heighten the awareness of my own feelings. There is no question of its importance. It is an unconscious force. It gives power, comfort, confidence, spiritual determination, peace. I experience it, touch it, feel it, taste it. Like an Indian's Totem, the Mountain becomes and hence is part of me.

Mount Lasen, my totem, my unity, my experience with nature

Mount Lassen becomes my first Sacred Mountain, a part of my life, my Totem. And it is still a Totem, a living symbol of the religious need for unity with and experience with Nature. I learn that we can go no further in personal growth until we accept its truth as our own. It must be recognized as part of our universal heritage. And so, it is the first step to discover the spiritual force of the Sacred Mountain and to connect to that force. What is on Mount Lassen, this home so hallowed to these Indians of California? Man can be whole, complete, entire only in union with Nature.

Our journey of discovery of mystery

The experience of Mount Lassen is essential to the whole search for myself. With it now a part of us, we can begin our own journey of discovery of the mysteries of the Sacred Mountains of the world.

Know nature, create personal Gods

We know Nature. We, like mankind, are now ready to create God. First, we must create a personal God. Where better than great Olympus, "Mountain of the Gods"?

Footnotes:

Peter Lassen

1. Named after Peter Lassen, a local adventurer and promoter of the immigrant wagon trail from the East into California.
2. Mount Helena in Washington was active as late as 1841 and Mount Shasta as late as 1786; Mount Mazama (now Crater Lake) collapsed about six thousand years ago much like Mount Tehama.
3. Bears were especially frightening; they had a reputation of eating any tribesman who violated the strict taboos against intercourse, sexual or even social, with in-laws of the opposite sex.

Four hunters womanized

4. To some Indians, "Coyote" represents good, not evil. "Cottontail (another Creator) placed stones in the fire and the men who were poor hunters were seated by it, the stone burst, cutting off their sexual organs, so they became women.

PART III

Sacred Mountains . . . Founders, Spirits, Religions

*One of the best appreciated and known
involvements of Sacred Mountains
and the spirit of their Mountain Gurus
has been their role in the creation of
new or vastly revised spiritual
or religious organizations.*

Songs and Psalms of the Mountain Guru*

The Guru and the People

My pilgrimage ends

Eventually, these pilgrimages were over. The circle was closed. On the long plane returning to San Francisco, I had time to sort out the memories of my Sacred Mountain explorations. As the moments of purge and the times of paradise flooded in on me, I became aware of the shadow that stood behind all. I had never been alone on this search. Wherever I went, that shadow stood above me, beckoning. The Sacred Mountain Guru would not come to me. So, I had to seek it. The Guru challenged me to appreciate the ecstasy. The Guru's presence, not a person, permeated my acts. When I was tired and discouraged, the Sacred Mountain Guru would comfort me. When I was overjoyed, the Guru remained strong and unflighty. If we were together and summited the holy Mountain, an object of the search, victory would be obvious. I was grateful to these shadows for showing me the way... the long, hard way was possible when I appreciated and followed Guru teachings. The Guru taught perseverance over pain. These shadows rewarded me with the inner and outer views of both the universe and myself. The more I traveled with them, the clearer the image of myself became. The more I became conscious of them, the more I wanted these shadows with me.

But when I finally came to the far country, to the sunrise of my own world of self-discovery, my shadow, my master, my guides faded into their own worlds. The stronger I became,

---

* Regent Press is also considering publishing separately in the future the Guru sayings and photographs in *Boy From Pocatello*.

the weaker the Guru's image became, until finally all that was left of them was the reflection of the Sacred Mountains that I climbed. And in their reflections, I see myself.

Personal findings

"Please fasten your seatbelts; we will arrive in San Francisco in twenty minutes," did not completely shatter my vision, did not bring me back to reality, for my reality was clear: the Mountains at least harbored my Sacred Mountain Gurus. I replayed my personal life on the images of my holy Sacred Mountains. A full panorama of my religious metamorphosis, my emotional experience, and my cognitive qualities passed before me, and I knew myself as I never knew before.

Pilgrimage people reflections

With this revelation, the people on my journeys began to reappear from different perspectives. I endured too many people: pilgrims on Fuji-san, monks in Greece, and tourists in Israel. They seemed to stand in my way, but contemplations of the Sacred Mountains showed them in a different tone. Were the solitary journeys of my Mountain pilgrimages a need to get away from people, hide some inability to love, to communicate with my fellow human beings? Can man ever do anything alone? The Mountains taught me that it is impossible. Man cannot learn alone. He cannot reach the holy summit alone and without support. Paradise is not a single blessedness. At the time of creation, "East of Eden" the Lord probably concluded: "It is not good that man should be alone" I previously thought that I could make this journey alone. It is not so; "Spirit needs company."

Fuji pilgrimage crowds

My mind flashes back both to Japan and to Sinai where I was so close to many others. While the crowds on Mount Fuji-san at first destroyed the Mountain for me and led me to avoid their crowded hostels seasoned with fleas, I now knew their presence provided significance to the experience, especially the sunrise and my special camp in Mt. Fuji's summit main crater." I remember the beautiful smile of a very old woman climbing Fuji-san with her friends, all in white garbs and coolie hats. I remember the friendly laughter of the hiking groups answering my greeting "*ikaga desu ka*" (how are you).

Support of fellow passengers

I hear the clapping again. I feel again the warmth of my welcome from my fellow travelers on the bus to Mount Sinai when I returned alone from my climb up Mount St. Catherine. Their concern about my absence was greater than their concern about my delaying their departure.

Women and spirit

The Journey clarified my impressions of women. Monks, like those I met at the holy Mountain of Athos, exist without women. The male-oriented Father-God religions of today have elements of misogamy, perhaps necessitated in origin by the need to rid man of the shackles of mother, mother nature, mother Goddesses, the terrors of fertility rituals, and the sacrifices of earlier religious history. Christ was unmarried and presumably born from a virgin; even his conception is said to not be a human male-female act of love or lust. Buddha abandoned his beautiful wife and small child to find his truths. Hindus, as did Ghandi, found spiritual merit in leaving the household and "semen retention." Only Mohammed kept his status as a "Messenger of God," husband and lover (several times over).

Monk celibacy

Celibacy is a requirement of devotion in many religions. Women are often in social history prohibited from participation in countless denomination monasteries. For example, Mount Athos monks, or Shugendo practitioners at Mount Omine in Japan. St. Catherine's Monastery at Mount Sinai was named for a female martyr but no females were ever admitted as monks. Sexual abstinence has historically been a condition of pilgrimages. I find concentration and the physical strain of climbing temporarily relieve the desire for sexual intercourse, particularly in the rough wilderness.

But the female role is critical in a different way.

The female in us all

To climb and conquer the Mountain, to overcome bigness, power, anger, and fear of such a phallic symbol, manhood (the Father) was a motivation, the driving force. But the result, the achievement, was an awareness that I cannot exist without the female. I wanted to lie on the peak after a long struggle and sleep in soft beauty in the lap of the Sacred Mountain, honored, comforted, at peace, in ecstasy at the end of the Journey. The sacred Mountain pilgrimage did not make me a celibate. It reminded me of the need for the Oneness in any successful search, the union of opposites, of male and female.

Purges and Paradise

Lost when alone and don't ask for advice

Coincidentally, I often became lost on each Mountain, sacred or not, when I climbed alone. This too bothered me. Getting lost meant more physical effort and discomfort from lack of food and/or water. I became lost because I was in a hurry, didn't ask for sufficient advice, and tarried too long in places that seemed pleasant. I used up my energy on side trips and unnecessary detours. Discouragement, fatigue, disillusionment, danger — these were the handmaidens of being lost. These things became my almost daily companions, especially in wilderness areas.

Psychological goals

But as I see them in the light of what I learned, what I became; they were all psychological tools I needed to perform my purging operation by myself. When I was over-desirous to get to the top, I hiked too fast. When I didn't know the way to go and concentrated on each step, I missed the path altogether. When I made it, I looked up to the Sacred Mountain, to keep the Mountain as a whole in mind. The closer I was to the peak, the easier it was. I now know that when I saw myself on the top, resting, successful and accepting this as one act among many pleasurable acts, each step of the way up and down the Mountain, then the fatigues and disillusionments were assuaged.

Actual and imagined dangers on the Mountain

Other purges are just as essential. Actual and imagined dangers in the Mountains produced in me real fears. That was apparent at the very beginning on Mount Lassen. Though I went to sleep easily the first night on the peak, several times oxygen starvation woke me so I was afraid I might be having a heart attack. I, a twentieth-century man supposedly unhampered by beliefs in demons and vengeful spirits, could still feel the fears of Mount Lassen that the Native Americans felt. I carried the memories of my ancient ancestors whose lives could be terrorized by Nature.

Mountains are about joy more than my fears

The Mountains taught me more about myself than just my fears. They exaggerated and emphasized my personality quirks. In business and social life, I was typically late. Without, at first being aware of it, I usually underestimated the return hike. I didn't want to leave so I tarried too long on the peaks of Olympus, Lassen, and Athos. My overstay at Mount Olympus almost left me alone at the bottom. My return from Mount Athos was a whole day late. At Sinai, I almost missed the bus at the bottom of the Mountain, which could leave me alone in that desert. I almost missed the plane leaving for Japan.

Mountain pains and stress

There were more pains to endure than the anxiety of being lost or late. The pain seemed to be the price of obtaining the Mountain treasure trove. If you press too far, especially in the desert areas, you risk collapse from heat exhaustion. To be without water for hours, climbing without shade in over 100° temperatures, with a mouth that was so dry and cracked inside that I was unable to talk, and suffered the pangs of the damned. Sometimes I became desperately tired yet was unable to sleep because of the heat, cold, sickness, or the insects. There were moments of terrible anxiety when I was unable to take a full breath of air, and no one was around to help. And there were the times when my legs, back and knees, ankles, and arches hurt so badly that each step ached. I wanted to drop but had miles to go for water or rest or a way out of the area. These stresses, along with loneliness, could create doubts about whether the whole Journey was a waste of time or an exercise in masochism.

Last night on Mount Athos at St. Gregoire

In the late evening of my last night on Mount Athos, I laid in my cell-like room at St. Gregoire Monastery, a room that overlooked the sea, and thought of my misadventures at Mount Athos, of being lost so many times on Olympus and then finally with the help of local Greeks finding my way. It became evident to me that night that contrasts are critical. When does a cool breeze feel the best? When your throat and mouth ache from thirst. Hunger before food. Restraint before elimination, exhaustion before rest, tension before peace. The pain of the climb, the thirst, the aching muscles, the hunger, the deprivation, and the tiredness only heighten the joys that the Sacred Mountain later provides. Man, I concluded, has the freedom to choose a neutral life without much pleasure or pain, an extreme life of ecstatic pleasures and excruciating pains, or somewhere in between (the ideal in many philosophies).

Ascetics and the Black Night of the Soul

Sacred Mountain purges body,

Ascetics voluntarily created painful conditions to enhance their spirituality. Buddha for six years in the hills of Nepal, Christ in the wilderness, Mohammed outside Mecca desert, and Moses at Sinai all chose grueling physical hardships, but they did not accept them as a way of life. Various ECK Masters of the modern age describe the black Night of Soul along the way but not as the end.

The Sacred Mountain purges the body, then the mind, and finally the spirit. The pains are preludes to inspiration, bliss, and growth. The Mountain proves not so much the beauty of holiness but the holiness of beauty. The climb is the teacher. The peak is the symbol of victory, of progress, of the new life. To be on the peak is pure joy. Paradise is the climb but descent from the peak can bring painful knees as well as bliss. It is why I instinctively looked up to heaven on my way down.

The Way to New Religion

Modern religions and their "izes"

I knew before I began my pilgrimage that man finds much that he seeks in drugs, philosophy, medicine, and more, especially in organized religions. Yet people in all the countries I visited seemed increasingly dissatisfied with modern religions. Have the belief systems of today fallen prey to the "izes" of religious degeneration: institutionalize, ritualize, philosophize, organize, monetize, and capitalize?

Organizational religions and their followers

The need to balance individual and organizational religious growth became particularly apparent to me at Bhagavan's Ashram in South India. The followers of Bhagavan there reminded me of the disciples shortly after the physical deaths of Buddha or Jesus. Why did they give their lives to Bhagavan's memory? Was it to help others; was it habit, or had they nowhere else to go? Raising their teacher's status may reinforce their own life significance.

Business of Religions

Religious Age — new understanding, consciousness, lifestyle

These devotees, like those before them of other new and old religions, seemed compelled in their founder's name to sell life memberships, hold "special" services, preserve relics, build buildings, publish sacred scriptures, employ officials and priests, and form branches. While these very procedures strengthened the "religion," they divert attention from the unchallengeable truths of their own lives and those of the person and the spirit they worship.

Religious Age — new understanding, consciousness, lifestyle

Yet the Sacred Mountains, where the religions of the past begin, leave no doubt in my mind that we live in a religious age. We seek new understandings and consciousness. We change lifestyles. We reject the illusory attractions of progress in politics, science, and art. We join unfamiliar sects and schools of thought and mysticism.

Sacred Mountain seeds of religion

And so, the stage is set. Within this century, there will be a new drama. To some, the new religion. How will the play move and end? The better soil in which the seeds of our present-day religions germinate is the Sacred Mountains of the Middle East and India. Why? What were the conditions that nurtured Hinduism, Judaism, Islam, Buddhism, Bo Po, and Christianity? Were these the same conditions inspiring a fresh awakening for me as with millions before me and as they may for some new founder of some new religion?

Roots of religious changes

The roots of new religions grow from long preexisting traditions in hot countries like India and the nations of the Middle East where there are sharp contrasts, crowded cities and isolated wildernesses, violence and peace, wealth and poverty. They grow out of dissatisfaction with the dominant religious forces of the time and a desperate longing of the people for physical, emotional, and spiritual healing. There is a strong intellectual base of understanding of many religions and, perhaps more importantly, there is inspiration from the Sacred Mountains.

Pedigree of theocracy

Egyptian, Hebrew, and Dravidian traditions precede by centuries their dissenting Christian, Islam, and Buddhist offspring. In fact, the tie is often personal in the form of a good pedigree in the old dominant theocracy: Moses is a courtier, Christ a Levite Jew, Buddha a high caste King's son, and Muhammad, a Hashimite, and Coreish. While they all grew up in towns except for Muhammad's years with the nomads) where it was easier to contemplate than to act, the opportunity to be alone was critical to their lives. Thus, Christ left Nazareth, Buddha deserted his palace community, Mohammed went out from Mecca, and Moses from Pharoah Ramses II in Egypt. They all experienced the hardships and beauty of out-of-doors life, the violence of warfare, depression and joy, success and failure. The social and individual symptoms of religious awakening seem to resemble manic depression with great highs and lows like Jesus' triumph and crucifixion at Jerusalem. In their lives, they need both human intercourse and isolation. They live, create, and pray where they can.

Old Jerusalem Church of the Holy Sepulcher

I experienced these contrasting needs strongly in the Church of the Holy Sepulcher in Old Jerusalem. At about five in the afternoon, I entered St. Stephen's gate in the Arab quarters of that walled city. I walked as fast as I could so as not to be a target for robbery. I lost my way. As I plunged deeper into the city, the lanes became darker and narrower with only enough room to get by the stalls; hawkers yelled at me and brushed past me. There were no signs that l could read, no one spoke English, no police and my map was useless. Finally, I found another gate, went outside again, and entered a third gate. By then, I was going in circles, seeing the same places over and over. In my confusion, I only wanted to escape. About seven o'clock in the evening, I turned a corner and found myself in the courtyard of a church. I entered its huge cavern and soon drifted into the inner grotto. Here

Re-stimulating my spirit

Christ is said to be first buried. The silence, candlelight, and smallness of the place restimulated my feelings of spiritual peace and my need for a world better than the worlds of the squabbling people above.

New Human guidelines

In such contrasts, I think people could accept the importance of new guidelines in our relations with each other. In the midst of human chaos, greed, insensitivity, and exploitation, the remedy became clearer: Love thyself. Love thy neighbor as thyself. Love thy neighbor better than thyself.

Religious Reformation

Moses, Jesus, Muhammad, and Buddha all believe themselves to be reformers of polluted, cynical, domineering, misogynistic, materialistic religions. As Jesus said:

House of Prayer

"My house shall be called of all nations, the house of prayer, but ye have made it a den of thieves."

Moses and Muhammad dealt violently with their idol-worshiping predecessors. Buddha rejected his Brahman position, his cultural heritage, and his privilege. Each of these founders was a "deliverer" of people's anger at religious exploitation, poverty, slavery, and illness. Christ healed; Muhammad inspired; Buddha taught; Moses led. The people who believed and followed them found release from their feelings of hopelessness and sickness. They cured themselves. "Your faith has made you free." In fact, the followers received much more. With one supreme powerful God behind them, Moses and the Jews had the confidence necessary to destroy their enemies as they wanted. Allah likewise gave great battle strength for centuries to the successful armies of Islam. Shintoism helps unify a nation. Christianity gives hope and thus makes life more bearable for the poor, the sick, the unfree, the misfits. (Judas mistakenly thought it was to give victory over Rome.)

Founders are deliverers of faith

Buddha history, individual, spiritual,

Buddha taught a personal way to resolve the practical problems of individual existence. New spiritual progress required the ferment of fresh ideas and a synthesis of diverse viewpoints. Such an intellectual milieu is present in the history of the Middle East and North India.

They were both crossroads for trade, in constant turmoil from military invasion and migrations, and included a potpourri of peoples. Muhammad's early life as a camel caravan trader exposed him to many different religions and cultures. Moses was obviously influenced by Aten (one God), whom Egyptian pharaohs worshipped, and other cults present at the pharaoh's court, then the capital of the known world. Christ grew up with Greek, Roman, Zoroaster, and even Egyptian and Jewish influences around him.

How to go to the Temple of Nature within

But the strongest need of religion is that the followers learn how to go to the Temple within to come in contact with the Holy Spirit. For me, as for the founders of these great religions, the vital contact was made on a Sacred Mountain, in a wilderness, with Nature. Moses at Mount Sinai, Muhammad at Mount Hira, and Christ at the Mount of Temptation. That cosmic power was the spirit and the stream of "Hu," a sound of God.

A Healing

It takes the power of illness to give me full insight into what happened to me. A few months after my return from the Holy Mountains, I attended a symphony concert at the San Francisco Opera House. In the middle of the concert, my left knee began hurting and swelling. I underwent two operations for cartilage removal in college before and after so I thought this new pain might be another dislocated cartilage. In the days that followed, I tried to work the pain out by playing tennis and other exercise. This made it worse. After I spent a few days at home in excruciating pain, my doctor ordered me into the hospital.

Understanding the power of an illness

Rare arthritis virus

All kinds of tests were done. No one knew what was wrong. A specialist from the University of California pronounced it a rare joint arthritis, seemingly causing an unknown virus. He advised me that there was nothing that medicine could do.

Having much time to "lick my wounds" I began to meditate on my search and its relation to this pain. I rethought my journey to the Sacred Mountains. I lost my uptightness about not being able to hike again, about perhaps losing the use of my legs for all time. And as I lost my concern, I was no longer so driven by unconscious forces. Meditation gave me new peace, new quietness, new patience. I found friends who were willing to pray for my healing. An old man who experienced a similar condition found love. All of these finds worked as cures; they all helped. I knew I would get well. As the daughter of one friend said, "I will be cured when the revelation of the Sacred Mountains is put into words that I can live by." Out of my illness comes my health.

Cure will come

Meditation, peace, patience, love

Out of our ilness comes health

The Essence

As time passes, the memory of my Sacred Mountains does not fade. It grows stronger. The Hindu Vedas are right: "Mountains are the filaments of the Lotus and saturate with their life-sap, the abodes of the Gods, the superhuman beings and the accomplished saints who bestow on the pious the fulfillment of their wishes."

Memory of Mountain will fulfill wishes

On my Mountains, I learned I must "climb up to reach down. "A Mountain, as a volcano or earthquake, is a beginning for man and a spiritual force, as well as an end. "In the last days… the House of the Lord . . . shall establish at the top of Mountains . . ."

The Nirvana of Buddha, "The Golden Mountain," is like a Mountain peak: "lofty, immovable, difficult of ascent where seeds (depravities) will not grow, and there is no cringing or repulsion."

Nirvana of the Sacred Mountain

And to the ancient Polynesians: "Where is the water Kane (the holy water; immortal life)? Yonder on the Mountain

Power of Nature

Holy Mountains a bridge between Mother Earth and Father Cosmos

path, on the ridges steep . . ." Man is always worshiping from a high place to a high place. With his spirit, emotions, mind, and socialization, he is more than Nature but less than the cosmos, the ultimate. The Holy Mountains of the world, the bridge between the earth and the cosmos, play their universal role in closing this gap between man and the mysterious unknown: the Mountain is the power of Nature, the Totem, the dwelling of the Gods, God's inspiration, the home of the saint and of the religions of Masters, the test of the pilgrim, the basis of knowledge and worship, and the light of self-realization and awareness. Though the high Mountain ranges appear formless masses, they are living. Like a snail or a turtle withdrawn into itself, it is only with experience that looking at a lifeless shell we know it contains a living being. One has only to live in the Mountains to see their life forces. They pull the needle of the compass and the minds and bodies of men toward their peaks; they grow and decay and pulsate with life; they create winds, clouds, rain, thunder, waterfalls, and rivers; they give shelter, food, water to people and animals; they collect invisible energies from the milieu of air, water, magnetism, and electricity. Their overwhelming power to attract, inspire, and destroy carries the respect of anyone who has known them.

Living Mountain Ranges

At first, Mountains (like all religions) seem to be similar. The brush, the trails, rocks, cliffs, wildflowers, grasses, forests, timber lines, streams, and animal and plant zones all seem the same. But also, each has an individuality. Each is a unique experience for the senses, the mind, and, the spirit.

Sacred Mountains are the way to growth and the peak of the Spirit

These Sacred Mountains are not themselves salvation. "Truly in vain is salvation hoped for from the hills and the multitudes of Mountains . . . "(Jeremiah) nor are they God. But Mountains are fountains for the spirit. The Mountain path is the way to growth, to the peak of the spirit. The Mountain is the undistorted mirror to see the inner Self unobstructed by smogs of civilization, the fog of nature, or the smoke of illusions.

Way to reality, the cauldrom of life

They are the Guru, the teacher, and thus show the way as they are the way. In the Mountains, the earth, dreams, and joy are the reality. The Mountains reawaken the soul. We become aware, alive, healthy, free, and calm with balance. Their memory, their power live on in the city and the office, in the cauldron that can be each of us.

Experience the cosmic force of the Sacred Mountains

The cosmic force is in the Mountain. Experience it, live and sleep on it, touch, taste, feel, smell and listen to it, accept its pains and joys, exhilaration and exhaustion without guns, paints, radios, TVs, cameras, pencils, and paper or other digressions. To see its greatness, keep your distance. To understand its form, walk around it. To experience its mood, see it in all seasons, at sunrise and sunset, in the sun, and in the rain and snow.

Sacred Mountains show us our way

Sacred Mountains showed me the way as they have and will for all who seek in them physically striving . . . self-knowledge of body and emotions, understanding of religions, awareness, . . . discipline . . . freedom from the tyranny of the "I;" the ego, . . . the perfecting self, . . . the realized soul.

The Truth

The Sacred Mountains still stand ready to unveil their truths to any pilgrim who seeks them.

Sacred Mountains unveil truths

The formal rituals that imprison their truths peel away with time. No longer does Lassen hold the forbidden secret of a totem nor Haleakala the sacredness of the dead nor Olympus' seat the Godly council. The monasteries at Athos, Tabor, and Sinai are barely maintained by a few faithful monks who

Formal rituals peel away

desperately hang on to a glorious past while the churches and mosques crumble with age. The Arunachala caves are almost deserted. Fuji-san is polluted and desecrated.

Future religions and spirit

What of the future? New rituals and different religions will appear. As always, their essence will be familiar. Or the core source of all religions will reappear publicly from an unbroken chain of Truth from the Living Masters — the Truth of the golden temples within, which only the soul perceives on its Journey to the God-head, the Sugmad, through the plains of Lok, of higher consciousness. Modern man, a world man in a technical age, an educated man or woman, a seeking man, will still find ultimate truths on the Sacred Mountain peaks.

Universal Indivisibles

Know and be the Self

Each of us is, as the earth's sacred high points show us, the universal, the indivisible "I".

Since I am the truth, the truth is me. I need not know the Mountain, only be the Sacred Mountain and know myself.

All living things are one

My being, my energy can never separate me from the Mountains, the sky, trees, flowers, sun, and rock, and all that is and grows outside the hand of man.

Free to be evil or a God

I am my God and all is me. I am therefore the good or the evil, free to be as I am, as I want to be.

Self essence is love, peace, joy, beauty

The essence of my Self is love,[*1] peace, joy, and beauty of this love is the quintessence. To forget my essence is to suffer hell.

Independent spiritual growing self.

My spiritual Self is a system independent of my physical, mental, and emotional Self. Growth is natural and necessary at all levels of the Self. It requires desire, effort, and discipline. To improve my body and my mind and free my emotional Self I must first know my Self; then I must forget my Self.

Moderation

What goes into the body and the mind is important — good food, knowledge, optimism, and challenge, all in moderation.

Way to the guru

I must find my guru-self and finally my Sat-Guru but Mountains, books and fellow pilgrims are on the way.

To search for wholeness without work is as stultifying as work without searching for wholeness.

Motive and spiritual key

It is not what is done but the motive, the spirit of its doing that is important.

I can enjoy the pleasures of this life without craving for success. I shall receive what I seek, be it good or evil.

As between the past, the present, and the future, the present is the more important.

Pleasure without craving

One with all

I am one with all people, those who have been, those who are, and those who will be. There is no death to fear or afterlife to know.

No death to fear or afterlife to know

My immortality is what I leave behind not where I go.

No Journey of a soul ever ends . . . before the next one begins.

Endless soul jourbney

Footnote:
1 "When the curtain of your limited 'I' is lifted-and it can only, disappear through love, and love alone-you realize unity and find me as your ideal self, i.e. God." Maher Baba (Needling, New Religion, p. 103.)

Sacred Mountain Spirits and Gurus

Sacred Mountains

Death Themes

Natural depression may not be dying but only suffering or sorrow

Experience natural depression from the loss of family or friends.

Mount "Diablo" ("Devil")

The Mountains that I describe are mostly well-known Sacred Mountains and relate to special attributes that provide experiences to humans that are common to spiritual Mountains.

One of the key aspects of both Mountains and religions is our human death experience. Religion's recognition of and involvement in the idea of rising from the dead, either individually or en masse, is significant.

Where I live, I am continually reminded of the important function of death as a human spiritual experience for us all, no matter how close or far we are from dying and trying to make the most of natural depression from the loss of family or others. Natural depression may not be our dying but only suffering or sorrow for those who are. We naturally experience "natural depression from the death of family or friends. Sacred Mountains are an important part of this experience and provide us with an internal course in compassion.

Others also influence our attitudes with their communications about death. Leo Tolstoy spent his last days writing a small physically but huge conceptually, book on the freedom of dying titled *Resurrection*. David Livingston, the famous explorer, on account of his travels around Africa and his exploration of its highest Mountains, alerted Europe to the deadliness of the slave trade.

Mount Diablo (Spanish for "death/devil") for years has been within my sight across the San Francisco Bay and has become part of my own daily spiritual consciousness. To the Native American Indians who lived here for centuries, Mount Diablo is where the souls of those American Indians go to be

185

Purpose Then/Now

judged by the sacred spiritual authorities who then designate each soul their appropriate eternal grounds, be it hell, heaven, or some other spiritual state. Mount Diablo itself is presently an oft-used park for hikers, cyclists, nature observers, and spiritual seekers. I have observed this Mountain for virtually a lifetime; for me, it is a shining sample of the importance of Mountains to the spirit.

Daily View

It is not insignificant that my daily view is of Mt Diablo—the Mountain of the "Devil" or the Mountain of "Death."

Richmond Bridge

I also have a view of The Richmond Bridge across the San Francisco Bay, an important human avenue of movement. This bridge across the Bay includes one of my most important objectives — to ride over the Bridge on a track reserved for bicycles. I'm proud to report that my goal has been met!

San Quentn Prison

And in this same view of Mount Diablo is the San Francisco Bay and the famous San Quentin prison for tragic and seemingly abandoned men. Although I do not have the experience of being incarcerated in that huge prison, I was asked and agreed to do photographic documentation of the whole prison and of its activities there, including Death Row for a San Quentin support group. (See bibliography: Nichols, "Behind The Wall.")

Past Personal Experience

Characteristic of my overall objectives in this book is to report on personal experiences that may be of value to others. Although it doesn't relate directly to Mountains, Sacred or otherwise, those Mountains that I relate to so much are a lifetime influence on me based on my Mountain experiences and my compassion for people whether they are prisoners, slaves, abused or anyone who I inherently feel sorry for.

Spiritual Leaders

Death Consciousness is one thing about which many Mountains are our teachers. Various spiritual leaders in our world history experience life in the Mountains. For example,

Mohammed communicated with God on Mount Hira, Jesus on Mount Tabor, Moses, and other "Saints" on Mount Sinai.

Spiritual Roles

The role of Mountains in matters of spirit is not so much related to their size, height, or prominence but to their role in human religions and spiritual lives. Examples include Mount Athos, once home to more than 1500 Christian monks, who celebrate the Christian religion with innumerable events, particularly Easter, glorifying Jesus' rising from the dead.

Easter on Mount Davidson

Easter day is also regularly celebrated on Mount Davidson in West San Francisco, near Forest Hills, where I have lived for many years. On Easter day, my daughter Sharon and I get up between 4 and 5 in the morning to attend a Christian Easter Revival on that Mountain and experience the spiritual thrill of worship with several hundred others.

Death Experience

Orthodox Christian monks in the monasteries on Mount Athos and on Mount St. Catherine in the Sinai desert are reminded of the spiritual experience of death by the eternal existence by the skeletons and particularly the skulls at the monastery stored and honored in a special area. This practice is important to these monks in their contemplation of eternity and plays an important role in emphasizing the immortal spirit, be it Christian, Jewish, Moslem, Buddhist, or other "believers."

In my life today, I relate closely to Sacred Mountains and discovering and participating in what is sacred, spiritual, holy, hallowed, sanctified, venerated, dedicated, and/or revered.

Extensive literature relates to sacred places and special Mountains.

"Our sacred spirit puts us on these six sacred Mountains. These Sacred Mountains are in the Four Corner Area of the American Southwest. And the six sacred Mountains are not outside us. They are inside. (Katherine Smith Diné, *Big Mountain*),

Sacred Places Source

Sacred places include graves, cemeteries, burial grounds, healing sites, sacred plants and animal sites, rock cairns, minerals, and purification sites). What makes them sacred sites is that they are places of spirit, myth and legendary happenings, fertility rites, sunrise ceremonials, rituals, and prayer. The "Sacred" is beyond "Religion."

Modern Dilemma

In modern times, sacred places create a human dilemma. Examples are a five hundred-million-dollar plant to be set up at Delphi in Greece; the infrastructure for 500,000 tourists yearly at Ayres Rock in Australia; the water polluting human activity in the Ganges in India; the government declared the illegality of a Masai religious practice on the ground that this traditional rite is against the law, disrupts education and natural development, justifying confining participating Masai to native reserves as in American Indian History.

Obstacles to preserving Sacred Places

Similar problems occurred in the United States where Supreme Court's Justice Sandra O'Connor denied a spiritual claim of the Karok Indians that a logging road through the rugged chimney rock section of the Six Rivers National Forest in the Siskiyou Mountains in California is a violation of an area that they see as significant as a stepping stone to heaven; or an appeal of the Chumash Indians in Southern California on the grounds that Point Conception is a portal where souls enter and exit from the earth plane.

Indian leaders, when asked what is the greatest obstacle to preserving sacred places, say that modern people just don't understand how or why these places are so special.

Joseph Campbell

Sacred spaces old as life

Joseph Campbell writes about the idea that a sacred place is apparently as old as life itself and can be traced back to Sumeria 50,000 years ago. It is obvious around the world that Sacred Places stir up feelings in humans, like Mount Ominesan, Mount Arafat, Mount Fuji, Delphi, Mount Kilimanjaro,

Mecca, Mount Sinai, Mount Denali, Haleakala Crater, Mount Kailash, Machu Picchu.

Pilgrimage to Sacred Places

"Loveless" points out that making pilgrimages to special sacred places is probably the most popular world tourism motive and the least understood. The English Tourist Board found that 72% of tourists who visit Britain come to visit churches, cathedrals, and shrines.

Sacred spirits arrive from nature

He also writes extensively about how the earth's surface is dotted with special sacred groves, caves, rivers, meadows, Mountains, and deserts that are rooted in the consciousness of early worship. "The essence of the Sacred spirit which justifies it as a sacred place the leaders say arises from Nature itself."

For everyone, sacred places are numerous points of spiritual power and our chance to live in harmony with Nature.

Dialectic of the sacrted

"The sacred expresses itself according to the laws of its own dialectic, and the expression comes to man from without." — Marcia Eliade

My Sacred Ring Mountain

Sacred Mountains are mythic sites, legendary sites, and dreaming places. There is a Mountain in the County of Marin in the state of California called Ring Mountain, near my former home in the town of Belvedere, which I frequently visit. It is, for me, a dreaming and spiritual place.

No conquest without peace

Carl Jung writes, "People cannot conquer a new land until they have made peace with its spirits."

Sacredness not only physicality

For some, Mountains are enchanting because of the steepness of their slopes or the roar of a nearby river. The pull of a sacred place is something more than just their physicality and the challenge to perform some physical feat. Many degrees of people love Nature, like Sacred Mountains and appreciate the power of places like them.

Psychology of the sacred

William James, a pioneer of the modern psychological study of the sacred, concludes that it involves a sense of ego, surrender to a higher force, and seven common qualities of feeling:

1. A sense of unity or a feeling of identity with all things.
2. A sensation of timelessness and spacelessness.
3. A sense of being touched with some sense of objectivity or alternate reality.
4. A feeling of blessedness or joy.
5. A sense of the divine presence or sacredness.
6. A feeling that the experience is unutterable or not capable of being related in words.
7. A sense of paradox or understanding the polarity of opposites at the same time.

Sacred Experiences

Peak Experiences

"Experiences or contact with sacredness results in emotional arousal and a sense of being guided by a higher power; encounter with a trigger in the environment which causes ego destabilization and begins a rapid shift in the state of consciousness leading to a peak experience. A peak experience with feelings of energy, bliss, wonder, joy, awe, and love; intense excitement, and relaxation at the same time. Manifestations of power such as visions, prophecies, interspecies communication, the hearing of music, etc. A return to normal reality, feeling inspired and deeply touched; a beginning of integrating the experience." (Osmond, *Sacred Places*, page 72).

Changing Universes and Spirit

When we Homo sapiens are forced biologically and environmentally to change universes, each of us or our ancestors still living will need all the spirit support they or we can get. Whatever new universe we pick for our own survival, it will contain many sacred Mountains based on our world and heavenly habitat. Here, now, in our world, our Sacred Mountains are important to our spiritual lives, that most of us admire and appreciate, let alone worship. My own Mountains in the Sierra

Spirit of the Wilderness

Nevada Range of California and the Western United States, especially because of the human interface with our indigenous American Indian population, teach us much about the "meaning of wilderness" and the sacredness of Nature.

Christ begins his ministry "in the wilderness," as did Muhammad. St. Catherine Monastery monks near Mount Sinai say it is made holy by the biblical reports of visitations of angels. Buddha spent part of his early ministry in the jungle wilderness of Asia. Muhammad traveled to many places in the deserts of the Middle East. More modernly, Bhagvan (Sri Mohatma) spent most of his ministry in a cave on Mount Arunachala in South Eastern India near Madaras until he moved to an Ashram outside Tiruvannamalai, a Temple town in India.

Spiritual Mountains indispensable

Assuming wilderness areas will exist on whatever planet we end up living on, we will need Mountains of spirit like those that are of such importance to our ancestors — Christ, Buddha, Moses, Muhammad, and innumerable leaders, moral and immortal, all over our world.

What do Sacred Mountain spirits mean

The goal of Part III of "Boy From Pocatello" is to study the role of Sacred Mountains to us on this planet and the possible immortality at least of the concepts of the eternal Father/Son/and Holy Ghost. It seems important to understand what "sacred" means to some of our personal Mountains.

Sacred beyond religion

"To be sacred is something beyond religion. In the face of True spirit, we are awed; and contained in that potent emotion are fear, wonder, and sacredness all rolled into one." — Mercia Eliade.

I was surprised when I realized how much time and effort I had spent writing this work and visiting Sacred Mountains all over the world. But I was equally shocked to discover the number of Sacred Mountains on our planet and their importance to me. I know I must limit the Sacred Mountains I cover in this work to include only (at least) Sacred Mountains, which I personally visited, climbed, explored, and attempted to find out why they are sacred and significant to me and the world.

I labeled my joint life with the Sacred Mountains in this book a "Pilgrimage." My Western spirit pushed me to summit, if possible, any Mountain that I explored.

Summiting is not always possible, but does not affect their holiness for me. For example, I am not equipped or qualified to reach the summit of Mount Everest. But I still consider it a Holy Mountain.

Mountains as Sacred Spaces*

Many varieties of Sacred or spiritual experiences are associated with Sacred Places. (Swan, pp. 86-104.)

For anyone who has any spiritual experience at a sacred place, the values of special places are forever understood. (Swan, pp. 114.)

Sacred places are a trigger to an Altered State of Consciousness (ASC), meaning a qualitative alteration in the overall pattern of mental function, personally experiencing a radically different way from the way it functions ordinarily. This resolves from a shift in mental years on account of the interplay between a person and the surrounding environment. This mental state is evidenced by ecstasy, often resulting from contact with the environment, beautiful, valuable, and both. (Swan, p.81.)

Nature has the capacity to facilitate people's altered states of awareness spiritually. Cognitive destabilization is needed to attain intuitive consciousness. Seekers should know that a pilgrimage may make a good person better, but it may also make a bad person better or worse. (Swan, p.84.)

Carl Jung reports his ecstasy experience while standing on the slopes of Mount Kilimanjaro in Africa: "The whole world around me was still in the primitive silence and knew not what it was. In this very moment in which I knew it, the world came to existence, and without this moment, it would never have been". (Eranos Jarhbuch [1938], p.115.)

* Unless noted otherwise references and quotes are based on *Sacred Places: How the Living Earth Seeks our Friendship* by James A. Swan.

Sacred Mountains

Sacred Mount Kailash

People View-Point

The rain falls cheerful on the wilted aspen . . .
Alone, I cannot sleep or dream:
Alone, I no longer feel hunger:
Alone, I often feel I am not a being
Alone, I'm lonesome just being all alone
Until I circumambulate holy Kailash
Around its God-made dome.

— Anon.

Location:	Tibet Autonomous Region, China
Range:	Gangdise
Elevation:	21,778 ft (6,638 m)
Prominence:	4,327 ft (1319 m)
Coordinates:	31°4'0"N
	81°18'45"E
Spirit:	Buddhist, Hindu, Jain, BonPo
Pilgrimage:	*Worship on a High Circle* (aka "Yatra")

ANGEL VIEW-POINT

Worship on a High Circle

Esoterica: Myths, Mysteries, Imaginables

Kailash is historically sacred for four religions: Hinduism, Buddhism, Jainism, and BonPo. Each has its own "Esoterica". There are many different names: KAILASH, Gang Rimpochi (Tibetan), KAILASH ("Crystal") (Sanskrit), Tise (water peak); Nine-story swastika (Bhutan BonPo),

Hinduism

The Hindu God Shiva residing in Mount Kailash with his consort Parvati and their children, Ganesha and Kartikeya, Shiva, who meditated inside Kailash, says, consistent with scripture, that Kailash is a "Stairway to Heaven." According to the "Ramayana" ("one of the more compelling Indian epics"), Ravana (a benevolent aspect of Shiva, existing and disposed to doing "good"), in revenge for Shiva's bragging about his own Mount Kailash home, Ravana, tried to get even by uprooting Shiva's home, Mount Kailash. Shiva, while seated within Mount Kailash, then retaliates by placing his right toe on the Mountain, trapping Ravana.

In another Mount Kailash Myth, the Pandava brothers, along with their wife Drapaudi, hiked to the summit of Mount Kailash to find "liberation," or "Heaven," known as "Swarga Loka," (a realm of gratification, where one is able to appreciate the divine, "the Celestial Abode of Light").

Kailash is still said to be the "pillar of the world", with its "four faces" of crystal, ruby, gold, and lapis lazuli, lies in the heart of six mountain ranges, like that of the Lotus.

Shiva still sits in the lotus position, deep in meditation inside KAILASH…

200

Jainism

Jainism is the religious teaching of a path to spiritual purity and enlightenment through disciplined nonviolence to all living creatures.

An important object of Jainism is moksha ("liberation, emancipation, nirvana, release"). According to the Jains, the holy word "Tirthankara" (savior and supreme leader of the Dharma) was carried to the Summit of Kailash by the legendary emperor, Bharata. Tirthankara was born after putting his mother in a deep slumber, bathed and anointed with precious unction.

Ashtapada is the site where this first Jain, Tirthankara Rishabhadeva, attained liberation. Here, his son built three stupas and twenty-four shrines with idols studded with precious stones.

Buddhism

Mount Kailash is recognized in Buddhism as Mount Meru, a major pilgrimage site connecting the earth with Heaven in the Buddhist tradition. Vajrayana ("a path to enlightenment") Buddhism is the home of Buddha Cakrasamvara or Demchok ("Wheel of Great Bliss"). Other sites in the area are associated with "Padmasambhava," whose tantra practices in holy sites around Tibet are thought to be the reason for establishing Buddhism as the main tantra influence in Tibet in the 7th and 8th centuries.

Milarepa, a Tibetan master, became champion of the Buddhist Vajrayana, "a route to enlightenment" as sorcerers and magicians battled to gain victory. Finally, they agreed that whoever could reach the summit of Kailash first, would be the victor at Kailash.

BonPo

BonPo Naro Bonshung rode up to the mountaintop of Kailash on his drum in a race. But Buddhist Milarepa suddenly overtook him by traveling on a sunbeam, thus winning the contest, so Buddhism became dominant in Tibet.

BonPo still refers to Kailash as "the Nine-Story Swastika Mountain" (the seat of spiritual power).

Lifetime love of Mountains

I would guess one thing becomes obvious: the Boy from Pocatello has used a lifetime living with and loving Mountains. This is likely my last book on that subject. Writing this has been an extremely vital memory of an extraordinary number of mountains in my travels, sacred and otherwise. In this time, I have only included mountains I personally studied, explored, and at least tried to understand. But there are many more mountains, some of which I have explored and many of which I have never even seen or known.

No time for one more Kailash Pilgrimage

So, why did I select Sacred Mt. Kailash as a key visit for a "Boy from Pocatello?" I didn't begin that way, but now, at 95 years old, I can, or more importantly, do not have the time to make one more pilgrimage around Kailash, or especially to complete an actual inner Kora journey around this mountain.

Kailash Summit still free of pollution

As far as anyone knows, no one has ever summited KAILASH. The guardians of this special Mountain, formal and informal, have guarded it for centuries against any such pollution. It is immoral and, nowadays, even illegal to summit Kailash.

Sinless Ascent

Several climbers familiar with Mount Kailash are asked if the Mountain is climbable, and they respond universally: "Utterly unclimbable, sahib. We can't climb that."

Sinless Ascent   Traditionally, natives claim only a man entirely free of sin could actually climb to the top of Mount Kailash. Furthermore, more likely no one could make it to the top on their feet, anyway.

Discovery snowed out   On one of my pilgrimages around Kailash, I thought I spied a route to summit Kailash, at least with the right equipment. But shortly after my first glimpse of this route, by a strange coincidence, a heavy snowfall came, making an ascent impossible in any event. The spiritual milieu of Sacred Mount Kailash is to do so would be immoral and also illegal. Admittedly with a smile, locals, particularly climbing Sherpas, would remind us that to actually accomplish such a feat, "you must turn into a big bird first and fly to the summit."

China permit to famous climber   Chinese invaders offered a permit to climb Kailash to a famous westerner, Italian Mountaineer Reinhold Messner. He realized this would give him the opportunity to be the first to even try to climb to the top of Kailash…. In the mid-1980's. He refused the offer, saying, "If we conquer this Mountain, then we conquer something in people's souls."

Ice, Clifts, Death   On the higher reaches of Kailash, shear walls of ice, rock cliffs, extreme winds, avalanches of rock and snow, and severe storms would likely make it impossible for any person, man or woman, except a skilled climber.

Spanish permit uproar   It was also alleged in 2001 that China gave permission to a Spanish climbing team to climb to the top of Kailash Peak. This caused an international backlash, opposition, and uproar against China. After that, China withdrew the permit and, as far as we know, has not offered a permit to anyone else thus far.

Outer Kora   It is still a form of worship to circumambulate on either of the two routes, the outer Kora and the steeper/more difficult inner Kora. The outer Kora route usually takes 3 days and 2 nights to hike the 32 miles around the mountain, either camping or staying in some shelter or temple at night and then finishing the hike the next day journeying around the Mountain by foot or using a pony or a domestic yak and takes 3 days on average, with night camp at Dirapuk Gompa about 1.2 - 1.9 mi (2 -3 km) before the Dolma pass and at "Zuthulphuk" (an important Yatra stop), we then climb a steep ridge on the "Kora" to the high point, the "Dolma La" of the outer "Kora" (over 18640 ft). There are huge boulders here, many of which have large overheads where one can camp or rest to avoid severe winds or heavy rains and snow. From below the overhang, there is still a mighty sight. The pilgrim sees incomparable, amazing views — a moon rise, a full moon, a moonset, more stars in the sky than I have ever seen, starlight brighter than the sun, spectacular sunrises and sunsets with extraordinarily vivid multicolor, and stunning, exciting skies to cap this vision. 1000 ft below is a small shining glacial lake. Tibetan and Himalayan Buddhist pilgrims, especially on this Pass sing Nyleu songs to promote fraternity with all those who cross paths on the Dolma La.

Sacred Lake Mansarovar

Another common journey for worshipers or those trying to understand spiritual invitations by emulating them is to circumambulate the sacred lake, Manasarovar, a beautiful bright blue lake that almost touches the base of Kailash. Lake Manasarovar is also known as Mapam Yumtso by Tibetans, along with several other namesakes.

While I was hiking in worship on the Lake beach, about halfway around the Lake, a Tibetan Buddhist Monk came out of his small Temple and invited me to stay the night and have some supper as his guest.

What an opportunity! I wasn't carrying the usual pack, tent, sleeping bag, food, etc., and we enjoyed an interesting, inspirational talk with my new Monk friend. It was an amazing event for me to have this chance to talk to the monk in English. And It also enabled me to remember the details of my circumambulation around the Lake and Mount Kailash.

Circumambulation around Sacred Mount KAILASH or Sacred Lake Manasarovar on foot, on my own pilgrimage, I confirmed to myself the beneficial spiritual practices and positive effects of these Pilgrimages, including, for example, collections of "meritorious Karma," "the cleansing of sins from one's consciousness" and "good fortune." Most Tibetan worshipers do not try to copy key competition by racing around KAILASH by prostrations. In my case, I walked the outer Kora five times. Although when I was there, I didn't see any other pilgrims walking around the lake, I proceeded clockwise around the Lake as well as Mount Kailash, like the Hindus, Jains, and Buddhists, while the Tibetan BoPos proceeded counterclockwise in their pilgrimages.

Inner Kora

In addition to the Outer "Kora" favored by most pilgrims, an Inner Kora can also be taken around KAILASH. It is more dangerous, steeper, more difficult, and requires full-blown climbing gear. I tried part of it personally before realizing it was beyond my ability, especially without a guide, skills, equipment, etc. The Outer "Kora" by "prostrations," on average, takes 3 weeks.

Counter-clockwise night stop

On my last pilgrimage (fifth) around Mount Kailash, I tried the BonPo route, counterclockwise, spending the first night in a small newly built Buddhist temple. The "Kora"

Woman Tibetan Prostrations

Never again

Thank you forever – Sacred Mount Kailash

passed close to the temple and interestingly provided a way for me to fully observe a Tibetan circumambulating Mount Kailash performing prostrations. More specifically, in a single prostration, the pilgrim bends down from a standing position, kneels, prostrates full body length on the trail, rises to his/her knees, crawls forward on hands and knees to the fingermark already made on the trail, the pilgrim does this over and over again to cover 32 miles.

Both "Koras" around Mount Kailash begin in the Tibetan village "Dashan" and end there. The Pilgrimage ends in the same place it began.... Just like We often end where we begin, I think. Figuratively, every expedition at Kailash and the Lake goes clockwise or counterclockwise on Sacred Mount Kailash; the only main religion that circumambulates counterclockwise is the ancient indigenous Tibetan BonPo.

In a final expedition to Kailash, for me, we spent the first night, after Darshan, at a newly built small temple on the counterclockwise expedition. The clockwise religions include Hindus, Buddhists, Jains and Tibetans, which together have a greater number of Kailash pilgrims or potential pilgrims than any other religion on the planet.

For me, the numbers make no difference....

But Sacred Mount Kailash has provided me, at least, and will as long as I live, an unexpected spiritual inspiration, wisdom, and enlightenment that will be with me until my own last days...

And possibly long after that – HOPEFULLY!

Sacred Mount
Olympus

People View-Point

Sacred mountain touchstone, breath, prayer,
    feast, hope, and home
Merge into a Godly Mountain Throne
Gold and silver, most durable and most sought;
Spirit lasts longer and is worth more
Glory is illusion.
                  . . . GREEK LYRICS

Location:	Greece
Range:	Olympus Range
Elevation:	9,573 ft (2,917 m)
Prominence:	7,726 ft (2,353 m)
Coordinates:	40°05'08"N
	22°21'31"E
Spirit:	Pagan
Pilgrimate:	*The Home Throne of Zeus*

Angel View-Point

The Home Throne of Zeus

*Spirit of Ancient Greece — Mount Olympus
Spirit power sits on the thrown of Zeus. Anyone
can appreciate their own Greek myth —
the primacy and joy of our Spirit*

Esoterica: Myths, Mysteries and Imaginables

Above the snow-fed meadow
Above the ancient Greek.
What Joy to drop my burden here
Where Zeus' Hermes built a fantasy:
There is no God above the earth.
There's only a mystery . . . and me.

The pain and exhaustion of the ascent is assuaged in this soft lap of the Gods and Goddesses. Here, in my imagination, Apollo brings beauty and moderation; Aphrodite brings love; Athena comes with wisdom; Hephaestus brings fire; Ares offers the power of war; Artemis, twin sister of Apollo, offers to guide in hunting; Demeter promises to teach about growing things; Hera and Hestia remind of home, women and children.

Return To Thunderbolts

Zeus and family overcome darkness and usher in new era of religion

The black sky flashes in white light. A thunderbolt cracks the horizon. Rocks hurl down from the high peaks onto the lower Mountains. By occupying the high ground of Olympus, Zeus conquers the Titans on Mount Ossa below, condemns Atlas to his eternal labor, and divides up the world with his brothers Hades (the underworld) and Poseidon (the sea).

Having beaten the enemy, the darkness of the past, Zeus ushers in a new era of religion, the beginnings of rational man.

The original name of "Olympus" is unknown. Various theories include the (translated) "pure foot," "blessed gods," "mountain," "assets of the gods" (Homer), and "heavenly threshold." Olympus has played an important role in the history of Greece as a hiding place and base of operations in the Ottoman Empire period. Olympus was declared an archaeological and historical site that should be preserved for its historical and archaeological importance. And it was critical to its declaration as a national park in 1938. It has also been designated by UNESCO as a biosphere reserve and by the European Union as a special protection area.

Inspiration from inspired poet

Zeus is said to have created the vale of Tempe between the Mountains. Though unnecessary militarily against the defeated Titans, it inspired generations of poets. No wonder. On its forested bank, I watched the setting sun reflecting in orange off the surface of the deep green waters flowing through the vale's gorge of granite.

Centralized father of Gods begins on Mount Olympus

Modern religions of the West begin with a concentration of authority, a single father, God of all Gods, "the cloud gatherer." They begin on Olympus. Here, Hermes (the clever God mechanic) builds for all the Greek Gods their temple homes above the clouds. The greatest, of course, is Zeus's throne. Behind the fearsome rock face is its "cushion," a snow-water-fed meadow of heather where I pitch my tent.

Gods build homes in a snow of heather

Gods' roles

Olympus topmost peak . . . dark, fearful, mysterious, powerful . . . potential danger

Being on Olympus's topmost peak reawakened me to "every man's history." In the beginning, in childhood, as in the Stone Ages, Gods or outside powers were everywhere — uncontrollable, fearful, and mysterious. The dark, the loud noise, and the potential dangers of everything are beyond current human comprehension. Magic and demons can be anywhere.

Thanks for bounty

Slowly, through acculturation, rationalization, and growth, the outside powers unified into an all-powerful God, and later an anthropomorphic God to whom man can relate:

"Please, God, grant our prayers."
"Why, God, are you angry with us?"
"Why do you hurt us?"
"Thanks be to God for his bounty."
"You give us your son because You love us so."

"You gave us your son"

Savagery, fierce slaughter of infidel enemies part of religion and fear

The savagery of human and animal sacrifice, voodoo, ritual, and the slaughter of the infidel enemy is a part of ancient Greek religion. The remains of this earlier period are less obvious now but still remain in the fierce destructiveness (in competitive games or wars, for example), the unconscious rituals or obsessions, the irrational instincts for self-sacrifice, and, finally, fear.

Outside powers unified into a powerful God, later on

Gods, like women or men, are a cornerstone in man's religious progress — to understand one's self is to understand one's Gods, a thinking process (Homo sapiens). The Greek Gods, though immortal, experience human pains, emotions, pleasures, and problems. Our human foibles and fights often erupted into serious jealousies and wars, some small and others worldwide. We are freed of the fear of the unknown since we learn to believe in Gods like ourselves.

The priests and creators of Greek religion are the artists, the poets, and the philosophers; men are also experienced in practical affairs — not so much theologians, prophets, or saints removed from ordinary life. There are no holy books, sacred commandments, authoritarian priesthood, or threats of damnation. The realization of beauty, perfection of reason, ethics of moderation, and pursuit of excellence are its precepts, sought for individually not 'en masse.' To such ideas many of us still subscribe. Thus, Phidias defines his religion, his Zeus, in his statute of "incomparable" beauty at Olympus, and I in my own "comparable" (as distinguished from incomparable) poetry.

A Study In Masochism?

Painful climb   The climb of Olympus from 300 to 9,600 feet above sea level is often painful. I anticipate less inspiration from a historical Zeus than from current religions. Thus, at first, the Mountain seems more impersonal. I am anxious about the lack of information about the trails as well as the pending thunderstorms moving in from Yugoslavia and Italy. The local guides at the base village of Litochoro are more interested in their rivalry with the Hellenic Alpine Hiking Club than they are in my need for information about the terrain and water. All they say is that it is not a one-day climb but a three-day trip and that I should not try it alone.

Litochoro

Guerrilla warfare here   If there is any armed forces opposition against the regime in Greece, it would be here. In these rugged Olympic Mountains, Greek fighters wage guerrilla warfare through modern history against the Turks, the Austrians, the Nazis and the Communists. This, no doubt, explains the new roads and army camps at the base of Olympus.

I soon discovered that my guide map was out of scale and misleading, particularly the "Routes Across Olympus in Hours of March." "Hours of March" must record mythological flight time for the Gods rather than a walking time for humans burdened with heavy packs.

Wrong way   The first two hours were depressing. I was furious at the tourist agency as their driver overcharged me for the drive to the trailhead. There was little wind to relieve the scorching July heat, roasting everything in and under my enormous pack. Almost immediately, I started up the wrong way, following a rough road being built on the lower slopes. A tractor driver working on the road shouted at me something that sounded like "No, no, no," but I couldn't be sure I understood. Unable to speak to me in English, he got off his tractor, took me by the arm, and pushed me in a different direction.

Dead end — Otherwise, I would have missed the trail and dead-ended in a valley of brush and boulders.

Canteen empty – thirsty — My water canteen was soon empty, all my lemons eaten; still, I was unbearably thirsty. Thirst forced me to ignore the advice of the local guides and to follow the Hellenic trail since

Hellenic trail — it seemed to cross the water sooner. At about 1:00 p.m., hours after my last gulp of water, I finally reached Prioni Falls. Here, I lay naked in the cold, shallow stream and drank my fill.

Back ache — My back, seriously strained and medically treated years ago, ached from the load.

I couldn't risk the added weight of a full water bag. I did, however, fill my canteen and took some extra water. That soon disappeared since I was drinking three-quarters of a canteen every hour. Sweat poured from every gland, soaking my pack and attracting flies and gnats to buzz and bite.

Five hour hell — The next five hours were hell. I struggled up the steep trail with short, plodding nine-inch steps. My legs ached. I was hungry, exhausted, and unable to stop panting even when resting. Even the ends of my fingers were raw from handling

Collapse under tree — the pack, cameras, tripod, knife, etc. At one point, I collapsed onto bushes under a tree. A rash like poison oak immediately

Poison oak — appeared on my legs and arms. By six o'clock, I was unable to go further.

Rest on trail — The only flat area on which to rest was right on the trail, in the dirt. The top of the Mountain was out of sight and obviously nowhere near. I munched two crackers, rolled out

Try to sleep — my sleeping bag, and tried to sleep. Exhausted and aching, I watched the stars. I dozed off and on. I was shocked into wakefulness by a howling animal that sounded like a wolf fifty yards above me. Just as I was about to sleep, time and time again, something started crawling on me in my sleeping bag. Apparently, I had flopped down on an ant hill! Large black and red ants kept crawling into my bag, seldom biting but still keeping me awake as I tried to flick them out.

Howling animal

Ant hill

Around two in the morning, I decided to give up. I packed and continued my upward climb. Another bellyful of water at Refuge A, with a Swiss family staff, kept me going. By noon, I reached the top meadow for my camp. I pushed myself beyond my body's limits.

Continued climb

Swiss refuge

Beyond body's limits

Reconsidering this climb the next morning, I wondered if this whole adventure was an exercise in self-torture. Why do it? For whom? Somewhere in my unconsciousness, hard physical effort was thought to be "good for me." Is my day and night rush up the Mountain, carrying over eighty pounds, even rational?

Masochism

Where better to test one's rational control system than at its source for Western man's world? The Greeks believed in moderation. They seldom, if ever, reported actually climbing Olympus. Like the Lassen Indians, did they fear the Gods and their Mountain-top home? No. The Greeks are relatively free of ghosts and demons. They are unafraid of the supernatural in Nature or in the Mountains. They are just too rational to voluntarily incur the pains of such a strenuous climb. Anything of importance that could be found on a Mountain could be attained at home and, particularly, within one's own psyche. They built temples to their Gods in their own cities on high places for the spiritual and aesthetic effect, but not on peaks. The Gods come to them, not they to the Gods!

Is not a prescription for attaining truth the avoidance of pain, notwithstanding the claims of Pilgrim's Progress, President Calvin Coolidge, and Jesus Christ? Still, that night, resting on the trail, I told my tape recorder: "Perhaps I'll be wise and strong enough and remember some Greek wisdom of moderation not to kill myself trying to make it to the top. If I don't make it, I don't make it."

But I was happy that I ignored my own practical philosophy. I survived the pain of the climb.

Olympus

I climb Olympus for her past
Though Zeus has long since left this home,
I reach to the sun to find the light.
I scale the peak for a glimpse of the God in me.
Exhaustion.
Fame.
Motion.
Mind and body put to the flame and molded to a new
 frame for the soul.
Or at least for peace in my own guts from maggot bites
 feeding future appetites.
I insist on my own resurrection, the summit.
I thus create my crucifixion:
My cross, eighty pounds of pack, cuts into my
 Throbbing back.
Muscles spasm'd.
Trembling legs. Sun-fevered.
Trail-blistered.
Grasping, sucking at the thinner air.
A parched mouth fed only dust to answer thirst.
Step by step, four inches each at most.
Spur'd by dreams, imaginings of future things?
Of adoration?
Of success?

Of peace — to see myself so strong? What do I seek?
 Diversion from the harder inner climb:
Or just to mask the passage of my time so age can 'suage my mind?

The victory over Olympus' crest goes to the will. Here on Zeus's throne, I cast my tent.

The soul's unloosened from the body's quests and soars from its eagle's nest
To the sun and moon,
In the wind, on the clouds,
Free in the sky
To feel the Greek in me,
My primacy,
Gods made in man's own imagery.

Mountain Harmony

Joy In Seclusion

Greek mythology erred in its physical description of the home of the Gods, but it described perfectly my joy at being on Olympus:

"Olympus. Whereas they say is the seat of the Gods that standeth fast forever. Nor by winds is it shaken, nor ever wet with rain, nor doth the snow come nigh thereto, but the most clear air is spread about cloudless, and the white light floats over it. Therein, the blessed Gods are glad for their days." (Homer's Iliad)

As Homer also says, "The Olympian Gods were not without their music." Their Mountain sang. Its ancient harmony is now and then shattered by the roar of Zeus's thunderbolts or chainsaws denuding the forest below. But I also heard the chirp of crickets and birds and the rattling crackle of grasshoppers, all mixed on the wind. As these sounds pass through the rocks and trees, they join the calls of woodsmen to their donkeys and shepherds to their bell-tinkling goats out in the valley

Euphoria of the ascent

The euphoria of the successful ascent, the peak, pervaded everything. Such feelings are beyond scientific explanation even though at high altitudes, different electrical charges (negative ions, for example) and cosmic and other rays and radiation that affects my cells, particularly those in the brain. My dinner of warm soup and crackers and cucumber is nectar to me, the ambrosia of the Gods. To breathe the air, divine ether is bliss. My mind is unfettered, unafraid. My body was painless, purged.

Negative ions Ambrosia of the Gods

Ambrosia of the Gods

Peace, serenity a natural Parthenon

Peace and serenity reign here among the Gods' homes, among the large rock crags, each a natural Parthenon, an immense temple. Water from the snow bank, food in the pack, a cozy tent, warm clothes, and a chapter of Greek philosophy were all anyone could need. The joy of isolation. Here I was, completely self-sufficient, needing nothing and no one. The reward was earned by carrying everything on your back, alone and thus owing nothing, being owed nothing. A single body, emotions, and spirit, all free to float with the clouds, unencumbered by pain, desire, and responsibilities. To be your own Ulysses.

To be your own Ulysses

Wild flower gardens

Rest and isolation

Resting alone in the wildflower garden of heather, rare violets, and bright yellow crocus, I was thankful for my isolation. But are such feelings a prelude to becoming a hermit or recluse? No, the splendor of this seclusion strengthened my attachment to the people in my life. Every time I used the knife my son gave to me, I silently thought of him, thanked him, and loved him. Lying in my tent, I talked to them via my tape recorder:

My sons love knife

Mountain Message

To: Lolita my wife

"Though I know it was hard for you, Lo (my wife), without your love and willingness I never could be able to make this trip.

Connie for arranging

Thanks to my loyal legal assistant, Connie, for all the arrangements.

Note to my daughter Sharon, who doesn't like bugs

Note to my daughter Sharon re bugs

— Except for a tremendous number of ladybugs, there are very few bugs up here; it's too windy. Lady bugs, though, are everywhere, perfectly harmless and delightful friends. I do bring up a spider and a couple of ants, but I think they were from my rest spot far below on the trail. They traveled here in my sleeping bag. They are disposed of rather ruthlessly.

Dinner with Connie's croutons

The last note about my cooking: I cooked myself a meal last night that was luscious. I put a can of salmon into the tomato bouillon soup that you threw in for me, Connie, and then I threw in bread like croutons. I also made instant applesauce. Alan, remember we made it on our last hike in the Southern Sierras.

Alan's apple sauce

Sharon's note

Sharon, the notebook that you made for me fell in the water and got soaked, but I've been able to dry it out, and it's fine again. Thank goodness you gave it to me. I'm using it for special notes, as you suggested.

Message to Jay, friend, photographer, and philosopher extraordinaire.

Studying for priesthood

Please go over the pictures from Olympus as fast as you can and send me a letter of any criticism in case, I am making any consistent mistakes. The camera is working well, in spite of the ubiquitous dust and dirt. Even though I clean it a couple of times a day, it probably isn't enough. Thanks for the quick photography course. So many of the things you told me keep coming back to mind. There was just enough that I could absorb. Your suggestions anticipated all the picture problems I run into. I hope they come out well.

Solitude forces yourself

Message to our landlady Mrs. Dresel:

Neighbor Seamstress support

I never would have made it through the New York, London, and Athens airports with all my overweight pack board, coat, and pack bag if you hadn't done such a good job sewing on the handle on my blue pack bag and the extra coat pockets.

Hiking strangers, Germans

As much as I enjoy being alone, I also am thankful for people. It was a pleasure to chat near the top of Mt Olympus the last morning with three German botanists studying the rare violets in "my meadow." It is a rare treat to talk in real English with a young man from Chicago I met at Prioni Falls on my way down. He is studying in Greece for the priesthood and, with four other Greek companions, on his way up Olympus. It's doubtful if they will ever make it in their street shoes, hanging on to lost luggage, obviously out of shape and exhausted.

Studying for priesthood

Solitude forces yourself

Not only does solitude enhance the desire for better personal relationships, but it also forces you upon yourself. Facing myself on Olympus, I know that the pilgrimage is only beginning, but the route is surer. More honest… more joyful, we must follow, not fly from ourselves. We can only truly live the essence of reality, Aristotle's "Good" within us; if we do, we cannot fail to be in union with excellence, our own Zeus."

Union with Zeus

Anxious Journey

Elysian Meadow delay

The ether and memories of the ancient Gods are exhilarating. I hated to leave my Elysian meadow atop Olympus. I slept late as the sun warmed me and broke camp slowly. I luxuriated in the morning freshness and sun, underestimating the terrain and difficulty of the return hike. I was unconsciously creating an overwhelming anxiety by being late to leave. It was eleven in the morning before I started down the trail, passing Refuge A at about one. I was taking almost as much time to descend as to hike up. My heavy pack and the

Pain and tiring delay

staircase-like trail forced me into small steps. My legs and especially my knees were in pain. But still, I had to pick up the pace and skip rest stops. Soon, my legs were quivering, and my knees and ankles were rubbery. This caused me to slow down and rest more often, whether I liked it or not. My back began to bother me again.

I didn't leave Prioni Falls until after three o'clock in the afternoon. It was at least three more hours to Starvos and another three to Litochoro. I was very worried. If the driver who was to meet me decided it was the wrong day or the wrong time and didn't wait there, I would be left alone in a military camp village, looking suspicious with a tape recorder and draped with high-powered camera lenses. Soldiers, military camps, and truck convoys were everywhere in Greece, on bridges and along rail lines in each town. There were signs everywhere celebrating the April 7 revolution of the Junta and prohibiting photographs. I have already been threatened while taking pictures in Athens and along the highway. The current rumors of torture and trial of Americans for spying were disquieting. Furthermore, no one I knew spoke English in the village. There were no hotels there in which to sleep, and it was over 150 kilometers from Thessaloniki, where I was to begin the next day's trip to Mount Athos. Aches and pains aside, I stumbled and rushed down the trail as the afternoon light faded into evening.

By 6:00 p.m., when I was supposed to be at Litochoro, I was still eight miles and a 3,000-foot drop from my destination. I was dog-tired and out of water. Luckily, at Starvos, a friendly patrol of Greek Mountain troops, through a combination of orders, laughs, and banter came up with a full canteen of cold water.

My spirits watered and buoyed; I hiked down the road to Litochoro in the dusk. A road worker commuting to his

Alone and suspicious in military camp

Picture taking threats

Greek patrol provides needed full canteen

village from the forest on his donkey made hand signs, apparently offering to carry my pack. I declined, not knowing where he was going, how fast he could go, and how much money he wanted. He and his friend nevertheless beckoned me to follow them down a trail off the road. I yelled, "Litochoro?" He nodded up and down (an international "yes" symbol). I needed a shortcut since it was two or three hours by road to meet my ride. But maybe these men and this trail weren't even going to Litochoro but to some other village or camp. A Swiss at Refuge A told me to follow the road below Starvos since there was no trail or shortcut.

Short cut ride offered but refused

Deciding quickly to take a chance, I plunged down the steep, rock-strewn trail behind the two men and their donkeys. To follow them, I almost needed to run on my already shaky legs and sore knees.

I run down the steep trail following the donkeys

As the trail turned further north (Litochoro is south), my heart sank, but it was too late. With neither the time nor the strength to climb back up to the road, I kept stumbling down. To my surprise, the trail came out on a switchback in the road to Litochoro, saving me at least three miles. By that time, my "guide" friends had disappeared. After finding my own way down the road and after another shortcut and more staggering through a few wrong turns in the town, I arrived at the village square. My driver was getting into the car to leave, probably thinking it was the wrong day. What a relief it was to find him there, waiting.

Hiking down the wrong direction . . . stumbled into Litochoro but my pick up was just leaving

He rushed me to Thessaloniki with no stops as a gorgeous red, orange ball of setting sun inflamed the sky over the whole Olympic range. Left alone with my immense pack in front of Thessaloniki's best hotel with a week's dirt, dust, and beard, I was sure the nervous manager was not going to "find." my reservations.

Thessaloniki

Dinner and sleep refreshing

Two baths, a huge dinner on the quay in front of the

hotel (tomato juice, asparagus, lettuce, and tomato salad, thick vegetable soup, five rolls, nine pads of butter, nuts, roast veal, vegetables, and watermelon), and a sleep refreshed me. By sunrise the next morning, I was up and ready for Athos, the Aegean Sea's "Holy Mountain."

Friendly strangers

In retrospect, it's fortunate I didn't accept the "expert" advice from the official village guides as to which route to take or that of the Swiss guide at Refuge A as to shortcuts. On the other hand, I was very lucky to receive the help of friendly strangers: the tractor driver, the army patrol, and the donkey "commuters." My own critical decisions were correct — to insist that the driver take me to the trailhead in spite of the extra money, to change routes so as to find water sooner, to rest the first night on the trail, and especially to take the advice of common people, not that of professional guides for sale.

Critical decisions

Patricide

Zeus had not been enough for me or the Greeks. The father must die if the son is to be free.

Zeus patricide

Zeus himself killed his father, Cronus. To allay the prophecy that he would be dethroned by his youngest born, Cronus ate his first five children on their birth. His wife saved Zeus by wrapping a stone in swaddling clothes, duping her husband into believing he had rid himself of another danger. Later, favoring her full-grown son over her husband, she provided the special weapon for his murder.

Dad's death reminder

Passing Thebes and Mount Cithaeron on my way to Olympus was a sharp reminder of my own father's death only a year before. Here, Laious (King of Thebes), fearing his own oracle's prediction that he would die at the hand of his own child, abandons his son, Oedipus1, on the open slopes of this Mountain. The resulting tragedy was further canonized in our time by Sigmund Freud's "Oedipal Conflict," a conflict so

Freud Oedipal conflict

Compare Moses and Christ

Aegis drowning

strong that Freud's own sanity is severely threatened by neurosis triggered by his father's death. Moses and Christ were likewise childhood escapees of the fatherhood fears from death prophecies, though on a more political scale — King Herod and Pharaoh. In a mythological variation, Aegis drowned himself in the sea, believing his son Theseus had been killed by the man-eating Minotaur with a human head and an animal body and wings. He took his own life to relieve the inevitable conflict that earns him immortality. From thenceforth, the sea is called the Aegean. (Aegean means "an animal that jumps.")

Universality of man's experience

These myths confirm the universality of all man's experiences, individually and socially. The father must die. The son replaces the father. The mother favors the son. The anger, inferiority feelings, fears, jealousies, hate, resistance to change, awe, and destruction that result devour many lives in wars, murders, neuroses, psychoses, and physical illness. The conflict between father and son, father and mother, sister and brother must be resolved. It entails the son's destruction of his father in his role as a tyrant, obstructionist, rival, and almighty.

Wars, murders, neuroses, psychoses, physical illness

Blessings to those who do it while both are alive so that they can enjoy the plateau of a new relationship.

Blessings on those who can enjoy a new relationship

Is this purely a male reality? As a male, my own experience vouches for these truths. However, the female role is critical in a different way. Just as in climbing and conquering the Mountain, the father is the essential process, the proof of manhood; the final object is to sleep in her lap, honored, comforted, at peace, in ecstasy at the end of the journey.

Accept mortal destiny

Changing the God

As my own enlightenment begins with the symbolic patricide of my God, Jehovah, Father, so the Greeks abandon Zeus. The seeds of his demise lie in an even higher power,

Fear is death and sad for her son Sarpedon

Moros, "destiny." Being supremely wise, Zeus does not fight with destiny; he only accepts it, the universal order. Thus, he bows down to the Fates, who set the hour of death for his own son, Sarpedon.

Liberation from 'father God'

The Greeks and their Olympus symbolize our transition of spirit: from fear of the uncontrollable spirits to Gods that are but super-humans to a single father God and then to liberation from that father God. This, historically and personally, is an enormous change before one is spiritually ready. In the next Mountains, we must understand what happened in Greece long ago (and in ourselves).

Plato suspects God is shadow of ourselves

Though an anthropomorphic God rids the Greeks of fear of the unknown spiritual world and is more easily rationalized and understood, he or she does not satisfy. We know we feel there is something more than our own image. We, like Plato, suspect a God that is like a man is but a shadow of ourselves — a shadow we see facing the blackness of a cave, our backs to the eternal light outside, the truth.

Moderation

Likewise, the Greek philosophy of moderation, the golden mean, was not enough for man. He seeks excellence, even though it may be painful to attain: "Heart racking sweat comes at manhood's height." To climb the highest peak, the home of Zeus, to be on his throne is worth the effort.

Zeus and Alan are highest point on Mt Olympus

> "Before the gates of excellence, the high Gods have placed sweat.
>
> Long is the road thereto and steep and rough at first, But when the height is won, then there is ease,
>
> Though grievously hard in the winning."
>
> — Hesiod

Zeus high God, Dionysus harvest God

Artist brings harmony out of confusion

Everything is excess

Greek Priest

Stage set for Paul's Dogmas

Poetry not admitted

Mountains not a playground for Gods but mystical experience for man

As Zeus is transformed into a loftier, single God, the Greeks graft a minor God (not even an Olympian), Dionysus, the God of wine, with Apollo, the artist God, the poet, the musician who brings harmony out of confusion. Apollo's shrine at Delphi, graven with its "Nothing in Excess," finally compromised with Dionysus, "Everything in Excess." Drunkenness, ecstasy, wildness. The Greeks do not become ascetics, finding liberation through the punishment of the body, but find new ground, mystical, mysterious, and new outlooks and goals — reverence, awe, purification, immortality, soul, unity, salvation. This new fusion brings renewed vigor. As men lose their isolation in the flowing Greek drama, the stage is set for Paul and the dogmas of Christianity.

"He who not being inspired," Plato said, "and having no touch of madness in his soul, comes to the door and thinks he will get into the temple by the help of art — he, I say, and his poetry are not admitted."

And because of the Greeks, the Mountain is no longer a playground for the Gods. It is a source of mystical experience for man.

Olympian Joy

I earned my proof.
Climbing, sweating, climbing, aching,
   climbing, climbing, climbing
Thirsting, panting, stumbling Up. Up. Up.
Fearing, trembling, thinking There is no God
That acts like me with love or jealousy.
Above the timberline.
I rose through the ether to his chair
Above the clouds to find nothing but loneliness
On Olympus' bare stone peak
Above the snow-fed meadow

Above the ancient Greek.
What Joy to drop my burden here
Where Zeus' Hermes built a fantasy:
There is no God above the earth.
There's only a mystery . . . and me.

Socrates Revisited

Socratic Revolutionary

Socrates best characterizes our philosophic transition. Often, the catalyst of change dies in the process, be it an individual belief or an original band of revolutionaries. So, it is with Socrates. Refusing to accept the old order, he prescribed activity for the soul. "Test your life, your beliefs; find your own truth." For refusing to give up his teaching, he is sentenced to death.

Soul activities

No evil can happen

"Be of good cheer," he told his followers while in jail, "and know of certainty that no evil can happen to a good man either in life or after death. He comforts his judges and speaks kindly to the jailer who brought him the deadly hemlock. Considerate always, he excuses himself: "But I really must go bathe so the women won't have the trouble of washing my body when I die." Suddenly, a realist asked, "How shall we bury you?" "Any way you like," chuckled Socrates. "Only be sure you get hold of me and see that I don't run away."

False words infect the soul

And finally: "Don't let them talk about burying Socrates, for false words infect the soul. Say, dear Crito, only that you are burying my body."

"And now we go our ways, you to live, I to die.

Which is better – to live or die. God only knows

Which is better, God only knows."

It was fifty years later that Aristotle saw the spark of divinity in man, the good:

Live according to the highest

"We ought not to listen to those who exhort a man to keep to man's thoughts, but to live according to the highest thing that is in him, for small though it be in power in worth it is far above the rest."

I am what I am
I am what I was

Two thousand three hundred sixty-nine years later, I climb Olympus to reach down into my soul with the power of Zeus's thunder and the light of ancient Greece. I am armed with the idea, "I am what I am, and I am what I was." I am a thinking man first but not last. Even though the Gods and The God have come down from the Mountains, the founders of the great modern religions, the priests, the followers, and now each of us goes up the Mountains to tap the spiritual energies that abide there. And now on to the Mountains of the New Religions.

Mountain spirit emerges

Today go to the Mountain of the new religion

Oedipus means "swollen foot"

Footnotes:
1. Oedipus means "swollen foot" since the baby Oedipus was left on the Mountain chained by the foot to a tree which caused the foot to be swollen.

Sacred Mount Fuji-san

People View-Point

No psalm, no seer nor darkness
can banish me from the Sacred Peak
Who's guru prayers it will always Be
So we will always BE.
　　　　　　　　　... The Mountain Path

Mount Fuji-San

Location:	Honshu, Japan
Range:	Dormant volcano
Elevation:	12,388 ft
Prominence:	12,388 ft
Coordinates:	35°21'39"N
	138°43'39"E
Spirit:	Buddhism, Shintoism
Pilgrimage:	*The Way of All Pilgrims*

Angel View-Point

The Way of all Pilgrims

Mount Fuji-san, Japan / Shinto & Buddha

Esoterica: Myths, Mysteries and Imaginables

Fuji-san, the epitome of Shinto and the greatest of all Shinto shrines has its own reason for being. Like all Mountains, she gathers the rains, controls the wind, attracts the lightning, and shades the land. But, more importantly, she gives the people of Japan beauty, challenge, unity, and esteem. What more can The Spirit do? She is a part of every person who lives in or thinks of Japan, whether they climb her slopes or not. She is more than a symbol. She is a religion.

Konohana Sakuyahime

The Mountains of the past were very close to the mood there. It was easy to imagine that Konohanasakuya-hime, the priestess of Mount Fujisan, beckoned me to mount her flanks to reach for the summer snow and the fiery sunrise.

Imperial princess Fujisan

In every flower, there was the beautiful Konohanasakuya-hime, "The lady who makes the trees bloom," the imperial princess of the greatest Mountain of all, Fujisan. To preserve the honor of her impregnation by Oyama Tsu Mi, chief God and Lord of the Mountains. To ensure that her son is recognized as a deity, the princess avoids any mortal sexual contact and gives birth without pain in the midst of the flames of her own prison.

Painless birth

Fuji-san

Born in pieces in a roaring volcano

And so, it is three hundred thousand years ago, in the fifth reign of Emperor Korei, as the written lore of the Shinto histories, the Kajiki and the Nihonshoki state, that Fuji is born from the Goddess and in one night becomes a roaring volcano. Later, the Mountain Gods themselves are created when Oyama, the Fire God, is cut into many pieces. Each piece becomes a different God of the Mountain — for example, "high slopes," "lower slopes," "steep slopes," "foot," and "minerals."

Two days in Japan revived me from my travels. I was well again. The smells, the harmony of the sea with the steep, forested hillsides, square green paddies, and the self-conscious friendliness of the people attracted me to this country. Even Tokyo's traffic, Americanized hotels, smog, and crowds didn't change my mood.

Two days of Japan cured me

On this trip, I was not alone. Steve Doi, a second-generation Japanese American friend, whom I had known for many years in San Francisco, arranged my admittance to Shugendo, an ancient Japanese Mountain religion. Its precepts were followed in the abstract by a modern Japanese sect, Gedatsu. And so, a Gedatsu representative picked me up at the airport in Tokyo and assigned "Subi," a young student instructor, to join me in my Sacred Mountain Japanese exploration.

Gedatsu guide "subi"

Before long, we were on the train going from Tokyo to Gotemba, where the ascent is to begin and end. I want to spend a night in a traditional Japanese inn. Instead, we spent the night in the village's best, somewhat seedy, westernized motel.

Train from Tokyo to Gotemba

All day, I strained for a glimpse of her, but the great Sacred Mountain stayed hidden behind the mists until sunset. Then, in a short splash of glory, her majestic peak showed above the black clouds. The remembrance of her, flooded with a pink rose light from the setting sun and reflecting in a small pond, still thrills me.

Thrill of splash of glory from Fuji sunrise

The next morning, we went around part of the Mountain by taxi and visited the nearby lake country where there are scores of vantage points to view Fuji-san ("The Hundred Faces of Fuji"); many are "Sacredized" by world-renowned artists who, like me, are enthralled by Fujisan's dominant beauty, drama, and constant change.

The hundred faces of Fuji

Hidden in a valley under towering pines at the base of Fuji-san is the Singen Shinto Shrine, a traditional starting

Singen Shinto Shrine, starting point for pilgrims to the peak

Do Sojen ancestors

Shrine reminder

Gods live on Mountain not inner sanctuary of shrine

Bus to lake to Fuji toll road to Station Five

point to begin a pilgrimage to the summit of the Sacred Mountain Fuji-san. We entered the Torii (main gate). Subi and I purified ourselves by washing our hands and rinsing our mouths. We stood before the stone Do Sojen, Protector of Travelers. We bowed and clapped three times before praying to his ancestors.

Those who came before built this temple, planted these gardens and trees, and preserved the spiritual tranquility of this forest at the foot of the Sacred Mountain. They planned a future for us. We are the beneficiaries. The shrine reminded me that I venerate those unnamed dead who contributed to my own awakening, my life, my sense of beauty, my knowledge of this Mountain, my chance to reach it, and live on it, and back through the generations, my very existence. Thanks to the fertile groundwork of those before us, we all can grow in spirit.

In gratitude, we left our offering in a wooden box in front of the sanctuary. There was no inner sanctuary at this shrine. The Gods here lived on the Mountain itself. In other shrines they dwelled in the shrine's inner sanctum where only priests can approach to recite prayers.

It is time to get ready to climb. First, we took a bus from Lake Kawaguchiko on the Fuji toll road partway up the Mountain. We took a bus through dense trees and underbrush, much like California's coast range. Then, I walked through pine and spruce forests similar to California's Sierra Nevada Mountain Ranges, also passing through aspen stands like those in Idaho. We finally came to Fuji's Station Five[*1] which is almost at the timberline (8200 foot level).

Fuji-san is one of Japan's "Three Holy Mountains" and one of Japan's "historic sites."

ALAN NICHOLS

The Vision of the Whore

There, up close, the Mountain that looked from a distance to be soft and immaculate, the innocent in the sunset glimpse became a degraded, diseased, pock-marked whore. We couldn't avoid people and their wastes — litter, pollution, stench, noise, hustling. This Mountain was crawling with humans, from five to eighty-five years old: men and women; hiking groups with their own flags and uniforms; teenagers with transistor radios blaring rock music; riders on horses and horse carts (to the 9000-foot level), old people in traditional clothes. Many pilgrims were making their first or their last Fuji pilgrimage.

"He who never climbs Fuji-san is a fool, but he who climbs it twice is even a greater fool."

On this Sunday, it seemed all 280 Fuji worshipping societies were in the parking lot at Station Five. There was a veritable traffic jam of buses, cars, and pilgrims. People were everywhere waiting, or starting up the Mountain, or coming down or just wandering around. And this was only one of the six routes up and down the Mountain!

And such was the case along the trail, on all the slopes and cliffs, from the Fifth Station to the top: garbage was scattered on the ground and blowing in the wind. It was difficult to take a picture without including half-eaten lunches, paper, lunch boxes and bags, toilet paper (used), Kleenex, soft drink cans, orange peels, food, and bottles. Such litter shattered any illusion of the neat, reverent Japanese. Later, I wrote to the Emperor of Japan, offering to bring friends and myself to clean up this sacrilege. He never replied.

Even more surprising to me was the series of stations, usually with places to sleep and to buy food and warajis (straw sandals to wear over my boots to save them from being

Fuji misleading from a distance

Crawling with Japanese

Mountain climbers are fools

Traffic jam of climbers ascending or descending

Garbage and litter ubiquitous

torn by the sharp volcanic rock). At each station, for ten yen, I could brand my walking stick with the signet of that place. Though most of the marks are oriental characters, a few stations that are pathetically modern, I think, would burn "Expo '70" or "The Top" into my stick.

Walking sticks and brands for sale

I didn't buy any water or any of the trinkets, soda pop, or candy available. Downwind from each of those stations, the strong smell of outdoor toilets and burning trash filled the air. Luckily, the stiff wind kept the flies away, except around the stations themselves.

Outdoor toilets and burning trash soiled the air

The Shinto Temple

I saw only a few very old people walking the trail, wearing the all-white garb ordained since 1532. Only once did I hear the ancient climbing chant and the prayer for purification of the senses against all evil. Its revered cry: "Roken shojo! Roken shojo!"*² was inspiring. The ancient prohibition against defiling the sacred Mountain with horses beyond the Fifth Station and women beyond the Eighth was, of course, long forgotten.

Old garb since 1532 Purification prayer "Roken-shojo"

To most of the travelers I saw, the Mountain was apparently neither sacred nor awesome. Why do they bother to climb it? Climbing is hard work.

Not sacred to many climbers

A steep trail rises five thousand feet vertically from the bus depot. Most of the "pilgrims" were dressed in street clothes. They climbed all day, slept on the rough floor at one of the crowded rest hostels at night, and arose in the darkness of early morning to finish the hike to the top, hopefully just in time to watch the sunrise. They usually descend the same day, their faces dirty and their bodies floundering with exhaustion. Yet they climb by the thousands. The wish to do so must be a part of their genetic inheritance. It must be an

Vertical 5000 feet to summit

Thousands of climbers

instinct, a bond of nationhood. They seemed unable to resist the pull from generations of ancestral veneration.

Fuji-Ichi dream

Ancient sacred history recognizes that Fuji-san is embedded in the Japanese subconscious. To dream of her, "Fuji Ichi," is to dream of the most beautiful, the most natural, the best in everything, and hence to assure yourself good luck.*3 In my quest for the true self in the Sacred Mountains, I too was drawn to this Mountain magnet from thousands of miles away with more knowledge and reverence for the Mountain than many but also less instinct.

Over 800 Gods homegrown shrine

Nowhere in the world can you find a closer connection between a Mountain, a people, and a faith than here. Fujisan, Japan's highest Sacred Mountain, is an integral part of her only "homegrown" religion, Shinto. This Mountain is sometimes called "Fuji Kami" (the Mountain God) in that its spirit "never dies." Legend has it that on this Mountain peak, earth and heaven begin. Shinto, meaning the "way of the Gods," has no founder, scripture, or dogma. It begins with nature, Shamans, and myriads of Gods (over eight hundred) with beliefs comparable to those of the Yahi tribe on Mount Lassen. "Shinto" seems more like a sentiment than a theology. An ancient poet expresses Mount Fuji's essence:

Fuji-Kami

"Unknown to me who resideth here; tears flow from a sense of unworthiness and gratitude."

Fuji first

Of the great earth forces, Mountains, and volcanoes, Fuji is thus the first in Shinto.

Coexistence with other religious especially Shinto and Buddhism

The heart of the Shinto religion, like the Mountain itself, is eternal. The surface changes . . . with the people, the weather or centuries of time . . . coexisting with, giving way to, reviving itself from Buddhism, Confucianism, Christianity, Emperor Worship, nihilism, and innumerable cults in between. Its essence does not change. Shinto absorbs,

Fuji provides beauty, challenges, unity, esteem

Fuji is a religion

Mountain blessing Communion challenge fatigue danger

Camp on the rim trail, very cold

Reward

Midnight scare

Pilgrim toilet

along the way, precepts of honesty, filial piety, veneration of ancestral spirits, meditation, orders of Gods, truth, purification, ceremony, harmony, and creation. Sacred Mountains and shrines are the centers of worship. They reflect both Shinto and Buddhist influences.

For two months (July and August), the Fuji pilgrims swarm up her sides to receive her blessing in the mist, the rainbow, and the sunrise; her warnings in the gray-piled thunderclouds distorting the sunsets of blood red and gold; her communion with all who together accept the challenge of ascent, the cold, the fatigue; and the danger. And they are rewarded. Fuji-san does more for pilgrims than most. She is Japan's Sacred Mountain for pilgrims.

Along with other pilgrims, we arrive at the summit of this national shrine just at sunset. I asked my friend, who had no sleeping bag, to stay in the warm station that first cold night. I dropped my pack on the rim trail in the shelter of a cliff. Putting on all the clothes I had, including my sleeping bag, I was still cold. The strong wind and freezing cold kept me awake most of the night. The reward for sleeplessness was the view of the magnificent star-scape above and flickering lights from the lakes and villages below.

In the middle of the night, I suddenly froze. A rustling noise comes from the rocks behind me, moving towards my bag. Is it a bandit, a Japanese war veteran, an anti-American student activist, or someone who resents an American on this holy peak? I got the courage to sit up and look. It was a large empty lunch bag blown towards me by the wind.

I dozed off finally. Just before dawn, groups of early risers stepped over my bag on the path and awakened me. There was a smell of urine in the air. My spot was sheltered behind a rock precipice. My fellow pilgrims obviously used this area to relieve themselves.

Walk the rim

Rock formations

Shinto priests

Weather Station

Japanese lieutenant frozen to death

Climbers / Pilgrim sacrifice

River Bed of Souls

Pile of rock "symbols" of names of hiking clubs
Crater camp

I picked up my companion guide at his hostel, and we walked the mile and a half around the rim of the volcano. This circuit is part of the ritual that two hundred thousand pilgrims observe every season. Every peak, rock formation, and vantage point had a special significance, and the names "Thunder Rock," "Buddha's Cleft," and "Peak of Mercy Goddess" are some of them. At the group of huts at the top of the trail, we joined the throng, and we walked clockwise to the Shinto Shrine dedicated to the Mountain Princess, first built in 27 B.C.

The first Shinto priests I saw on the Mountain were dressed completely in white and were selling curios and water from the "Golden Well." We rang the bell three times, entered a grotto that was full of the odor of incense and climbed to the weather station on the west rim.

One winter, a Japanese lieutenant attempted to live on the summit with his wife. Though knowing the risk of freezing to death, he refused to allow a rescue team to remove him. On the second try, the rescue party found him so weak that they removed him forcibly. No one since then has tried to live there, although expeditions, at some loss of life, climb the peak in the winter. Such stories were reminders that Fuji takes its toll on pilgrims (even Boy Scouts in 1971). Every year accidental sacrifices to her frigid temperatures, sudden storms, and perilous cliffs and slides are experienced by nameless pilgrims.

Stone rock cairns mark the "River Bed of Souls," where fifty pilgrims froze to death.

Heaps of piled stones were above my camp. For centuries, the faithful piled these stones to help the souls of dead children condemned to fill with rocks, the Buddhist equivalent of the River Styx. Nowadays, the stones prove "they were there" in rock symbols of names and hiking clubs. I found a small crater with its own snow bank where I could pitch my tent. I was comfortable there off the beaten track where I could rest, read and be by myself. Though alone I was in full view of people hiking the ridge above, which made going to the bathroom a challenge. I ordered my guide Subi back to the station for one more night even though he wanted to stay with me outside of my tent.

Explore craters

Using my tent as a base for meals and naps, we enjoyed exploring the craters. The gigantic center crater, over a third of a mile across, fascinated me. Subi asked about it but was warned not to try to go down to that crater without ropes or climbing equipment. It was regarded with reverence, and descent into it is taboo. An emperor long ago was lured to his death in its rocky bottom hole.

Descent into crater taboo

Slip to oblivion

All this only made it more interesting to me. Since Subi refused to join me, I tried it alone. One slip on the long snow bank and I would take a fast ride into oblivion on the boulders at the base. The cliffs were impossible. There was a steep slope of loose rock and shale that appeared to be a way down. It turned out to be easier than it looks and Subi finally followed.

Crater silences

The bottom of the crater is strangely silent, like another planet. We are entirely alone inside the Mountain one thousand feet below the rim. A lively but gray stream flow from the huge snow bank into the sandy soil. The water is cold and refreshing. Immense volcanic bombs, flint, black and hard, are left on the smooth sand floor "helter-skelter" like toys of a child God. It is not hard to imagine the force that in 1707 exploded, burying Tokyo in ashes seventy-five air miles away and covering the surrounding countryside in lava.

Hallowed ground

Echos of three claps and ritual calling of Roken-shojo

This is hallowed ground. I feel it. I clap three times and call "Roken shojo" nine times. The sheer, darkly multi-colored cliffs that surrounded me replied in crescendos of echoes fading, fading, fading into some other world. Here is the womb of a nation, a race, a people . . . me.

Fuji-san sunrise a national symbol

Fujisan's sunrises are themselves a national symbol. But there is no guarantee. It's often too rainy or cloudy. Happily, my penchant for good weather holds. On two mornings, I chilled to the cries of hundreds of voices, their cry, "Banzai!" ricocheting on the wind from the inside walls of the volcano just as the first tip of the sun broke the horizon. Soon, the wide rays burst upon the whole sky, bouncing pink, then red, gold, and finally yellow on the fields, the lakes, and the clouds below.

"Banzai" shouts ricochet off the volcano walls

The impact of this sight is not so much from the rising sun as from the watchers of the rising sun. I know again that there is no religion, no feeling, no appreciation, no inspiration, and nothing without people, believers, and fellow seekers. Here, the light of morning is transfigured into gold, and the brown Japanese faces are turned to the east.

Pilgrims mesmerized with strength and nature

Mesmerized, these people stand on every rock, cliff top, and cranny along the east rim of Fujisan. The Mountain brings strength to them and to Nature. The sun receives her due. In turn, the sun infuses her newborn strength directly into those chosen for this gift.

Sliding to Kyoto

We were late leaving this Mountain of magic and people. Taking the "Sliding Sands" descent route, we literally skied down the steep ash and cinder slopes. For every ten feet we slid, huge clouds of dust stirred up with each step. Myth holds that the sands that slipped down the Mountain by our movement are returned to the top by the Gods each night. People in the fog above and below create their own dust clouds that look like walking fires and vapor trails.

Sliding sands descent

Slipping sands

Upon our arrival at the Sixth Station on the Gotemba side of the Mountain, my strong need to be alone with nature reached a crisis. There were buses here to take hikers down the rest of the way to the train. I wanted to walk down by myself, so I asked my companion to take the bus. He refused even though he had complained of being very tired. Just as the bus was about to leave, I got mad: "You have to get on that bus; I'm going to walk alone!"

It was drastic and upsetting to both of us, but so suddenly, he obeyed.

It was also a mistake! The hike is too long. As soon as I started, I realized I didn't have any idea which way to go except down. I had sixteen miles to go. I was thirsty. My legs already ached. I was a victim of my own stubbornness, my continuing drive to do it the hard way, to go it alone. Miraculously, I made some correct turns and chanced upon a shortcut through a forest and wildflower meadow. I avoided heading in the wrong direction by some road workers who understood my "Gotemba Gotemba?" A friendly Japanese soldier, in response to my gestures of thirst, filled my canteen with all the water he had (we both had U.S. Army canteens). Apparently, my route had been straight through the middle of Japanese Army maneuvers — firing, squad tactics, tanks, trucks. Though I was being stared at, I wasn't bothered. Hours later, I arrived at the station barely in time to meet my friend, have a ham sandwich and a coke, and catch the last train to Gora (ten minutes), Odawara (thirty minutes), and our next destination, Kyoto via Osaka (two hours).

Everything on the new Tokaido Express train to Kyoto was first class (reserved seating, dining car, automatic ticketing, air conditioning, clean, speedy (ninety miles per hour) except me. Covered with Fuji's dirt and grime, bearded, and struggling to carry my bulky pack, camera, and walking stick onto the train, I was an ugly sight. I was embarrassed. Everyone else was neat and well-dressed. I felt sorry for the Japanese woman

Order "Subi" to complete descent by bus

Luckily I found route down with help of workmen

Japanese soldier gives me his water

Japanese army troup maneuvers

First Class Tokaido Express train to Kyoto

who had to ride next to me. She turned out to be a charming schoolteacher. We shared our food — her raw fish and my canned nuts. She even spoke some English with the help of my fellow hiker, Subi, across the aisle. When asked how old she thinks I was, she said, "about sixty." At least in Japan, that was a compliment! Maybe it is my growing white beard?

We shared our seat and our food with Japanese teacher

A Fellow Pilgrim?

By the time we descended, Fuji-san was on our way by train to Kyoto; I grew to know my companion, Subi, better. In the early evening of the first night on Fuji-san, he came from the summit station where he was sleeping to see if I was all right. He took some night pictures of the moon and lights in the valley for me since my hands were too cold to function. It was kind of him.

It is only in Japan that I am with another person for any length of time on this exploration. I have had the chance to try every method of travel to the Sacred Mountains: alone in Israel by car, in India by bus, with private drivers (and a boat) in Greece, and a tour bus in the Sinai Desert to Mount Sinai.

Travel to sacred Mountains in Israel and India private drivers and boat

Subi, my guide in Japan, was a sincere and devout follower of Gedatsu. This burgeoning new religion was an outgrowth of Shugendo, abstracting and generalizing that religion's specific Mountaineering concepts into a modern religious philosophy.

Gedatsu

Shugendo

New Religion

My introduction to this was at the San Francisco Gedatsu church before I left on this trip. In answer to the visiting Bishop's question as to whether I wanted a companion in Japan, I thanked him and asked that the person selected "be sure to understand I am on a religious quest and would want to be alone a good deal." I didn't receive word until long after I left that they would accept me as a novitiate. I met my

SF Gedatsu

Novitiate

guide companion on my arrival from India via Hong Kong. We were introduced and taken to the hotel by a Gedatsu representative. He was friendly and solicitous. We were together for about eight days. This trip was an opportunity for him to see and do things he had never done before. He took full advantage of it. His English was sufficient for tourism but not for religious philosophy.

Gedatsu rep friendly together for 8 days

He turned out to be much more determined and self-effacing than he appeared. Although I wanted to rent a car, he insisted (correctly) on using trains to save time and money. There was a hardness and even a deception in his politeness. I became furious at him a number of times. He would not leave me alone unless I "ordered" it. Though I was too tired to walk on our arrival at the Kyoto temple, he told the priest (in Japanese) that I wanted to hike to the hilltop temple in the middle of the night. On the way to Omine-san, after I told him "No detours," he maneuvered me unknowingly on and off trains and through a village to see a temple he wanted to visit. I was tired and exasperated but unable to do anything since I didn't know where we were. He couldn't bear to follow directions or suggestions as to how to take photos for me.

Guide determined to take me where he wanted to go by transport he selected

On the other hand, there was no question of his desire to do a good job. Also, he introduced me, at the temples where we stayed, to one of the world's great pleasures, a traditional Japanese bath in a wooden tub: soap up first, rinse, soak in the tub brim-full of very hot water, rinse again in cold water and then repeat it all. His matter-of-fact attitude reduced my embarrassment at the close quarters and complete nakedness.

Introduced me to one of world's great pleasures – Japanese wood tub

It was almost impossible to say goodbye even when we returned to Tokyo. First, he made it very difficult for me not to take him to dinner. Our meal in the nightlife Ginza district wasn't as sumptuous as he wanted, but I pretended

Hard goodbye

Ginza district restaurant bit disappointing

Inside issues

not to understand his veiled complaint. He led me to a poor but expensive tourist restaurant in Kyoto, and I didn't want that to happen again. He carefully rewrapped the expensive Mountain books I bought for him. I guessed he was going to exchange them. I think he did appreciate it.

The gift of my sleeping bag made me feel obligated to visit his friend with him at the Gedatsu College in Tokyo. He gives the cab driver directions in Japanese. I was tired and didn't want a social occasion. He telephoned this young man every night we weren't on a Mountain during our trip.

Apparently, this other man wanted to join us, but thankfully, they decided against it. We are all friendly and informal, having beers in his friend's apartment. Somehow, it began to make me uneasy.

Marriage

The subject turned to sex. Subi and I hadn't discussed it before except momentarily when I joked with him upon his return from a two-hour absence in the village near Ominesan; I remember his prior mention of the town's reputation for carnal relief from the rigors of Shugendo. In answer to my question about marriage, he said that the problem was money, a job, and his desire to travel. But here in his friend's apartment, he seemed to be trying to explain something. "We (he and his friend) are different . . . girls only make problems." I knew what that meant, but I didn't want to or even try to pursue it. Subi went with me to the airport when I was to leave Japan. He seemed unconcerned and almost pleased when we found out that my reservation had not been reconfirmed. I was upset. His callous and unsympathetic attitude was a problem for me and I told him so.

Different attitude but we parted friends and I could never have climbed Mountains without his aid

But we parted as friends. I was deeply grateful for his help. Angry and irritated at times, I was never lonely, thanks to him. Without his aid in and out of train stations, taxis, towns, and temples, I would never have climbed both Mountains, Fuji-san, and Omine-san, during my short stay in Japan.

"Kokoro" the spirit of things

I tell you this story of Subi because he made clear to me the Japanese idea of "Kokoro": What matters is not the surface, whether it is litter on the mountain, formal politeness, commercial concessions in temples ("gum-wrapper" Buddhism) or even transitory human foibles, sexual or otherwise. What matters is the spirit of things — not so much what is done but the feeling, the concentration, the power of how it is done. It is not climbing that is important; it is the soul of the climber.

Followers make a religion

Fuji-san, despite my Western irritations, I learned again from Subi and my fellow pilgrims that the followers make the religion. We must look to the climbers of the Sacred Mountain more than to the Mountain to find what we seek. But every climber, every follower, needs a Mountain, whether in Tibet, India, China, the Sinai, or Mecca.

Those who are on Mt. Fuji-san with me teach me more about religion than any book, holy or not. A pilgrim is never all alone.

Footnotes:
1. 'Each station on the trail up Fuji-san takes theoretically forty five minutes to the next so the true pilgrims could climb one thousand feet in altitude each day as prescribed. Stations were named in order of height from "ichi-gome," first station, to "ju-gome," tenth station. There is no "shi-gome," fourth station, since the other meaning of "shi" is death. Many have other special names to commemorate deaths, exhaustion, the hope to succeed, etc.
2. Chinese chant: "May our six senses be pure and the weather on the honorable mountain be fine."
3. 1t is better than dreams of the falcon (straight forward, honest, clean living since this bird can gaze at the sun without flinching and eats only living warm-blooded animals) or the egg plant (most beautiful color) which brings a lesser good luck.

Sacred Mount Omine-san

People View-Point

We are all pilgrims

day or night

male or female

wrong or right

We all have the right

To hear the voice of the Sacred

    Mount Omine-San

And learn from the Mountain Guru's Spirit.

Amen

      ... A<small>NON</small>

Location:	Nara, Japan
Range:	Omine Mountain Range
Elevation:	5,640 ft (1,719 m)
Coordinates:	34°15'10"N
	135°56'26"E
Spirit:	Shugendo / Buddhist
Pilgrimage:	*The Ascent To Buddahood*

Angel View-Point

Step 1: Jigoku. A body experiences hell.
Two Shugendo priests hold the author by the ankles over a 1,000 foot clift.
It was truly terrifying.

The Ascent To Buddahood

Shugendo
Mount Omine-san — Japanse Central Alps

Train from Fjui-san to Kyoto

The train trip from Fuji-san to Kyoto took less time than I had spent waiting for a taxi to take me to the Diago Temple, where we were supposed to stay that night. This huge temple was on the outskirts of the city. Its manicured grounds, ornate gates, Emperor Diago's quarters and large temples, the temple was built a thousand years ago and rebuilt every hundred years since then, were another inspiration and reason to admire Japan. My companion, Subi, asked that we be permitted to stay at the upper hilltop temple. The hike up the trail in the dead of night was almost too much after my eleven-hour hike down Fuji-san and the strenuous trip to Kyoto, Japan's old capital. But I restrained myself from complaining. I knew I was at the beginning of a mystical discovery, a renewal of the self in an unusual religion, Shugendo. I was so taken with this Mountain religion that the experiences there, the trip by train, the taxi from one temple to another and the climb itself are still standard floating dreams for me.

Morning meditation

My Shugendo began for me on this hilltop temple. I dozed the next morning, half awake in a warm cocoon of thick, fluffy bedding. Dreams and thoughts drifted and mixed into my natural meditation:

Soft, happy comforting

The morning sun . . . is long since topping the trees around my hilltop temple . . . asleep on the dark polished floors – everything and everyone is One. The valley breeze slid through

256

gold-painted panels. A forest . . . a green meadow . . . too far away . . . better to imagine than be . . . to see than hike . . . no challenge . . . a vision of greens: dark, light, yellow, brown. . . tree filters the sunshine . . . light spots with their own sets of greens. The God's breeze . . . everything's soft: me, my bed, my inner being, happy, comforting, conflict fading, assuages my future thoughts of . . . climbing the sacred Omine-san, to become a Shugendo . . . Lying, luxuriating in nothingness, aware only of the morning. I am my altar, my essence a woman's breast, a woman's thigh, her caress, love, an idea, quietness, a communion of silence, Sacred Mountain Man softness . . . hides within my center core.

Climb sacred Omine-san to become a Shugendo

Is it safe . . . to be so female? Is it so female?

I remember the bath of the night before: Ah, the bath — easy, satisfying. Steam, soap, hot water seeping, then breaking through the barrier into my soul. Like a massage ... the ultimate of love, of touch . . . the tub . . . needs, craves. . . a woman I love . . . where come, my darling.... my back, shoulders, spirit . . . a baby, one, two, three years old . . . me . . . can't remember bathing, powdering, holding, rough-housing, cuddling, playing with me. I remember now my greatest pleasure: to be touched, fondled, caressed by a woman I loved.

Baths fondling caressing, pleasures of being touched with love

From baths to Shugendo . . . a short step . . . my ultimate merger . . . of Sacred Mountain climbing and religion . . . of the physical and spiritual . . . a debt to the Founders, also the Preservers . . . to feed my inner thirst for discovery and truth. Who is watching? Subi . . . the priests . . . the villagers?

Baths a short step to Shugendo

Mountains, religious inner thirst for truth discovery

After we visited part of the temple shrines and gardens that bring Nature and man so close, the Bishop interviewed me. He told me that I was accepted as a Shugendo novitiate. In our talk, the Bishop asks, "What do you like to eat?" Not to impose on his generosity, I say, "Thank you. I like everything."

Bishop tells me I'm accepted as Shugendo novitiate

My answer to question as to what I would like to eat was "everything"

When we arrived in the evening at the next temple, near Omine-san, my answer as to the dinner question was translated into a "thank you" dinner of "everything"! And that's what I received. Hot steaming rice, fish, soup, veal steak, tomato, cucumber, eggplant, stuffed eel, beer, pressed fish strips, cabbage and tea. The food prepared and served to me in my room on two trays had a unique taste and was an experience, an observation and participation in Spirit itself.

After dinner priest brings me Shugendo clothes

After dinner, a priest brings me Shugendo clothing, the largest sizes he could find: a white cloth coat, broad coolie straw hat, white cloth headband, shiny black head shield, straw sandals called Waraji (two pair), a bell with a white ribbon waistband to tie around me (so that it will ring with each step to remind me and the Gods that I am with them), a large fir walking stick with symbols burned on it, and finally white leggings and arm coverings.

Walichis too small to stay on

Only the warajis (sandals) were to prove a problem. Being too small, they wuldn't stay on. I retied them almost every step when we began, or walked in my socks. The latter would have soon meant walking barefoot on the hard rock trail that not even the mud and rain could soften. The blisters on the bottom of my feet started to ache again and open up.

At that point, I felt stupid for trying to dress like a Shugendo. But Subi saved the day by tying them on differently so they remained on my feet perfectly for the whole climb.

I enjoyed the footwear rituals of the temple itself: shoes off at the entrance and slippers on, new slippers in the hallway, socks only in my room, wooden shoes in the bath and special slippers for the toilet.

God bless my feet; they do everything I really enjoy!

A Shugendo Nirvana

But before I continue this narrative, some understanding of Shugendo is necessary to experience this Mountain. Shugendo is practiced on the Sacred Mountain at Omine-san, another Sacred Mountain in Japan. For centuries, Mountains have been the central nucleus of worship for a whole group of Shinto sects. Deities reside on certain sacred Mountains. In Japan, the foremost of these sects is Shugendo. Mount Omine-san in the central Alps of Japan combines the spirit of Shinto and Shugendo with the teachings of Buddha.

Shinto Shugendo on Mount Omine-san

Climbing is the ritual; the Mountain's Nature is the sanctuary. To that extent I follow Shugendo. It has none of the trappings of success of the main religions of the world. There are comparably few followers. Without separate priests or temples, Buddhist clerics keep it alive in Shinto shrines, the surrounding forests, and on the Sacred Mountain Omine-san. This is not unusual in Eastern religions, whose tolerance for and assimilation of other beliefs is almost incomprehensible to competitive Western religions.

Climbing ritual for followers without separate priests

Tolerance and assimilation of others beliefs

Shugendo is the only formalized religion that consciously accepts the generally unnoticed but omnipresent role of Sacred Mountains in worship. Its founder and most of its believers, especially nowadays, have always been both Shintoists and Buddhists. Because of its priests, in the main temples at Kyoto and Dologawa (at the base of Omine), most Shugendo are now Buddhists. In these times, Shugendo was considered a Buddhist sect. In the past, Taoism and Shinto predominated, with Confucian characteristics evident. Originally as in all religions, the Mountain is the God and, in later spiritual focus, the place where the Gods live.

Unnoticed but omnipresent role of Mountains

Mountain Gods homes

Shugendo was revised in its present form in the ninth century by Shobo Taiski. He and the founder, Jimpen Dai Bosatsu,

Shobo Taiski Jimpen Dai Bosatsu

Spiritual John Muirs

Shugendo simple with Mountain as place of worship

were spiritual "John Muirs" of eastern mysticism. They worshipped at Omine, feel that desire, greed, temptation, and sorrow can best be shed on Mountain heights and spiritual knowledge and peace can also be found on the Sacred Mountain.

Shugendo precepts are simple, but its place of worship, a Sacred Mountain, is a precursor to man's need to build religious structures. Almost all the world's churches, mosques, synagogues and temples have a peak or a high point somewhere. This intentionally or unconsciously could be man's attempt to duplicate a Sacred Mountain, a symbol of eternity, mystery and sacred power. That object is also frankly recognized in Hindu sacred architecture. Shugendo returns to the beginning and strips away the symbolism. Thus, the sacred place of worship, the seminary, and the whole religion is the Mountain, Omine-san.[*1] To climb Mount Omine-san is a holy act.

There are ten steps of Shugendo practice (Shugyo):

10 steps of Shugendo Meditation

Jigoku
Gaki
Chikusho

Shura

Ningen

Tenkai
Shomon

Engaku

Step 1. JIGOKU. The body experiences hell.

Step 2. GAKI. Survival, hunger and thirst.

Step 3. CHIKUSHO. Bearing the hardships of animal existence.

Step 4. SHURA. Dispelling feelings from competition, reproach, antagonism.

Step 5. NINGEN. Understanding the transient nature of man.

Step 6. TENKAI. Realizing our vulnerability to downfalls.

Step 7. SHOMON. Listening to the Mountain manifestations of the divine consciousness.

Step 8. ENGAKU. Grasping the truths and causes of illusions (entire Mountain).

Step 9. BOSATU. Spiritual enlightenment and salvation of others through compassion.

Step 10. HOTAKE. Supreme enlightenment, Nirvana

Bosatu
Hotake

Buddhahood, Nirvana, each step must be experienced on the Mountain, physically, mentally, emotionally and spiritually.

The climb of Omine-san, the goal of each Shugendo, is also the path of supreme enlightenment or Buddhahood. Since most Shugendo are also Buddhists, the Mountain has little meaning apart from a knowledge of Buddha (See Part III, "Founders").

Ready for Omine-san

I am ready to look inward. I am ready for Mount Omine-san. The Sacred Mountains strengthen my body and spirit. Buddha opens my mind. The Shinto spirit pervades around me. The memory of the climb is still the present, not the past.

Buddha history

Cold Warm-up

4AM ready for step 1

"It is four o'clock in the morning, damp, cold and slightly rainy. I crawl bleary-eyed from my bundle of heavy, warm comforters on the floor. I sleep soundly in the temple. Some reserved willpower puts me into my hapi gown, and I stand outside in the rain. I am ready for Step I. JIGOKU

Step I. Hell: JIGOKU

"This Shuygo is for the Initiate to persevere in the most extreme form of physical, mental, and material hardships and discipline his mind and body."

Hell

The black, wet cold of pre-dawn starts me shivering violently. Practicing my Sutra[*2] prayer is a helpful diversion. The water in the "golden pool" flows directly from an ice-cold spring called "The Dragon's Mouth." Deciding to wade in suddenly before losing my nerve and determination, I stripped quickly. But it was too painfully cold. I stepped in inch by inch; my toes, feet, ankles, legs, testicles and waist sent new shock waves to my brain, leaving the submerged parts aching. The

Golden pool, "the Dragon's Mouth", painfully cold

pain reminds me of frost-bitten hands, the kind I received as a child playing in the snow in Pocatello, Idaho.

It took every ounce of "perseverance" to squat into the water to cover my shoulders. Before me were the statues of the God of purification and spiritual energy, Fudo-myo, and Jimpen Dai Bosatsu. I chanted my sutras. The pain subsided into numbness. Getting out was still a relief. The morning air and mist seemed almost warm by comparison. With this cleansing initiation, I began the ten steps of the Shugendo. The service, the ascent of the Sacred Mountain, follows.

Cleansing initiation

To Soar

What is it to soar? To feel the heat of my body; to see the overcast day. To almost taste the cooling fog. I couldn't stop for rest. Climbing here was soaring. Every part of my body flowed without effort. I was exhilarated in my heart, in my peace. I was laughing going faster up the trail. My steps lengthened. No panting even. I was not tired, nor did I feel hunger or thirst even at 'Otaska Misu, "Saving Water Springs."

Climbing is soaring, exhilarating, laughing

The forest was a part of me, along with the clouds, the lush ferns, flowering bushes, and the varieties of pines. I yelled the first line of my Sutra. "Han·Ya Shing Gyo!" "I cannot die.' My spirit is free of everyone, of everything, of the world. I am the inner light of joy. Nothing else interferes. Was this not the reason for my quest, to be free? This was no climb; this was a flight. An effortless, soaring, beautiful flight. Is it too easy? Must I question, analyze, dissect . . . or only absorb and appreciate? What I am doing is not a thought, an act, or even a feeling. It is a distinct, separate force, a compulsion that drives me to seek the core, the cell, the reality, within myself.

Sutra

"Han-Ya-Shing Gyol"

*Death fear
Free
Joy
Soaring in flight*

Compulsion that drives me to my core

The force follows the will. It comes after the body, after the emotions, and after the mind has been experienced and controlled. It leaves them all behind. They are but milestones, obstacles and opportunities, initiators and obstructors. They show the way and bar the way.

The way

Mountain keeper of the Holy Grail

And there was the Sacred Mountain, keeper of the holy grail. The spring of my new joy poured into the ocean of my entire life. I love, I experience, I am. Thank God, thank me. Thank reality that I know my happy freedom and float up the Mountain without climbing. To see without seeing, to find happiness within myself, to translate nature around me into a personal joy, to stand aside and watch my body, my work, my mind, my struggle with good humor, detached from the sorrows or the strain, the fleeting disappointments of nothingness.

The fleeting disappointments of nothingness

Fear of death and life

I am unafraid of life, even of death. My Self needs no one even though the body, the emotions, and perhaps the mind needs others. But they can be assuaged with only a few selves: one woman to wife, children, a companion, a fellow worker, a friend.

Pilgrims

Shugendo

Fudo-Myo

Over precipice alone

Squeeze up rock chimney

I followed at least thirteen hundred years of pilgrims seeking to be closer to their God. I went through the next steps of Shugendo: on cliffs that frighten; "Ants Pass" (only ants can make it alone); mazes through the rocks. I was required to find my own way alone over a precipice.

I explored a cave, climbing alone down inside the world in darkness to the bottom of the pit (there was a single ray of daylight from somewhere high above that pin-pointed a statue of the God, Fudo-Myo, a now familiar personal idol). I squeezed up a chimney of rock barely wide enough for my head to burst again upon the world from the womb to be reborn yet again.

Rain

Past, present, future Buddhas

The rain came in sheets, making the highest temple of this Mountain a nest of incense and candlelight. This temple is overseen by the three gold Buddhas, one each for the past, the present, and the future. I struggled to forget the past, ignore the future, and be the present. Again, I know others watched me because I was a unique figure in this house of worship, built in three layers thirteen hundred, eight hundred, and one hundred years ago. Shall I give money to the watchers or would that be an insult? I tried. The priest refused. Subi recommended that I give it anyway. I insisted, and they took it. It was good advice. Could there be more to this experience? I seemed saturated. But I am a Shugendo. I completed my climb and all the Practices. Was the peak an end, an experience in disillusionment? I had nowhere to go, literally or spiritually, except down.

Tips

Shugendo dead end

"... (T) the Initiate has gone through the hardships of the lower realm, and he is approaching the summit of the Mountain. However, when he arrives at the summit, the only path which leads from it is the one going back down the Mountain. The Initiate realizes that attainment of only the physical goal does not give him true security and peace of mind, since he is vulnerable to downfall at any time."

Physical goal not enough

Step 6. TENKAI.

But more is to come.

"Satisfaction cannot be attained by the mere efforts to reach the summit in the previous steps. When man begins to contemplate how he could attain true happiness and peace of mind, then he begins to cultivate a mind that searches for spiritual truth. This is the ignition of the divine spark latent in each person. It may consist of acts such as listening to the teachings of the one who initiated or recited the Sutras. He listens to the sound produced by the wind and the sound of birds and beasts of the Mountain and discovers that all of this is the manifestation of the divine consciousness. This realization is the object of the "Shomon."

Spiritual truths

Step 7. SHOMON.
Listening to the Mountain manifestations of the divine consciousness.

Shomon – divine consciousness

"The Initiate learns fearful truths and becomes awakened to the hidden meaning of life. He observes that the forms of nature are undisturbed by the effects of the wind and rain and that the grass and trees appear to die during one season, but they return to life with a seasonal cycle and cover the Mountain once more. The animals and birds prey upon each other, but their lot does not become extinct. He realizes that human life carries forth in cycles of birth, growth, and destruction. But life and its activities do not cease . . ."

Step 8. ENGAKU.
Grasping the truths and causes of illusions.)

Engaku

Now a priest took me by the hand to the darkness behind the huge altar, to a place only for those who practice Shugendo on this Mountain at least thirty-three times. The smaller altar here has no Buddha. It was covered by a curtain. A gong sounded through the whole temple. It seemed to echo to the beginning and the end of time. A chant begins as the candles are lit. Strong incense is lighted. I am swept up by the strange ritual: The curtain is pulled back. The strange wailing guttural chant grows stronger. In the dim candlelight, I see a wooden self-sculptured statue of Jimpen Dai, the founder, twelve hundred years old. When the sacred recitation stops, the curtain is drawn. Time dissolves. The atmosphere is heavy with life and desire, past and present. My spirit touches Jimpen Dai's. I am with one who attained Buddhahood, the last step of Shugendo. "He comprehends the sanctity of spiritual enlightenment. He strives to work for the salvation of others with compassion delivering all mankind his wisdom. He finds affinity in all creations."

Statue of Jimpen Dai, founder, twelve hundred years old

With Jimpen who attained Buddhahood

Jimpen works for salvation of others

Bosatsu

Step 9. BOSATSU.
Spiritual enlightenment and salvation of others through compassion.

"He is the person who attains supreme enlightenment … who imparts spiritual truths to others by applying it to their lives. The whole universe is the substances of universal consciousness. Buddha is the enlightened one who is part of this all-encompassing consciousness. The Initiate realizes that he also is a part of this consciousness. Through the experiences of the Bosatsu Shugyo, he suddenly awakens to the ultimate reality and becomes merged with our universal consciousness."

Hotake

Step 10. HOTAKE.
Supreme enlightenment, Buddhahood.

Life and death, and the encompassing consciousness are revealed to me on this Sacred Mountain. But I have one final test to meet — death."

The Fifth Shugyo-Death / NINGEN

It started to drizzle again by the time we scaled the first rock ledges on the west shoulder of Sacred Mount Omine-san.

Need for others while climbing

The climb was a lesson to show me my need for others (part of Step 4. SHURA.). For a short person, like a Japanese, the steel grab-rings are so far apart that the climber could not make it without help from his fellow climbers. Being so much taller and somewhat experienced, I didn't need any help. Nevertheless, I let the priest give me a boost and I gave him my hand over some of the steeper parts. But this effort was an anti-climax to my earlier experiences. There was a Disneyland feel to this part of the climb: "Watch the pilgrim climb the death-defying cliff with only his Shugendo priest behind!"

Disneyland

My leader now tells me in poor English but easily

understood gestures not to worry. The next practice apparently was not as bad as I anticipated. Secretly I was disdainful. The last event was too easy even though slippery from the rain and mist.

Natural and practical spirituality

Nevertheless, I liked my guide and priest. As a man of nature, a Mountaineer, he had a natural and practical spirituality about him. But I had no idea then that he would have my life and death in his hands, literally. My guide seemed truly concerned. I am too stupid to be. My Japanese guide entered a small hut, emerged with a rope, and signaled me to follow him up a flat rock about twenty feet square.

Step 5. NINGEN: Life is a composite of joy, anger, sorrow, pleasure, goodness, and evil. Realizing that he is living in a world of such illusion, man still cannot escape from its effect. Observing the grandeur and imposing appearance of the Mountain where he is doing, SHUGYO; the Initiate, realizes

Selfish desires

the unworthiness of his selfish desires. From a precipice, he looks down into a bottomless abyss and contemplates the tran-

Bottomless abyss

sient nature of his existence. To transcend the illusions of the mind through such contemplation is the next step."

Transient existence

We walked to one side. Finally, I was beginning to understand what I had to do. This is the top of a sheer rock cliff face; it is almost one thousand feet straight down to the rocks

Cliff down to boulders, forest below

and boulders and forest below. The thick hemp rope had two loops with a splice to a straight rope about twelve feet long. The

Rope me up and we crawl to edge

priest put the loops around each of my shoulders. The assistant holds the straight end.

We crawled closer to the edge. The priest chained himself to the ledge. His chain was attached to a steel "eye" which was made a part of the rock. I lay on my stomach and snaked my body toward the drop-off. Unfortunately, it wasn't difficult since the main rock sloped downwards. But looking straight down and slipping further out terrified me. I tried to stop my slide by grasping for a rock, but there was nothing to hold. The priest yelled something to me, yet, in my fright, I couldn't understand. I felt the priest's hands on the back of my legs, but instead of pulling me back, he pushed me further out. The rope tightened on my shoulders. My whole body, from the waist up, was hanging out over space. I was too far out to grab anything. I knew I was going to die. The priest started a sutra. I tried to repeat mine but couldn't remember it. I couldn't remember anything. Finally, the priest and his assistant started to pull me back. It is over. By now, it was pouring rain, so we ran for a nearby climbers' hut. Inside, they took the white band from my head and stamped a Japanese symbol on it, indicating that this step of my novitiate was complete. The event was recorded in a large book, a rare entry considering my race and nationality.

Push me out further

Whole body hanging in space

Couldn't remember my sutra

They pull me back

Stamp for symbol and my initiation completed text entered into record

Yet something was incomplete, wrong. I could feel it. As the violence of the wind and rain increased outside, the priest and his assistant talked to each other in Japanese. Finally, I asked, "What's wrong?" Only then did they tell me that although I qualified, I had not really done this part properly. It was unbelievable. I go to hell and back but they are unconvinced. I failed to hang out over the precipice far enough! In addition, I used my hands to grab the rock cliffs. This was improper and also dangerous since the rope could have slipped over my shoulders unless I kept my hands tightly together.

Something wrong

I didn't do it "properly"

I flew from the United States over twenty thousand miles to this Sacred Mountain. I could not fail. I told them I will "face death" again. Before I had time to change my mind, we took the same positions as before. It was still sleeting rain, and I was again sick with fright. Back on my stomach, my hands tight together, I again "worm" out on my belly over the edge. This time, the priest pushed harder. I entered into shock. I pictured myself falling out of the ropes into a legs-over-head

I agree to face death again

Repeat ritual

Held by my ankles

Unconsciously shout my sutra

Rope slips, facing death

Fear, my whole body shook

I couldn't talk, heart beating wildly, oblivious to rain

To death and back again . . . twice! Resignation to death

Blackness without fear

Golden Mountain taught me freedom from fear and the power of meditation

somersault. He kept pushing me. Finally, I hung down held only by the rope and the priest with his hands on my ankles. My ankles were the only part of me on the rock edge of that cliff. The priest chanted his sutra. Again, I couldn't remember mine. I shouted words that, unknown to me at the time, were my actual sutra. Somehow, yelling kept me alive in spite of such fear, dangling head-first over that cliff with the blood running down my head. I was terrorized even more when the assistant stepped forward, so the slack in the rope suddenly dropped me further. I was facing death. It was a blank, black, nothing.

Fear eliminated all thought except the thought of dying. Finally, my aides pulled me back. I crawled to a stone and sat up. My whole body shook uncontrollably. It is impossible for me to stand up. My heart beat wildly. My lungs were about to burst from the heavy frantic breathing. I couldn't talk. I just sat oblivious to the rain. Slowly, my strength, my thoughts, and even joy returned.

I then knew that I had experienced death and returned again. There was no revelation. But the second time, there is resignation. If it is my time to die, so be it. I am now free from death's anxieties: the next time I face death, wherever it comes from. I am ready. No longer do I fear death. I know that at death after the fear is over, there is only blackness. If I am prepared, the blackness will be warm and beautiful.

To Meditate

When death is removed from the Self, only eternity remains. Buddha "The Golden Mountain" teaches me freedom from the tyranny of the body, the scourge of inner conflict, and the slavery of the mind. He shows me the Trail of Meditation, which is a way to paradise that waits now within each of us, a way to self-realization. It is not the same as "contemplation," "pondering," "thinking," "musing," "reflecting."

"It is abiding as one's Self without swerving in any way from one's true nature and without feeling that one is meditating. One is not in the least conscious of the different stages (waking, dreaming, etc.) in this condition. The excellence of the practice lies in not giving room for a single "Mental Concept."

Give room for a single concept

You are in your heart

It is our inner thoughts that govern our lives, but
"As we thinketh in our heart, so are we."
— (Proverbs XXIII, 7)

So that since:

Regulate well your inner heart talk

"[m]an holds an inward talk with himself alone,
. . . it behooves him to regulate it well." (Pascal)

Climbing Omine-san as a Shugendo was a meditation

When I climbed Omine-san as a Shugendo, it was a meditation. True meditation, prayer and even silence and sleep are the same experiences where the inner self may be awakened and freed from the bonds of everyday thought and action. The climb was neither a ritual nor a thought process*3 but a discovery of the sacred Self. It makes no difference where that Self resides — the right side of the chest as the Hindus believe, the God on the Mountain, the Sacred Mountain, the God in heaven, or the God in contemplation. Nor does it matter that others meditate differently; it isn't unimportant that they sit, stand, kneel, or gaze at their belly buttons, concentrate (Zen), chant (Stati) or keep silent, utter Mantras like "OM" (Japa), separate themselves from their senses (Dhyana), fix on psychic centers or extend the mind to effortlessness (Janana).

No matter that others meditate differently

Meditation, like the Sacred Mountain, begins in confusion, a hodge-podge of ritual, silence and bells, nature's structures and man's buildings, sutras, chants, statues of Gods, semi-Gods and heroes not yet Gods, symbols, conglomerates of several types of worship; post-card and candle sales.

I am too ignorant to understand the language and too wise to regret it. Even the ten steps of Shugendo confuse physical practices in climbing the Sacred Mountain with the philosophy of life, rules of conduct, and religious objectives.

But to know, and appreciate the essence of this Mountain and of meditation is easy, beautiful, and enlightening:

First, I must forget the externals and most of the internals. The ritual, the symbolism, the method, the culture, the language, and even the emotional and physical state make no difference. Man, so often makes things difficult with books, buildings, words, and emotions; religions and meditation systems are the worst offenders. To meditate, to climb, clear the mind of detail. For fun, conversation, or to earn a new living, you can return later to learn or add any new complications you want.

Secondly, regardless of the form, there is only one object: to still the mind and experience, make contact with, or realize the inner Self. The inner Self is the central core of existence; its title is irrelevant: Self, God, or Totem. Where is it? That, too is insignificant, except perhaps negatively if the location becomes a fetish.

Finally, while the object and result are the same, the particular way of attaining the goal is unimportant. Prayers to Allah, Christ, Om, Ram, God, Yahweh, one of a million Gods, a Mountain totem, a God-like man or a man-like God, are the same. Even ideals, goals, drives become sacred in their importance and catalysts for meditation.

You can adopt any method of meditation that meets your needs and maturity. The only question you need to ask is: Does it work for you? If it's not working, it diverts you to other purposes and brings other results: acceptance by others, material success, or just exercise (mental or physical), for example, or if

Too ignorant to understand the language and too wise to regret it

Appreciate essence of Mountain and meditation

Man makes things difficult with books, buildings, words and emotions

Clear the mind of detail

Only object to still the mind and experience

Prayers to Gods all the same

Adopt any method of meditation that moves to your needs
Only question: does it work

it creates an inner illusion of spirituality. That is simply remedied by humility and continued striving (no less than twenty minutes each day in a quiet place).

Quiet place 20 minutes per day

For me, religions, forms and prayers, as well as other special concentrations, interfere with and delay the search. They do not help me, though they help many others. I must search alone, without form or guru', but meditation is now an important part of my life.

Meditation, searching alone, all help considering "Who Am I"

Most helpful in meditating is the thought "Who am I?" As the mind wanders toward problems, activities, body, ask "Who is thinking this? And this successfully pulls one to the function and essence of the Self, towards pure consciousness.

The result is to feel me, to be myself, to become aware of all that is, then, now, and forever. I smile or laugh with the pure joy of being. Waves of beauty surround me. Pain disappears. A quiet peace opens my inner eye to the aberrations of my emotional, physical, and mental conflicts. I am reminded that only through my love of others can I keep my peace, my beauty, and my joy alive. I am open and receptive to destiny and to the people in my life.

Joy of being

Waves of beauty surround me

Love of others keeps my joy alive

My Self becomes an image. . . a tube of light . . . a door to the infinite that enlightens, controls and watches. I am not, need not be a prisoner, physically, of my mind or of conscious or unconscious drives and conflicts.

My self

And when I am free, even the Sacred Mountain Omine-san that served me so well is gone.

Footnotes:
1 Although women were historically prohibited from climbing the Sacred Mountain, a neighboring peak, Enna Moora has a summit temple on top, especially for women with its own God and Buddha.
2 I was given a Sutra to memorize. It is a Buddhist prayer for wisdom, not really translatable except for the last line: "Let us go, let us go, all of us, helping each other to the shore."

Sutra memorization

"Let us go"

Six perfections:
giving
morality
forbearance
striving
insight
meditation

Calming section of
Lam-rim-chen-mo

3 Intellectualizing meditation can be a fatal diversion to the real object. The categorization and detailed formula and directives on the meditation of Tibetan Buddhism, for example, have that effect on me: To mature the Buddha nature for oneself, according to the Bodhisattva Practice of Lam-rim-chen-mot, six Perfections are required: (1) giving; (2) morality; (3) forbearance (4) striving; (5) insight; and (6) meditation. Each is divided into subcategories.

As to meditation, for example:

"It was already mentioned that possession of the first four Perfections enables the Bodhisattva easily to master Meditation. Moreover, certain "equipment" or accessories are specified to serve as a foundation for the speedy and pleasant accomplishment of Calming. These are (from the Calming section of the Lam-rim-chen·mo): residence in a favorable place (good access, good settlement, good soil, good companionship, good usage); meager desire; contentment; elimination of multiple activities, such as buying and selling; purity of morality; elimination of discursive thinking of craving, and so on. Purity of morality, seeing the disadvantages in craving, and residence in a favorable place are the chief ones."

There are many schools of Tibetan Buddhism with their own complex ways of meditation, e.g., Nyingmapa, Kargyodpa, Sakyapa and Gelgpa.

Reputedly, this can be dangerous, especially in Tantric meditation, where death or serious injury can result.

Sacred Mount
Sinai

People View-Point

The flow of Moses', Christ's and
  Mohammeds spirits
swirls on these Mount Sinai peaks . . .
On ancient deserts with their divinities
These three great religions and their founders
all began their desert origin.
.   . . . THE MOUNTAN PATH

Location:	Sinai Peninsula of Egypt
Range:	Sinai Mountain range
Elevation:	7,497 ft (2,285 m)
Prominence:	1,089 ft (334 m)
Coordinates:	38°32'21.9"N
	33°58'31.5"E
Spirit:	Judaism, Christianity, Islam
Pilgrimage:	*In Moses' Footsteps*

Angel View-Point

In Moses' Footsteps

Mount Sinai — Sinai Desert
Immortalized by Moses' footsteps
Important to Judaism, Christianity, Islam

Esoterica: Myths, Mysteries and Imaginables

Here, in the blazing brier, God calls on Moses to return to Egypt to free the Jews from slavery. Here, He gives Moses the golden tablets which Moses breaks. Here, a second time, the stone tablets with the Ten Commandments and hundreds more are provided. Here, Elijah, like Moses, lives for forty days to find solace from the errors of Israel, to hear God, and to select his successor. Here, Muhammad finds refuge in his flight and inspiration in his night journey to heaven. Here, according to the prophets, the Jews must return. And finally, it is here that thousands of Christians for over sixteen centuries have come to escape pagan persecutions, to talk directly to God in their lone caves, and to prepare for the final judgment day.

And here, too, I went to talk to my God.

The Scientific approach to finding the location of Mount Sinai, where Moses is said to have talked to God. The Biblical Old Testament description of that is a very significant, allegedly historical event. It is epitomized in a scientifically described mammoth study, *The Mountain of God* by Emmanuel Anati (360 pages published by Rizzoli, New York, 1986). It is a detailed scientific review of the evidence of the actual location of Biblical "Mount Sinai" concludes at least tentatively that Mount Sinai is actually a present-day mountain "Har Karkom" location. This conclusion is based on a detailed analysis of historical, archaeological, biblical analysis, artifact discovery, relative chronologies, reviews of other relevant studies, narratives, and extensive analysis. The author in his "conclusion" to this study states about his work The

Mountain of God: (page 291)

"Much still remains to be accomplished. The archaeological work at the site of Har Karkom will require many years. In addition, new prospects of research can already be discerned in the field of comparative literature of ancient Egypt from the end of the third millennium BC. This work will certainly contribute substantially to a better understanding of the Biblical accounts of the Exodus.

The research presented here is in its initial stages: there will no doubt be further developments in the near future. This exceptional sacred mountain must still hold many secrets. Perhaps the Mountain of God contains other messages and clues, yet to be discovered." Success Needs A Prophet

Bus to visit Mount Sinai and St. Catherines

The only way for me to get to Mount Sinai was by a combination of buses. Time is too short to risk being turned back by roadblocks or held up in a military firefight or an Egyptian attack. On the plane to Tel Aviv, a young man who had journeyed by bus for months in Israel tells me the dangers of traveling alone with Arabs thinking I am a Jew, Jews thinking I am an Arab, or Bedouins thinking I am for the "other" family in a blood feud. Snake bites, heat exhaustion or listening to travel agents seemed the more likely catastrophes for me.

Bus leaves

The bus left Jerusalem around six on an overcast hot morning. Every seat was filled, mostly by Israelis, but there were a few Jewish tourists, a young couple from Australia, a single girl from New York, and a family from Cleveland, Ohio. We breakfasted in Beersheba to bypass Gaza because of the rioting there, crossed the Negev Desert, followed the recent battle route through central Sinai, and turned south along the Gulf of Suez. The guide talked for hours along the way about one subject — the Six-Day War between Egypt and Israel in this desert, a fantastic Israeli blitzkrieg of armor and air that demolished an entire Egyptian army supplied, supported, and

6-Day War Battleground

encouraged by the Soviet Union. The desert is cluttered with what is claimed to be only five percent of the destruction by the Israelis. The rest is salvaged — burned-out Egyptian and Soviet tanks, demolished trucks and personnel carriers. Even guns, gloves, canned goods, beds, and gas masks are scattered for miles along the roads, realistic memorials to the Israeli's armed victory.

Wasteland of cluttered military equipment from the recent 6-Day War

The huge abandoned Egyptian military bases are only partially occupied by their Israeli conquerors. A large part of the Egyptian force tried to escape Suez back to Egypt through the Mitla Pass. Our guide, an Israeli reserve army officer, told us that five of the nine tanks in his platoon had run out of gas, so the remaining four tanks proceeded on alone to this defile. Those four tanks blew up every vehicle that tried to go through the Pass without opposition. With reinforcements, the Mitla Pass became a shooting gallery and slaughter of Egyptians.

Every tank was blown up

Although almost all of our passengers were going to Mount Sinai, no one asked the guide a single question about it. War, not Moses, was on their minds. They were rightfully proud of their splendid military, superb mobility, air control, and high morale. It was equally obvious that the Egyptians were extraordinarily inept.

Israel proud of mobility air control and high morale

Does Israeli pride come before a disaster or assure future success? For an army or an individual?

"Pride goes before destruction and a haughty spirit before a fall."

Pride before destruction

If the Israeli armor was modest about its initial victories, it would have been more cautious, less sure of itself. It might have lost the war.

Such military victories more than match the material accomplishments evident everywhere: new highways and roads, agriculture, factories, and modern structures. Yet Israel seems to need a new prophet for her soul. Her whole success seems focused on buildings, tourists, farms, and war, not worship, God, or their religious heritage. They have even become intolerant towards non-Western Jews. I saw a Jewish Boy Scout troop beat up Arabic street urchins and heard Jews in the hotel berate Arab servants and humiliate an employee who spoke favorably of Islam as a religion. The most sacred place seems to be not Mount Sinai, but Masada, where the Jews massacre themselves rather than give up against a Roman siege centuries ago.

Sacred Places

Their humor reflected their disdain for Bedouins. For instance, there is a commonly told tale about a Sheik riding in his Cadillac limousine who picked up a hitchhiking girl. Unable to seduce her, he started to force her into intercourse. She warns him not to because her father is a Sheik in the area and will punish him severely. It then becomes clear that this man is her father, but he has so many wives and children that he doesn't know her.

The Bedouin Daughter

While Israelis condemn Bedouins for begging, they encourage it by promoting tourist travel for the same reason: money. These desert tribes-people are of the same stock as the twelve tribes who, a few thousand years ago, followed Moses into this same land but are now poorer, dirtier, and more outcast than their cousins of today.

Israelis encourage Bedouin begging

"Ask what you will, and you shall have it." A nation or an individual can have the luxury, comfort, even joy, of material success, but it can also be all-absorbing, leaving little time for one's inner spiritual growth. Many find success breeds more success, more money, more work, more recognition, better homes, better schools, better neighborhoods, more parties, and more desire for more, as well as less time, less health, less peace, less character, and stunted growth, both spiritually and emotionally.

Inappropriate material success

Israel is fighting for, praying for, and receiving her triumph — security, joy, and wealth. Will her victories be hollow?

Will her people be able to refocus on her spiritual needs? Or do those voices rolling on the thunder from thousands of years ago still ring true?

Focus on spirit more than security

"Isaiah: Woe to the rebellious children, sayeth the Lord, that takes counsel but not of me; and that cover with a covering, but not of my spirit."

Rebellious

"Hosea: They sow the wind and they shall reap the whirlwind." (8.7)

Sow/reap this wind

"Jesus: No man can serve two masters … Ye cannot serve God and Mammon."

Can't serve God and Mammon

"Isaiah: Woe to Israel for she forgets her God." "Hear, O Israel … and thou shalt love the Lord thy God with All thine heart and with All thy soul and with All thy might." Deuteronomy 6:4-5

Love the Lord

Rattling through Sinai, only at infrequent rest stops did we have a chance to be a part of the desert, the hot wind, the openness. It was a relief from the dust and rattle of our bus, incredibly held together over endless bumps; the highways were made by paving over the desert, lumps and all. At noon, at a road construction detour stop, Arab road workers in 105° heat were cooking their hot tea over a fire of camel dung. We lunched on box lunches in the shade of the administration building of an abandoned oil field. The whole complex of buildings, oil wells, and tanks were intact and operable but deserted, with windows open and doors flopping in the wind. By an unwritten pact, neither the Israelis nor the Egyptians destroy oil facilities along the Suez; they are too valuable to waste on a war— lives, yes; but not oil wells!

Paving the desert

Camel dung fires for tea

Oil well complex saved

I was attracted to a young woman traveling alone, and we ate lunch together. She was a teacher from New York spending the summer in Israel, intelligent, and with a nice personality. When I asked her that evening to walk over to the mess hall for a beer, she said she would see me there.[*1] Five men on the bus had already suggested the same thing!

After six hundred kilometers of a tiring bus ride, we arrived at Abu Rudeis on the Suez, an oil town and a converted Israeli army base, by late afternoon. This was an active Israeli defense complex with slit trenches outside each barrack, barbed wire, and mobile fire units and artillery. We enjoyed a swim in the warm water sea and a typical meal of cucumbers, pickles, tomatoes, and canned sardines with vegetable soup. All this raised our morale for the next day's trip to Mount Sinai. That night, Arab Radio from Damascus reported an amphibious attack on Abu Rudeis, destroying the Israeli forces there and killing a busload of tourist Jews. That could have been our bus. Since, luckily their radio propaganda is bigger than their military capacity, I slept all night without a scratch.

At 5 a.m., we are on an open-air bus, going south along the Suez to another ghost town, once a thriving port of embarkation for Moslems going to Mecca. The early morning sun in a cloudless sky brightened to a sparkle in the waters of the Suez and flooded the foothills with golden shadows. Turning eastward into the open country, we followed dirt wheel tracks in the sand of a Wadi (like a valley or a wash) that narrows as we go further into the Mountains. It is striking to see, now and then, a few Bedouins appeared from nowhere in this absolutely barren Mountain wilderness with only rocks, an occasional thorn tree, and overwhelming heat, two boys racing their camels, children who learn to beg persistently, a lone old man appearing from nowhere. The wall of the Wadi becomes steep cliffs, often with caves or rock fortresses used for centuries for warfare against caravans, travelers, invaders, or for hermit retreats.

This is part of a caravan route thousands of years old. Surely, it was part of the trail followed by the wandering

New York teacher

Oil town Abu Rudeis

Mountain road

Bedouin in the barren wilderness

Children beggars

tribes of Israel on their way to Mount Sinai. At the Valley of Inscriptions in the Wadi Sidri Nubian, we saw writing in stone caves three thousand years old.

3000 year old Wadi inscriptions

Suddenly all was green. Here at Feron Oasis, we have lunch in a garden of Eden with water, palm trees, fruit trees, vegetable gardens and vineyards. But Eden's bathroom was a shock. It is so filthy the daughter of one of the passengers fainted on sight.

Lunch at all green Feron oasis

Beyond a large palm tree forest of which each specific tree was owned by a family, we stopped for a drink of dirty pop at an Arab outpost. It is here that I tasted the tamarind from a tree with long lacy pine-like needles, whose jelly-like sap is now conceded to be Moses' "manna."

Eden's bathroom

Though bitter, in August and September the sap falls to the ground and can be made into sweetbread.

Tamarisk

God's Fortress — The Wrong Mountain

Moses' manna

We returned to the desert and a new Wadi, skirting ranges of cliffs and hills. In my expectant imagination, I thought that I had seen the Mountain of Moses several times. Beyond a mosque standing alone on a wide plain, we head south into a smaller rock valley guarded by some unoccupied stone huts. Suddenly a huge monastery with walls fifty feet high loomed in front of us. A shaded garden with a running stream softened the environment's hardnes.*2

Mountain of Moses

This fortress was to be my lodging for the night. Built to resist marauders, it originally had no entrance except by a rope and pulley. Even today it has at ground level only a small passageway through the mass of stone. For fourteen centuries, orthodox monks (often those out of favor with the Emperor) operated this monastery, preserving its art treasures and maintaining its precious library, including a scroll of protection with a signature "X" by Muhammad himself and a document

Monastery

Rope pulley entrance

Art treasures

Mohammed "X" and Napoleon Signatures

of protection by Napoleon Bonaparte. The monastery survives Crusader occupancy and Moslem siege destruction, thanks to the mosque of Islam built inside its walls and the persistent folklore that Muhammad took refuge here during his "Flight" to Heaven. Is it teetering on extinction now? I saw only two or three young monastics and one or two older ones. Someone told me that petty criminals or recalcitrant religious are given a choice of duty here or physical punishment. Allegedly, they usually chose the latter.

Tiny cells

The tiny cells where monks lived their entire lives were unforgettable. A few are still occupied. In times past, monastics sealed themselves with stone and mortar into an eight-foot by ten-foot prison without light or any furnishings, received their food through a small slot, and passed out their excrement through the same slot. The only way anyone knew of their death was when they stopped taking food for a sufficiently long period.

Skeletons in chains

In penance for murdering their uncle, two brothers chained themselves together in such a cell; after their deaths, they were buried, then dug up, and their skeletons are still visible in their chains. An extreme way to serve God! At least their fellow celibates who retreat to caves on the hillsides are with nature in their life of self-sacrifice.

Yet we cannot condemn these men. They live their beliefs and hurt no one else by such extreme asceticism. Such loneliness, one-sided devotion, masochism, and apparent "withdrawal" from the human race are not unknown in present times even.

Monk asceticism

Each monk here is assured of at least one kind of immortality. Three years after burial, his skeleton is exhumed, his bones are washed in wine, his spirit consecrated at a special service, and his skull stored in a separate chapel. I obtained permission to visit this locked holy storehouse. It was an eerie

Burial procedure

Thousand years of skulls

St. Stephen's skeleton

Locked in for sleep with very old linens

3 a.m. camel drivers begin trek

Light of pre-dawn

sight in the afternoon light to see the huge crib piled high with over a thousand years of skulls. The dusky smell of death and all those empty eyes watching for the last day, the Judgment Day, is a striking experience. Saint Stephen's complete skeleton, in full dress, stands guard in silence; somehow, he demands that I leave quickly..

Though the Monastery is very interesting, I felt the pressure of too many people. I preferred to spend the night alone on Mount Sinai. But it was after sundown; the only entrance and exit were locked. The abbot in charge pretended he didn't know what I wanted when I asked to leave. So, I went to sleep in a monastery fourteen hundred years old, in a dormitory nine hundred years old, and in a sway-backed bed two hundred years old with sheets at least a hundred years old.

Movement in the courtyard woke me at about three in the morning. The camel drivers were preparing to take visitors to the "Moses" Mountain they call Jebel Musa.[*3] Since the door was now unlocked, I escaped. I walked gingerly by the grunting camels. It was dark. I felt the trail with my feet. The black Mountains silhouette against a dark sky, moonless, almost starless. Unsure about my direction, I stumbled over boulders every time I strayed off the path. Progress was slow. In fact, I was too far east, just as my Swiss friend advised me not to on my climb up Mount Athos. On the shoulder of Sinai, beyond the hill where Aaron, according to history, speaks to the seventy elders, the light of predawn appeared. Lines of charcoal-gray mountains were touched at their crest with gold; the new sun left silent black shades in the valleys.

Racing the last 734 stone steps, I watched the sun flash a light over the world below me from the peak. I wanted to bathe in the beauty of new light. I wanted to pray as Moses did. There is a small chapel to Christ directly over the cave where Moses once prayed. There is a mosque of Muhammad higher up`. Christ's house though is not open. I entered the open mosque, kneeled on an oriental rug left there for believers, and faced Mecca; the sun shone on my face through a slit window: "ALLAH, BE PRAISED!"

"ALLAH"

View from Sinai

By nine-thirty that morning, I was out of water. Moseying around the summit, I watched the camels miles below moving up like toys in a long line, casting shadows on the trail switchbacks. The sun bathed the Mountains and valleys below me. About thirty yards from the mosque was a well with a pitcher and rope. I drank my fill and filled my canteen with water. Then I felt something gnawing at my stomach. The rising sun and the Mountain were inspiring, but there was another force, a pull from somewhere else, a dissatisfaction. I was not with Moses. Moses saw this Mountain but, I'm sure instinctively, this was not where he heard the voice of God. It must have been elsewhere.

To the west was St. Catherine's Monastery

Some force turned me toward the west! There, across a deep valley in another range was Mount St. Catherine, named in honor of a Christian martyr and queen, as is St. Catherine's Monastery below. This range is obviously higher than Sinai. Allegedly on this Mountain, St. Catherine's bones were found. She miraculously survived the torture Coliseum and the wheel in Rome. But her head and body were not cut into pieces by order of the Roman Emperor. Her bones are still preserved as holy relics in the central church at the nearby monastery They are displayed on holy days. St. Catherine's peak showed far off, challenging, beckoning.

Time was short, but I had to follow an instinct. I had to climb this "Jebel Catrina," on a mountain across a valley far below me.

I scale down the steep rocks and terrain on the west side of Jebel Musa. In two hours, I was in the valley and crossed the white stone camel caravan route which traverses from the east to Egypt and Africa over five thousand years ago.

Camel Greeting

Suddenly around a turn I came upon two camels alone. They passed, casting haughty looks at me, a stranger, ill-equipped with neither hump nor enough patience to survive in their country. A few minutes later, I was surprised by an Arab on the trail. Not knowing what to do, I smiled and put out my hand. He shook it and we went our separate ways.

A few fruit trees and the smell of water

Between these two Mountain ranges is a small oasis, an incongruous green patch in the barrenness. In the oasis is a rock house, a few fruit trees, and the smell of water. In the morning sun, it is cool, comforting, restful. It attracted my innermost being. It is a Shangri-La, a perfect place to live, to be happy, to be at one with the world and myself on a small human scale. It is a place of peace, in isolation, yet close to history, with clean air, a garden for one's own needs, room for a few intimate friends, and the high Mountain desert at the doorstep. Though hot at midday, it is a dry heat, and the mornings and evenings are cool.

But such thoughts are only dreams. In real life, I was out of water again but afraid to drink from the trickling stream; it was green and stagnant. An Arab appeared over a rock fence. He didn't seem friendly. I walked quickly by without asking for water. We smiled in passing. Soon, the climb began on a good pathway up the Mountain.

No drinkable water

The trail was steep, with no vegetation. About two hundred yards down a ravine is a lone green tree, undoubtedly the site of an underground spring. Did Moses find his water there for the forty days and nights he spent on this Mountain or for his parched followers? Twice, I sprawled out for a rest on the trail in the shade of a rock. Creeping exhaustion, thirst, and hunger were making this detour dangerous, especially since I was alone. Yet I felt I had to climb this peak. The cliffs, the

Walkable trail

trail, the caves, even a soaring vulture seemed to say, "This is the way. This is the hallowed high ground, Mount Horeb, that Moses, Aaron, Joshua, and Elijah walked."

Mount Horeb

On the lower reaches, a long way above me, a few black dots moved across the Mountain. Two white dots started racing over the boulders toward the trail higher up to cut me off. I picked up a rock and took out my mace to prepare to defend myself. There is no other trail to follow. As I climbed up closer, the black dots turned out to be goats and the white ones, small boys, my son Alan's age. They abandon their goats to greet me. One of the boys had a wooden shepherd's flute. He played it. The sound echoed from the rocks and valleys. It was haunting and lonesome, yet in perfect tune with the empty landscape as it met the sky. The other boy, more fearful, hid behind a ledge with two large rocks in both hands.

Goats and boys

Finally, I went up to them and sat down. We talked without understanding and smiled at each other. I showed them my camera and sang them a song, "God bless America;" they broke into laughter. I think we are friends and feel they like me.

"God Bless America" friends

Then they started begging, screaming, and holding out their hands. The begging occupation, to my surprise, permeated even the young people far from the tourist routes and main oases. Begging, an end product of tourism (and with the same object, money), spreads its debilitating hopelessness like a drug culture. Angry, I gave nothing, stood up, and started climbing as fast as I could. They had to run on their short legs and bare feet to keep up; but they followed, always demanding money. Though they were breathing hard, I was panting. I shook my head, "No! Go watch your goats!" Finally, I was exasperated. I turned around and yelled at them, "Get the hell out of here! Beat it!" They retreated a few yards behind me, followed at a distance for a while, and then gave up. Their pleading dark brown eyes still affect me. Now that it's too

Bedouin friends become innocent beggars

late, I realize my anger stemmed from disappointment, rejection, and egotism. What I imagined to be two young Bedouin friends are really only two innocent young boys putting touch on a stranger the only way they knew.

Of course, these sons of the desert people will survive. They always escaped from invaders, friends, enemies, tourists, and even civilizations. It is really their country, though someone else seems to be their conqueror. When the Egyptians control the area, the Bedouins work for them, for pay, of course — building roads, carrying supplies, furnishing information as to Israeli army movements, and spying against their benefactors for the Israelis. Now, they do the same, only for and against the Israelis. For centuries, occupying nations have tried to resettle them, nowadays providing education and medical care. The Israelis, in their thoroughness partially succeed with Bedouins from the Negev desert further to the north. But the only people who really live in, own, and love this beautiful, harsh land are the Bedouins. I suspect they will still be there when the next invaders come and go. For their sakes, I hope so... unless the begging is too successful and the affluence weakens them.

St. Catherine's peak

Here I talk to my God

Exhausted, dehydrated, and soaked in sweat, I finally staggered to the top of St. Catherine's Peak and collapsed on a rock wall outside the locked stone chapel. The view easily overshadowed my discomfort. Here, even I could talk to God. The whole world was here; to the west, the Suez Canal; to the east, the Gulf of Aqaba; the alleged Mount Sinai, miles away, looked like the lawgiver himself with a flowing square beard and skull cap. The bright sunshine and shimmering heat waves distorted the rows of desolate rock Mountain ranges into a fantasy, a collage of color, undulating into indistinct motion on the horizon. Each range reflects its distinct colors from granites, limestones, lavas, blacks, whites, and reds, fading into grays, purples, and blues until the vast Sinai wilderness below merges with the sky.

Breakfast With Moses

Moses' Mountain

There was no doubt in my mind. This was Moses' Mountain. Not Jebel Musa, as claimed by the monastery. At first, this was only a hunch, intuition, but when I reached the top of Mount Saint Catherine, I knew it. Years of study of Mountains and religions intellectually confirmed my hypothesis. The founders of the Monastery of St. Catherine were undoubtedly devotees of Christ. They are pioneers and scholars, but they weren't Mountain men. Otherwise, they wouldn't have mistaken where and how Moses talked to God.

Christians, St. Catherine's Monastery

Whether or not Moses is a Jew or a former follower of Egypt's Ikhnaton, Moses is, at the very least an important historical leader.

Moses as leader

If Moses did exist as a person, if he led the Jews from Egypt into the Sinai wilderness; if the tribes were anywhere near this part of the Sinai Desert (where there are oases and main camel routes); if Moses retired to the wilderness to meditate alone, away from the others; if he climbed a Mountain for this purpose — then this is the Mountain!

Gold tablets

Stone tablets

My studies of Moses, the Old Testament, commentary on his life, and the lives of religious leaders in Mountain areas all support this historical hypothesis. A great man is attracted to the highest place, literally and figuratively. God's presence would not be on the lower of two almost adjoining Mountains, assuming they are both accessible to man. If God is close at seven thousand five hundred feet on Mount Sinai, God is closer at eight thousand seven hundred feet on St. Catherine's Peak.

By now, hunger and thirst triumphed over speculation.

My last meal had been a very small dinner the night before of bread, soup and a few beans. I ran out of water several hours earlier. Here in this desert wilderness, I was seriously thirsty, at least two hours from water and six hours from safe water. Furthermore, I was tired, especially my knees. That wasn't surprising since I started hiking at three o'clock that morning. As usual, I was late in starting my return — this time to catch a ride from the monastery back to Abu Rudeis on the Suez.

Pushing myself back up on my aching legs, I walked up the south shoulder.

In about forty minutes, I walked into a field of barbed wire strung in layers to prevent enemy infiltration. Although no one was in sight, a small flag with the gold star of David whipping in the wind proclaimed this an Israeli army unit. There were two high radio antennae, some scattered small Quonset huts and fortifications. At the lower end was an opening in the wire and a pathway through. With the brazenness born of necessity, I walked right through the wire and gate. I shouted "California! Water!" and held up my canteen. "California" in Israel and Greece (and later in all countries I visit) is a word everyone seems to know and like. You get the feeling the whole world desperately wants to become another California.

Soldier sleeping in sentry shack suddenly wakes up!

Probably because of the wind and the generator's motor noise, no one answered. There is a sentry shack about fifty yards beyond and above the infiltration wire. Inside the guard's house, an Israeli soldier slept on his bunk. When I knocked on the wall, he jumped up, grabbing his automatic weapon. He was going to fire on me before he was sufficiently awake to realize I was not an Egyptian commando. Egyptian units and Arab guerrillas probe these areas for intelligence and interdiction.

Soldier is surprised. I am scared

The soldier was surprised. I was scared. He saw before him a strange bearded figure in dirty army-green shorts and yellow shirt, with a telephoto camera around his neck and a canteen in his hand upside down. Maybe my shouts of "California" and "Water" helped. He didn't fire but trained his weapon on my chest, making it clear I was not to move. Keeping an eye on me, he rang his field telephone, and a long conversation ensued. He seemed defensive, trying to say the same words over but obviously being cut off. He finally finished and ordered me, with his gun, to sit down.

Sentry rang his field phone and ordered me to sit down.

About five minutes later, two more soldiers came from the buildings higher up the slope. One spoke a little English. When I told him I needed water, he took my canteen and disappeared up the hill, leaving the other to guard me. Enough time passed to make me wonder if he will return.

Two soldiers joined us and took my canteen to get water

When he did come back, he ordered me to follow him. A little nervous, I explained I was late and that I would be on my way if he would give me my canteen. He made it clear that it was not my choice. At the buildings higher up, the number of men standing around surprised me. There were at least fifteen soldiers and no officers. A strong, good-looking man, about forty years old, in shorts and no shirt, came out of one of the huts. The soldiers stood around while he talked to me in English. He was obviously well-educated and asked many questions. He was interrogating me. Where did I come from? How did I get here? What was the name of the Abbot at St. Catherine's? Was I in the army? He was dubious when I said I had hiked from the monastery over Jebel Musa. He didn't believe that I came up this Mountain just for a hike.

I was ordered to follow Israeli soldier

Buildings higher up

40 year old well educated Israeli cross examined me

Slowly, everyone, including me, became more at ease. My questioner became friendlier, and the soldiers talked and laughed at jokes I couldn't understand. They brought me another canteen full of cold water. After I drank most of it in one long swig, they filled it up again. My questioner turned out to be the unit

We became more at ease
Bring me canteen full of water

Israeli Unit commander offered me breakfast.

I ate everything offered – delicious

I refuse officers offer to drive me back

They radio my ride to pick me up in another area.

I agree to call his mother-in-law when I return to NYC

We shake hands

Moses must have walked here

commander. He asked if I had breakfast or lunch. When I told him no, he offered me anything he had. I weakly declined.

He didn't accept my refusal and took me by the arm into a small mess hut higher up the slope. His men took his orders to give me whatever I wanted literally and with good humor. They brought out hot cocoa, two oranges, milk, cereal, three hard-boiled eggs, butter, toast, jam, and sardines. I ate everything. The decor was rugged and dirty, but the meal was delicious. Everyone was friendly. Afterward, I chatted with the officer and visited his hut, a small room about five feet by fourteen feet, with a chair, field desk, cot, and field telephone. He was a reserve captain of a Signal Unit, a university graduate, and a tour guide in civilian life.

He offered to guide me back to St. Catherine's monastery, but I told him it was unnecessary. His men radioed my bus driver where to pick me up at the mouth of another valley to the north. That made the trip down faster and easier for me. It eliminated a whole valley and Mountain range from my return hike.

He did not accept my offer to do something for him, except for one request. Would I call his mother-in-law and tell her that he is all right and convey his love? He wrote down her name and address. When I saw it, we both laughed at the improbability of all this — two reserve officers in the American and Israeli armies meeting in the middle of the Sinai Desert on a Mountain; and where does his mother-in-law and my mother live? New York City, New York, U.S.A., where my mother also was at the time.

We shook hands. It felt as if I were leaving a long-time friend. Soon, I am on the same trail once the crossroads of civilization (Babylon, Palestine, and Egypt), in the same footsteps that Moses must have walked thousands of years ago coming

Moses

Elijah

Jesus

Joshua

Muhammad

I enjoyed my "Breakfast with Moses"

down this Mountain.*⁴ I imagine Moses still keeps an eye on "his" Mountain from his consciousness in the next world. He is probably smiling, even chuckling, that day at the scene. He must be proud of his progeny — swift destroyers of the Egyptian enemy but so kind to a stranger, especially here.

Full of spirit, water and food, I truly enjoyed my "Breakfast with Moses."

Footnotes:
1. A weak excuse just to enjoy the company of a woman, since I dislike beer.

Built by Justinian

2. It was first built by the Emperor to protect monks already living there and was dedicated by a stone tablet: "Built by Justinian, the lowly king of the Romans, dependent on God and hoping in the promise of his Lord in eternal remembrance of himself and his consort Theodora, completed in the 30th year of his reign, the year 6021 since Adam and 521 since Christ."
3. The Arab name for Mount Sinai, literally "God-trodden mount."

Limit on food and water for migration

Golden Calf

4. There isn't enough food and water anywhere in the Sinai to support 600,000 migrating people in one place which is one estimate of the number of Jews with Moses. Perhaps excess numbers was an unconscious reason for Moses directing the murder of all the Jews who worshiped the Golden Calf while he was away talking to God on Sinai. In any event, the number 600,000 is too high, considering other references to Moses ordering only 3,000 killed.

Sacred Mount
Arunachala
(Red Mountain)

People View-Point

No matter the rare beauty of nature
We the living do not respect our talk
   about a dead corpse
Root out the eagle of those
Who meditate with the heart
On you my sacred Mount Arunachala
. . . and Guru Bhagavan.

   . . . Anon

Arunachala

Location:	Tiruvannamalai, Tamil Nadu, India
Range:	Eastern Ghats
Elevation:	2,671 ft (814 m)
Prominence:	N/A (it is a hill)
Coordinates:	12°14'28"N
	79°03'26"N
Spirit:	Hindu
Pilgrimage:	*Who Am I*

Angel View-Point

Who Am I?

(Hinduism) — South India
Tiruvannamalai, Annamalaiyar Temple Ashram

Esoterica: Myths, Mysteries and Imaginables

Hindu myth reports that Parvati, consort of the God Shiva, once in a moment of Godly mischief in a flower garden at their home atop Mount Kailash, gently closed her sleeping husband's eyelids, throwing the whole world into darkness. If God's light is lost even for a moment, all light is taken from the universe and the earth submerges into darkness for years. Parvati tries to give shy and humble penitence to the other devotees of Shiva. Shiva then appears as a large column of fire on the summit of Arunachala, returning light to the world. Shiva then emerges with Parvati to form a different half-female/half-male form of Shiva.

Arunachala, or 'Red Mountain,' lies behind the temple. The hill is sacred and considered an iconic representation of Shiva.

Other myths relate that Shiva, in a contest with Brahma, another Hindu God, appears as a flame and challenges Brahma to find his source. Brahma becomes a swan and flies to the sky to see the top of the flame, while Vishnu, another god, becomes a boar Varaha. This scene is called the Lingodbhava (an iconic representation of the Hindu god Shiva), and the picture is on the western wall in the sanctum of most of Shiva's temples. Neither Brahma nor Vishnu could find the source. Vishnu considers this a defeat. Brahma lies and says he has found the pinnacle. In punishment, Shiva ordains that Brahma will never have temples on earth for his worship.

In the Tamil language, the word "arunam" means fire or red and "aslam" means hill. Since Shiva manifested himself in the form of fire in this place, Arunachala has come to be associated with the hills and the city. The history of this town revolves around the temple beginning in the 9th century. In both Hindu and Muslim history, the stewardship of Shiva's temple is included.

Feeling India Through a Hard Seat

Mountain of Light

Airport to Downtown Madras

Met English girl who looks like a "buttercup in the middle of an umber field."

Ashrams

Mount Arunachala, the Mountain of Light, lures me to India. I fly from Bombay across the Deccan Plateau and the Eastern Ghats to Madras. I take a bus from the airport to downtown Madras. Every bus ride in India can be a traumatic experience. Anything can happen. On this particular ride there was a most attractive English girl about twenty-five years old, dressed in a beautiful yellow dress that made her look like a buttercup in the middle of an amber field. She was an experienced traveler in India, much less perturbed by the hubbub, dirt and crowds than I was. She was interested in Ashrams, not Mountains, and she, in a moment of euphoria, the kind travelers always feel when they meet another traveler who apparently speaks the same language, asks me to go with her. Ashrams, a peculiarly Indian phenomenon, are communities of people seeking a higher plane of contemplative spiritual experience than the one in which they live. They are usually organized around a particularly spiritual person with a gift for the esoteric. Strangers and foreigners are often welcome and sometimes never leave.

Travel by bus, not private car

I would enjoy joining her, but I must stick to my own search. She provided advice that I followed: "Travel by bus, not private car in India. The bus will give you the feel of psychic India."

I got off the bus at the best hotel in Madras, a relic of old British colonialism. The hotel was overflowing with white-turbaned, barefooted staff. The hotel operated its own travel agency that pretended to know all there was to know about South India. Yet no one in the hotel could produce a bus ticket to Mount Arunachala. All anyone could do was hustle me into a taxi with such vague directions that neither the driver nor I could understand where we were to go. This fact became obvious when the taxi driver left me with my heavy pack at a bus terminal that had no relationship whatsoever with my destination.

No bus ticket to Mount Arunachala

In a short time, I was surrounded by dozens of people who begged or gawked, believing that this foreign traveller in full hiking gear, ten-pound boots, army green shorts, canteen, old yellow shirt and a fancy Nikon camera was fair game for anyone over the age of three. To cover my bewilderment, I asked many people where I should go. After receiving conflicting directions from many people, it became quite clear that I was at the wrong terminal: I couldn't get to Mount Arunachala from there.

Conflicting directions

I finally learned from a ticket agent that if I went to the government terminal I might get a bus that would at least take me in the "direction" I wanted to go. A woman behind me in the line told me how to get there. I should go a few blocks to the government terminal and find a bus to a place called Singarapettai. I was relieved that I would not have to spend the night on the streets of Madras.

Government terminal with buses to Singarapettai

Getting aboard a bus in India, a singular feat in itself, does not settle the matter. I learned I must have a ticket. I also needed the conductor to approve that there was space for me, pack and all, on his bus. Finally, I must be assigned a seat. I found the conductor, and he assigned me seat number 49. It was a tight squeeze to get my bulky pack past everyone to the rear of the bus. But the last seat on the bus was number 43. And so, with the cunning of the desperate, I grabbed the rear corner seat, piled everything on top of me and settled myself like an over-sized egg under a mother hen.

Need ticket and conductor's approval

Thirty bus stops and five towns later, we arrived at Singarapettai. A friendly, well-dressed young man, probably a student, with an English accent, helped me pay the fare as we traveled. He also told me when to get off and pointed the way to another terminal where I was to take another bus. He shouted, "Good luck!" as the bus pulled out. I felt lonely.

That didn't last long. I was soon surrounded by about two hundred people, including the local police chief. But they were friendly, and soon, my loneliness went away. They enjoyed the pictures I took of them. They even enjoyed the speech I made thanking them, even though they couldn't understand a single word except the word "California." But though they couldn't understand, the thought got through to them where I wanted to go, and they escorted me, Mardi Gras style, with smiles and laughter and gay gestures, to the bus I was supposed to take.

No traveler is eligible for initiation into the rites of a journey into India until he or she takes an open-air bus.

My bus to Mount Arunachala was an open-air bus. It stopped at every crossroad, every village, and whatever came in between. I think it stopped so that the dust that was everywhere had a chance to settle. The hard benches were only softened by the passengers' bodies pushing against each other by the jolts of the road. We were all in suspension on our fellow passengers' hips in an arch of bottoms. For 137 miles, I breathed dust, fell on people, and smelled smells I never wish to smell again on our ride to "feel" India.

India is a natural home for the manic, the schizophrenic, dogs, rats, dirt, animals, filth, and the unreal. Disease and poverty smother and ooze into the lives and bodies of the masses so that they are callous to others and either desperately aggressive or catatonically passive on the knife-edge of survival. The unreal world of dreams, Atman, and the spirit are reality.

---

30 bus stops and five towns later switch and pay fare

Local Indians couldn't understand me but escorted me to bus needed

Open air bus in India an initiation, hard seats, ubiquitous dust

India natural home for the manic

Atman and Spirit are real

Our bus stopped at several villages. I often got out to stretch. If I appeared at all receptive or made any motion towards my wallet, the beggar pros from five to seventy, limbs rotting from leprosy, running sores and piercing eyes crowd me, touching, polluting, demanding. In India when hate and fear purge me of all compassion, someone offers me love — a small boy some nuts, a holy man his peace, a complete stranger his home. No wonder the new religions and my own spiritual insight blossom in India. From despondency and physical hell is best seen in the freedom and bliss of spiritual peace. From the darkness, the light. From India, God.

From darkness, light. From India, God

You do sense all of this on an open-air bus. By the time I arrived outside my destination, the town of Tirunvannamalai, I was happy to be there alive and well. I felt the beggar's stare, the children's poverty, the mystic's spiritual peace. And so, when I put my dirty, bearded self, with my hiking gear, off the bus in the twilight of July 22, I was ready for whatever India has to offer. I put on my pack to walk through the town. Urchins swarmed around me shouting "Coolie . . . you coolie boy!"

I walk through town wearing large pack

"Coolie boy"

The very first thing one must get ready for is the inevitable contrast. Amid dirt, dust, smells, weariness, and poverty, over the crowds, the shops, the cars and trucks, the noise, even over the spires of an imposing temple is the Sacred Mountain, Arunachala; a vast pyramid, solitary on this plain, fading into a charcoal silhouette against black skies with streaks from the fire of sunset. No wonder the Hindu Gods frequent this Sacred Mountain.

Arunachala charcoal silhouette against black skies streaked with sunset

Home is an Ashram

Tirunvannamalai

Sacred Mountain

It was completely dark by the time I walked the two miles through and beyond the village of Tirunvannamalai to my destination, an Ashram at the west base of Arunachala Mountain. The soft light of something inside the Temple cast an almost green glow on three young men dressed in white who sat inside the stone entranceway to the Temple. I walked with a full pack to ask them a traveler's question — where do I stay? Without answering they hissed me away, pointing at my boots. I got the point and retreated into the darkness. Just as I had unlaced my boots, a short, white-haired old man with the brightest, kindest eyes I have yet seen greeted me warmly. He said he knew that I was coming and that he had a room for me. I felt his kindness and I'm sure he felt my appreciation.

Hissed away to remove my boots

Kindly old man takes me to barren room

Locks everywhere

He took me to a barren room with only a table, a bed, and a lethargic overhead electric fan. Locks were everywhere: two to get in; three to get out to the open pit toilet. He told me that the puja (the religious service) was almost over. I went with him to worship in candlelight and circle the inner sanctum's phallic symbol of Shiva, and hear the chant of the repetitious "songs from the breath of God" (Reg Vedas). I breathed the camphor smoke of the incense as it clouded the heads of the worshipers, their faces daubed red and white with ashes. As I wondered about the ceremony, the old man explained the details of much of the symbolism, the reasons for the rituals, and the contents of this and all Hindu Temples. The fascination with the ritual and the strangeness of the scene almost made me forget my hunger pains.

Candlelight inner sanctum with phallic symbol of Shiva

Swamis eat cross legged in rows

I imagine beautiful blond in white sari, silent, pale, withdrawn

Supper, South Indian style, brings my hunger to my attention. The eating place was filled with Swamis, clad in orange or white, temple workers, strangers, two Englishmen and me. We all sat cross-legged in rows. Suddenly like a vision of loveliness, a beautiful, pale, young woman with light blond hair appeared at our supper. Her dress was a white sari. She was silent, mysterious, and withdrawn. I never saw her again anywhere at the Ashram. I came to believe that I imagined her.

A serving boy walked by us with a bucket of rice. He dumped rice by hand onto a large banana leaf in front of each of us. The banana leaf rested on the floor. Another boy passed by us and ladled warm milk into our tin cups. He also ladles a predigested-looking goulash over our rice. With every bite, my teeth ground down on grits of dirt from the leaf. I disregarded my usual caution about native foods and ate with great hunger, grit and all. Without the use of a spoon or fork, with my elbows dripping and the floor a mess, I managed to get some of the slippery, wet, rich mush from the leaf to my mouth. Later I wished that I had not succeeded.

After supper, I washed the food from my face, my legs, and even my arms, went to bed, and immediately fell asleep. The day that began on an old bus from the Madras airport ends here in this serene Ashram on a hard bed. Here, time is unknown.

The next morning began with a breakfast of warm milk and rice cake wet with something other than milk. After breakfast, I wandered around the Ashram founded by Sri Ramana Maharishi (Bhagavan) to get my physical and spiritual bearings. The gardens were lovely, and the climate of the place was serene. In the two adjoining Temples puja services were held daily plus special services on special occasions. A gray granite samadhi with two elaborate towers, a memorial to Bhagavan's mother, is one, and a modern marble-floored rectangular edifice in memory of Bhagavan is the other. In the modern temple, a gold screen curtain separated the open hall from the polished black stone symbol of Shiva and a full-sized, electrically lighted photograph of the recently deceased founder of this Ashram.

The sales and administration offices of the Ashram are coldly and officiously operated inside the old temple. They are complete with telephone, clerks and files. In addition, there are a number of other buildings with rooms for devotees and

Serving boy dumps rice onto my banana leaf along with gritty goulash

Regretted ingesting slippery rice mush into my mouth

Breakfast of warm milk and rice cake

Ashram founded by Sri Ramana Maarishi

Memorial to Bhagavan and his mother

Full size black stone symbol of shiva

Sales and administrative offices cold and officious

staff, plus a five-bed hospital and a library. Everything is spotlessly clean, including the building set aside for the breeding and caring of the sacred cows.

A swami, the son of the President of the Ashram, showed me Bhagavan's room, the room in which Bhagavan spent his last year of life. This room was cluttered with mementos, books, pictures, pill bottles, canes, shawls, sandals, and all things associated with Bhagavan. To cap the tour, the swami, who seemed so anxious to please and impress me, took me outside to a place near a small bridge that leads up to Mount Arunachala. Here, true to the Hindu's deep compassion for all animals, Bhagavan's favorite dog, cow, and monkey were enshrined, preserved, and cherished.

In a short time, I prepared myself physically for the experience of the Sacred Mountain. I had my geographic bearings; I entered into the life of the Ashram. Spiritually, I was not ready for the search. And so, I began to put into place what I read and my experiences, including the things I found out about the Hindu Gods and their relationship to Mount Arunachala.

"Millennia ago, two of the Hindu Trinity fought over who is superior. Shiva, the Absolute God (destroyer of man's ego and imprisonment, sometimes called the "Mountain Lord"), appeared as a column of fire and challenged the other Gods to reach the ends of the column. One God flew as high as he could to reach the top while the other God bored into the earth to find the bottom. Both failed, but in failing, they found the truth in their trial. When the column of fire cools, it becomes Mount Arunachala."

"Long ago, Shiva's wife, Parvati, was banished to the plain below Mount Arunachala as punishment for her practical joke of closing Shiva's eyes, thus plunging the world into darkness. Shiva appears as a ball of fire, much as God appears to Moses at Sinai, to forgive Parvati. Where she watches his personification, the Temple of Arunachala, the "unapproachable Mountain," now stands. Thousands of gurus, ascetics, holy men and worshipers come to the Mountain to follow in the footsteps of their Gods."

A Hindu Freud

And who is Bhagavan? And what do I need to know about him to make my ascent of the Mountain more meaningful? These questions need answering before I am ready.

Bhagavan, when seventeen years of age, went to the Temple of Arunachala. The year is 1896. For three years, he sat in the temple making no sound, speaking to no one, eating only a few morsels brought to him. Boys and strangers scoffed at him and threw rocks at his body He moved to the basement to continue meditating silently, oblivious to the swarming mosquitoes and rats that chewed his flesh, permanently scarring his legs and his torso. For more than twenty years after that, he lived in complete silence in the caves of Arunachala. From such meditation and study Bhagavan developed his own truths.

His spiritual psychoanalysis combines the essence of Socrates and Buddha. It is grounded in Hinduism, which is much older than Christianity, Buddhism, or Islam. It is a religion so individual that each household can have its own God or Goddess in addition to the one God in triple form — Vishnu, Brahma, and Shiva. It is broad enough to encompass every religion at every stage of growth. It does not matter to Bhagavan what you call the object of your pilgrimage — nirvana, liberation, self-realization, heaven, peace, or immortality. To benefit from his existence and teachings, you need not accept the Hindu concepts of detachment, non-violence,

Shiva forgives Parvati

Thousands follow footsteps of Gods at Mountain

Who was Bhagavan?

17 years of age

Bhagavan made no sound

Bhagavan in a cave alone

Vishnu, Shiva, Brahma)

Multiple spiritual objects

time as a pool rather than a river, and Karma (rebirth depending on your prior life's behavior), but you will grow to accept Hindu ideas of unity with God, self-control, and charity. Nor is it necessary to abandon any other religion. Bhagavan often refers to "Hindu literature".

I need to refresh my own understanding of the Puranas, Bhagavad Gita, Upanishads and especially the fifteen thousand song stanzas of the Reg Veda. Bhagavan's most important addition to such literature is that "the person who embodies religious truths has no use for them." What is needed in my preparation for my search is "How important is this Mountain going to be to my own understanding of truth?"

Mount Arunachala is Bhagavan's teacher and guru. Could it be mine? He believes the ancient Purana scripture when it states:

"This is the holy place! Of all Arunachala is the most Sacred! It is the heart of the world! Know it to be the secret and sacred Heart center of Shiva! In that place He always abides as the glorious Arunachala.

What cannot be yours without endless pains — the absolute truth — is easily attained by all who can either directly sight this hill or even mentally think of it from afar."

Slowly the truth of Bhagavan seeped into my Spirit. He taught that Arunachala is the embodiment of God (Shiva), a mirror of the Self and thus truth. I once read this as information and now it seemed personal, the answer to my question, "What will I find when I climb Arunachala?" Certainly, this was an opportunity to find myself. This mountain mirror of Indian spiritualism is reflected, as well as my image, and I was on to a new plateau, a new dimension. Bhagavan taught that no special ritual, yoga, austerity, knowledge or withdrawal is necessary to the discovery of self, or Atman. Only freeing

Person who embodies religious truths has no use for them

Mount Arunachala was Bhagavan's guru. Could be mine?

Glorious Arunachala

Absolute truth from Arunachala

Truth of Bhagavan seeped into me

I will find myself on the Mountain

Mountain mirror

Own image Self or atman

yourself to see yourself is important. And out of such teaching I also came to realize that I have to meditate on one question, "Who am I?" Who am I who thinks these thoughts, who prepares himself for search? In such meditation, I am lifted out of the anxieties of the moment, raised above the hate, trials, disasters, and sickness of the world to new levels of self-meaning. The example of Bhagavan warms me greatly.

When about forty years old he broke his silence and came down from the caves of Arunachala in the place where his mother is buried, now the Ashram. His followers gather around him with questions of how to liberate themselves. They ask him: "Should we follow your path, renounce the world of work and home?

"No," he answers. "Perform your duties in life without self-interest. Whether in society or in the forest makes no difference; the mind is the difficulty — change it, not the environment. As the wise man's activities exist only in the eyes of others and not in his own, he really does nothing although he may be accomplishing immense tasks. Therefore, his activities do not stand in the way of peace of mind."

"What are the rules or conduct," ask the followers. "Moderation in food, moderation in sleep, moderation in speech."

"What will happen in the future and what happens after death?"

"Why do you want to know what will be in the future or when you die before you know what you are now? First, find out what you are now. Take care of the present and the future will take care of itself."

"What is God?"

"God, guru' and Self are not really different but the same."

"What is happiness and how can I be happy?" "Getting

Free yourself

Who am I meditation

Bhagavan broke his silence and came down from caves of Arunachala

Perform your duties without self-interest

Change your mind not your milieu

Don't stand in the way of peace of mind

Moderation

First find out what you are now

Same guru and self

rid of non-existent misery and attaining the bliss that is always in you. Everyone has supreme love for oneself; as happiness alone is the cause for love, to gain happiness, which is your nature and which is experienced in the state of deep sleep where there is no mind, one should know oneself. For that, the inquiry 'Who am I?' is the principal means of the path of knowledge."

Getting rid of non-existence

"Who am I?"

"I am not the senses, the organs, the functions, the mind, the unknown. I am awareness; existence consciousness-bliss."

Who am I? spiritual duty to find mysteries of Mount Arunachala

In light of this study, in the clarity of this review of what Bhagavan believes in and where his thoughts come from, I accepted his Hinduism. I was ready to practice the essence of his truth. And being ready I was in tune with my spiritual desires to find the mysteries of the Sacred Mountain.

Circling God Shiva

And now, I slipped away from the Ashram itself and began my pilgrimage around Hindu God Shiva's home, Sacred Mount Arunachala. It was consistent with Hindu tradition to circle the object of worship clockwise. In the first mile of my journey, I rammed a thorn a half inch into my big toe. It was so painful that I limped the rest of the way. I took slim consolation, however, in the fact that my painful walk was still easier than rolling on the ground for the full eight miles of the pilgrimage, the traditional method used by the "holy roller" pilgrims. Along the way, I passed many rundown Hindu shrines usually with stone statuary of animals, sometimes with a swami. At various points on my circle of Arunachala, I rested and gazed anew at the steep granite Mountain, which constantly changes shape with the

Hindu tradition to circle object clockwise

Jam thorn full inch into my big toe

Pass rundown Hindu Shrines occupied by animal statuary and sometimes by swamis

Arunachala steep granite that changes shape in changing light

Bhagavan's semi-annual pilgrimage around Arunachala

Holy Bowl

Arunachala image an elephant with a peaked cap

Temple, farmers, kindness to holy man. I will never forget him.

Main road with 6 pagodas over 11 stories high

changing light. On this hot, gray day the Mountain was an entity of reddish rock ledges, massive boulders, splotches of green from bushes and grasses, with the great peak dominating the two shoulder peaks and the ridges spread out to the flat plain below it.

The past and the present flooded in as I walked. Bhagavan made this same pilgrimage around the Mountain at least twice a year. But he discontinued it when it became Tiruvannamalai's semi-annual charade. Hawkers sell food and religious trinkets to pilgrims and holy men. With an advertising agency and TV coverage, I had the feeling that this could become India's Holy Bowl game of the year.

I rested on a small bridge halfway around the Mountain. From here, Arunachala looks like an elephant's head with a peaked cap. The long trunk points to the small village behind me.

Two hundred yards away a family was working their tiny field with their wooden plow. I saw a small boy who had left his family and came running to me. He was frightened by my strangeness and was shy himself. But he continued to approach me with his hands closed together. He held out his hands. He opened them. There were a few nuts in his hands. He offered them to me. He was willing to share the little that his family had with me. I hoped that he could see, beyond my beard and my foreignness, a holy man with whom he wished to share his worldly goods. I will never forget his kindness.

Finally, I was back on the main road which led to the outer gate of the Temple of Arunachala in the town of Tiruvannamalai, about two miles from the Ashram. This gate is one of six pagodas that stand over 217 feet and eleven stories in height. On each square foot of the gate is an intricate stone sculpture of everything that is or is believed, including thousands of animals, people, plants, symbols, and Gods. I worked my way to the entrance wondering if I could go inside. All the people around the gate — loafers, kids, holy men, stall operators, beggars — suddenly were aroused and raised a furor. Apparently, I could enter the gate only if I removed both my slippers and socks. A magnetic force mixed with curiosity overcame my concern about cutting my feet or about picking up some disease through open blisters. I stripped my feet bare and entered the Temple.

Allowed to enter but required to remove shoes

Being a part of this temple was a spiritual pilgrimage for me. It was a place (walled from the outside world) set apart, a place of spirit. I felt impermanent, insignificant, and tired in the face of such a timeless colossus of towers, lakes, staircases, shrines, statuary, walls, and courtyards. The infinite meanings, symbols, statues, and mosaics of man, of cows, of Gods, plus a live elephant, all need a lifetime of study to understand. A serenity comes from the beauty of this quiet place. A mystery comes out of the dim half-lights and darkness inside the great caverns of the central temple. When I entered into three rooms, each smaller than the last, at the womb of this great Temple, I found intimate acceptance and peace. The five-foot by ten-foot inner core was lit only by flickering candles and the spiritual light of the chanted puja in a thick smoke of incense. Even as I returned to the outer gate, I was renewed, enlightened, and made ready for the climb.

Temple my religious Pilgrimage

Beauty

Mystery of dark corners of temple . . . intimate acceptance, peace

Renewed, enlightened, ready for the climb

Up the Down Mountain

At three the next morning, I began the climb from the Ashram. I wished to avoid the oppressive heat and the crowds. In mid-July in South India the heat and humidity are extreme. The early hour also assured me of privacy; no one would be awake in the Ashram, and no one would give me

Begin climb early (3AM Monday)

advice I didn't need. I would not have to answer questions about where I was going. I wore boots. I had to profane the Mountain since my sore toe compelled me to wear boots. I knew, no matter how I felt bare feet and slippers were no match for Indian thorns and rocks.

Sore toe requires boots

At three o'clock, it was dark, except for the stars. I skirted beyond and around the Ashram compound and struck out across the flat plain, unable to see my footing but ready for the wild dogs or beasts with a can of mace in my belt. Arunachala in the night looms black and huge about half a mile ahead.

Carried mace for wild dogs

Once onto the Mountain, I stumbled across a main trail. Soon I came to a small temple with locks overlooking the town of Tirunvannamalai. There is a spring from which I filled my polyethylene bag. I now made my own trail straight up the Mountain. I scrambled in fast spurts over rocks, up small cliffs, through brushy areas full of thorns and poison oak. A steady step-by-step ascent was impossible. My extra supply of water made my pack much heavier. The water bag continued to shift, throwing me off balance. Fear of poisonous vipers that may strike in the dark made me extra careful. I often couldn't see my feet in the high grasses, even with my flashlight. Just as a gray, gold dawn begins to lighten the sky, a strange hooting noise (like that produced by blowing breath over the lip of a bottle) preceded me up the Mountain. I was further unnerved by a sudden loud sharp crackling croak of another animal. Something or somebody unknown was tracking me. My mind imagined a jaguar, a saddhu (strange holy man), a blow snake, a lizard. What was worse was that the sounds were directly above me. I had to climb towards these frightening sounds. I never found out who or what makes the sounds.

Found main trail and came to locked temple and spring

Dangerous

Something or somebody tracking me

ALAN NICHOLS

Pack, heat, sounds, my scramble wore me down

"*Shiva, you bastard!*"

"*Thanks Shiva*"

I summited, threw off pack

Didn't notice threatening weather, rain streaks, thunderhead

Misery distracted by brilliant sunset

Shiva's column of fire, forgiveness of Parvati, Hindu priests ritual

The sounds, the heat, the heavy pack and my scrambling action forever upward wore me down after only a few hours. My head ached. I felt weak. Frustration set in. As I mounted one rise, another loomed in front of me, hiding the top. My leg was bleeding from the worst fall so far on my trip. In rage but filled with hope that a verbal complaint might help, I yell: "Shiva, you Bastard! Why do you do this to me? Why are you so mean?" I haven't talked to God like that for a long time. And, strangely, after much cursing, the irritating, strong, hot wind stops. In awe, I said: "Thanks, Shiva," and I meant it.

I reached the summit of Arunachala. I slammed myself to the ground and took off my pack. I hardly noticed the blue Mountain ranges to the west or the panorama of green, brown and yellow farm squares and the temples and villages dwarfed by distance all stretched before me. Even the threatening weather seemed unimportant. Although the sky overhead was azure, lined with white cloud strata, to the southwest, a gathering storm of violent black thunderheads was firing grey rain-streaked lightning threads to the earth. I lay on Arunachala uninspired, trying only to avoid the sun. I cooked my "Mount Athos goulash" of tomato bouillon powder, dried peas, and carrots on my Mountain stove, but I couldn't eat it. All I wanted was water mixed with lemonade crystals. My misery was complete, even though the sunset was bursting in brilliant scarlet and orange through bright indigo gaps in dark clouds.

Here I was on the blackened rock that is a part of Hindu history Here I was on Shiva's column of fire. Here I was, where Shiva appears to forgive Parvati. Here generations of Hindu priests memorialize each year the event with their own ball of fire of camphor and butterfat oil. And I was too tired, too dulled to think through the significance of my act. Could my sickness and my fatigue be confirmation of the ancient

Hindu belief peaks dangerous to man

Hindu belief that Mountain peaks are dangerous to men? Was this source of all energy and life, this symbolic vulva holding this symbolic phallus of fire too much for me? Was I exposing myself to an overdose of cosmic spiritual radioactivity?

Poncho and food blown away

Almost full moon filtered through clouds

Brilliant stars and sounds . . . sublime

After sunset, I lay down and slept for an hour or two. A strong wind awakened me. Before I could protect myself, my poncho and some food packets were blown away, yet Shiva aroused me to the beauties of this moment. Toward the east, in the midnight blue sky an almost full moon filtered through the clouds. Its bright yellow accentuated the black monsoon clouds crossing its path and brilliantly reflected in blazes of light from silver clouds. Its rays beamed God's blessing to the villages and fields. The scene was sanctified with the twinkle of a few brilliant stars and wavering sounds of bells and chants from the temple far below wafting on an unsteady breeze incensed with pungent grasses. Sublime, I neither slept nor remembered my bodily complaints.

Wake predawn

Weakened I leave Arunachala

I dozed off. But before dawn, I woke up in the bright sun of early morning. I am much sicker. The night seemed only a dream. I took a Belladonna capsule. It didn't help. My water ran out. Without food or sleep, I was progressively weakening. If I didn't get off Arunachala soon, I would be too weak to carry myself and my heavy load. It is past time to begin my descent.

Use rope to lower myself down cliffs

Difficult trail to Ashram

The direct route down to the Ashram proved difficult. Twice I needed to use a rope to lower myself and my pack separately down granite cliffs. I followed the high contours to avoid heavy thorn brush and deep valleys. I finally came out in the spring on the other side of the Mountain.

Small temple

Two holy men welcomed me with kind smiles, helped me off with my pack, and offered me buttermilk. The small temple there was the entrance to a cave. Bhagavan, like these holy men, spent over eleven years here. The cave has been converted *cave entrance Cave converted to room, a peaceful Mountain haven*

Bhagavan not an ascetic

Didn't need much food, speach, social interactions

Hell/torture not necessary preludes

Return to quiet, shaded ashram

Nap brings peace

Police search party can't find me

Meditation Hall where Bhagavan answered questions silently and

into a room with a whitewashed door and is comfortable and pleasant. The burbling spring and the large trees make this a peaceful Mountain haven on this hot Indian day.

For the first time, I understood that Bhagavan was never an ascetic. The early photos of him, calm, alert, healthy, and clean, had previously disconcerted me with my Christian concept of salvation through suffering. He neither emaciated nor tortured himself. He ate only one cup of food each day because that was all he needed. He did not speak because he did not need to speak. He did not want sexual or social intercourse, wealth, power or recognition because he did not need them. Here, I suddenly realized that crucifixion, hell, and torture (physical or figurative) are not necessary preludes to liberation. Early in the afternoon, I returned "home" (it feels that way) to the Ashram, took off my boots, and walked through the cool shaded grounds, quiet except for the occasional wail of a peacock. I was glad to get back to my room to sleep a few hours.

Revelation

My nap brought peace, in my stomach at least. I woke up and walked around the Ashram. People seemed genuinely pleased that I had returned. They admired my going alone to Arunachala's heights. Only later did I learn that a police search party was sent out but never found me. It never occurred to them that I could be on the summit.

I gravitated to the meditation hall. It is in this same hall where Bhagavan lived for over twenty years after coming down from Mount Arunachala. He was always available to answer questions both silently and verbally. This hall is about twenty-five wide and seventy feet long. Vines grew around the windows, the black wood frame and walls, and the dark stone *verbally Bhagavan slept on davenport here for 20 years*

Room open for silent meditation night and day

Who am I meditation

Yoga

Swami

tile floor darkened the room even at midday. At one end is the Davenport, where Bhagavan would sleep or sit. His three-by-five-foot oil portrait is illuminated by candles, which are always burning and draped with fresh flowers. This room is open for silent meditation day or night.

This place continually attracted me. Often, I picked up a grass mat from the stack by the door and sat in the hall cross-legged with my back against a side wall, directly facing the picture of Bhagavan. Here I stayed quietly for as long as I wanted. My mind ranged freely or focused on "Who am I?"

When I left this room, on the afternoon that I came down from the Mountain, a young swami came up to me. He is the exact picture of my image of Christ except for his orange robes. His flowing dark beard and warm, knowing eyes seem to reflect both the pure light of the sky and the depth of his mind. His face is clear, perfectly proportioned and calmly active. I noticed him at the first night's dinner and was impressed. He is teaching Yoga at the young yoga students' request.

He asked me in English if I had any interest in yoga. Admitting my ignorance, I told him I had not been interested in the past because I thought yoga stresses form over essence. His very invitation made me somehow anxious. He persisted in inviting me to his room to learn the fundamentals particularly the positions of yoga. I finally agreed. I set our visit for seven-fifteen that evening, if I could by then complete some photographs. Both consciously and unconsciously I stalled the picture-taking until dinner to miss the appointment. I was not aware of any reason for my concern. My dinner of a small banana and a glass of warm milk with honey was my first food for a long time.

Meditation on picture of Bhagavan especially his eyes followed by flowing tears

After dinner, around eight, I walked as usual into the meditation hall, picked up a mat, and sat against the wall looking directly at the picture of Bhagavan, particularly his eyes. Without any warning, tears flood down my face. I was shaking and sobbing, yet I made no attempt to hold my tears back. A sentence repeated itself to me — I felt the words were not really mine. They seem stilted and meaningless. They just existed and came to me from somewhere else. They were: "I treasure nothing that I can buy." They overwhelmed my being so that no other thoughts, words, or actions were possible. I returned to my room about forty-five minutes later, feeling refreshed and uplifted.

The thought, "I treasure nothing that I can buy" expanded and repeated itself. The words began to have personal meaning. They seemed self-revealing to me. Other seemingly unrelated thoughts were in my mind. I lay down, naked in the night heat. The old overhead fan slowly turned above me. The room and my mind swirled. My room periodically lit up with bright lightning flashes. Thunder roared, sometimes distant, sometimes close. It was an explosively strange storm without rain. I couldn't sleep. Then the storm ceased, and a full moon flooded the clear night moving brilliantly into my room. Some animals began to howl. I stepped out into the night to quiet it. The howling stopped. I went back in, and the sound began again.

After seven fitful hours, I got up to write about what was searing my brain. Seemingly without thought my words from the darkness, from the void, from words of Bhagavan; a mixture of thoughts, dreams, and revelations flowed out: "Thanks to an old man and Mrs. Osborne for showing love in their kindness to me. Hope to a penniless young man, Krishna, needing a job; a rebuke to the President for doing business in his mother's Temple; a direction to the Swami to free Bhagavan's deathbed of the clutter fast becoming sacred relics except for his cane, water pitcher and leopard shawl. A note of apology to the priest who offers to teach me yoga: "I

"I treasure nothing I can buy."

Lay down naked in my bed

Room lights up with lightening, thunder roars.

Full moon floods my room.

Animals howling goes on and stops

After 7 hours I get up to write about what was searing my brain

like you; You look like pictures of Christ. I fear that you want to teach me yoga not from the heart but for money or something more. I feared to put you and me to the test by taking you up on the offer. I hope you can understand."

For me, the treasure of Arunachala was revealed. It was simple, as all great truths are. My treasure from Arunachala is within. I treasure nothing I can buy be it knowledge, wealth, wisdom, or friends. I treasure love, being alone, my wife, children, and those I call friends. I treasure creation, sharing, meditation, silence, beauty, simplicity, openness, Mountains, spirit, inner consistency, the certainty of Atman, death, God, soul, the uncertainty of life, joy, love, and giving.

Shiva's Five Holy Places

In the State of Tamil Nadu, Arunachala has become one of Shiva's five holy places. Tamil Nadu is in the southernmost state of India and is the home of the Tamil people, who speak one of the longest-surviving classical languages in the world. Their motto is "Truth alone triumphs." Tamil Nadu has been continuously inhabited by humans since 15,000 BC. After the British occupation of India ended, this area became the Madras State of the Republic of India. This state was renamed as Tamil Nadu in 1968. It is also the home in India of many historic buildings, ancient relics, religious pilgrimage sites, hill stations, and heritage sites. The Tamil Film industry, called Bollywood, is influential in the state's popular culture. One of the highly recognized spiritual Ashrams near the Sacred Mountain Arunachala is in the town of Tiruvannamalai. Tiruvannamalai, aka Trinomoli or Tiromalee, is a spiritual, cultural, and economic hub and the headquarters of Tiruvannamalai in the Indian state of Tamil Nadu. The city is also home to the renowned Annamalaiyar temple, Annamalai Hill, and is a prominent tourist destination for foreign visitors.

I am joyful at my awakening, O Mount Arunachala, you showed me how to discover myself. It will take a happy lifetime to analyze all the meanings of this revelation.' The change of my attitudes from negative to positive, the consistency of love with my nature, my relations with others, and the role of money, security, recognition, and success.

When I left the Ashram, I was still weak and sick. I wanted only to get out of India. On my flight thirty-three thousand feet over Burma, I was free. I could only laugh at my dinner salad before me: on the lettuce next to the tomato is a dead fly.

My message from Arunachala: There is a God. You can find God. To succeed, you must use what you have. You must use nothing less than your spirit, your mind, your body, and your desire. "When," not "if" you find God, God will make you free and happy. God will give you love, direction, meaning, and fulfillment. For YOU are your God!

The Five Tao Sacred Mountains of China

Taoism Unveiled

The Great Tao Mountains

My earlier Tao Sacred Mountain explorations in China were on the Five Taoist Sacred Mountains:

T'ai-shan (Shantung Province)
Heng-shan North (Shansi Province)
Sung-shan (Honan Province)
Heng-shan South (Hunan province)
Hus-shan (Shensi Province).

In the course of many trips to China I observed and experienced Taoism along with my Sacred Mountain summiting explorations of China's Tao Sacred Mountains. For me, this included temple visiting, reviewing my special study on the Sacred Mountain and personal interactions with the Chinese Taoist priests, their temples and their religious services. Sacred Mountains and particularly these mountains have been important to China and its citizens for millennia.

Pilgrimages to the Tao Sacred Mountains were once, and probably, even now, a critical part of some Chinese citizens' lives. These pilgrims, in expeditions to the Tao Sacred Mountains, endured hardships, lengthy travel, and undoubtedly a change in their normal routine, especially sleeping, eating and the physical difficulties of summiting these mountains of China.

Of course, for me, climbing, interviewing participants and reviewing my special mountain notes on these Sacred Mountains was a major part of my own effort and strains.

Overnight stays on any Sacred Mountain require lodges or similar places for nighttime and necessary foods provided one way or another to the Pilgrims. All of these mountains were places of active monasteries; even spiritual emotions provided motivation to explore all these mountains. In the course of this, I learned about China's four Buddhist Sacred Mountains. Unfortunately, I had neither the time nor the opportunity to visit them, except for Sacred Mount Omei-shan.

Chinese Taoist Pilgrims experienced many different psychological problems, as well as physical issues. I am positive that this Pilgrimage and opportunity to interact with Taoist priests and the Sacred Mountain provided inspiration to everyone... As it was to me, a Westerner, although undoubtedly in different ways, I found special interests and appreciation of the Taoist philosophy. The Taoist organization operating these Tao Pilgrimage programs not only provides the Taoist pilgrims information and inspiration but also lodging and food. This required active operating monasteries for thousands of years, sharing the benefits of understanding and practicing Taoism.

"Taoism" and "Daoism" are really the same; a literal translation means the "way," "road," channel," "path," "doctrine," or "line." The Tao is "a natural order that enables all things to exist and dominate every action, not so much through force, but through "a natural curvature of space and time." Tao is the origin and power of all creation. Its essence is unknown, but observable in manifestation.

---

*China's four Buddhist Sacred Mountains
1. Wu-t'-shan (Shasi Province)
2. P'u-t'-o-shan (Chekiang Province)
3. Chiu-hua-shan (Anhwei Province)
4. Omei-shan (Szechuan Province)

Beyond the origin and beyond all power and creation, it is said to be "the underlying cosmic power that creates the universe supports culture and the state, preserves the good (confirming the moral order of the universe), and punishes the wicked (persons going beyond reasonable or predictable limits)." *The Way* is the way things develop naturally… the *Way* Nature moves and living beings grow and decline in accordance with cosmic laws. The Tao is untimely and claimed to be indescribable. It transcends all analysis and definitions. The Tao is also said to be a process of reality and a way for everything to change and gather together. In fact, change is actually said to be a fundamental characteristic of all things symbolized by numbers representing 64 related force relationships, known as *hexagrams*. The Tao mostly refers to this change by the forces of *Yin and Yang*.

Historically, the Five Taoist Sacred Mountains, particularly the Sacred Mountain Tai-shan, are associated with the supreme God of Heaven and the main cosmic deities of traditional Chinese religions. All of China's Sacred Mountains have been important destinations of Pilgrimage which is characterized as "paying respect to a holy mountain."

The Taoist Sacred Mountains, also often referred to as the Five Great Mountains, are arranged according to the five cardinal directions: North, South, Center, East, and West. These Chinese Sacred Mountains are said to have cosmological and theological significance. Of course, they are also natural landmarks in Chinese history, the sites of imperial worship and sacrifice by Emperors. The Emperor's Imperial Sacred Mountain expeditions became state rituals as prescribed by Confucianism. Every new dynasty and emperor used these expeditions to establish his claim to all his newly acquired domains.

Two Taoism Sacred Mountains are referred to by the same name, "Heng-shan." One is the Tao Sacred Mountain

North, and the other is the Heng-shan Sacred Mountain South. Sacred Mount Heng-Shan in the south has an extraordinary history and many summits. Hunan Province, where Heng-Shan South is located, is also the birthplace of one of China's modern "emperors," Mao Tse-Tung.

It is said that these Tao Sacred Mountains originated from the body of Pangu, "The first Being," the "Creator of the World." In ancient times, particularly, Sacred Mountains were places of authority and fear, ruled by the "dark force", yet faithfully worshiped. They were indispensable to human existence, welfare, fertility, rivers, herbs, and medicinal plants, as well as the source materials needed to build homes and tools. Taoists have a strong intuitive connection with Nature.

The one hundred and eighty precepts of Taoism are set up as a guide to living a good honest life; 20 of these precepts explicitly refer to Conservation of Nature and many others, at least indirectly, are aimed at preventing the destruction of Nature.

Like Mount Meru to the Japanese and Buddhists, Taoists consider Mountains as a channel of communication and the connections between heaven and earth. It also is the place to find personal pleasure and immortality!

My early Sacred Mountain explorations in China included the Five Chinese Taoist Sacred Mountains. In the course of four trips to China to explore the Sacred Mountains, I experienced extraordinary events and inspirations from each of these mountains that I studied, visited, and summitted. In history these mountains are particularly important in the life of the Chinese Taoist.

These Chinese pilgrimages to the Sacred Mountains of China were once a critical part of Taoist life in China. The Pilgrims also endured many different physical and physiological problems as well as psychological issues. They also went to the Sacred Mountains for inspirational opportunities to participate in the Tao rites on Sacred Mountains surrounded by Tao priests and information as well as other presentations relevant to Taoism.

Although I was surprised by the thought for years, I thought of these Tao Mountain Pilgrims as experienced predecessors to the same kind of experiences we moderns enjoy on ski trips, like Squaw Valley, for example, in California. Difficulties of travel, changes in life routines, expert ski instructors (instead of priests), physical exhaustion, and outstanding lifetime memories from a week with the great outdoors and Nature.

Esoterica: Myths, Mysteries, Imaginables

In the beginning, everything was featureless, formless, and primordial; it all came together into a cosmic egg and included the principles and the development of "Yin and Yang."

"Pangu" appeared then in the universe as a primitive hairy giant with horns. Pangu began creating the world by using his giant axe to separate Yin and Yang and create and raise the sky. Years later, (18,000), after Pangu died.

"His breath became the wind, mists, and clouds;
his voice became the thunder,
his left eye the sun,
his right eye the moon,
his head and body turned into mountains and streams
    of the world,
his blood into rivers,
his muscles into fertile land,
his facial hair became the stars and Milky Way above,
    his fur, brush, and forests,
his bones valuable minerals;
his bone marrow to precious jewels,
his sweat to rain, and even the little fleas on his fur
    carried by the wind became animals."

A mountain Guru claimed that the inner organs of Pangu

were also transformers; a combination of Pangu's liver, his heart, and his brain became two of the highest components of human consciousness once humans were in the world: LL (love and longevity).

All this may seem a long story, but it's only a tiny summary and illustration of the huge volume of Chinese Esoterica as to the creation of "everything."

Tai-shan is the Taoist Sacred Mountain of The East and associated with sunrise, birth and renewal; it has been a place of worship for at least 3000 years; it was one of the most important ceremonial centers in China; and is now a UNESCO World Heritage Site.

The "Mount Tai Earthquake" in Taishan is considered by most scholars as the first recorded earthquake in Chinese history. Historically, Tai-shan has been considered the premier Taoist Sacred Mountain, probably because of its connection with China's emperors as well as its notable connections to China's artistic world. Seventy-two Emperors were recorded as visiting Tai-shan.

Temple complex at Mount Tai

Royalty Rules...
TAI-SHAN
Tao Sacred Mountain

The South Gate To Heaven at Mount Tai

Elevation: 1,532.7m (5,029ft)
Prominence: 1,505m (4,938)
Coordinates: 36°15°21°N
117°06°27°S
Type: Climbing
Age of rock: Cambrian
Spirit: Tao / UNESCO World Heritage Site
Cable cars available

Esoterica: Myths, Mysteries, Imaginables

Tai-San favorite

Donahue Emperor is said to be the supreme God of Mount Tai. He claimed to be the descendent of Pangu, the Creator. Originally Sacred Mount Tai-shan, The Taoist Sacred Mountain of the East, was the favorite and most often visited by large numbers of Chinese. In those early days

Chinese Emperors in effect adopted Tai-shan by making the Pilgrimage to Tai-shan personally.

I still remember all the special Chinese Groups, organizations and individual groups hiking on Tai-shan. In the course of its history, parts of the steep areas of Tai-shan were transformed from trails into thousands of stone mountain steps. This made it easier, especially for the older Pilgrims.

Shoeless old ladies

I noticed a group of seemingly very old women high on the mountain at a rest stop dressed like traditionally fashioned Tao Pilgrims, including bare feet! ("There's no way that I would be able to do that!") The whole women's group seemed to be laughing and cheerful as they climbed up Sacred Mountain Tai-shan. At the summit, an available lodge was provided for Tao Climbers during the night for them and anyone else wanting to stay overnight. In the early morning, they could welcome and celebrate the next day's gorgeous, inspiring, and memorable rising sun.

Hua-shan v. Tai-shan

In more modern times, Hua-Shan, now the Sacred Mountain of the West, probably attracts even more people than Tai-shan because of its amazing sunrise and lights. Later, we take that journey to Hua-Shan when we visit the Taoist Sacred Mountain of the West, Hua-Shan.

A Cliff Hanger...
HENG-SHAN
Taoist Sacred Mountain of the North

Hanging Temple at Heng-Shan

Location: Shanxi, China
Elevation: 2,017 M (6,617 ft)
Coordinates: 39°40°26°N
113°44°08°E

Double Heng-shan

Esoterica: Myths, Mysteries and Imaginzbles

Sacred Taoist Mount Heng-shan has been the site of Chinese Pilgrimages since 1045–256 BCE. This Mountain is not to be confused with Mount Heng-shan in the South (Hunan province). Both Sacred Mountains of Heng-shan are Taoist and are considered one of the Five Sacred Taoist Mountains of China. One of the Eight Immortals of Taoist Mythology on Heng-shan North, and is still said to be there somewhere practicing Taoism.

Dedicated to God inside Heng-shan

Also, according to myth, the Heng Shan temple was dedicated to a God residing inside Sacred Mountain Hengshan North. After an emperor named the mountain as one of the most Sacred Mountains, it was regarded as the second greatest mountain in the world and one of the 12 most Sacred Mountains by the Emperor in 206 BCE.

Hanging Temples

Today, the 'Hanging Temple' alongside the Beiyue Temple has survived more than 1,500 years on the side of a rock Mountain cliff. Interestingly, the temple is dedicated to Buddhism, Taoism, and Confucianism. Two of the temple's water wells, very close together, are about halfway up the slope. One well is sweet and refreshing, while the other is bitter and has an unpleasant aftertaste.

While the sweet well is shallow, its waters are inexhaustible, and Emperor Xuanzong christened that well "Dragon Springs."

Mystic Sites

Other seemingly mystical sites on the mountain include "Cloud Out Cave," "Wind Gap," "Flying Stone Cave," "Tiger Wind Gap," and "Sister-in-law Cave."

The Sacred Center . . .
SONG-SHAN
Taoist Sacred Mountain of the Center

The Song-Shan Buddhist Academy

Location:	China 33°54°N 113°30°E
Highest Elevation:	2,413.8 m (7,919.3 ft)
Demographics:	Chinese Haun:98.6%/ Other: 1.4%
Language:	Zhongyuan Mandarin, Jin
Religion:	Pilgrimage Taoism

Esoterica: Myths, Mysteries, Imaginzbles

Once upon a time, a long time ago, many factions were trying to take control of the Chinese empire. One of these factions was led by an evil warlord. Their first error was to kidnap the Prince. The evil warlord then ransacked the Shaolin Temple on Mount Song.

According to the story, 13 Shaolin monks joined together to defeat the warlord's guards, kill the warlord, and rescue the Prince. The Prince then became the emperor and in honor of the monks, he granted the Shaolin Temple extra land.

To this day, the Chinese word for Pilgrimage means "paying respect to a Sacred Mountain."

Center of Heaven/Earth

In Taoism, Sacred Mount Song, similar to Buddhist Sacred Mount Meru, symbolizes the concept of Sacred Mountains as the connections between heaven and earth.

Pangu's Creations

The myth of Pangu reports that when the Creator Pangu dies, after 18,000 years, Pangu's belly becomes the present-day Mount Song, the Taoist Sacred Mountain of the Center.

Along Yellow River

Song-shan is part of an isolated mountain range along the Yellow River and one of the five Taoist Sacred Mountains known by Chinese Astronomical Mythology as the "Center of Heaven and Earth".

. . . Yin/Yang Peaks Balance

Mount Song is often referred to as having seventy-two peaks, though this is likely a mystical figure (sometimes rounded to 70). In the ancient myth, Shaoshi Mountain (meaning all peaks west of the valley) and Taishi Mountain (meaning all peaks east of the valley) are said to have 72 peaks, respectively, representing one set of "Yin" and one set of "Yang," which cancel each other out at the monastery, achieving zero… meaning a complete balance of Yin and Yang.

Kung Fu / Shaolin

The monastery at Mount Song and its monks are known for their knowledge of Kung Fu, spiritual and physical exercising, martial arts, and the Shaolin Temple.

HENG-SHAN
Taoist Sacred Mountain of the South

Trees on the snow covered Zhurong Peak at Mount Huangshan Scenic area.

Location: Hunan, China
Elevation: 1,300 m (4,266 ft)
Prominence: 1,130 m (3,710 ft)
Parent Range: Hengshan Mountains
Type of Rock: Granite

Esoterica: Myths, Mysteries, Imaginables

Myth tells us: China's Yellow Emperor, an individual deity known also by His Chinese name Huangdi, is a mythical Chinese sovereign and culture hero from the story "Three Sovereigns and Five Emperors."

The Yellow Emperor appointed Zhu Rong, the God of fire, to administer his kingdom. In that capacity, Zhu Rong taught the local residents how to keep warm, how to cook food, and how to drive away wild animals.

A peaceful morning on the top of Mount Heng-shan.

Zhurong Peak

To commemorate Rong's good works, the people named the highest peak of Sacred Mount Heng-shan after him. This peak is also the highest one in the Mount Heng-shan range and, of course, the best place to welcome the sunrise, admire the ocean of sky clouds, and, in winter, enjoy the snowy scenery.

The myth also has it that a Gold Bull lives at the bottom of one of the Sacred Mountain pools. The Bull was forced into the pool while in a fight with a dragon, trying to drive the dragon away.

Temple/ Academy

Sacred Mount Heng Shan is a famous Mountain home for its majestic scenery as well as a Sacred Historical Cultural Site. At the foot of the Mountain lies the largest temple in southern China — the Grand Temple of Mount Heng (Nanyua Damiao), built in 725 CE during the Tang dynasty. This temple survived four dynasties and six fires and was finally rebuilt in 1882. Heng Shan, also at one time, housed the largest academy in China and was known for its fighting history against fascism.

At the foot of the peak, a stone staircase leads to the top of the mountain and, halfway up, a rising sun view platform.

At the top is a famous hall temple made of granite with a roof covered with rows of iron tiles to protect the roof from the wind, ice, and snow; it's esoterically implying that the temple mated with the peak and became a part of it.

On the west side of this mountain temple is the "Moon Watching Alter," the highest point on Mount Heng. "Water Curtain Cave" houses bubbling springs, flying waterfalls, and a harmony of Nature's magnificent sounds, light and shadows, making the cave one of the "Four Wonders" of Mount Heng.

In the Mountains, the Nanyue Great Temple on Chidi Peak was built in a royal architectural style and featured Taoism, Buddhism, and Confucianism.

Zhu Rong took charge of the southern affairs of his kingdom as the God of fire. Zhu Rong taught the local residents how to keep warm, to cook food, and to drive away wild animals. In an effort to commemorate this God, people named the highest peak of Mount Hengshan after his name.

The Zhurong Peak is the best place to see the sunrise.

Sacred Mount Hua Shan

People View-Point

I am Mournful,

I ache,

I am bitter

With the pain and rejection

That God puts on me . . .

And Grateful

For all God's ecstasies.

       . . . Greek Lyric

Location:	Huayin, Shaanxi, China
Range:	Qinling Mountains
Elevation:	7,067 ft (2,154 m)
Prominence:	1,083 ft (330 m)
Coordinates:	34°29' N
	110°05'E
Spirit:	Tao, Buddhist
Pilgramage:	*Trespass into and escape from the Holy Sacred Mountain Hua-shan, "China's Taoist Sacred Mountain of the West. A Hua-shan summit trail to heaven*

Angel View-Point

Trespass into and escape from the Holy Sacred Mountain
HUA-SHAN
Taoist Sacred Mountain of the West
A Hua-shan Summit Trail to Heaven

Esoterica: Myths, Mysteries, Imaginables

Hua-Shan is alleged to have received its striking visible features when the God Juling-Shen cut off Mount Hua from the surrounding mountains with a huge blow of his ax. The effect was to move the mountain to the other side of the Yellow River and create a channel to free the river flow to the ocean. The supreme deity of Sacred Mount Hua is Xiyue Dadi, with the power to gather clouds and rain to nurture the growth of everything, grant blessings, and provide prosperity to the people. This God's daughter, Huayue, known for her extraordinary beauty, disobeyed her father by marrying a mortal.

She faced imprisonment under Mount Hua as punishment for violating such rules of heaven.

Tang flower Hua-shan summits and sun rituals in the earlier days were attended by imperial and local Pilgrims but not well attended by Pilgrims from the rest of China. It was also, however, an important Pilgrimage for seekers of immortality, herbal Chinese medicines and drugs, and places for hermitages. Mount Hua grew and flowered during the Tang Dynasty, 618 – 907 CE. From that period, Hua-Shan's fame began as a Sacred Mountain officially revered by the Emperor of the Tang Royal Family.

The Mountain deity, "The King of Metal Heavens," is now the deity of sacred Hua-shan at the Chinese Taoist Sacred Mountain of the West.

Mount Hau is also called Hua-shan, its literal name, as well as its other name, "Mountain Under Heaven." This mountain is located near the city of Hunayn in Shaanxi Province, about 120 kilometers (75 mi) east of Xi'an. It is the "Western Mountain "of the Five Great Mountains of China and has a long history of religious significance. Originally classified as having three peaks, in modern times, it is classified as having five main peaks, the highest of which is the South peak at 2,154.9 meters (7,070 ft).

Ax-splitting rock

Hua-Shan's Western peak still has a giant rock known as "Axe-Splitting Rock." It is 100 feet high and neatly divided into three parts. The story claims that a mother's son made a heroic attempt to split the rock in order to attempt to rescue his mother by dividing the Mountain.

The Underworld

In the second century BCE, a Taoist temple, "the Shrine of the Western Peak," was built at Mount Hua-shan's base. According to Taoist beliefs, the God of the Underworld resides at this Shrine. This mountain was often used for spirit mediums to contact the God of Fire and his underlings....

Nature/Sun Time

The sacred mountain of the West, Hua-Shan, for me, and apparently for the crowds of Chinese Pilgrims I experienced there, is clearly an exciting opportunity for people to participate and spend time with Nature and, like many Sacred Mountains in China, an opportunity as a group to welcome the sun rising.

Hua-shan/Xian

Hua-Shan's entrance is often referred to as "being connected" to the old capital of China, Xian. In my several attempts to be admitted to Sacred Hua-Shan, I either began or ended up staying in Xian and taking the train from Xian to a stop next to the entrance gate of Hua-Shan.

Danger!

My inability to even be admitted to Hua-shan Mountain reflects claims there are discrete military security facilities… so no foreigners are allowed. I suspect one of the other problems was that the mountain trails to the peaks and infrastructure of Hua-shan were actually dangerous. It might have been embarrassing to authorities for the world to know that China was operating a highly visited holy Mountain that could and probably did result in a lot of injuries or even deaths. I can remember, for example, one of the trails along a sheer rock cliff that was basically a few planks stuck into cracks in the rock cliff and a rope to hold onto.

Tresspass easier . . .
Escape harder . . .

After four unsuccessful trials and two arrests, I made it to the sun summit and joined the pilgrims at the top to welcome the morning sun without realizing that it could be more challenging to leave Sacred Hua-shan than it was to get in.

First trespass fails

Four times, I came to Hua-shan in the hopes of just entering the entrance gate, but failed. The first time, they wouldn't let me in because I was a foreigner. I tried to go in without realizing that foreigners were ineligible.

Second trespass fails . . .

The second time, realizing how well-guarded the entrance was, I took a very early train — and since the guards were actually sleeping when I arrived, I boldly walked in. Still, I was soon discovered and escorted out — by the police. They seemed to naturally accept the idea that Americans were dangerous. No way would they allow an American to visit their Holy Mountain; in fact, there were signs in English along the trail going up stating it was a criminal offense to attempt to enter the area without a permit. Based on my understanding, that applied especially to foreigners (like me).

Third trespass fails . . .

On my third attempt, I assumed that because the entrance was already crowded with Chinese people, they wouldn't notice me. So, instead of attempting to breach the entry myself, I climbed the facility fence out of sight of the guard's actual entry. I then crossed over a steep area, waded through a small stream, and I was finally headed on the trek up Hua-shan.

Fourth trespass succeeds

About the time I began to feel confident hiking the summit trail, I admired this very good trail, at least here. I now emotionally began to celebrate summiting and seeing the glorious light of the sunrise! Yet somehow, the police spotted me. An unnamed uniformed person escorted me back down to the entry to be ejected. They didn't realize that this was my third trespass offense at Hua-shan. If they had, I would probably still be in jail today as a triple offender!

Still determined, I made a new plan to try again while on another expedition that I had planned in China about three years later. Finally, on that expedition, I took a train diversion to Xian. I knew the train passed by the entry point of Hua-Shan. I got off that train one stop before the Hua-Shan entry station – about midnight – and walked the track alone in the night, arriving at Hua-shan entry at about 2:30 in the morning. To my surprise, the gate guards were again sleeping on duty; I was again able to walk right through the main gate onto the summit trail. A little fearful, I walked as quickly as I could.

Shouting with the Sun!

I made the eastern summit before sunrise and had the joy of shouting my own welcome to the sun along with several hundred Chinese Pilgrims who were also yelling our greeting.

Escape impossible

By this time, I was very hungry and realized that my next problem would be exiting, as the entry was also the way out and probably guarded. I began the hike back down to the entrance. As I approached the bottom of the trail and started for the exit, a friendly Chinese person struck up a conversation with me. He then invited me to breakfast at one of the food places near the bottom of the trail. I was as pleasant as

I could be — but I wasn't going to trust anyone until I made it through the exit, which looked very difficult at that point, as there was a larger police staff to handle the exit from Hua-Shan. I refused my amicable companion, "Thank you so much for your courtesy, a complete stranger, but I need to catch the next train soon leaving for Xian." That seemed to satisfy him. He left for his breakfast without finding out who I really was and whether I had a permit. We shook hands, I continued towards the exit, and he went into a shop for his breakfast.

Warning: Undercover police

Shortly afterwards, another unknown older Chinese man passed me on the trail, whispering in English, "Don't talk anymore to your hiking companion. He's undercover police." He rushed on without another word. I stood there in shock for a moment.

Panic

To avoid suspicion, I slowly walked on to the actual exit. To my dismay, it was guarded by two policemen sitting on each side of the trail with their knees touching each other. There was no way anyone, including me, could get by. The police could have easily seen that I was a foreigner and shouldn't be there. I choked down my panic about my four trespassing offenses that would surely result in at least some Chinese jail time. I "delayed," really "froze," and pretended to adjust my pack while I tried to figure out what I could do. If I walked back up the trail, I would immediately be suspected. There was no other available way to leave from here.

Disguise

But time and the Gods at Hua-shan, for some unknown reason, decided to help me. A group of about ten Chinese Pilgrims walked up to the same exit to leave; putting on my very dark glasses, I pulled back my hat over my face and joined the Chinese group. The guards then had to stand up to let the Chinese group out.

Thankfully, I didn't need to crawl on my knees to exit.

Victory/Free

By bending my knees as I walked, I didn't stand out as a foreigner. (I was probably about a foot taller than most of them).

All of us then went through the gate, and suddenly "I was free!"

I walked down the railroad tracks to the next train to Xi'an. Once in Xi'an, I soon deboarded and took a taxi back to a hotel in Xi'an, pre-arranged by my fellow explorers.

Years later, I understand that foreigners with a permit are now allowed into Hua-Shan. In fact, the crowd of visitors increased so much that a tram was constructed from the entry gate to allow more people to take part in Hua-shan's glorious sunrises.

Since the original times, most of the near vertical rock aspects of Hua-shan were only accessible by stairs cut into the rock face with chains hung down as handrails. Hua-shan historically has been a place of retreat for hermits, Taoists, Buddhists, and others. Access to Hua-shan was only available for many years to the Chinese, the strong-willed, or others who had found "The Way" (Taoists).

Imperial Pilgrims, seekers, immortality, herbs, hermitages.

The historical and actually dangerous trails on Hua-shan were transformed in order to avoid the dangers to pilgrims. Different trails and summit routes were used to increase the safety and accessibility of Hua-shan for pilgrims.

In addition, a tram has been installed from the base of Hua-Shan to the summit in order to avoid these formerly dangerous mountain trails.

In spite of it all, it seemed sacrilegious to let machines take over access to the Great Sacred Mountain, Hua-Shan, the Tao Sacred Mountain of the West. But for me nevertheless I felt privileged to finally be able to attend the sunrise ritual on Hua-shan.

It turned out well worth all that trouble and anxiety… now that I am safely home!

CONFIDENTIAL

NO TRESPASSING

SACRED MOUNTAIN
X

PEOPLE VIEW-POINT

If a Blessed Mountain's treasure
          closes before you
The Mountain disappears.
It will show a hidden nothing.
Where nothing's now known.
          . . . Anon

DANGER CONFIDENTIAL

If I give too much information, anyone, any nation, any group, especially China or Mongolia, will excavate and destroy the billion-dollar value (probably now the trillion-dollar contents) of Chinggis Qa'an's grave. And we will lose an important part of the story of the largest empire and most successful conqueror in history.

Artist's View

Mountain X

The past governs here.
The future is always another story.

The first question any reader may ask: what kind of foolishness is it to hide the name of what you claim is an historic Sacred Mountain with the title "X". That's a fair question. I spent ten years studying, visiting, and writing about Chinggis Qa'an, the most famous warrior in history in terms of people conquered, nations destroyed and slaves and artifacts taken. Everybody seems to understand that, but they don't recognize or know anything about his generosity, his fairness, and his support for his family and friends. He is also brutal in his attitude and in warfare against his enemies.

It is a common practice for famous leaders like Chinggis Qa'an to create extraordinarily large important homes, palaces, museums, public and private temples, and to record and celebrate their own death and lifetime accomplishments.

Chinggis Qa'an has been notably realistic and decisive. He understood that any enemies, friends, political leaders, scientists, artists, or anyone else would give or do anything to excavate his tomb after he dies. He orders his family and friends not to reveal or otherwise communicate to anyone where his corpse and treasures are buried. And anyone who knows or is connected to Chinggis Qa'an or part of his extended family will obey him to the letter or die prematurely.

Anyone knowing his burial place in 1227, when he died, did not survive more than 10 years as they got older, so Chinggis Qa'an's tomb still remains a secret, as originally intended and ordered, over 798 years later. Recent historic and scientific exploration findings on what we call "Mountain X." It is necessary to protect the sight by not revealing its exact location other than Mountain "X". Once the United Nations or other major international organization, public or private, obtains an excavation permit, the almost last step is completed and this mystery will be solved.

Naturally, since 1227 when Chinggis Qa'an died. all sorts of "crackpots" claim that they have found his tomb. Whenever that happens, and it has happened many times in the last almost 800 years, the story has been debunked by scholars. Such as the construction worker who discovered a lot of bones and skulls while building a road. It was widely reported and claimed that the bones found while building the road as Chinggis Qa'an's tomb, but the claim was debunked by academic experts.

Crackpot claims,

Mountain X historically is archaeologically in a rare situation. Other world leaders who recognized the importance of maintaining secrecy of their burial places, knew that if they don't, someone or some organization may excavate it for their own advantages, honor, financial wealth, or academic fame.

Chinggis Qa'an and his army in the process of conquering and destroying major civilizations in the 13th century, burned down and destroyed the infrastructure of other leader's fame, particularly spiritual. But almost all of such facilities are major building and monuments that make their leaders death places obvious and subject to robbery for the wealth, artifacts or recognition involved. Other research shows that Chinggis Qa'an directed he be buried with him a significant portion of his extraordinary acquisitions from his military successes worth, probably in today's dollars, trillions of dollars.

Intuitive recognition as well as facts, histories and logic are part of locating hidden tombs. Many important discoveries, including finding Mountain X, often stem from instinct. Some discoveries are just "luck," synchronistic events, or discoveries while looking for something else like Howard Carter's waterboy stumbling on a stone that turned out to be the top of a staircase leading to Tut's tomb.

My own experience typifies the role of intuition in finding Mountain X. A stranger suggested years earlier that we divert from our Bike Expedition from Istanbul, Turkey, to Xi'an, China, to a Sacred Mountain in a well-known Mountain range {where Chinggis Qa'an is probably buried}. This granite range contains many impressive Mountains rather than a single one like Sacred Fuji-san in Japan, Shasta in California, or Kang Rinpoche in Tibet. On our explorations of Mongolia, we noticed a granite pyramid shaped Mountain bathed in sunset light, seemingly too steep to be climbable but somehow, someone, sometime long ago built a small temple on the summit.

It wasn't until our return to continue our bicycle journey across China that my wife Becky and I saw the Mountain bathed in a golden light of sunset. Instinctively we both became confident this is Mountain X, the sacred death ground of Chinggis Qa'an.

Applying historical records of explorations, instincts and scientific techniques particularly ground penetrating radar and magnetometry we confirm our historical and expedition findings that Mountain X is Chinggis Qa'ans grave.

Since this find will be an extraordinary discovery it will take a United Nations project to obtain a permit to physically confirm the find with excavation and analysis of the evidence. We are confident this will confirm the existence of Chinggis Qa'an's burial place.

We are awaiting the day when the world is ready for an accurate and full report of Chinggis Qa'an's life and burial, and the availability of financing for the huge excavation and inevitably extensive government permitting,

Until then, in memory of Chinggis Qa'an's extraordinary accomplishments, the secret of Mountain "X" will never be revealed, at least by me.

Sacred Mount
Tabor

People View-Point

On the trails/roads to the

Sacred Mountain summit,

Some live some die;

We dont' known when

We don't know why.

. . . Anon

Location:	Israel
Range:	The mountain is in the area of Nazareth Hills in Galilee southeast of Haifa
Elevation:	1,886 ft (575 m)
Prominence:	n/a
Coordinates:	32°41'14"N
	35°23'25"E
Spirit:	Jewish, Christian, Moslem
Pilgrimage:	*Voices From Sacred Mountains*

Angel View-Point

Voices From Sacred Mountains

Mounts Olive, Temptation, Tabor and Calvary
— Israel —

Is it God or Moses? Is it Christ or Jesus? Is it Mohammad or God who speaks on Mount Tabor?

Esoterica: Myths, Mysteries and Imaginables

I have never literally seen or talked to God from a cloud, a bush or a lake. I do talk more clearly to myself on a Mountain. Alone on a Mountain I have only myself to talk to, to search, to see, to feel. I dream more vividly. The unreal becomes more real. I understand my harmony with Nature, earth, the cosmos. Whether it is the tiredness, the dreams, the concentration of negative ions, or God, the Mountains do have such spiritual influences. I know. Their imagery becomes reflected in my own spiritual eyes. My own thrust to the heavens, my own climb. My exaltation at the sight of wider and wider worlds within me.

Inspiration and revelation from Mountains

Mountain Voices

We do not know exactly how Christ felt at the critical events of his life. We do know that it is on a Mountain top, if anywhere, that God spoke to Christ and now speaks to man. It is on a Mountain summit that the future is foretold, mysteries arise. The Bible just states that confrontation with God does occur. It gave strength to Jesus, to his disciples and to Christian believers afterwards. It is no coincidence that after the crucifixion, the eleven disciples, at Jesus' bidding, "went into a Mountain in Galilee to meet Him and receive His words."

"God" spoke to Christ and now to man

After crucifixion, Jesus reportedly went to a

"Go ye therefore and teach all nations, baptizing them in the name of the Father and of the Son and of the Holy Ghost."

Both Moses and Elijah talk to God on a Mountain, at Sinai. Muhammad, too, found his solace and his revelation on Mount Sinai. Every year he withdrew for a month to Mount Hira near Mecca.

"By the Mountain of Sinai and by the book written in an expanded scroll (the Qur'an) and by the visited house (Kaaba in pilgrimage) and by the elevated roof of heaven: and by the swelling ocean: verily the punishment of thy Lord will surely descend: there shall be none to withhold it. On that day the heaven shall be shaken and shall fall and the Mountains shall walk and pass away."

Crying with Christ

It seems sacrilegious to me to luxuriate in a hotel in Jerusalem atop the Mount of Olives, the geographic center of the religions of Moses, Muhammad and Christ? On this same hill Jesus meditated and was betrayed. From Calvary He Ascended. The impact of all this struck me late in the afternoon of my first day in Israel.

It was afternoon when I regained consciousness from my twelve-hour sleep. I lie in unaccustomed comfort surveying my room. What a contrast. Parts of my pack, dirty clothes, papers, supplies, food, equipment are scattered all over the room on the floor, bed, dresser and closet. They obviously didn't belong. They were from a world other than the world of clean, orderly luxury, the world of bright new colors, deep green carpets, packaged soaps and covered water glasses, toilet-seat bands, neatly stacked white towels.

The first thing I did after breaking out of the bonds of ease is to visit the Information Director of the Tourist Ministry. I wanted to request special assistance in reaching my Mountain

---

Baptism in name of Father, son and Holy Ghost

Moses/Elija talk to God on Mount Sinai

Mohammed went to Mount Hira for a month annually

Recitations from St. Gabriel

Hotel atop the Mount of Olives

12 hours sleep in luxurious room

Tourist Ministry won't help on Jordan and Sinai

objectives in isolated areas along the Jordan Valley and in the Sinai Desert. It didn't take long to find out I won't get it. The Ministry, through the Director, doesn't want me to go on my pilgrimage at all. Unconvinced, I leave his office but secretly determined to go ahead on my own.

Garden of Gethsemane

Later that afternoon, I felt the urge to wander on this sacred hill. Here was the Biblical Garden of Gethsemane. It was a favorite place for Jesus to be alone and away from the city. Here Judas betrayed Him with a kiss.

My own Christ consciousness

Christ was and continues to be a real (though supernatural) person to most Christians. My own experience with Him is not unusual: When I was very young, I prayed and appealed to Him for what I wanted (sometimes in formal prayers and often for specific favors). I prayed to Him as though He were a father who could give me my requests. He evolved into a model whose life, as I imagine it, guides me in my actions and dreams. Then He becomes more of a friend, a comforter. In times of anxiety and stress I feel His comfort. Finally, He is a personal and living symbol of my natural need to love. His betrayal and crucifixion deeply sorrow me.

Visit huge cemetery with caskets above ground

Now I was on His hill. I climbed to the top, then proceeded through a huge cemetery. All the caskets of marble and stone were above ground. It was easier here to cut marble and stone than to dig holes in this rocky, sunbaked clay. The cemetery was like a baby giant's playroom, with blocks of all sizes strewn over the landscape. They seem to be man-made counterparts to the dead volcanic bombs on the barren rock fields at Mount Lassen. Both the caskets and these bombs experienced the heat of life in the womb of Mother Earth and now lay heavy, stone-cold, where fate has left them. These caskets and tombs were ideal camera platforms and resting places from which to view the old walled city of Jerusalem in the afternoon light. The Cemetery, like the adjoining churches and buildings, is surrounded by a wall about twelve feet high.

High walls, wide pathway, beautiful gardens

Because of the high walls, I saw nothing but the sky and some treetops while walking from the cemetery down a wide pathway. Now and then I glimpsed beautiful gardens through the cracks in the great wooden gates. It was terribly depressing. I wanted to be like Christ, to feel love, warmth, beauty — as I imagined He must have felt these things when alone on this hillside. But the gates were locked and shut.

Depressing

Outside walled in and restricted to dirty walkway

Christ's garden is taken over by His followers. The traveler, the stranger, the outsider is walled in and restricted to a dirty walkway. If you want to see these gardens of Jesus, you must trespass or buy the antiseptic guidance of a tourist group leader with special arrangements of course as to time and payment. The price includes a lecture, post cards and trinkets of whatever religion or sect you profess.

Loneliness overwhelming

My loneliness was overwhelming. It is unbelievable that from this bitter soil Christ's message of love grew. Anticipating Jesus there, I gulped long draughts of this presence, only to find too late that I was polluting Christ's nectar.

In this mood, I crossed a paved street and stepped over a low, crumbled wall into a vacant area of about ten acres. It contained rocky soil, scattered garbage and a few weeds. The smell of urine permeated the still air. An emaciated donkey hobbles and is tied to one of the few scraggly olive trees growing on this stony terrace. Was the poor animal a descendant of Christ's immortal donkey he used for His triumphal entry into Jerusalem, or Mary's ride to Bethlehem?

In one corner is an overhanging rock, almost a cave. From the smell, the cans and old papers, squatters with nowhere else to sleep or wash must have been the occupants.

I walked to the far end of the plot to a thick ten-foot

fortification. Climbing an olive tree, I looked over it. It was nothing but a vacant lot of rubble and a few more olive trees. However, its message to "Keep. Out, Stranger" was clear: Broken glass with the sharp points embedded in the cement top. It would cut my hands and arms to shreds if I tried to scramble over that wall by jumping for a handhold without seeing the top.

"Keep out, stranger!"

I was apprehensive. Everything was getting darker in the later afternoon shadows. I was a lone American in this Arab sector. In history this very ground was taken by Israeli forces from Jordan backed, as many Arabs and Jordanians believe, by the United States. Nationality in this part of the world can be a matter of injury and death. I am a lucrative target for armed robbery though bearded and not dressed like a tourist; my special boots and expensive camera make me stand out as a rich man. An emaciated dog, frothing from his lower jaw, followed me, snarling and barking.

Late afternoon darkness.

Tourist target

Emaciated frothing dog follows me

Yet somehow, this place fascinated me. It was dangerous and saddening, but I had to stay. I looked at Jerusalem from this "garden" and hated it.

I hated the "garden"

The brilliant orange sun setting behind the Islam Dome Mosque, and the spires of the imposing churches, synagogues and Temples, seemed the devil's creation. This city is impersonal, filthy, grasping, unfriendly, and overbuilt. It is operated to relieve the visitor not of his fears and sins but of his money. It preys upon his religious simplicity, stupidity, and credulity. It exploits his mystical and spiritual needs. The hypocrisy and the pollution seem worse at the very center and tradition of three important religions: Islam, Judaism, and Christianity.

Sunset and the devil's creation

Pollution at center of religion

Then comes the shock: I was feeling Christ. Like Christ I wanted to throw out the money changers from the temple, as he had done. I understood his unusual violence. I agreed with

St. Jerome's words as he castigated the city before retreating to Bethlehem to write his Bible.

I bowed toward Mecca rather than Jerusalem as does Muhammad. (During prayers he dramatically turned away from Jerusalem. And his believers face that way ever since.)

It's lucky for Jerusalem on that afternoon in July that I'm not a conquering general with the power of destruction. I might strip the city of every religious building and phony commercial enterprise. In their places I would build open gardens where everyone could worship and feel his or her own religion, be it Islam, Judaism, Christianity or other spirit groups. Purged by my hate but unrequited, I broke the hold this place has on me and started toward the Old City.

Broke hold on me of this holy place

A few hundred yards down the hill I found to my surprise an open church with a small garden in front. At the gate is a tourist bus and the usual Arab hawkers.

Elbowing my way through them as they tried to force postcards into my hands and hands into my pockets, I came into the churchyard. The church was about to close. A last busload of tourists was still standing in the garden listening to an English lecture about some tree that was allegedly two thousand years old.

It was easy to slip past the tourists and a monk into the church. The only illumination in the church is from the stained-glass windows over the alter and along the rear. I sat alone in that darkened cavernous hall. I wept. Love returned. The warmth of love, Christ's spirit, was everywhere. His own betrayal occurred in this same garden. He feels the putrefaction and exploitation of persons and religion. He was sad. He cried. Finally, He died so that everyone, including me, might know and feel His message of love here. He helps me to love. I am grateful, uplifted. I understand. Love can prevail against

Jerusalem, against hate, against anger, against sadness, loneliness and disillusionment.

Pilgrim on Wheels

Resolve to track Jesus along the Jordan, atop Mount Tabor

I resolved in that church to track Jesus' footsteps through the open country where He traveled alone*[1] — in the desert hills, along the Jordan, atop Mount Tabor. He was an outdoors-man, like all the founders of today's major religions.

Rent a car and drive to Bethlehem

To carry out my resolution, l rented a car and drove to Bethlehem. Joseph and the Wise Men could easily find a place to stay overnight there now. But finding a safe spot to park is another question. Bethlehem is geared for automotive pilgrims and is determined not to repeat its neglect of two thousand years ago. A plaza has been converted to a parking lot. It is in front of a basilica, hovering in Mountainous stone over Christ's simple birthplace.

Basilica over Christ's birthplace

My car mobbed by vendors

When I entered this area, my car was mobbed with guides and kids with things to sell, particularly protection from each other for my rented car. I hired a guide to the church (five pounds).

A few donations later, I was admitted to a dark crypt below the grandiose altar, lit only by candles. Everything is in small intimate scale. My heart beat faster. I felt the thrill at being so close to the place believed to be where Christ was born. I still get a fast heartbeat with this memory

Dark crypt below grandiose altar

From Bethlehem, I headed for the desert. Beyond Jericho was the Jordan River where John began Jesus' ministry with his baptismal rites. But the road was blocked with barbed wire, tank traps, and a sign in three languages:

"War Area, Do Not Enter"

DANGER!
Frontier Ahead Restricted Area Unauthorized Entrance Endangers Your Life

I turned back and headed for the wilderness.

Christ's next journey was to that wilderness area between Jerusalem and the Jordan River. The weather was scorching. Even the Dead Sea below seems to seethe, a boiling cauldron. There was no drinkable water nor shade. The hillsides, barren of any vegetation, were rock, sometimes a deep red or dusty white. It's no wonder that Christ had visions after forty days and nights alone here. Or that Bishop Pike (from San Francisco's Episcopal Cathedral) died in these same steep ravines after he ran out of water and gas.

I am grateful that I saw nothing of the beasts or angels Mark describes when he writes:

"And there came a voice from heaven, saying thou art my beloved son in whom I am well pleased. And immediately the spirit driveth him into the wilderness. And he was there in the wilderness forty days tempted of Satan; and was with the wild beasts; and the angels ministered unto him."*[2]

And let alone the devils and temptations more colorfully recited by Matthew*[3] and Luke*[4].

In fact, it is hard to maintain the mood of Jesus' wilderness. Military units kept appearing or following me. Bishop Pike's sensational, world-publicized death here a few months before made the Israelis more anxious to control tourists. This is also close to the Jordan border where patrol warfare was a daily occurrence and guerrilla attacks a constant threat. The signs of this war are everywhere — tanks, military camps, convoys, barbed wire, thousands of abandoned homes and refugee camps. At one point, driving up the valley, I noticed in my rearview mirror I was being followed by a motorized patrol — a gun-mounted half-track, jeep and personnel four-by-four. Whenever I slow down, stop or speed up, they do too. It is a stern reminder that this is no game, a disconcerting, escorted invitation to leave. The map reading "War Area, Do Not Enter" must have been accurate.

These desolate areas contrast sharply with the fertile green valleys, the blue sea of Galilee, the farm towns. I imagined these areas, except for the modem military equipment, must have looked much the same during the Roman occupation long ago.

Sea of Galilee

I drove through Shechem and Samaria, stopped at Mount Gerizim and arrived at Nazareth at dusk. There were no signs to Mount Tabor, my destination. Nazareth is a small, dirty village on a steep hillside. As usual, massive churches cover everything conceivably significant: the carpentry shop where Christ grew up; tombs of biblical characters; Jesus' childhood Synagogue; Mary's well and the seat where she watches Jesus jump off a cliff to escape; the rock where Christ and his disciples meet after the resurrection. Two rival basilicas marked the exact location(s) where St. Gabriel announces the impregnation of the Virgin Mary or actually plants the seed of life (Greek Orthodox and Roman Catholic6 version).

Shechem and Samaria

Impregnation of the Virgin

It is obvious that Jesus preferred the Open Road for his ministry. Maybe because he was not welcome in Nazareth.

Jesus preferred his "open road" ministry

The Nazarines in those times were offended by Jesus. But Jesus told them, "A prophet is not without honor, save in his own country and in his own house. And he does not do mighty works there because of their unbelief."

Prophet without honor

Like Jesus, I have no desire to stay that night at Nazareth but there are too many people to make camp nearby. Looking for someplace to stay, I drove towards New Nazareth, an apartment complex for Jews. It was different — modem steel and glass, garages, community buildings, like a California suburb or an occupation army headquarters. No one in new or old Nazareth seemed to know how to find my destination

Nowhere to stay in Nazareth and no one knew

Mount Tabor. They knew where all the stone monuments are but not where Jesus talked to God and was transformed.

Because I wanted to see "everything" and not knowing where to stop, I ate nothing all day except wheat crackers and lemonade extract. Hunger finally forces me into an Arab grocery store. It is run by a friendly woman. The prices are cheap and her young son speaks English. He even directs me to Mount Tabor. We all like each other but I wanted to keep moving. These days of rushing around Israel in a car were low points of my journey, too much like San Francisco.

Arab grocery store son of owner directed me to Mount Tabor

With nowhere to sleep, I decided then and there to drive the twenty-two miles to Tabor that night. From the main road, a small, narrow one-way track starts toward the Mountain and up a steep hillside. It is paved and has scores of hairpins turns. This long road is risky at night in Arab country near the border, even though occupied by the Israelis. The zoom and boom of rocket artillery sounds in the distance. Often jets scream close overhead.

Drive 22 miles to Tabor at night

War zone boom of rockets and jets

Suddenly truck lights flashed full on me directly ahead and on two sides. I hit the brakes and was immediately surrounded by automatic weapons. In the glare it was impossible to see who is behind them. The soldiers ordered me out of the car. My eyes could now focus on about eight trucks and forty to fifty soldiers, including eight or ten women, part of an Israeli infantry company on patrol. No one spoke much English; however, they seemed to understand my "church," "Christ," "Mountain, "Tabor" Apparently, no civilians were allowed to be there, but they waved me on.

Surrounded w/automatic weapons

50 Israeli infantry patrol

It was midnight when the road levels off into a parking area. A huge monastery looms in the dark under the stars. A light inside goes off just as I arrived and two viciously barking dogs circled the car. My fear of strange dogs and my desire

Monastery Midnight parking area

not to infuriate their owners by squirting the dogs with mace forced me to sleep in the car. Every time I stirred, they started barking again. I kept wondering when the monks or Arabs would roust me. It was too hot with the windows rolled up, but there were too many mosquitoes to roll the windows down. I finally settled for the mosquitoes; their powers assuaged slightly by a repellent. The back seat is too small. It is difficult to curl myself around the front gear shift and steering wheel. It was a bad night. But the discomfort was minor compared to Jesus' state of mind when He came here in secrecy and in concern for His own life.

Mosquitos

The Un-transfiguration

With the first sign of predawn, I was more than ready to get up. To my surprise, the two dogs not only had bigger barks than bites but were friendly tail-waggers, happy to be patted and to follow me around.

Predawn light transforms vicious dogs into friendly tail wags

Matthew, Mark and Luke all wrote different versions of this Mountain and of the transfiguration of Jesus here. Jesus, like Moses with Joshua at Sinai, brings some disciples, Peter and James, with him here to pray. He is transfigured in their presence:

Jesus' transfiguration before Peter and James

"His face did shine as the sun and his raiment was as white as light." (Matthew)

Matthew

"And his raiment became shining, exceeding white as snow; so as no fuller on earth can white them." (Mark)

And Moses and Elijah appear in glory and talked with Jesus. The disciples propose that a temple be built for Moses and Elijah on this ground. But then a black cloud overshadows them all and a voice from it says:

Moses and Elijah appear

"This is my beloved Son in whom I am well pleased. Hear Him." (Matthew 3:17)

God: "This is my beloved

Jesus predicted his own death

Jesus calms his disciples' fear but speaks mysteriously of suffering and death at Jerusalem and "the Son of God." The disciples are instructed to tell "no man what they see until the son of man is risen from the dead."

Striking early dawn view in all directions, Nazareth and Mountains.

In the early dawn light on the top of this Mountain it was easy for me to picture Jesus. The once formal gardens and walkways have so deteriorated that the growth is more natural. Beyond the monastery is a steep hill of sunbaked clay and lava. There are a few oak trees, cactus, bushes and dry grass. Tabor stands by itself in the plain of Jezreel with a striking view lit by the rising sun in all directions, towards Nazareth, fields and valleys, Carmel Mountains and northwest to the open desert. Of course, the top is dominated by the mammoth stone basilica.

Franciscan temple originally built by Greek Orthodox

Friendly monks give canteen of water and tour of monastery

American monk here 25 years decides to stay for life

I entered this temple first built by Greek Orthodox, now run by Franciscan monks. The enormous stained-glass windows facing the east glow with the rising sun. A series of masses are being held, each priest performing his own mass. The monks were friendly and gave me a complete tour and a canteen of clear, cold water. One of them was an American from the midwest. He lived here twenty-five years. He now has a chance to return home, but decided to remain for the rest of his life.

The monks weren't without a sense of humor, judging from the sign at the entrance: "If you believe in God, you are welcome to visit. If you are vain and calloused about the rights and property and feelings of others, write your name on our walls."

I discussed with many whether the transfiguration of Christ took place here or on Mount Herman[*5] further to the north. Mount Herman is higher, but it is much farther from Nazareth and was less familiar to Christ. Both are a "place apart." But I don't think Jesus would have walked from

Caesarea to Herman in six days as is described in the Bible. On the other hand, Tabor might have been populated but is less likely to have snow on it. (Some believe snow accounts for the gleaming whiteness of everything at the transfiguration.) It is unlikely that Christ and the disciples could have stayed at the top of Mount Herman very long because of the cold weather and their light clothing. The best support for Tabor comes from careful, Byzantine biblical scholars who over a thousand years ago studied this question, and selected Tabor and built temples there to Jesus, Elijah and Moses.

Test of spiritual truth is feelings

Does it make any difference? Mount Tabor was in no way a transfiguring experience for me. Someday I'll stay on Mount Herman to see if there is any different effect.*6 But the ultimate test of truth is what one feels and believes, particularly in matters of Spirit.

Hike up and down Mount Tabor uninspiring

That morning, I hiked down the Mountain and back up again. Although it is but a short climb, the lack of sleep and food for the last few days, the black snakes, and the windless, terribly hot day kept me flat, without inspiration. The heat and desolate views must have reinforced Christ's depressive thoughts about his coming death. The thorn bushes trigger my remembrance of his pain at Jerusalem. I was sad. Did they affect him that way too? Was he specifically aware that they are to be his crown on the cross?

Although a monk invited me to stay at Tabor's monastery for the night, I discovered that the Mountain urges me to move on, to continue my quest, to continue my own perhaps transfiguration already begun.

I felt as I imagined Jesus, Muhammad*7 even Moses and those who follow do; the inspiration and revelation I seek comes from the Sacred Mountains.

But until the final day, the Mountains are close to God.

God is "up." Mountains are isolated in places where man's mind can focus on "up" without the distraction of people and events, where no one else has a chance to witness any holy meeting or to claim that it did not happen. Mountains are concrete symbols of man's aspiration to raise himself to new heights. He must do so. His body, made of earth, must, like the Mountain, be harder, larger, more visible, more real, more permanent than it seems. It is man's need, spiritually.

The same will be true of every climber of Sacred Mountains. The Mountains support the growing concept that Sacred Mountains are an integral part of the living earth.

Footnotes:
1. "Do not imagine that something will be lacking from your faith because you have not seen Jerusalem, an overcrowded city where there is a curia, a garrison, prostitutes and buffoons just as in other cities."
2. Mark, Chapter I, 11-12
3. Matthew, Chapter IV, 1-9
4. Luke, Chapter IV, 1-14
5. Originally a Samaritan holy Mountain, its religious significance is attested now only by a Muslim mosque.
6. By far the larger one. In fact, one of the largest in the Middle East.
7. The Qur'an.

Sacred Mount
Hira

People View-Point

Belief in all other worlds
Celebrate the holiness of the Sacred Mountain
Perpetuity for fifty thousand years

                       . . . THE MOUNTAIN PATH

Location:	Makkah Province, JeHejaz, Saudi Arabia
Range:	Hijaz Mountains
Elevation:	2,106 feet (642 m)
Coordinates:	21°27'29"N
	39°51'41"E
Spirit:	Islam
Pilgrimage:	Allah's *Desert High Points*

ANGEL VIEW-POINT

Allah's Desert High Points

Muhammad, Archangel Gabriel, and The Cave

Esoterica: Myths, Mysteries and Imaginables

Qur'an: "Muhammad (peace be upon him) received his first message from Allah through Archangel Gabriel, the "Angel of Revelations".

On the Night of Power in the last third of the month of Ramadan, Archangel Gabriel appeared to the Prophet Muhammad (p.b.u.h.). Archangel Gabriel appeared to Muhammad in the cave of Sacred Mount Hira and said:

"Read"

Prophet Muhammad replied, "I cannot read." "Read"

"I cannot read" "Read"

"I cannot read"

The Prophet then received the first lines of the Qur'an and understood from a sudden illumination that "read" really meant to "receive and understand God's message to man." After leaving the cave, the Prophet Muhammad walked down the mountain. He then heard a voice:

Muhammad considered suicide on account of voices

"Muhammad, thou art the Messenger of God, and I am GIBRIELL" (Gabriel).

"Your Lord is the Most Beautiful One, who by the pen has taught mankind things they did not know."

Mountains will turn into dust 50 thousand years from Muhammad's death

It is on this same Mountain that Muhammad considered suicide because he was afraid, he was "hearing voices." The Qur'an makes clear the role of Mountains during man's life. But on the day of judgment when none but angels and believers shall survive, there is no need for Mountains since God will be there for everyone. Thus, on that day the Mountains will disappear in dust.

Founders

Buddha . . . Moses . . . Muhammad . . . Jesus

After my pilgrimage in Greece to Sacred Mountain Olympus, it was time for me to return to Western man's religious birthplaces to try to find the power of the Mountains that sparked four great religions . . . Buddhist, Jewish, Muslim, and Christian.

Morning Boat to Airport

The morning boat from Daphne in Athos to Tripite was late, so I missed the noon plane to Athens. Left alone at Saloniki Airport, I soon discovered the travel agent had not booked me on any plane. If I missed the last plane, which was about to leave, there was no place to stay in tourist-crowded Saloniki, and my Israel reservations would also be lost. A seating chart hung on the wall with tags posted for each seat on the last plane. The agent assured me that even though the aircraft was overbooked, someone would not show. The tags began to disappear as each passenger checked in. As take-off time drew nearer, other stand-by Greeks started shouting at the harassed agent and giving him money. Tags were exchanged until only five were left. I panicked and shouted. Two tags were left. In desperation, I grabbed the agent, tears in my eyes:

Flights to Athens Full

My Appeal with Bribes and Tears

I shouted, "I am a Californian! I must get to Israel! I have nowhere to stay here! I am alone! I'll miss my connecting flight in Athens!"

Soon there was only one tag left. The din of demanding Greeks crescendoed. The agent reached up, took off the last tag and gave it to me! My two-dollar gift to him was more an offering to the Gods than a bribe! I was the last and most thankful to get aboard – to be on my way to my own spiritual beginnings, the Holy Land.

I'm on my way to the Holy Land

387

Hotel on Mount of Olives

To my surprise, my pack, coat, and equipment made it through the x-ray machine and search guards without opening for the TWA flight to Tel Aviv, Israel. With current Arab guerrilla warfare, plane hijackings and bombings, close inspection of everyone's hand baggage in Israel was now standard procedure.

About one o'clock in the morning, after the flight to Tel Aviv and a taxi ride to my hotel, I was ready to sleep in my room atop the hotel near the Mount of Olives. My room overlooked old Jerusalem. This Jerusalem I was looking at under the stars must have looked much the same as it did to Jews two thousand years ago.

Founders

Here I was to face, understand, and be a part of my own formal religion, Christianity, explore its roots in Judaism, and examine its sister religion, Islam. This is where it all began and now begins for me on these Mountains: the revelations to Moses at Mount Sinai, the temple at Mount Zion, Christ's temptations and his Mountain sermon, his transfiguration at Mount Tabor, his betrayal and ascension at the Mount of Olives and his crucifixion at Calvary. And here is Muhammad's enlightenment at Mount Hira and his sanctuary at Mount Sinai. Buddha has a similar history, but his life and "ministry" was in a world, culture, and area different from that of Moses, Jesus, and Muhammad. But an area with its own important Sacred Mountains featured in "Boy From Pocatello"

Sources of Founders Greatness

These Founders' religions are the product of man's universal need. Man was ripe for them in His time and for centuries afterward. But the catalysts and salvationists for Buddhism, Judaism, Islam, and Christianity were individuals: Buddha, Moses, Muhammad, and Christ. The true greatness of these men is not in their being "at the right place at the right time", not in their words or even in their ideas, but it is in their very beings. Their own immortality comes from the actions, motivations, and beliefs they inspire in their disciples. They changed the world by changing those near them and those not near who followed their teachings.

Thought and words of the Founders

If we would understand their places in the world, their importance, and their power, we must know them and the holy writ they inspired. For my own understanding, I put together profiles of the essence of Buddha, Moses, Muhammad, and Christ in my attempt to summarize their lives and thoughts and rely on their own pronouncements. They are included so that the reader may become, as I am, involved in the very words and thoughts of these four great religions and their respected Founders.

I give you first, Buddha's concepts of truth*[1]; "Song of Moses"*[2]; Allah's "Our Messenger Mohammed"*[3]; and finally, "Parable of the Man"*[4] about Jesus Christ.

Concepts of Truth

I am The Buddha

I Am The Buddha. I was born a prince, an heir to a kingdom in India in the 6th century before Christ. The sages and Brahmins of the time predicted that I would grow to transform this kingdom and small nation now ruled by a King, by my father, into an empire or possibly a unique people and kingdom that was "not of this world". When I grew older I became concerned about the hypocrisy of political leadership and yearned for answers from my own and all men's suffering. As a young man, I gave up my legacy of Kingship, my wife, and my newly born son to become a wandering holy man. For years I sought my teachers. I lived alone in mountain caves. I begged for food. I finally starved myself almost to death until I decided asceticism is the wrong path. Finally, after 49 days of quiet meditation under a Sacred leafy fig tree (called the

Buddha Story

Bodhi or enlightenment tree), I found my own truths and wanted to share them with any person interested.

For example:

Conquer Self

"One's own self conquered is better than all other people conquered."

I found my Nirvana on a 40 day journey to the Sacred Mountains, jungles, openness, and with Nature. I experienced and found sorrow outside my old palace walls as I spent 6 years in the hills and mountains of Nepal, starving, freezing, and injuring myself.

First Sermon

My talk at the Indian Holy City of Varanasi was my first initial "sermon":

Avoid Extremes

"By avoiding the extremes, I gained the knowledge of the Middle Path that leads to wisdom, calm, knowledge, Supreme Enlightenment, and Nirvana."

Limits of Moderation

But mere moderation alone does not assure such ultimate success for most of us, "Sorrow" does not seem to be the touch stone of today's quest as it was for me. My advice to others to rid themselves of all desire may seem unreasonable, for desire is a natural part of life, a humanness, and a joy. Elimination of craving rather than ending desire, seems more modern. Although complete elimination of desire may seem unreasonable, my Noble Eightfold Path to enlightenment can be a true road to enlightenment:

Noble Eightfold Path

> Right Knowledge.
> Right Intention.
> Right Conduct.
> Right Means of Livelihood.
> Right Effort.
> Right Mindfulness.
> Right Concentration.

Human Suffering

My own truths relating to suffering may not be a satisfying answer, reason, or cure of suffering, but to suffer is a true human condition for everyone: and can be cured, at least assuaged, by my suggestions if recognized and adhered to:

1. Suffering is universal.
2. The cause of suffering is craving or selfish desire.
3. To cure suffering, rid oneself of craving.
4. To eliminate craving, follow my Noble Eightfold Path.

Four Percepts

Accept Doctrines of Karma, Cycless of Birth/ Death

As I see it, "Buddhism" is an individual matter and doesn't require dogmatic acceptance of all my concepts. There's no need to consider me an especially holy individual or whether ones experience and understanding leads him or her to accept the concepts of karma, the cycle of birth, death, and rebirth or the philosophical trappings of Tibetan(Tantric) Buddhism, Theravada Buddhism (known to its detractors as Hinayana, "the lesser" Buddhism), Mahayana Buddhism and variations of them, nor the Four Precepts–"begging, merits, accumulations, monkhood". Many Buddhists create their own miracles, rules, organizations, cults, and other recognized aspects of other religions not based on any "truths" that I have espoused.

I am not bothered by the many people who say I seem more like a philosopher than a holy man or a philosopher rather than a priest. I never pretended to be a God or even a sacred person. I only wished to show the path of my own enlightenment to those who are interested; so called "Buddhahood" is available to every man and woman.

For forty-five years after my own enlightenment, I offered myself and my truths to anyone interested. My personal gift to any person, man or woman, wishing it is a path to enlightenment, an awakening to reality through meditation, the treasures of love, joy, peace, and beauty within each of us. I tell others that only in this way can anyone walk the path to inner understanding and ultimate truth.

A SONG OF MOSES
CHAPTER I

Rule-Maker Founder

I am Moses, the Rule-maker, A Founder.

I am drawn from the waters, the dawn, the fire.

Without Aaron

I sing alone of God without Aaron for it is I who spoke to Him at Horeb and none other.

So, as I "speak," God speaks.

Son of a Pharaoh

I was born of Merneptah, the Pharaoh, the father of the world, from the desert of Libya, from the fourth cataract of the Nile, to the Euphrates of Syria.

Fatal jealousy

Condemned like Zeus or Romulus, Cyrus or Oedipus by the fatal jealousy of my father to His son.

I was abandoned in the marshes of the Nile.

I was raised to sing, hunt, play in luxury, rule, hate, and love as royalty.

Rageful leader

Quick to rage, desperate to lead, I heeded the voice of violence, murdering in stealth, hiding the body, disgracing my father,

Flee to Sinai

And then fled to the desert, my beloved Sinai, to nurture in the hot winds,

The cloudless sky, the loneliness, Zipporah's love, the wildness, a seed, Yahweh, to burst the cosmic bounds beyond the dreams of pharaohs, emperors, and kings.

Later:

Leader of Jews

I was the leader of the Jews from the thirst of the red Nile, from the stench of the frogs and the filth of the flies.

From the disease of the herds and pus of the boils.

From the hail and the fire. From the plague of the locust.

Angel of Death

From the three days of complete darkness from the angel of death passing over.

From the blighted land of Egypt. From the marshes of the Red Sea. From the barren rocks of the desert. From hunger, thirst, and pain.

Pain

From fear and depression.

Fear

From the wanderings in the wild lands. From the wounds of battle.

To the land of Canaan as I had promised.

The Jews were my children whom I governed with punishment and with hopes and with rods and clouds, acacia bushes and visions of angels and with God.

I found the core that activates an inner force to fight, to follow, and to live beyond its strength: the ark, the tabernacle, the candlestick, the curtains, the sacrifice and Aaron's dress, a signet, Holiness to the Lord, the mercy seat and all the rest, bejeweled, crafted in such detail that even their added weight with Levite care raised the heart of each Jew there.

Wrath of Pharaoh and Jehovah

Nine times I faced the wrath of Pharaoh. Nine times I faced Jehovah's anger.

Each time I was the stronger one. Each time I doubted, I recovered; each time I feared, I overcame.

Drowning Pharaoh

I hated the Pharaoh and all who broke their covenant; they drowned or died in violence.

Hated and killed women and children

I hated mine enemies and scourged them from the earth and all their women and children, the Amorites and Jebusites, the Moabites and the Canaanites.

Hated Jews who blasphemed

I hated those Jews who blasphemed my God, betrayed our cause, who broke the Sabbath, worshiped others or whored in their father's house; and they were slain in their tents or stoned to death outside the camp.

Hated disobeyers of my laws

I hated those who disobeyed the laws I made, everyone:

The "shalt nots" that cover history's pages: There are no other Gods but me. No adultery. Make no Hebrew your slave for over six years. Don't steal or kill, with some exceptions.

— like enemies or witches or whores or priests who burn the wrong incense. Don't lie against or envy neighbors, live with lepers or carry tales. Eat only flesh without cloven feet that chews the cud or swims with fins and scales (the sheep but not the camel; the quail but not the hawk; the locust but not the ant) and bread unleavened at the feast. Never wear a cloth of wool and of linen nor eat the blood of anything.

Eye for an eye

A wound for a wound. Five oxen for an ox. A foot for a foot. An eye for an eye.

Obey all these matters I decree and hundreds more to survive my jealous wrath.

CHAPTER IV

I loved the mothering Jewess breast, the father's daughter who rescued me, the warmth of Jethro, Ziporah's lap, and all that gave me kindness on the way.

Loved children

I loved my children as they followed me.

I loved the Mountains of the wilderness, and the highest of them all, Sinai, where with myself and my own God I learned all that need be known, "I am that I am."

For on Sinai's slopes, I first met God and received his laws. Finally:

I sinned for claiming miracles and never tasted the honey of the land of Canaan.

Liked the battle more than the victory

But it was well, I was old. I liked the battle more than the victory.

I was buried, as I began, on a Mountain overlooking the Jordan.

My seeds

But from my own beginnings and from my seed grew the greatest of them all: the prophets, Christ, and then Muhammad.

Jews will succeed   And the Jews will succeed for their strengths, those I imbued them with. They will be wracked with heavy pain for their rebellion and their religious fame.

Jews will not die   But they are now a source of man. They will not die in any land.

I am what I am   For they are me, my immortality, since I am what I am and what they are.

As Moses might have described himself in the "Song of Moses," imagine with me how Allah might have spoken of his Messenger, Muhammad:

OUR MESSENGER

Allah   "We, Allah, the Most High, the Mighty, the Wise, the Compassionate, the Merciful, King of Judgment Day, the Day of Doom, By the fig and by the olive,

Laws to Moses   By Mount Sinai where We gave Our laws to Moses,

By Mount Tabor where We gave Our blessings to Jesus,

By the barren desert and the black tents where We gave Our character to Muhammed,

By the great caravans where We taught Him of men,

Cave at Mt. Hira with Gabriel   By Abraham and the black stone of Paradise of Mecca,

By Mount Hira where We first spoke to Him through Gabriel, Muhammad is "the praised one."

Preseverance   "We were well pleased by His perseverance: Over early death of those closest to Him, His father (before He was born), His mother (He barely knew her), His patron grandfather, His most beloved wife, His eldest son and two daughters, His close companions in His cause;

Poverty   Over poverty (for He had only five hungry camels, one old slave and a hovel as His inheritance); Over the hunger, the fears, the hardships of the open desert, and the terrors of the hunted and His flight from home;

Over His doubts of His sanity from Our Revelations and His desire for suicide; Over the scorn, slander and humiliation of fellow tribesmen and enemies;

Over the betrayal of His followers.

Man, not God — We were well pleased by His understanding that He was only a man not a God.

Normal Life — His acceptance of the mundane, the marketplace, the flocks that he shepherded, the normal needs and pleasures of life: "Praise be to Allah;" He said, "I fast and eat, I keep vigil and sleep and I am married."

His words: "The things in the world which appeal to me most are little children and women and perfume, but I have only found complete felicity in prayer."

Compassion — His compassion: "He who wrongs a Jew or a Christian will have me as his accuser;"

Wives — "Treat your wives with kindness and love."

Lovers — His love for His followers, for practical Halima's breast, ideal Amina's short lived motherliness, Khadija's loving care, and Ayesha's couch of joy;

Humility — His humility, for on His tomb at Medina He had written:

"O Lord, let not my tomb ever be an object of worship."

Personal Character — His personal character, even His faults: Anxiety about clouds, winds, darkness; the Desert Arab in Him — Spartan, loyal, reticent, a man of few words and common tastes; solitary, eager to learn of other faiths and lands; friendly with a charming smile, a strong handshake and hearty laughter; moody with fits of anger that made the blood vessel in his forehead throb and turn black; superstitious about drawing His blood and obsessive about cleaning the wide spaces between His large white teeth; desirous of and squabbling with His wives (requiring their veiling with His advancing age); trustworthy in business (they nicknamed Him "Al Amin," the reliable);

courageous and cowardly, leading and withdrawing, patient and vengeful, clever and stupid; But most of all for refusing to be considered a God, Our Son, a worker of miracles, a divine.

"We were well pleased that He delivered Our Message as We gave it to Him:

Not a God

We, Allah, are everywhere, The All-Knowing King. The Only God. Idolatry, be it stones at Mecca, Christian Saints, Sons of God, or blasphemous Goals. Our will explains and accounts for all that has been or ever will be.

Our Will

Angel

We have angels — Gabriel for Revelation, Azrael for the dead, Azrafel on Judgment Day and Michael for the living — and prophets free of sin — Adam, Noah, Abraham, Moses, Jesus, and Muhammad.

Each man or woman is free to choose the path: Surrender themselves to Our Will.

Surrender

Those who do, go to Paradise, where lies that which is most missed on earth. To each male believer from the desert, foundations and springs and seventy-two black-eyed virgin nymphs, never touched by men or jinns, of resplendent beauty with retiring glances and swelling bosoms; to avoid disturbing jealousies, we never specified the pleasures of Paradise for Our Women believers.

Paradise

Those who do not, go to hell, lost forever, their skin to be scorched with fire, with only boiling water to drink and decaying filth to eat.

Hell

We gave Moses the Pentateuch, Jesus (the Messiah) the Gospels, Muhammad the Qur'an, and Buddha the truth.

Every Believer must give alms to his kinsman, the poor, the wayfarer. It is their due as We own all that is.

Alms

There will be a Judgment Day, a Day of Reckoning when Jesus will return, the ledgers of each person balanced and everlasting doom or paradise assigned.

Judgment Day

Ritual

"Our ritual is simple; follow it well: Recite: Ash-hadu La ilaha illa Allah, Muhammad rasul Allah (I testify that there is no God but Allah and "Muhammad is the Messenger of Allah).

Prayers five times a day

Pray: after cleansing with water or sand, five times a day facing Mecca at dawn, noon, mid-afternoon, and sunset, two hours after sunset. (It would have been every hour but for Our Messenger's persuasive argument in heaven on his Night Journey.)

Make a pilgrimage to Mecca if you can afford it.

Pilgrimage to Mecca

Keep sacred Ramadan by fasting every day during daylight for one month (before and until after a white hair and a black hair held at arm's length are indistinguishable in natural light).

"We know each of you and need no mosques to hear your prayers or the help of any priests nor penances, chastity, or ascetic proofs.

Sacred Ramadan

There is no piety in turning your faces to east or west. But he is pious who believeth in God, and the last day, and the angels, and the scriptures, and the prophets; who, for the love of God disburseth his wealth to his kindred and to the orphans and the needy and the wayfarer and those who ask, and for ransoming; who observeth prayer and payeth legal alms and who is of those who are faithful to their engagements when they have engaged in them, and patient under ills and hardships and in time of trouble. These are they who are just and these are they who fear the Lord. (Sura al Cow)"

Mosques not needed

No piety in directions

And finally, how better to tell of the beginnings, the founding of Christianity, than with a story, a "newer testament".

The Parable of The Man

Christianity

And one of the priest classes asked: "What is Christianity?"

"It was like unto a man whose life seemed a failure, born of a laborer like an outcast among the animals, fortunate to survive mass killings, ordered by a King fearing patricide. Though showing signs of more potential, He learned only to work with his hands outdoors as a carpenter. But that didn't really interest Him. Lonely, odd, by age thirty He had neither a wife nor friends.

Carpenter

His consolation was to wander in the wilderness and the hills where He could dream of His special importance unhampered by reality. Such dreams were inflamed when a wild evangelist baptized Him in the muddy waters of a murky stream. Immediately, He returned to the barren desert Mountains and there conjured His God and Himself as a miracle worker and victor over the devil.

Wandering in the hill

Convinced by His own consuming need that He was the Word, He became an itinerant preacher, attracting a small group of followers and a few women. At times, ecstatic with His God and at times morose and fearful, He predicted a violent day of judgment for everyone (especially Jerusalem) and a fatal betrayal for Himself. Such paranoid-type illusions were mixed with what many considered delusions of grandeur — He thought He was the Messiah the Jews had prayed for and fantasized about for centuries. Nevertheless, He began to have a wider following: the sick and the poor (materially, mentally, physically, spiritually) with nowhere else to go came to Him for comfort or hope. He told them what they needed to hear... it's easier for a camel to go through the eye of a needle than for a rich man to reach heaven. The first shall be last and the last first, the meek shall inherit heaven and earth, etc. His God was easier than the Old Testament Jehovah-softer, kinder, more personal; one God, Ten Commandments, Sabbaths, and justice were all right, but more important was to love your neighbor as yourself.

Jesus believed He was the World

Simple and uneducated, He was praised in stories but

Jesus uneducated

wrote nothing. But there was a country folk shrewdness about Him. He knew how to avoid trouble with learned Rabbis (If David called Him Lord, how is He, his Son?) and Roman police (Render unto Caesar that which is Caesar's). As psychiatrists, priests, Christian Scientists, leaders, and healers of all types have discovered, He found that a few followers could cure themselves of their illness with their strong beliefs in His presence. These instances became known. However, His ministry in the surrounding areas, and even in His hometown, was short-lived and unsuccessful.

Roman Record Silent

He had little effect in His time; the careful Roman record keepers didn't even note His presence.

To add new life to His sagging movement, He and His disciples reported a new meeting like that of Moses with a transfiguration by God at Mount Tabor. They planned to build a temple there but never did in His lifetime.

Jesus wrath at Passover

In His middle thirties, He enjoyed a flicker of popularity during Passover in Jerusalem. He used His popularity to vent His wrath on the establishment's money exchanges. But His acceptance came too late for Him to enjoy it. He chose martyrdom, welcomed His betrayal, and refused to defend Himself.

Jesus unknown while on Earth

He was sentenced to death, reluctantly by the Romans and happily by the Jews. Too weak to carry His own cross, abandoned by all his followers, He died like a non-Roman thief, like a slave with a crown of thorns and nails through His body. His life as he knew it was a failure. His fellow Jews and contemporaries were unaffected in any significant way either by His teaching or His presence.

Christianity

Yet, after His death, His memory and the memory of Him have dominated two thousand years of history.

Men and women still die and kill for Him, curse, and pray to Him. In fact, at least twice a year, over nine hundred and fifty million people worldwide call Him Jesus Christ, the

Love

Son of God.

And His Word is still "Love"!

Thus, armed with the words and thoughts of these four Founders, we can together make a pilgrimage to the Sacred Mountains and Nature from which their revelations still came, and their religions blossomed.

Footnotes:
1. Based on Carus, "The Gospel of Buddha ... Compiled from Ancient Records"
2. Based on the "Pentateuch" (the Torah is the first five books of the Jewish and Christian Holy Bible ..."Genesis", "Exodus", "Leviticus", "Numbers", "Deuteronomy".
3. Based on Pickthall (translator), The Glorious Qur'an, Yayinlari, Istanbul, Turkey, 1930
4. Based on The Holy Bible and the Britannica website, "Religious Personages and Scholars.", Jesus."

Buddha

Moses

Muhammad

Jesus

PART IV

Mighty Himalaya

Cave Myth & Sacred Peaks

Spirit

> *Spirit is not measured or judged by the size or popularity of the Sacred Mountain. There are Sacred Mountains that are almost hills rather than mountains . . . Sacred Mountains that are true mountains but are relatively unknown to the worlds public . . . Sacred Mountains that are widely known to the world's public . . . and Sacred Mountains that are unknown to the world's public but well known to local residents.*

Himalayas

> *But those Sacred Mountains that live in the mighty Himalayas are widely known by the public. This chapter recognizes and includes four mighty Himalaya peaks celebrated here for their world wide popularity, well known to millions of people, and significant for their contributions to Sacred Mountains lore, religions, and spiritual forces separate from their almost virtual, international recognition.*

Size irrelevant

> *Spirit is not judged by the features large or small of Sacred Mountains, spirits are also not reduced or denigrated to a minor significance just because of their popularity and mightiness as Mountains.*

Sherpas

The Sherpas left Tibet more than 400 years ago and settled in uninhabited Himalayan Valleys. They believe that mountain peaks, foothills, ridges, passes, and fields are the abodes of deities; they celebrate the presence of supernatural forces by hanging prayer flags and other rituals.

Five Zangma Sisters

The esoterica relating to the above-mentioned Himalayan Sacred Mountains is about the traditions and myths of Five Zangma Sisters.

The Sisters are part of a class of worldly deities and reside on Himalayan Peaks on the Tibetan/Nepal border, protecting the area from harm and giving spiritual support to those residing on the flanks of these peaks.

Goddess Jamo

Spiritually, the Everest Summit is home of the Goddess Jomo Miyo Lang Zangma, and at times her other four Long-life Sisters. They are dedicated to the longevity and prosperity of all local Himalayan Mountains' human residents.

Although varying names and designations are made for each of the Five Sisters most sources refer to them as:

Sisters names

One	Miyo Lang Zangma
Two	Tashi Tseringma
Three	Ting Gi Shual Zangma
Four	Chopen Drin Zangma
Five	Alkar Dro Zangma

Sisters in Bhutan

The traditions and Myths of the Five Sisters tell us that all the Sisters sometimes reside in the Paro Valley in Bhutan.

Reward

The local residents at least in these parts of these Sacred Mountains believe they will obtain the reward of good fortune including wealth if a person visits the Five Sacred Sites where these Goddesses live on a single day. They will then be rewarded with good fortune and wealth.

The Long-Life Sisters ... Himalayan Sacred Mountain Imaginables

Sister Names	Animal Rides	Animal Gender	Holding Artifacts, Treasures	Residences	Color	Personal Sister Titles	Clothes Accessories	Physical Attributes
1. Mayo Lang Zangma	Tigeress / Red Tiger	Female / Male	Tray of Wealth and Riches Bowl of Food- right hand Mongoose that spits out jewels- left hand	Tancient Gonpa to the South. (All Sisters Reside For Varying Lengths of Time on All Himalayan Peaks Including our Featured Mount Everest, Kangchenjunga, Makalu and Gangkhar Puensum.)	Orange Skin; Yellow	Long-Life Sister Goddess of Inexhaustible Giving Resident Goddess of Mount Everest Mother of Mountains.	Bright flower head reef Mostly colored silk garments	All Sisters are reported to have "one face and two arms"
2. Tashi Tseringma	Lioness / Lion	Female / Male	Gold nine-prong Vajra-right hand Long-Life flask with auspicious knot and swastika- left hand	Drengje Gonpa (All Sisters Reside For Varying Lengths of Time on All Himalayan Peaks Including our Featured Mount Everest, Kangchenjunga, Makalu and Gangkhar Puensum.)	White	Long-Life Sister	UNKNOWN (See Artist Imaginables)	All Sisters are reported to have "one face and two arms"
3. Ting Gi Shula Zangma	Mare / Wild Ass	Female / Male	Silver mirror- right hand Banner of Gods- left hand	Ramna Temple to the East (All Sisters Reside For Varying Lengths of Time on All Himalayan Peaks Including our Featured Mount Everest, Kangchenjunga, Makalu and Gangkhar Puensum.)	Blue	Long-Life Sister	UNKNOWN (See Artist Imaginables)	All Sisters are reported to have "one face and two arms"

4. Chopen Drin Zangma	Doe Stag	Female Male	Wish-filling jewel-right hand Jewel incrusted casket	Dzongdrakha to the West (All Sisters Reside For Varying Lengths of Time on All Himalayan Peaks Including our Featured Mount Everest, Kangchenjunga, Makalu and Gangkhar Puensum.)	Red	Long-Life Sister	UNKNOWN (See Artist Imaginables)	All Sisters are reported to have "one face and two arms"
5. Talkar Dro Zangma	Dragon Turquoise Dragon	UNKNOWN UNKNOWN	Bushel of Durva grass-right hand Snake noose-left hand Silver Ladle of Milk	Gangteng Temple to the North (All Sisters Reside For Varying Lengths of Time on All Himalayan Peaks Including our Featured Mount Everest, Kangchenjunga, Makalu and Gangkhar Puensum.)	Green	Long-Life Sister	UNKNOWN (See Artist Imaginables)	All Sisters are reported to have "one face and two arms"

At least I can imagine the effect of their names - first, middle and last;
Why the specific riding animal?
Why a turquoise dragon?
Why are all the riding animals females on one list and males on the other?
Is there any special significance of a female dragon, compared to a male dragon?
Is there any reason to each artifact held by each sister?
Why is each sister a different color?
Does each color have a special meaning or any meaning?
Why is anything made of their universal physicality "all Sisters have one face and two arms"?
Why is Paro Valley in Bhutan the only other research-claimed "residence"?

Developed and authored by Alan Nichols, "Boy From Pocatello"
Produced by Kirstena Gonzalez

Sisters / Buddhism

    In the 8th Century the Five Long-life Sisters agreed with Guru Rinpoche to become protectors of Buddhism. Later it is said they went to India for further Buddhist instruction.

Sisters / Milarepa

    In the 11th Century, the Sisters created ghosts while trying to distract the great Tibetan Yogi Milarepa from his meditation. They failed, but a few days later, the Sisters returned to humble themselves before Milarepa and also offered to protect the Buddha Dharma; they suggested their "life sentence" be included in the form of mantras. Milarepa gave them the "enlightenment thought" and various other Buddhist practices, including later, detailed instructions.

    There are many variations in the Ancient Historical Records in the names, designations and descriptions and even the activities and Sacred Mountain residences of the Sisters.

Descriptions and Variations…
The Five Sisters of The Himalayas

Sisters / Myths

    Finding at least current research on all Long-life Sisters has been an exciting development personally. I knew about Mayo Lang Zangma because it has been reported along with everything else about Mount Everest. For me, this discovery raises so many other questions, because I know that these Myths, every word, and every description that we do find, have some direct and interesting information about each of the Long-life Sisters.

    The Long-life Sisters of the Himalayas are known at least esoterically by the animals they ride and the animals' gender, the artifacts and treasures they held, their residencies, their color, their titles, their clothes and accessories, and their physical attributes.

Everest / Makalu / Kanchenjunga / Gangkhar Puensum

    They all inhabit the Sacred Mountains of the Himalayas including featured mountains in this book Sacred Mount Everest, Sacred Mount Makalu, Sacred Mount Kanchenjunga, and Sacred Mount Gangkhar Puensum.

Sacred Mount Everest

People View-Point

The Sacred Mountain postulates:
"Deceptions" and "soul" never cease.
... Together almost as powerful
as The Sacred Peak.
... GREEK LYRICS

Mount Everest

LOCATION: Nepal & China
RANGE: Mahalangur Himal sub-range of the Himalayas
ELEVATION: 29,031.7 ft (8,848.96 m)
PROMINENCE: 29,031.7 ft (8,848.96 m)
COORDINATES: 27°59'17"N
86°55'31"E
SPIRIT: Tibetan
PILGRIMAGE: *Elevation Doesn't Raise Holiness ... Necessarily.*

ANGEL VIEW-POINT

Elevation Doesn't Raise Holiness . . . Necessarily

"To achieve anything you must be prepared to dabble on the boundary of disaster."
— Sterling Moss

Esoterica: Myths, Mysteries and Imaginables

Scientists tell us nothing biological can live on the Summit of Mount Everest. Climbers are only allowed a short time to enjoy the view, assuming it's not raining, snowing, foggy or too windy to even stand up.

The Sherpas are critical to the survival and ability of climbers to summit Mount Everest and other Himalayan peaks.

Miyo fortunes

One of the Long-life Sisters, Miyo Lang Zangma, also known as Miyo, according to the Sherpas, distributes wealth and good fortune for climbers and expeditions on Mount Everest, as well as local residents, particularly resident Sherpas. Miyo Lang Zangma, "The Goddess of Inexhaustible Giving", is one of the Five Long-life Sisters and the Goddess "Mother of Mountain", as well as the resident "Goddess of Mount Everest and the Khumbu Region".

The Five Long-life Sisters, their animals and treasures are said to be:

Sisters, animals and treasures

One Miyo Lang Zangma — riding a tiger, holding a tray of wealth and riches

Two Tashi Tseringma — riding a snow lion, holding an arrow and a dice

Three Ting Gi Shual Zangma — riding a wild ass,

holding a divination mirror

Four Chopen Drin Zangma — riding a stag, holding a treasure vase

Five Talkar Dro Zangma — riding a dragon and holding a silver ladle of milk

Locals

The Locals believe if a person visits all Five of the Sister's Sacred Sites in a Single Day, they will obtain the reward of good fortune, including wealth!

A reincarnate Llama of Tengboche Monastery and an expert on the Five Sisters tells us Miyo Lang Zangma is very pretty, rides a red tiger, "wears" an orange skin and a wreath of bright flowers on her head and multicolored silk garments. She holds a bowl of food in her left hand and a mongoose that spits out jewels in her right hand. Her stern benevolence seems to require her beauty and generosity to be reciprocated with respect and offerings.

Sisters favored playground

The Sherpas thought Mount Everest and its valleys to be the "palace and playgrounds" of the Five Sisters. The flanks of Everest and the other mighty Himalayan Peaks carry Miyo's spiritual energy.

Hillary and Norgay summit Everest

The generally understood story is that Miyo Lang Zangma guided Tenzing Norgay in 1953 safe passage to the summit of Mount Everest. The story goes on that Edmund Hillary, on that expedition, was not only rescued by Norgay, but that Norgay was also in turn led by Miyo Lang Zangma to the summit, followed by Hillary. These two climbers were the first humans to summit Mount Everest.

Finding at least current research on the Long-life Sisters has personally been an exciting development. I knew about Miyo Lang Zangma because it has been reported along with everything else about Everest. For me, this discovery raises so many other questions, because I know that these Myths, every word, every description that we do find, has some direct and interesting information about each of the Long-life Sisters.

Tibet railroad genocide

While a marvel of construction, the Chinese railroad to Lhasa completed the population transfer and genocide in Tibet. Over 6,200 monasteries destroyed; six-year-old children, monks and nuns jailed and tortured for loyalty to the spiritual leader, Dalai Lama; all in clear violation of the Geneva Convention prohibition of population transfer; and 1.3 million Tibetan deaths from China's occupation.

One of the saddest things in human experience is to be misled. Where is the Dalai Lama now . . . Russia, Ukraine . . . and what does he have to say today? (2024).

I will never climb Mount Everest

Mount Everest, like many of our featured Sacred Mountains in this work, is a high point I have long read about, dreamed, and imagined climbing. I won't make it, however. It's too late. I never took the time to obtain and use the equipment needed for a Mountain like this. I observed the summit from both the Base Camp in Tibet and Everest Base Camp in Nepal. I also explored Makalu's lower reaches nearby to the south.

Blum invites me to eaverest and Makalu

My closest opportunity comes from another exciting and positive happenstance. I'm invited to join a group of men going to the Everest Base Camp in Tibet, including two University of California track athletes and a prominent California stockbroker, Dick Blum. It's at least a chance to explore the Everest Base Camp and some adjoining areas on Mount Makalu.

Fly to Lukla

We fly together to India and then take a light plane flight into Lukla, a small village. However, we are at such an altitude here in Tibet that when I leave the plane, all I want to do, on this beautiful, warm sunny day, is take a nap behind a

Bush nap

bush to keep out of the wind. Our young Cal student companions are so energized from the altitude and the pure air that they walk down a steep trail, two miles to another lower village and then return uphill to join me and Dick.

We arranged a Mountain hotel for all of us to stay and have dinner that night. The two younger men, even though they have lots of Mountain experience and are members of the University of California at Berkeley track team, are feeling altitude sickness from their hike from our landing place down to the village. They become worse during the night. The only cure for altitude sickness is to move downhill. The two young men are disappointed but we advised them to return to the United States. They both board the small plane the next morning for a lower location leaving Dick and me by ourselves.

Cure for altitude sickness

Dick and I then put together our own expedition, gather our sleeping equipment and food, and hire a team of Sherpas to carry our bags. We begin our own hike towards Everest Base Camp with a stopover at a Buddhist Temple, Tengboche Monastery. I've been here before. The setting for me is perfect – to the highest Mountain in the world, Everest, the Buddhist Spirit and Tengboche Temple, and what I consider the most abused and yet the most admirable people in the world, the Tibetans.

Tengbouche Monastery

Neither Dick nor I are qualified with the skills, the experience nor the proper equipment to conquer the summit of Mount Everest, so Dick suggests we explore the neighboring area of Sacred Mount Makalu. It is higher but to the south of the main Everest trail and Base Camp.

Makalu not Everest

We adopt Dick's suggestion and our visit at the Everest Base Camp and observe its operations from a Mount Makalu ridge above. The camp is full of climbers' expeditions down on the Base Camp and the tents of the climbers preparing to attempt the Everest summit. By this point we are on a high ridge southeast of Base Camp.

Snow starts

Two feet of snow

Message from Dharamshala

Meet the 14th Dalai Lama

Freedom without actually fighting for it?

About the time we think to start the home trip; black thunder roars in and dumps at least two feet of snow onto us in two hours. The only way to survive is to set up our tent and hunker down. For a couple of days we stay in our own tents and eat food that is brought to us by a couple of Sherpas. By the third day we decide to risk hiking back down the trail to the village below.

I have described our encounter with the Dalai Lama and my developing feelings towards him in an earlier chapter.

It is only in recent years that Everest has been recognized and confirmed at 29,301 feet to be the highest mountain on our planet.

As a result of this special elevation status and the effect on its human admirers, Everest is called Qonalangme, ("Holy Mother"). The shining translation from the 1721 Kangxi Atlas, besides the name's recognition, includes Chomolungma. There is a long list of other names for Sacred Mount Everest and disputes on the subject of the name as well as its pronunciation; several more claim the correct name is translated as "Goddess of the Sky", "Head of the Great Sky", "Geohungha", and "Gaurisankar".

Everest in upper troposphere

Everest has also been confirmed by many experts and others that the world's highest mountain ascends into the upper troposphere*. Its altitude exposes the summit to the fast and freezing winds or the jet stream often exceeding 100 miles per hour (160 kilometers per hour). As with most Himalayan Mountains, histories of these mountains are dominated by special technical climbers. Sherpa Tenzing Norgay and mountain climber Edmund Hillary are the official first people to summit Sacred Mount Everest. They summited at 11:30AM local time on May 29th, 1953. On top of Everest, they buried a few candies and a small cross in the snow, before starting back down.

*The troposphere is part of the atmosphere extending about 7 to 10 miles [11 to 16 kilometers] from the surface of the earth. Its temperature is reduced quickly and clouds form from the automatic circulation of fluids and transfer of heat due to gravity and density variations.

Everest death toll

Up to and through the 2010 climbing season, approximately 700 climbers successfully summitted Everest. Meanwhile, the total number of verified climbing deaths on Mount Everest exceeds 350, about 4 people a year since keeping records began in 1922. The total reported annual cost of Everest climbs exceeds many millions of dollars.

Everest still dangerous

It is still a dangerous climb in spite of the installation of permanent climbing facilities, important safety regulations, rescue teams, helicopter evacuations, permanent rock stairs and other rock safety works.

The Death Zone

Although the figure is probably higher now, at the time of this report, "almost anyone", can summit Mount Everest with the support of other climbers, a Sherpa climbing team, and the payment on average of at least $50,000.00

$50,000+ to Summit

It is still a dangerous climb, in spite of the installation of permanent climbing rock stairs and climbing facilities, important safety regulations, rescue teams, and even helicopter evacuations.

I don't have and never had the money, the time, the equipment, the skill, or the opportunity to summit mighty Mount Everest.

Holiness

On the other hand, I'm fortunate to still be alive and able to understand for myself at least the holiness of Sacred Mount Everest.

Sacred Mount Makalu

People View-Point

O, holy mountain, set me free

From doubt and sorrow;

So I realize

My true heart's desires.

      . . . GREEK LYRICS

Mount Makalu

Location:	Nepal, Tibet/China
Range:	Mahalangur, Himalaya
Elevation:	27,838 ft (8485 m)
Prominence:	7828 ft (2386 m)
Coordinates:	27°53'23"N
	87°5'20"E
Spirit:	Buddhist, Hindu, Jain, BonPo
PIlgrimage:	*Snow Bound Spirit , , , Sacred Mount Makalu*

Angel View-Point

Snowbound Spirits ... Sacred Mount Makalu

Esoterica: Myths, Mysteries and Imaginables

Some esoteric forces, like the Long-life Sisters, are a part of all Himalayan Peaks and the local characterizations. The Sisters are included in the Himalayan indigenous peoples' consciousness, especially the Sherpas. See chart of text relating to Sisters in the introduction of Part IV (pages 406-407).

Makalu Barun National Park

Sacred Mount Makalu is now a part of the Makalu Barun National Park. That park contains many high Himalayan Peaks. It is a rugged and traditional area that has long been considered "prime Yeti country". Unfortunately, my planned expedition to explore this isolated and rugged Himalayan area, and at least keep our eyes open for a Yeti while there, was not able to be carried out. I was of course disappointed; on the other hand, there is good news: Barun Valley contains extraordinary biological plant and animal life and is being surveyed in order to become a New Protected Area. Inaccessible valleys of the Barun River encompass some of the last remaining pristine forests and alpine meadows and has already been designated as a "strict nature reserve", the first in Nepal, "in order to protect the natural ecosystem and processes in an undisturbed state for scientific study, environmental monitoring, education, and the genetic resources."

"Strict Nature Reserve"

As made clear in the previous piece on Sacred Mount Everest, the other Four Long-life Sisters are on many or maybe all other major Peaks in the Himalayas including Sacred

Mount Makalu, Sacred Mount Gangkhar Puensum, Sacred Mount Kanchenjunga and Sacred Mount Everest …

Base Camp Expedition

We visit the Everest Base Camp and observe for ourselves base camp operations for Everest from a Mount Makalu Ridge above. The Camp is full of climbers' expeditions, preparing to attempt the Everest summit. We observed this all from the high ridge on Makalu and observed 3 Expeditions starting up the trail for the Everest Summit. The weather looks bad and, to my surprise, I'm glad I'm not going with them.

Snowstorm

While we were exploring the lower reaches of Makalu, several hours later we think we should start for home. A black thunder then booms in, and dumps at least 2 feet of snow on to us in 2 hours. The only way to survive such a snowstorm is to set up our tent and hunker down. For 3 days we hole up in our own tents and eat food brought to us by a couple of Sherpas. By the third day, we decide to make "a run for it" and risk hiking back down to the Everest trail and the village below.

Invitation to Dharamshala

On the way down, Dick tells me he has just received a message from Dharamshala, India, a small refugee town for Tibetans and their leader, the Fourteenth Dalai Lama; this was granted by J. Nehru and India in a humanitarian action to save the Tibetan people's government from China's attack. The 14th Dalai Lama accepted India's generosity and now lives there with his administration.

We tour a number of Temples in a long valley as we hike to the border with India. We talk to Tibetan monks fortunate enough to escape over the Indian border with Tibet and avoid China's vicious PLA (People's Liberation Army).

Audience

We then hitch a ride from the end of our hike to Dharamshala, in India, where the 14th Dalai Lama lives and is headquartered and where Dick and I are to have an "audience" the next day.

Dalai Lama Success

The Dalai Lama at the time was one of the most admired persons in the world, beloved and praised by world and country leaders, the recipient of many national awards, growing wealthy from his multiple book sales, appearances, talks, etc. Unfortunately, his extraordinary international sympathy and admiration actually results in an increase in the torture of his Tibetan people who cannot escape from Tibet; they suffer, death, torture, and injustice beyond measure. Much of the rest of this tragedy is the subject of Part 1, "Dalai Lama, Go Home".

Tibetans Tragedy

Makalu is the 5th highest Mountain on our planet (27766 feet), (8463 meters). It is 19 km (12 miles) Southeast of Mount Everest. As a prominent mountain in the Makalu Barun National Park, it shares the international Border with the Qomolangma National Nature Preserve of the Tibet protonic region.

"Makalu", derives from the Sanskrit "Maha Kala"; the Hindu God Shiva and translates as "Big Black". It is one of the world's most difficult Mountains to climb with very challenging steep pitches and a summit pyramid, pure tactical rock climbing.

Fewer Climbers on Makalu

Nevertheless, while Makalu doesn't draw the climbing community anywhere close to Mount Everest, at least many fewer climbers die trying to summit Holy Mount Makalu compared to Sacred Mount Everest.

Sacred Mount Kangchenjunga

People View-Point

Mountain passion and Love

Steal soft hearts from inside hard bodies.

I can always feel but never see

The deepness across my eyes.

Beneath my heartstrings,

Until I hear the Spirit Mountain groans

        . . . Greek Lyrics

Mount Kangchenjunga

Location	Sikkim, India
Range:	Himalayas
Elevation:	28,169 ft (8848 m)
Prominence:	12,867 ft (3922 m)
Coordinates:	27°42'12"N
	88°08'51"E
Climbing:	Fist ascent 25 May 1955 by Joe Brown and George Band during the 1955 British Kangchenjunga expedition.
Spirit:	(current) Hindu, Singh
	(historic) Tibetan Mother Goddess
Pilgrimage:	*Cave Hermit Rock Paradise . . .*

ANGEL VIEW-POINT

Cave Rock Hermit Paradise . . . Sacred Mount Kangchenjunga

Esoterica: Myths, Mysteries and Imaginables

Kangchenjunga is said to be the home of a mountain deity, Dzö-nga (aka Kangchenjunga Demon, a type of yeti). In Tibetan Buddhist cultural traditions, the original inhabitants of the area are the Lepcha people and the Limbu people.

Valley of Immortality

Generations of legends recounted by the locals around Kangchenjunga, both in Nepal and Sikkim, speak of a Valley of Immortality that lay hidden on the slopes of Kangchenjunga. In 1962, Tulshuk Lingpa, a Tibetan Lama, led over three hundred followers into the high slopes of Kanchenjunga to open the way to Beyul Demoshong. (The story of the expedition is retold in a 2011 book *A Step Away From Paradise*). The followers' goal was to open a crack in the fabric of reality and go to a land we'd all like to be, a place of peace and comfort. This work involves the Tibetan tradition of "Hidden Land" and claims to be a riveting tale of adventure, consistent with the real spirit of Tibet.

"Knott of Attachment"

Tulshuk Lingpa's *Guide Book to the Hidden Lands* advises: "Don't listen to anybody. Decide by yourself and practice madness. Develop courage for the benefit of all sentient beings. If you do this, you will be free from the knot of attachment. You will continually have the confidence of fearlessness, and you can attempt to open the Great Door of the Hidden Place."

Hermit Caves

There are pros and cons of the life of Hermits living in caves, whether on Sacred Mountains or otherwise.

Many Himalayan Mountains, sacred or not, house one-man hermitages — once more extreme than in older times, or even ancient times, when the hermit experience was more popular.

The historical, traditional definition of a "hermit" is "one that retires from society and lives in solitude" particularly for religious purposes. A hermitage is a secluded habitation or private retreat. It usually contained a solitary resident, especially on a Sacred Mountain like Kangchenjunga. It is claimed that while this involves extreme hardship, some services from others, including providing food and removing waste. In most cases, it is a complete solitary experience.

Advantages

The advantages to a cave hermit, includes a discipleship to a concept, empowerment, constructions and hopefully liberation, with luminosity, the observation of miracles, substantial, insubstantial and both, avoids personal disputes from jealousy, "spiritual ripening" from liberation, and spiritual courage including self-honesty, faithfulness and renouncement of this world and this life, practices and observation of miracles that promote joy. True hermits live an unusual existence. Key questions involve individual, environmental and spiritual issues.

Isolation

Personally, and on occasion, even in a monastic state as I experienced at Mount Athos, isolation in a monastic situation may look attractive at first but cannot be measured in a day or two. My own solitary experience in a hermit's cave on Kangchenjunga is obviously an insufficient test, at least for me.

Hermit Prayers for Others

Hermits often consider their prayers and penance not only to absolve them of their transgressions, but even other peoples'. Many consider it not to be a selfish act to live as a hermit and aesthete, but rather to serve others spiritually. Hermits sometimes have powers which in turn attract followers: it then becomes difficult to remain "solitary". The Italian word hermit — "eremita" means desert. The harsh, hard desert nature becomes a means to surrender to God, physically and symbolically.

No Human Relations

From the earliest times Christian monastic communities incorporated the basic premise of a solitary life without the necessity of human relationships. The hermits seek quiet lives in the rhythm of solitude and devotion and often include giving up worldly pleasures to find insight, wisdom and peace.

Mount Athos Monasteries

While exploring Mount Athos monasticism, I finally decided not to even consider becoming part of a monastery, let alone living in a solitary cave in the desert, on Kangchenjunga, or anywhere else.

Hermit Caves

Sacred Mount Kangchenjunga

Kangchenjunga, the third highest Mountain in the world, is a Sacred Mountain in Sikkim on the border between Nepal and Sikkim, now a State of India. It is named from four Tibetan words and interpreted in Sikkim as the "five treasures of the great snow". It holds an important position in the religion of the local inhabitants, many of whom believe that Spirits live on the peak, so no one stands near the peak out of respect. They say anyone trying to reach the peak fails or is killed. It is considered a difficult Mountain to climb. The area on the way to Mount Kanchenjunga contains hermit cave houses: several hermits live for years or even an adult lifetime in the caves.

Short Term Cave Hermit

While on my expedition to Kangchenjunga, I had the opportunity to be a 'cave hermit' and spend a couple days by myself meditating in a cave, once the home of a hermit, absorbing the beauties and wisdom that can come with such an experience.

Climbing Difficulties and Inspirations

The risks, struggles and the special adventures on Sacred Mount Kanchenjunga makes it clear to me that Kanchenjunga is beyond my climbing capacity–rock faces, technical climbs, ice, unstable snow slopes, avalanches, falling rock, cliffs, and difficult weather, especially snow. It requires not only personal skills but the unusual and indispensable climbing guides. I am with an expedition that is only able to go high enough to be inspired by the views and enthralled with our association on this powerful Sacred Mount Kanchenjunga! Although it isn't clear on our hike up this Mountain, when we return down, I also appreciate the difficult, emotional importance of the black and white Mountains nearby.

Cave Hermitage Decision

But I would not try to live the life of a cave Hermit. As I see it, a Hermit's life involves extreme isolation and vulnerability... physically... mentally... emotionally... spiritually. "My" cave I was in, was small and could be kept warm with a small fire. A little stream of drinkable seepage water trickles out of one place in a cave wall. It was possible to sleep since the floor was softer sand and I added some tree and bush leaves from outside. At least in late fall, a well-organized effort might make the cave comfortable at times since it was large enough to keep out snow, rain, wind, animals, most bugs and insects well.

"My" Cave

But even now I'm sure that a solitary cave hermitage here or anywhere else is not for me.

I would prefer a small, secure house on a warm beach... at least for a while!

Sacred Mount
Gangkhar Puensum
(Dzongkha)

People View-Point

If the Sacred Mountain provides the gift
That opens our heart every day
*   while we are together,*
We would never be misled
Thanks to our love for Blessed Heights
*   . . .* G‌REEK LYRICS

Mount Gangkhar Puensum

Location:	Bhutan China border
Range:	Kulakangri, Himalayas
Elevation:	24,840 ft (7570 meters)
Prominence:	9826 ft (2995 meters)
Coordinates	28°2'54"N
	90°27'15"E
Spirit:	Buddhist
Pilgrimage:	*Three River Unifiers . . . Sacred Mount Gangkhar Puensum*

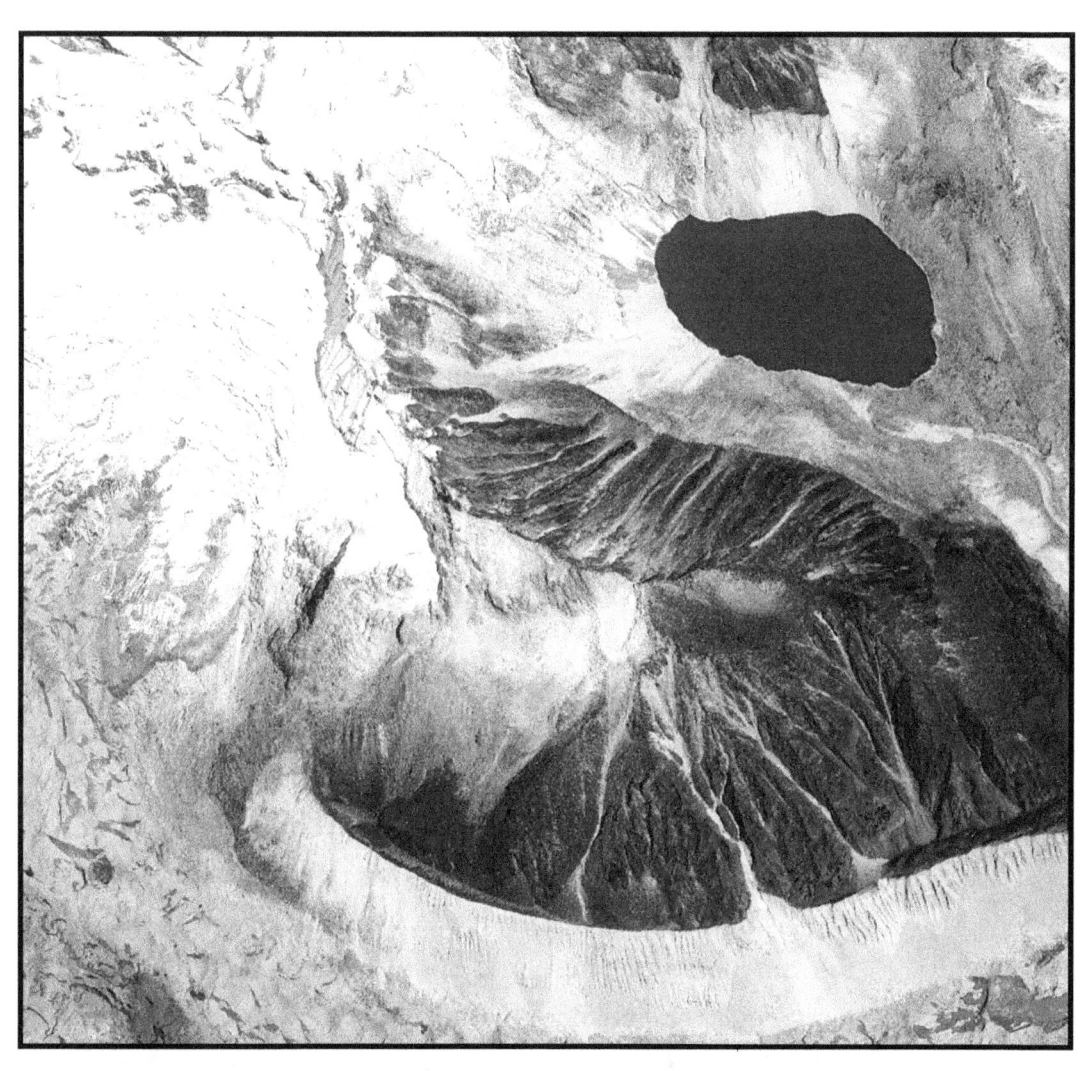

ANGEL VIEW-POINT

Three River Unifiers . . . Sacred Mount Gangkhar Puensum

Esoterica: Myths, Mysteries and Imaginables

Long ago at Gangkhar Puensum, ("the white Peak of the Three Spiritual Brothers,") which is the highest Mountain in Bhutan at 7,570 meters), three lakes were blessed. These brother lakes realized that because of this blessing they had a responsibility for the well-being of sentient beings, the regular people who lived in Drukyul (Bhutan).

Three Rivers

The brothers decided to flow three rivers from the three lakes, to drain the valley, and create fertile soil so the dwellers would have a bountiful food source every year. But the brothers disagreed how to do this, each concerned with the credit the other brothers might receive. Before going to sleep that night, the brothers agreed they would take their own route the next morning and compete in a race. They also agreed to meet at a common point after draining the valley. From the valley drained by the first and second rivers they would harvest paddy (unhulled rice), the main staple food at the time, while the valley drained by the third river would reap only common cereals and not rice. All three brothers agreed to this. But no mention was made about the timing of the race.

Brothers Agree to Race

Eldest Brother Flow

The next morning before dawn, the eldest brother silently woke up and flowed down the mountain to the valley of Drukyul. Afraid the noise would wake up his two brothers,

438

he picked the most comfortable route and flowed slowly and silently. But he was so slow he couldn't reach his destination first even by taking the plain through the valley of Bumphang.

Second Brother "Easy" Route

When the second eldest brother awoke, he found that the oldest brother had already left, so he started moving down also, taking easy routes but at a faster speed and then penetrated the valley of Trongsa. His river was swifter and noisier than his brother's.

Youngest Brother Wins

When the youngest brother awoke late in the morning and was about to wake up his two brothers, he found both of them gone. He searched for them at high speed and flowed fiercely through any terrain in his way be it jungles or swamps or cliffs and drained the valley of Lhuentse.

3 Brother Rivers From Manas River

These brothers were all different rivers. When the second river finished his route through the plains, he thought he was the first to complete the race but then found the trail of his brother ahead of him and could only join him. For that reason, the first brother river lost to the second brother river in the race, but was relieved that at least he could bless the valley he drained with growing rice. The two brothers continued but found that their youngest brother had already gotten ahead of both of them. The three brothers then proceeded together and formed the mighty Manas River which flows through the Indian plains to reach the great ocean.

Final Unity

This is how the youngest brother won the race, followed by the second brother and this is why Bumphang does not grow rice even though it has a fertile valley to do so and the two other valleys do grow rice: The final unity among the Bhutanese is recognized when the three rivers flow together, all forgetting who won and who lost . . . . But don't worry, global warming has already helped Bumthang grow.

The bad thing is that the peak of Gangkhar Puensum is apt to wither by day unless precautionary measures are taken

Summit Permit

beforehand by anyone reaping its blessings one way or another.

Bhutan opened Sacred Mount Gangkhar Puensum for expedition in 1983. Four permitted expeditions to the summit failed. The government permitted summit attempts in 1985 and 1986. Mountaineering is now subject to a ban in Bhutan since 2003. Sacred Mount Gangkhar Puensum now seems able to "breathe" without summit expeditions.

Crown Prince

I have the pleasure and the honor of knowing the Crown Prince of Bhutan and, as the President of the Explorers Club, a worldwide organization, invited him to attend an Explorers Club Annual Celebration at our headquarters in New York City. The Crown Prince was very much admired by the Explorer Club members.

Pilgrimage

I took five expeditions to Bhutan to explore and camp in this beautiful friendly country, even mountaineering at lower permitted levels. Although climbing higher than 6000 meters is prohibited on spiritual grounds, hiking and climbing is encouraged as well as participation in Spiritual and Cultural Buddhist activities, events and worship.

Remote

I was disappointed of course when we were not able to carry out our expedition to one of the most remote parts of Bhutan. If there really is a yeti, they are understood to be very shy, especially with humans so that any chance of finding them would have to be in a very remote area, with very few humans around. If they were to be anywhere, the yeti would be living in very high elevated forests, cliffs and mountains in Bhutan not usually visited by people. It was a pleasure to do the planning. And in any event, our anticipation likely vastly exceeded any reality.

Better men than I have tried to "discover" the yeti and even written books about it. So, if there even are any yetis, there is still a possibility they may be "discovered" one day. Hopefully, after I have "moved on."

PART V

Sacred Mountains Can Be Anywhere

The Sacred Mountain is more popular

with the closer peoples

There are probably thousands of Sacred Mountains, some well-known, some less so, and many unknown. They are the Way in the religion and the special spiritual aspects of an area. Their significance in terms of number of followers varies significantly.

This part of "Boy From Pocatello" provides some examples from all over the world of Sacred Mountains included here that I have personally studied, explored and made a part of "Boy From Pocatello". In that process, the Sacred Mountains and the Sacred Mountain Guru, as well as my own personal observations on my pilgrimages to the Sacred Mountain. It has been proved to me at least that different concepts, localities, and holy aspects of Sacred Mountains that are everywhere and anywhere on our planet…

Part V "Sacred Mountains Can Be Anywhere" is proved in this book's featuring Sacred Mountains in Scotland, Iran, Uganda, African Jungles and Open Space, Switzerland, Morocco, Costa Rica, Belize, Aegean Sea Peninsula, California, North and South, Tibet, Greece, Japan, Egypt, India, China, Israel, Saudi Arabia, Nepal, Bhutan, Mongolia, Alaska, Washington State, San Francisco, Kuai and Maui, Hawaii, and New Hampshire.

Sacred Mount
Ben Nevis

People View-Point

Nothing is better for a man than a good wife.

And nothing worse than a bad one.

According to the Guru's Sacred Mountain.

     . . . **Greek Lyrics**

Mount Ben Nevis

Location:	Scotland, United Kingdom
Range:	Grampian Mountains
Elevation:	4413 ft (1345 m)
Prominence:	4409 ft (1234 m)
Coordinates:	56°47'49"N
	5°00'13"W
Spirit:	Christian
Pilgrimage:	*Spirit, Like Mountains, Has An Easy Way and a Hard Way . . . Sacred Mount Ben Nevis*

Angel View-Point

Spirit, Like Mountains, Sometimes Has An Easy Way and a Hard Way . . . Sacred Mount Ben Nevis

Esoterica: Myths, Mysteries and Imaginables

Ben Nevis is not just a mountain to be "conquered" by climbers but also home to Scotland's creator Deity, The Goddess of Winter… the giant Cailleach. This God is described as an old hag with rusted teeth, a single eye, blue skin and white hair.

Giant Goddess: Cailleach

Once upon a time when she walked, huge chunks of earth fell from her clothes and formed islands like my ancestors' "Isle of Skye". She shaped mountains with her magic hammer, carved out glens, and filled the lakes. Her stories across the country created place names still used. Her throne was on the top of Sacred Mount Ben Nevis and she would ride out across Scotland every winter from the heights of Ben Nevis to the gulf of Corryvreckan. She washes her enormous plaid in swirling waters until it is shining white and then casts it over the mountains of Scotland dusting the land in light snow. As she travels Scotland on long, dark nights she strikes the ground with her staff covering with frost and ice. The Cailleach is especially protective of animals, particularly deer. Scot hunters are always mindful to protect the herds around Mount Nevis.

Throne

Snow dust

Bride Prison

Out of jealousy, Cailleach imprisons a beautiful young girl named Bride deep inside Mount Ben Nevis. She forces Bride to carry out chores for her until King Angus of Summer sees her in a dream. Angus tried to rescue Bride and went to Scotland to do it. With his presence, winter started to retreat. In the Spring, flowers began to appear and the old hag feels her power waning. But she wasn't powerless yet. So, she raised storm after storm to prove her might, But the exertion was too much. The Cailleach began to grow weary and Angus was able to free Bride from her prison inside Mount Ben Nevis.

Release

Summer was coming and Cailleach had to rest until fall. But she knew that she would regain her strength, capture Bride again, and take back her throne on top of Sacred Mount Ben Nevis.

Every year this same cycle takes place as seasons pass. No matter how harsh the Winter or wild the Spring, the people of Scotland can be sure that Angus will rescue Bride and Cailleach will be forced to rest.

"Winter might be here but doesn't last forever!"

....

Ben Nevis

Ben Nevis is the highest Mountain in Scotland, United Kingdom and the British Isles. The Summit is a collapsed dome of an ancient volcano comparable to Mount Rainier in Washington. It is a Mountain for mountain and ice climbing. The first recorded ascent of Ben Nevis was made on Aug 17th, 1771.

I am on my way for my first and only visit to Scotland's Isle of Skye, my own ancestral Scotch family home as I understand. A few members of my family came from this place in Scotland.

Climbing Mountain?

While driving, I, as usual, become fascinated thinking about an island with a climbing Mountain on it that I am unfamiliar with.

A dirt road seems to go towards the top so I decide to see where it goes. Actually, I discovered it goes to the summit of Ben Nevis.

Why "climbers"

Several British climbing groups are resting on the summit from their mountaineering. While I could summit without knowledge of the mountain, any guide, or technical climbing experience, I am surprised that the groups already there have ropes, pitons, and the equipment required for climbing cliffs, ice, and overhangs. All presenting considerable hazards. When I inquired of a climber why they need all that equipment, he directed me to the other areas of the summit with cliffs, ice falls, and other serious climbing areas. Ben Nevis is indeed a serious climbing Mountain.

It is also a mystical moment for me and the ghost of my family on the Mountains on the Isle of Skye across the nearby bridge.

Sacred Mount Damavand

People View-Point

Only in stillness and in movement
Only in Spirit can the Mountain speak
On earth and in heaven.
The person who knows does not speak.
And those who speak do not know.
The spirit and the Sacred Mountain
Are most Real

. . . ANON

Mount Damavand

Location: Iran
Range: Alborz-Azantaran
Last Eruption: 5350 B.C. (plus or minus 200 years)
Elevation: 18,402 ft / (5,609 m)
Prominence: 15,312 ft (4,667 m)
Parent peak Mount Elbrus
Coordinates: 35°57'04"N
 52°06'32"E
Spirit: Islam, Ancient Persian
Pilgrimage: *Wrong Interpretations Become Pleasant Surprises . . .*
 Sacred Mount Damavand, Iran

Angel View-Point

Wrong Interpretations Become Pleasant Surprises... Sacred Mount Damavand, Iran

Mount Damavand is a dormant stratovolcano and is the highest peak in Iran and Western Asia, the highest volcano in Asia, and the 3rd highest volcano in the Eastern Hemisphere at an elevation of 5,609 metres. Its last eruption was in 5350 B.C.(± 200 years).

Damavand has a special place in Persian mythology and folklore. In Persian poetry and literature, the mountain symbolizes Iranian resistance to despotism and foreign rule. Zoroastrian mythology emphasizes a chained three headed dragon, Azi Dahaka, inside Mount Damavand who is supposed to be there until the end of the world. In a later similar myth, the tyrant Zahhak was also chained in a cave somewhere within the mountain after being defeated by Fereydun, a "mythical hero". The famous Persian poet Ferdowsi wrote about this in what most people consider his masterpiece, the Shahnameh: "He brought Zahhak like a horse to Mount Damavand, and tied him at the peak tight and bound."

Damavand is said to hold magical powers in the Shahnameh. The Mountain has also been named in the Iranian myth of Arash as recounted by Dal'ami as the location

Esoterica: Myths, Mysteries and Imaginables

Iran resistance to Despotism

from which the hero shot his magic bow to the corners of Iraq, during a border dispute between Iran and Turen. Also, the poem "Damavand" by Mohammad Bahara is a fine example of the mountain's significance in Persian literature: "O white giant we see in chains / O dome of the world, O Damavand."

Multi Names / Multi Myths

While the origins and meaning of the word "Damavand" are unclear, prominent researchers have speculated that it probably means "the mountain from which snow and ash arise." The mountain was mentioned under several different names in antiquity and many myths and legends were recorded in Arab histories and Persian epic literature. Likewise, the villages around the mountain have several legends and tales featuring the mountain, and many names for it found in its archaeological remains like rock carvings and prehistoric tombs.

For example, in the upper valley a small ravine sprinkled with marshes, hot springs and geysers, is named Div Asiap (the Devil's Mill). Other translations of the name include: "The Mountain of Many Faces", "Snowstorm", and "Magical Mountain".

The first king of Iran resided on Damavand. Another historical personage was said to have traveled in the air from Damavand to Baylon, arriving in a chariot made and driven by demons. And there is a story about the two cooks of the tyrant Zahhak who are ordered every day to kill two men in order to feed two serpents growing from Zahhak's shoulders. The cooks kill only one man and send the other to Mount Damavand, thus saving many people who resided there. These two cooks were noted to be ancestors of the Kurds. Finally, Zahhak was defeated and sent to Damavand where he was chained at the bottom of a well.

Damavand is said to be a mountaineering challenge as part of the volcanic seven summits. It is very close to the Caspian Sea in the North.

Volcanic Summit

Most of the volcanic activity originates from the summit in addition to a few flank vents. A secondary creator, Haji Dela, exudes lava flow near the summit. The last eruption was around 500 BCE.

Thermally Active

Mineral hot springs are located on the volcano's flank and at the base. In fact, the area around the volcano is the most thermally active in Iran.

16 Summit Routes

There are at least 16 established routes to the summit with varying levels of difficulty. But the most popular is the Southern route which features a camp midway, 13,850 feet (4,220 meters).

Mountain Lodge

We spent a few nights in the area with my wife, Becky, in a hotel at just the right time. The setting sun provided a stunning view of beauty and majesty on the sea. I also took the opportunity to stay at a lodge part way up the mountain so I could climb to the summit and return the same day.

Thanks to the kindness and even the friendliness of local Iranians it was a very enjoyable visit in spite of the repression of the anti-American signs and commentary on television. The police seemed to be everywhere, there were special police to assure compliance with policy, particularly by women as to activities, dress and attitude. In our hotel 24-hour "moral police" sat in the lobby to make sure all the rules and requirements were strictly followed. While the official presence of Iranian police created a fearful atmosphere to personal activities, the attitudes of regular Iranian citizens was completely different.

Government Propagands v. Friends

In fact, to keep to our schedule, we had to leave Tehran before we wanted to.

On our way out of Tehran, I realized I enjoyed being an unofficial Iranian. I still remember their helpfulness and even positive reactions to America and Americans in spite of the constant flow of anti-Americanism in the media. In fact, it shocked me when I was riding my bicycle on the freeway coming into Tehran and a car pulled up beside me; the driver rolled down his window, and shouted, "God Bless America" and then sped on ahead.

I was a little surprised at the Iranian official police and governance people who allowed me to bicycle clear across Iran with no attempt at control or harassment on my biking activity… I just had to survive the cars and trucks on the highway, especially on the freeway into Tehran.

I took pictures of every factory I saw.

Atomic Sites for the C.I.A.

I surmised while being all by myself on the highways in Iran that the factories, especially the ones that were off limits, were atomic facilities of one kind or another. The newspapers in America had all kinds of articles about Tehran's growing atomic operations and the future of what was considered a rogue nation having a military atomic potential. Of course, one has to have the necessary information to decide how to analyze the actual situation based on facts. I thought that taking pictures of factories from the highways would provide useful information. But, in spite of my efforts, after I returned and offered the pictures to the CIA, they listened, thanked me, in effect said "Thanks, but no thanks". I never heard from them again. I have no idea why. I even talked to some people I knew who were familiar with the security world and they didn't clarify it for me.

Bike Security

So, with that I want to make clear, I really enjoyed the Iranians even on a very difficult part of my bike travel. I'm no smarter, in fact even dumber, about the huge security operations in both Iran and the United States.

Sacred Mount Karisimbi

People View-Point

The valient hero

Who subdues hate with love

Evolves "to angel", even Saints or cooing doves,

Man or Woman, gorilla or human.

                 . . . THE MOUNTAIN PATH

Mount Karisimbi

Location:	Uganda, Africa
Range:	Virunga
Elevation:	14,787 ft (4,507m)
Prominence:	10,866 ft (4,027 m)
Coordinates	1°30'30"S
	29°26'42"E
Spirit:	Modern Religions, Aboriginal African Tribal
Pilgrimage:	*Sacred Mountain: Gorilla Eyes*

ANGEL VIEW-POINT

Sacred Mount Karisimbi Gorilla Eyes

Esoterica: Myths, Mysteries and Imaginables

BOY FROM POCATELLO
I looked into the jungle
Of Holy Karisimbi
To find a bold Gorilla
To see and talk to me.
But when I saw gorilla eyes
Of compassion, interest, joy,
I ask you, Sacred Mountain Guru,
What should I really do?

GORILLA
I looked outside the jungle
Of Holy Karisimbi
To find a friendly boy
To see and talk to me.
But when I saw human eyes
Of love and great surprise,
I ask you, Sacred Mountain Guru,
What should I really do.

The Darisimbi Sacred Guru replied:
"Be kind to your neighbor as yourself,
        animal or human-kind.
Then all will be happy, all will be fine.
Especially if your eyes still shine."
Humans can learn from gorilla eyes.
Gorillas can learn from human eyes.

ALAN NICHOLS

Saccred Mount Karisimbi is the highest of the eight major mountains of the Virunga Range and Western branch of the East African Rift, and the 11th highest mountain in Africa. Between Mount Karisimbi and Visoke, is the Karisoke Research Center, where Mountain Gorillas living in that area are officially observed. But it is a thrill to find your own gorilla group, especially to really look at each other.

The Mountain is a special inspiration to me since I was able to spend some time personally observing two subspecies of the Eastern Mountain Gorillas. One of the major populations of gorillas is found in the Virunga Volcanic Mountains of Central East Africa inside 3 National Parks. Another population of gorillas is found in the "Dwindi Impenetrable National Park".

After some time with these "other" animals, I feel they are my cousins and well worth efforts to preserve our "relatives" for future generations, and even more convincing to have the chance to look at each other for a while.

While we were in this jungle, we "roomed" in a treehouse here in Uganda in the jungle hills for a few days exploring some trails and to observe local gorillas.

Their gorilla eyes told me much; it was all an esoteric experience that became my own "myth, mystery, and imaginable". My message from "Gorilla Eyes" seemed to come from the Sacred Mountain Guru of Holy Mount Karisimbi.

Sacred Mounts
Kilimanjaro and Meru

People View-Point

The fox knows many tricks
The seaman, a few.
The hedgehog only one.
And the Sacred Mountain none.

> . . . Greek Lyric

Mounts Kilimanjaro and Meru

Location	Tanzania, Africa
Range:	Eastern Rift Mountains
Elevation:	19,341 ft (5,885 m)
Prominence:	19,308 ft (5,885 m)
Coordinates:	03°04'33"S
	37°21'12"E
Spirit:	African
Pilgrimage:	*A Black and White History*

Angel View-Point

A Black & White History of Sacred Mount Kilimanjaro

Africa's Highest Mountain

Esoterica: Myths, Mysteries and Imaginables

Spiritually speaking, it has been difficult to find specific information about the original religious or spiritual role of Mount Kilimanjaro and Mount Meru, especially from the indigenous natives. Adjoining Kilimanjaro is Mount Meru, much smaller and less geographically important than Kilimanjaro, Africa's highest mountain.

However, Mount Meru arouses a special reaction to anyone who thinks about it. Mount Meru is a significant Mountain designation used often in far eastern religions, particularly Buddhists in Asia, in reference to any Sacred Mountains that bring the earth and heaven together into close contact. So where does the designation of Mount Meru or Kilimanjaro as Sacred Mountains come from? Particularly, from what indigenous tribes and peoples in Africa, who may be thousands of miles away from Asia's "Meru"; this name-sake for a Sacred Mountains is ubiquitous in Asia but not in Africa. There seems to be no evidence that "Meru" is the Sacred Mountain name relating to a local African tribe, the "Ameru".

The Chagga natives who originally lived on the slopes of Kilimanjaro speak about a man named Tone, who once provoked a local God to bring famine to the land. The people were aroused and angry and forced Tone to flee. While nobody else wanted to protect him, a lone dweller who had already turned stones into cattle, told Tone never to open the stable of cattle. But when Tone did not heed the warning, the cattle escaped.

Tone followed them but the cattle threw up hills to run up.

Tone finally collapsed, ending the pursuit.

Another Chagga myth tells about ivory filled graves on Kilimanjaro and of Rayli, a cow, that produces a miraculous fat from her tale glands. If anyone tries to feel the gland, but is too slow, Rayli will blast a powerful snort and blow the thief away.

. . . .

When in Africa, I hiked from Atisha, the closest city to Kilimanjaro, on the road in the lower foothills of Sacred Mount Kilimanjaro. I am unable to find anything obviously accepted at least academically or otherwise as to an ancient spiritual role of Mount Kilimanjaro or even Mount Meru.

Every Environment

Kilimanjaro contains an example of virtually every environment on earth – glaciers, snow fields, tropical jungles, very hot, arctic environments – all in the spaces of a few kilometers. The Mountain's peak is 5,895 meters (19,341 feet). At the summit the atmosphere contains less than half the oxygen available at sea level. There is a significant amount of literature about the Mountain but little history on the record of the indigenous people's religion and spiritual interest in this Mountain prior to the invasion and occupation of this part of Africa, mostly by colonial European powers.

Dormant Volcano

Kilimanjaro is a dormant volcano with three volcanic cones and is the highest mountain in Africa and the highest single freestanding mountain above sea level in the world, as well as the highest volcano in the Eastern hemisphere.

Pre-Christian

There is significant religious activity by European occupiers and conquerors in Africa, but little reference or history of any pre-Christian religions.

Johannes Rebmann

Johannes Rebmann is the first European to see Kilimanjaro. He reports that while the coastal people understood Kilimanjaro as meaning a "Mountain of Greatness", it could also translate as "Mountain of Caravans", recognizing the Mountain is a landmark for caravans in Africa that can be seen from afar. Reportedly, the Chagga people, who live in the Kilimanjaro area, call the peak Kibo, which Rebmann thought translates to mean "snow".

From then on, several men make their fame and reputations as explorers of this area of Africa, including Rebmann, Cooley, Krapf and David Livingston.

Western Breach Route

Our own expedition climbs Kilimanjaro from a less common vantage point, the "Western Breach", rather than the normal easier but longer northern approach to the summit of Sacred Mount Kilimanjaro.

Slave Trade

This whole area was once a source of a brutal slave trade. Any slave that dies on route from the Mountain to the slave ships on the coast, or those who were too exhausted to continue, were just left on the Mountain to suffer. One woman had her child taken from her by guards and the child's brains dashed out on a stone.

David Ligingston

The planters and politicians observed little of this kind of colonial abuse. Left to them, the trade might have continued even longer than it did, but the public of Britain and Europe were incensed by David Livingston's reports based on his solitary journey to Africa where he saw more of the slave trade than any other white man. (*Kilimanjaro*, 1982)

White & Black Men

Africa was dominated by the colonial powers, mostly referred to as the "white man". There's almost no reference to the fact that the natives, the blacks of Africa, were eager to sell out their fellow black people to slavery for what they could get out of it.

Johannes Myer was praised as having made the first ascent of Kilimanjaro in 1891.

At the summit we look for the now eulogized, but apparently removed, painted sign that once marked where the

"Snows of Kilimangaro"

leopard immortalized by Earnest Hemingway in his book *The Snows of Kilimanjaro* died on the crater rim photographed in 1926 by nurses from the Lutheran Mission and Marangu.

High Campt to Summit

It is a difficult hike from our high camp adjoining the huge ice field and ice caves on the Mountain via the Western Breach route to a campsite. Early on the next morning, we continued to the summit. The ice field was melting away, not because of alleged world global warming, but because of the scientifically observed local warming in Africa.

Summit Sign

It seemed a little anti-climatic when we actually reached the summit. We finally found a faded sign posted in the sand held down by a few rocks, to keep from being blow away by strong winds. It was just a board in the rocks with the name and altitude of Kilimanjaro painted on it.

Slide Down

It is also very cold and windy here. There is plenty of evidence that the summit is full of climbers and visitors almost continually. The walk down, really the slide down, on the sands of Kilimanjaro, is exciting, much shorter and a lot easier than the climb up.

I still want to explore Mount Meru next door but I can't interest anyone else in our group to join me. I am so tired, that our leader won't allow me to go alone. That is fortunate since I later discover Mount Meru is 70 kilometers away.

On the other hand, I am also more than ready to sleep off this adventure at our modern hotel in Atisha.

Colonialism

My only excuse for not being able to perceive an indigenous spiritual basis for Kilimanjaro is colonialism. Not only did the European traders encourage a continuous slave trade, but they required the indigenous people, upon pain of death, to accept and observe European culture, which demanded a denial, non-recognition and non-acceptance, or even kindness to the local indigenous people, or allowing other indigenous religions or spiritual practices.

The Ameru Tribe

There is an African tribe, the Ameru, but I am unable to find any information relating to any Buddhist conception of the Asian Meru in the local mythology that might solve this mystery of how "Meru" is used as a name for a Mountain in Africa.

Native Culture

Kilimanjaro's history, interesting to me spiritually, is not a matter of record or authentication. When the colonial powers, mostly European, first recognize what they could get out of Africa that justifies their commercial exploitation, they determined to destroy past African culture and native spirituality.

It's difficult to dig out what the historic spiritual importance of Sacred Mountains truly is. Kilimanjaro is the highest Mountain in Africa, so the current knowledge of that Mountain environment by the locals is recognized. Like Everest, people climb it all the time. The world knows about it.

Thanks to David Livingston

The huge slave trade that once existed at now Sacred Mount Kilimanjaro is a reminder of the potential horror of human brutality. Few people nowadays pay any attention to the major slave trade once on Mount Kilimanjaro. But thanks to David Livingston and many other concerned authors, the record of our human slavery and brutality by blacks *and* whites on Kilimanjaro rises to a condemnation of our human species, no matter what the color of their skin.

Sacred Mount Matterhorn

People View-Point

Rid yourself of the Idea Of The I-Am-The Body
Merge the mind into body
Know the self as a non-dual being
Experience darshan,
At the center of the universal Godliness

> . . . THE MOUNTAIN PATH

Mount Matterhorn

Location:	Aosta Valley, Italy and Valais, Switzerland
Range:	Pennine Alps
Elevation:	14,692 ft (4,478 m)
Prominence:	3,412 ft (1,042 m)
Coordinates	45°58'35.0"N 7°39'31"E
Spirit:	Christian, Italian, French, Roma
Pilgrimage:	*A Time to Kill? A Time to Die? Sacred Mount Matterhorn*

ANGEL VIEW-POINT

A Time to Kill? A Time to Die? Sacred Mount Matterhorn

Esoterica: Myths, Mysteries and Imaginables

The Matterhorn history states between 20 million and 90 million years ago the African and Eurasian continental tectonic plates slammed into one another and forced the ground upward into the peak of the Matterhorn on the border between Switzerland and Italy. At 14,692 feet, the Matterhorn reaches higher than the tallest summit in all the contiguous United States. Nevertheless, the Matterhorn is not the highest peak in the Alps (Mount Blanc is more than 1,000 feet higher). By any measure, the Matterhorn is one of the more striking, recognizable, and photographed peaks on our Earth.

In Medieval times, the locals told stories about the Matterhorn as a home for dangerous, aggressive dragons and beasts. The natural result of course, is the understanding and advice that anyone climbing the Matterhorn would suffer. Today of the approximately three thousand people who summit the Matterhorn annually, an average of three or four of them die.

Climber Deaths

Statistically, almost 500 people, according to current records, lost their lives on the Matterhorn, comparatively more fatalities than Mount Everest, Mount Rainier, or Mount Denali.

Giants/ Mountains

To this day, there are often many legends and myths describing mountains as being once giants. The Matterhorn was often referred to as a mystical place where some creatures (climbers) paid for their mischief. It is also said that the summit contains souls of the injured mountaineers whose climbing of the peak is associated with enlightenment around the world and associated with the divine as well as the connection of the earth and sky.

Myths/Tourist Attractions

Occult myth in Switzerland about the Matterhorn attracts tourists in the thousands.

The Matterhorn's mythology has affected many cultural fields including well known literary works. One of the more relevant ones to our story is about the Northern Giant (Gargantua) who actually lived in Italy and decided to explore the world further to see what was behind the Alps. After a few powerful, huge steps into Switzerland from Italy, all the surrounding rocks collapsed leaving the rock that is the Matterhorn. Gargantua was powerful and his long hair disappeared into the clouds, and his huge body shook the earth as he walked. He collapsed during his journey in the Alps. The only thing left was the part of the rock between his legs. That is now the Matterhorn. More imaginative people claimed Gargantua's heavy footsteps can now be traced on the rocks on the Mountain. The idea of attributing the creation of Mountains to giants is a regular mythical theme photographed by tourists consistently in their Mountain pictures.

The Matterhorn is a mountain in the Alps straddling the main strip between Switzerland and Italy. The Matterhorn is a pyramidal peak within the Monte Rosa arc of the Pennine Alps, and one of the highest Alp summits in Europe with four steep faces, facing the four directions. The Matterhorn overlooks the Swiss town of Zermatt and the Italian town of Breuil-Cervinia in the Aosta Valley. Theodul Pass, between two valleys on its north and south sides, has been a trade area since the Roman times.

While I was doing business in Switzerland, I found myself near a forest through which I was taking an evening walk.

Golf Course Trailhead

The forest is surrounded by a golf course essentially closed for the night. Nearby, I stumble onto a trail to the summit of the Matterhorn. I considered it a fantastic opportunity to climb the Mountain.

The weather was nice. There was plenty of light from the sunset and later from the moon and stars. This trail at least didn't seem to require climbing equipment. However, after a couple of hours, trying to climb further didn't seem like such a good idea. I had no climbing gear, no guide, no supplies or particularly no warm clothing. I sat on a log to ponder my next move and soon concluded that my temptation would probably kill me and I imagine how my stupidity can and will be used by anyone advising Mountain climbers. While experiencing foolish climbs before, I became convinced this is the most extreme. These thoughts were enough for me to decide to turn back down even though the Mountain did not seem as dangerous as it looks practically or as difficult as it might be higher up. In any event, I sat for a while and then returned. I arrived at the "Gold Coast" at 2:30 am where I was staying that night, happy to be alive.

Return to Room

Pierre-Auguste Renoir, famous painter of over a thousand pictures, once advised "one must, from time to time, attempt things that are beyond one's capacity."

Moment of Wisdom Saves a Life

This isn't the time for me, thank goodness . . . Better described as a moment of wisdom that saves my life.

Sacred Tan-Tan

People View-Point

Here on Morocco's Tan-Tan beaches,
The west Sahara Mountains.
Preserved, cherished, honored
By Morocco's King and Prince.
Here Nature governs
The sacred sand, sun, mountains.
Where the sea celebrates the holiness
of creations
We all thank our godly universe.
Here in this home of history, royalty,
"The Venus of Tan-Tan."

... Anon

Location:	Tan-Tan, Morocco (Western Sahara)
Range:	N/A
Elevation:	167 ft (51 m)
Prominence:	N/A
Coordinates:	28°26'N
	11°6'W
Spirit:	Ecumenical / Christian / Islamic
Pilgrimage:	*"I Am the Venus of Tan-Tan"*

Angel View-Point

"I Am The Venus of Tan-Tan"

Esoterica: Myths, Mysteries and Imaginables

It is a "little" difficult to tell how old I am. Modern scientists say I am 200,000 or maybe 300,000 to 500,000 years old, BCE (Before the Common Era aka BC). They also say I am made of quartzite rock.

Carbon Dating Me

Anyone, especially an architect, can better predict and estimate my age with "carbon dating", but so far as I know, it has never been used on me. Maybe it is because I'm too small. But in light of all the controversy about me, I'm surprised whether my age is really relevant anyway. For your information, I'm made of quartzite, a very compact granular rock composed of quartz and derived from sandstone by metamorphism (a ground change affected by pressure, heat, and water that together create a more compact and more highly crystalized condition; a condition that resembles a crystal, and is transparent, and clean-cut.)

Dug up in 1999

It is also reported that I was taken by manuport (a natural object deliberately taken from its original environment and relocated without further modification). The manuportist, Lutz Fielder, the German State archeologist found me in 1999 and dug me up from the North bank of the Draa River, about 6.2 miles (10 kilometers) from Tan-Tan in Morocco.

Earliest Human Representation

Headlines and scientists proclaim I'm the earliest human representation of the human form. Some say and publications have proclaimed I am the earliest representation of the human form. Robert Bednik, President, International Federation of Rock Art Organizations academic at the International Center of Rock Art Dating, Hebi Normal University, Shisyzhuame, China, has pointed out that he has published more than 1450 scientific articles, including many written articles about me.

 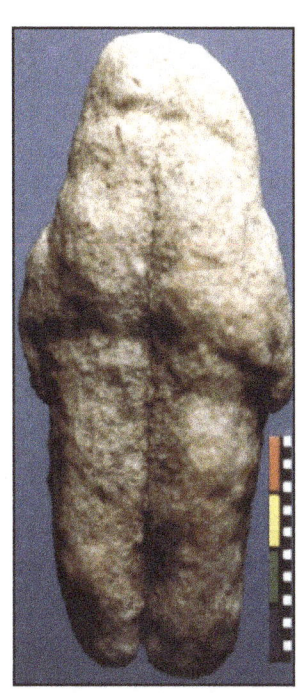

"Oldest Human Sculpture in the world. One of the oldest examples of prehistoric art known to archeology."

2.4 inches (6 centimeters) long
.47 inches (1.2 centimeters) thick
1 inch (2.6 centimeters) wide
3.35 oz (10 grams) heavy

Nature/Human Creation

Even I, of course, admit that my overall shape is Nature's work, but some of my grooves making me look human were made by "repeated battering with stone tools "and" my greasy flecks of iron and manganese could be red ocher paint which later was a regular technique of human art." "The specks of iron and manganese on me don't resemble natural iron oxide; that is a natural substance not a human created substance.

Homo Erectus Homo Sapiens

Incidentally, the references to "humans" at this time apply to homo erectus, a predecessor to you, homo sapiens. While Nature probably created my shape, homo erectus created the lines and ochre coloring.

I'm not sure why even though I am part of the Morocco Royalty, I have been held in Spain's Museum of Human Evolution.

Just because I'm small does not mean that I can't be an honored, extraordinary artifact for the world."

Thank you,

The Venus of Tan-Tan

Explorers Club

While I was President of the worldwide Explorers Club I was invited by the Moroccan King's brother to participate in the Tan-Tan festival to honor the Royal Court's figurine "The Venus of Tan-Tan." Dated 2000-5000 BCE, this "Venus of Tan-Tan" is considered one of the oldest human formed sculptures in the world.

Tan-Tan Festival

As President, I was asked to invite some outstanding Explorer Club members to also take part in the event. We all were extremely gratified by the generosity of His Majesty King Mohammad VI, and the direct hosting of our team by His Royal Highness Prince Moulay Rachid. It was an overwhelming experience and an extraordinary opportunity for all of us. We were all most grateful that the Prince, at our invitation, then agreed to join our large annual Explorers Club annual membership meeting in New York City. The membership was enthralled with his presence."

This journey was also a way to experience the silent Western Sahara Desert, now a part of southern Morocco, and to mingle with the Moroccans and gypsies (Roma) at the festival. The leadership of the Explorers Club were able to enjoy a unique tour through Morocco, the vitality of the Tan-Tan festival and a desert/ocean/mountain meditation.

The flat-topped Tan-Tan Mountains hover over the town of Tan-Tan. They are found in the southwestern regions of Morocco and bounded by the Atlantic Ocean westward and Sahara Desert southbound. It is a holy festival attracting many Moroccans along with tourists, mostly from Europe.

The Tan-Tan Festival in southern Morocco sponsored by Morocco's royalty is held where the West Sahara mountains meet the Atlantic Ocean. The Festival's activities include thousands of camel trades, a spiritual worshiping ceremony and people from all over the Sahara Desert and beyond, who come to celebrate the Quran. The fairground promotes craft-fair exchanges, sales, and displays.

The Tan-Tan was an unusual chance to honor Morocco's history and our joys of exploring.

His Majesty
King Mohammad VI of Morocco

His Royal Highness
Prince Moulay Rachid of Morocco

Sacred Mount Chirripó

People View-Point

Life continues

Though the cherry-blossoms fall.

And loose their enchanting gleam

The Sacrted Mountain Tree softly sings

of happiness

Beyond it all.

... THE MOUNTAIN PATH

Mount Chirripo

Location:	Chirripó National Park, Costa Rica
Range:	Cordillera de Talamanca
Elevation:	12,536 ft (3,821 m)
Prominence:	12,228 (3,727 m)
Coordinates:	9°29'2.7"N
	83° 29'19.2" W
Spirit:	Indigenous (Cabécar)
Pilgrimage:	*A Miracle Can of Chicken Noodle Soup on the Sacred Mountain*

ANGEL VIEW-POINT

A Miracle Can of Chicken Noodle Soup on Sacred Mount Cerro Chirripó . . . Costa Rica

Esoterica: Myths, Mysteries and Imaginables

Sacred Mount Chirripó is Central America's most prominent peak. Its elevation is above all other mountains in Costa Rica. Because the Mountain is the source of lakes and streams around the mountain, "Chirripó" translates to "Land of Eternal Water".

Costa Rica volcanoes

Costa Rica is home to five active volcanoes and 61 dormant volcanoes. In recent history Arenal was the country's most active volcano, although it went into a resting stage in 2010. Most of Costa Rica's volcanoes are considered caldera volcanoes, whose crater may be full of water and rising steam.

Costa Rica is part of the Ring of Fire created by plate tectonics on Pacific Ocean Coast that explains why five volcanoes out of 290 are classified as active. Officially the Mountains name is Cerro Chirripó with the elevation with 12,536 feet (3,821m). The Sacred Mountain is part of the Chirripó National Park, famous for its ecological wealth.

Old man?

I am an old man. Annie tells me not to say so. My only solution is to die young. Too late for that. Or die laughing. I'm too serious for that. So, I'll just keep my eyes open for miracles.

Contra Costa miracles

A good place to find miracles is on Sacred Mountains, like Costa Rica's highest Mount Chirripó. For those geographyphiles, the trailhead is 17 kilometers out of San Isidro.

Costa Rica + +

Annie puts down the phone, jumps up and down, and announces, "We're going to Costa Rica. How you'd like to bask in the sun, sip margaritas, frolic in the Pacific Surf, rest under the palm trees, go shelling on a deserted white sand beach, all smack in front of our home-to-be for a month? An added bonus: three bedrooms, so friends and children are welcome."

Costa Rica – –

I may be a senior, but I'm not that dumb. The correct answer to her enthusiasm is "Yes. Wonderful, dear!" Then I rush out to buy a Costa Rica travel guide to discover some escapes from the sun's melanoma, the tropic's bugs, the dementia of 24-hour relaxation and familial boredom. My rescue appears on pg. 283, "Climbing Mount Chirripó." Even a hint the peak was once a home for local gods.

Who climbs Costa Rica

The natives are too smart to waste three days on Chirripó, ruin their knees coming down and their hearts and lungs going up. To say nothing of freezing at night, boiling in the afternoon, and walking on rocks for days. This leaves the mountain to the tourists, you know the type, a few backpacking, free loading American hippies, Dutch waddlers, and the Germaniers out to "conquer the mountain". Now and then, to be contrarians, small back packs of young Costa Rican try it. Talking a lot, panting more, usually smiling, sometimes lying on the trail, and in all stages of dress, from street shoes to mountaineering boots.

Autobiography of soup can

In the meantime, thousands of miles away, Campbell's produces a can of soup. A farmer and his illegal immigrants grow the grain, spices, and whatever else goes into noodles; the lumber man cuts the trees, the miner shovels the metal; someone else makes a self-respecting can with a red and white label, "Campbell's Chicken Noodle Soup." Thousands contributed to this can of soup, however minuscule their individual participation. Think about it, they will either go to sleep or go crazy. For this story, just take my word for it. Not one of them knew they were actually creating a miracle.

I/ Annie / Soup Can

Suffice it to say, Annie and I and the can of Noodle soup make it to Costa Rica; San Jose for us and Porto Limoa for a can of soup along with hundreds of other tourists and millions of other cans. We make it to our haven in Elaya Seco, and the can to a native grocery store in San Juancito, and administrative center on the Pan-American highway in South Central Costa Rica.

We all meet

It was a miracle that we all survived to meet. In this country, travel by car or truck is only for the vehicularly challenged: Ready and willing to pass on curves and cross double lines, dodging serious chuck holes, avoiding the on-coming trucks with cliffs for road shoulders, and beating the on-coming traffic over one-way bridges without a head on collision.

Death travel

Bicycles, motorcycles, pedestrians, dogs, cows, and occasional iguanas are fair game for road kills. The only long-term solution to Costa Rica's International record for highway killings is to drive only diesel semis. Then it's the other fella that dies. Or buy an armor-plated Hummer, like the bright red ones we see all over the country.

Treasures

And speaking of National Treasures (we were, weren't we?) you can't help treasuring the breast, fertile and uncontainable in brassieres and blouses of Costa Rican ladies, young and old, prominently on display in every city, town and village, emphasized by tight, clean, bright dresses at least a foot above the knees, good posture, self-assurance, hairless underarms, and roving eyes. Even these treasures pale compared to a single can of Chicken Noodle Soup.

No permit to climb

Meanwhile back on the Mountain, Annie and I scout out the idea of climbing without the required National permit. One psychological impediment is overwhelming — while not having the required permits doesn't bother us, not having any food, sleeping bags or warm clothing makes us a little anxious. There's supposed to be a hostel 14 kilometers up the mountain where we can rent blankets, but the owner of the Inn at the trailhead, thinks it's closed and knows it's below freezing at night up there. With more wisdom than courage, we take a consolation hike into a rain forest reserve near-by.

Hypothermia / frost bite / malaria / heart attack

We have no idea that climbing the mountain, risking hypothermia, frostbite, malaria, and a heart attack are nowhere near as dangerous as the 8-hour drive to San Jose that night on the narrow, two-lane Pan-American highway in the fog, rain, and sleet, facing the bright lights of oncoming traffic, especially on curves too sharp to squeeze by on-coming semis. Exhausted, without food for 8 hours, we get lost trying to get through Cartago and San Jose for two hours. It's two more miracles when we stumble onto a Pizza Hut and even find a comfortable hotel.

Car wreck

Broker / cancelled permits

Back on the beach, to my surprise, Annie says "how 'bout climbing Mt. Chirripó tomorrow?" Thanks to a Costa Rican couple who canceled their permit, I am back in San Isidro with Juan Carlos — a pleasant young ranger and the broker of canceled permits. $75 buys the permit, two nights at the hostel, including the extra "gringo fee."

Climb begins 5:10am

At 5:10am we're an hour late starting the climb. Eleven hours later we arrive at the hostel fourteen kilometers from the trailhead and 5,000 feet higher. We rent three blankets each and head for our assigned bunkroom #6A. Annie claims "we're in a refrigerator with the door closed and the lights out." Our fingers frozen, we eat most of our remaining nuts and crackers. To try to get warm, we snuggle fully dressed into a single lower bunk, worried that we only have a few crackers and some granola to get us down the mountain, and we're still 5.2 kilometers from the summit.

Mountain refrigerator

We never see our roommates. Two sleeping bags and several other blankets are piled on two other bunks; an open bottle of wine, a can of Campbell's chicken noodle soup (probably empty) and some other garbage are scattered around the room.

Laughing wine

The open wine bottle in the corner reminds me of my days as a garbage man at Idaho State College. When I brought down the garbage from the third floor of the women's dormitory, I brought along a half full bottle of wine. My truck driver boss grabbed it. When we were both in the truck driving to the dump, he took a long swig from the bottle, turned red and gasped, "it's piss". I laughed all the way to the dump.

More blankets

Annie and I try to sleep, but it's too cold. I get up and rent six more blankets so we finally fall asleep, until about 3am. When I get up to find the bathroom, it occurs to me to see if there is anything left in the can of soup on the shelf. To my surprise, it is unopened. I put it in my pack and jump into our blankets. Annie is also awake and says,

"I can't go the last 5 kilometers; I hurt everywhere."

"Don't worry," I say, "we'll go back down tomorrow from here."

"No," she replies, "hiking the peak is your dream."

"Its the mountain, not the summit"

"That's OK," I whisper to her. "It's the mountain not the summit."

We finally decide I will get up in an hour, about 4:30am, and climb to the peak while she stays in the new warm blankets.

"I'll be back by ten, I promise."

Back by ten

But when the time for me to leave comes, and we're both more rested, Annie says, "after all this, I want to at least see the top from somewhere…. But after the sun is up."

Climb reversal

I agree, "nobly" in my mind, and we sleep until sun-up.

Joy of leaving the refrigerator

The day is clear, the trail broad and gradual; we both feel rested and hungry but glad to be out of the "refrigerator". At a trail junction we sit for twenty minutes trying to figure

Which trail?

which way to go. Maybe we're more tired than we think. Annie investigates the right trail across a small bridge; I follow a trail East towards the highest peak we can see, thinking it must be Chirripó. We both return to the junction. By then it is obvious that the third alternative with a "2 Kilometers" sign is the only way to Chirripó.

"You can rest here and I'll be back soon," I say.

Climb plan reversals

"I'll go just far enough to see the top," Annie counters.

But the peak is nowhere in sight until we cross a high pass ridge. Then Chirripó appears, a sharp pyramid with a flag on top, less than two kilometers away.

Annie sits down, "looks like some rock climbing at the top. I'll wait. You go ahead."

As I start to leave, she gets up again, "that's not fair. I've come all this way. I'm going."

It's a scramble made much easier by some steps cut into the rock. On the summit in our ecstasy we hug, have a long kiss, take many pictures, and start back just as a Costa Rican TV documentary crew is arriving to picture the early morning for a show about the mountain.

By 1pm, we're back at the trail's junction with 3 more kilometers to the hostel.

"Never back to refrigerator"

"I want to get off this mountain. The thought of another night in the refrigerator gives me the chills."

I reply, "Me too. But it's a long way. Let's see how long it takes to go the next 3 kilometers. We don't want to hike at night on this trail."

Another plan reversal

An hour later at the hostel, I warn Annie, "at this rate it would take us 5 hours to the trailhead, so we won't be there til 7 or 7:30 at night."

Time and distance mistakes

"Let's do it."

"OK, but we have to rest thirty minutes, eat the last of our granola, and rub down our feet."

"Let's do it, but, first, to lighten your load, leave that can of soup up here for someone who might really use it."

The first one and half kilometers down takes us an hour. "That's too long, but the trail's extra steep," I think to myself. We make what I think is the next kilometer in twenty minutes. At that rate, we can still make it by 8pm. But Annie's knees and hips are painful, increasing as each Advil wears off. The next kilometer takes an hour.

"Annie, I made a mistake. That 20-minute kilometer was really half a kilometer. We'll be really late. Shall we go back to the hostel?"

A foolish question. We are too exhausted to go back the steep 4 kilometers. We just plug along ever more slowly. The only miracle is my remembering, a neighbor gave me a small package of biscotti to put in my pack "in case you should ever need it." It was a gift from the gods for us — sweet, full of nuts. It assuages the weakness from not eating these many hours of heavy exertion.

Just another miracle

With sore legs, we spend the next four hours climbing downhill, swishing away the swarms of gnats and mosquitoes and avoiding the loose rock. At one point, sitting on the trail for a ten-minute rest, we hear a sharp crack and discover, fifty yards down the trail, a tree has fallen across the trail that could have killed us. Just another miracle.

Bad news

In the dusk, after hours of downhill walking, around 7pm, we arrive at the 7-kilometer emergency shelter. The bad news is that it is only halfway and it will be dark in half an hour. A clean cut young American, in a bright blue down coat, comes out of the shelter.

"Welcome. Will you be my roommates or continue on down?"

No choice – keep going

We sit down. Annie and I hesitate, but it is too cold. We have no tent or sleeping bags and no food so we decide to keep going. He tells us he is out of food and does not offer to share his one-man tent with us. At least we can get water, but Annie fills up only the smaller one-liter bottle; that will keep my pack lighter; and we won't need much water in the night cold. That's a mistake.

To tired to give someone soup

Annie whispers to me to give him our soup, but I am too tired from not eating after many hours of heavy exertion to take off my pack and give it to him.

"We might need it," I respond selfishly, just avoiding the effort.

Walking plan doesn't work

The next 2 kilometers through the forest are easier, but soon it is pitch black, so we turn on our single flashlight, trying different combinations of walking, so we can both use it – walking side by side is best, but usually the trail is too narrow for that. My pack seems oppressively heavy. Annie hangs onto the straps. Annie can't see the trail if I have the flashlight shining ahead, and I can't see if I hold it back for her. I re-swear I will never carry a pack again.

Trail steep, rock-strewn

We keep slowing down. The trail is steep with sharp cliffs on either side and is rock-strewn. Our fatigue scares us. Annie tries to hold me steady since I am beginning to stagger and stumble. We try to sit down every thirty minutes, but Annie complains, "It's not worth resting; it's so hard to get up."

Hypothetical question / wrong answer

While perched on an uncomfortable root, trying to rest, Annie asks, "What would you do if I hurt myself and couldn't make it?"

"Make you comfortable and hustle down to get help."

"Promise me you won't do that… you 'll stay with me."

"I don't think that's smart, but I promise."

"Even if I'm dying?"

"Yes."

We sweat, even in the cold night air. By 8'o'clock our

water is gone. Annie keeps taking Ibuprofen pills to relieve her knee and back pains.

Finally, about 8:30pm, we give up and lie down on the trail. On our backs, looking up, we can see the stars through the trees. Small, white lights flash in the forest – more like fairies than fireflies, but stunningly beautiful in the black night.

Fireflies

Still, and lying together, the mosquitoes find us and attack. Annie is on a flat rock, but I can't lie around two sharp rocks. Exhausted, we can't rest, so we stagger up and move. At this point, the flashlight begins to dim, a dangerous development, since neither of us thought to bring extra batteries. We cross a sharp ridge with the jungle on one side and an open, grassy, steep slope on the other called the "Coffee Plantation."

Injecting mosquitoes

Annie stops. "We have to stop now. That flashlight is about to die. I know. I had one just like it."

Flashlight dies

Too tired to argue, I stop, shine the light around, find a rare, flat grassy spot next to the trail, and collapse on it. It is the only resting place within 5 kilometers. Annie falls on it too, without even checking for snakes, thorns, fire ants, ticks, centipedes, or anything else that could hurt. I turn off the flashlight.

Give up / lie down

The plants make the ground almost soft, but, of course, the mosquitoes, gnats and ants soon find us. We have at least 5 hours until pre-dawn. Annie starts to shiver and whimper. Holding her helps… until it gets colder.

Trail bed

Then Annie remembers the plastic emergency ponchos buried in my pack. We spread one on the ground and one over us. Lying together, we actually sleep 3 hours.

Poncho discovery

We suddenly awake with two flashlights in our faces. Two young Costa Ricans stand over us.

Costa Rican discoveries

"You okay?" one asks

They offer to take us along, and even to give us batteries. Annie smiles, "I can't believe it; we've been rescued!"

Lost / rescue

However, it turns out they are going uphill, not down, and none of their batteries fit our flashlight. We pretend everything is okay and tell them to go ahead, forgetting even to ask for water.

Pack horse visitors

Two hours later, two pack horses coming up the trail rear and shy seeing our legs sticking out on the trail; luckily; otherwise, they could have broken our legs passing over us. By 4:30am, there is enough light to walk. At first, refreshed from the rest, we walk steadily. Soon, we realize we're desperately thirsty, having been without water for nine hours and no food. I start staggering again. Annie takes each step gingerly, and slowly, to avoid the excruciating pain in her knees and back.

Annie stops on the trail, "I cannot take another step without taking another Ibuprofen."

"You're not supposed to take it on an empty stomach, especially such a big dose, 600 milligrams."

"Miserable hell. I can't get off this mountain."

"Okay."

Ibuprofen failure

We sit down on the trail. She gets out her last pill and puts it in her mouth. She tries to swallow, but has no water nor saliva left. She can't swallow, but chokes and throws up the pill.

Pain panic

I panic. It could be hours before we see anyone. We're dangerously fatigued. I imagine what Annie's reaction to the pain could be. It might be dangerous to both of us.

Dawn soup discovery

Dawn begins. It dawns on me that I have a miracle. The can of Campbell's Chicken Noodle Soup is still in my pack. The broth is an answer to our prayers. The two tiny pieces of chicken, exquisite; the noodles, fantastic; and even too much salt tastes glorious.

Pill rescue

Annie picks up her last pill from the ground and swallows it. Twenty minutes later, she can walk. The last 4 kilometers

Last 4 kilometers

are long and painful for her, but we make it back to the trailhead, breakfast, and four hours sleep.

Pack miracles

Miracles are where you find them, usually, right next to you, in your own pack.

Soup miracles

*Koan: "A can of soup can be a miracle… when you're looking for it."

Intuitive enlightenment

*Footnote: A paradox to be meditated upon to train Buddhist monks to abandon ultimate dependence on reason and to force them into gaining sudden intuitive enlightenment. The difficulties of this expedition seemed endless. As I see it, here are a few of my faults:

Victory Note . . .

Footnote to victory

1. I failed to adequately plan and prepare
2. I didn't bring a sleeping bag
3. I failed to carry enough drinking water and food for the length, steepness, and needs of this expedition
4. I failed to plan and use available lodging
5. I failed to find a sleepable area along the trail
6. I vastly underestimated the difficulty of the exploration
7. I failed to research weather and temperature on the higher reaches

BUT WE MADE IT!

Sacred Victoria Peak

People View-Point

We hynn: truth wins the victory
through aspiration.
No matter . . . that the Sacred Mountain
offers only hopeless climbs.
No concern . . . hear the symphony
of the Holy Mountain . . .
with discipline . . .
Brings a sacred spirit
To the psyche and to the tangled jungle.

Location:	Belize
Range:	Maya Mountains
Elevation:	3,688 ft (1,124 m)
Prominence:	N/A
Coordinates:	16°48'44"N
	88°37'13""W
Spirit:	Mayan, Christian
Pilgrimage:	*A Coconut Miracle . . . Sacred Mount Victoria, Belize*

ANGEL VIEW-POINT

A Coconut Miracle . . . Sacred Mount Victoria

Earthquake Lore

It is believed that the heart of the Mountain, the Tepeyollotl, was originally ruled over by the Aztecs who governed earthquakes. It was pictured in drawings and petroglyphs as a dangerous jaguar leaping up to the sun, Tepeyollotl was the perfect representation of the power and danger of an earthquake, imaged as a chief force coming from the very heart of the Mountain and jumping like a jungle cat to topple its prey unexpectedly.

A Nahua creation story explains the shaking of the land as the ubiquitous twisting of the giant Capacei.

Esoterica: Myths, Mysteries and Imaginables

Serpent/Lake

Once upon a time, a group of unknown Indians came into a Huetar Tribe village. The people there gave a tree in exchange for presents. When a reptile came down the tree, starting a large flow of water, the inhabitants agreed to take only a tree so the visitors were left with a serpent in the exchange. The mountain top where they left the serpent, was filled with water creating a lake. A few days later, the serpent went from the lake to the top of the mountain and ate a few children. In order to rescue the settlement, the people were told they should sacrifice children and told the parents who sacrificed their children that they could use all the wood in the forest around the lake. But, if someone from whose family no one had been sacrificed entered the forest, they'd never came back.

Today the snake's lake is called Barba and is situated on the top of a volcano with the same name.

. . . .

Belize

Victoria Peak is on the mainland of Belize in Central America. Belize itself is an island about 290km (180 miles) long and 110 km (68 miles) wide. It is the least populated and the least densely populated nation in Central America and is formerly a British Colony. Victoria Peak is in the Cockscomb Basin Wild Life Sanctuary and is home to many special flora and fauna common to Belize. There are over 300 species of birds in the Cockscomb Basin. This includes endangered species of the ornate hawk-eagle, keel billed marmot and the scarlet macaw. The sanctuary also hosts the worlds densest jaguar population as well as pumas, ocelot, armadillo and many other special mammals.

Endangered Plants, Animals

Recently, the height of Doyle's Delight elevation is measured to be 3,688 ft (1,124m) while Victoria Peak, 3,670 (1,120m) had for many years been considered the highest peak in Belize.

We camp on the island of Belize but hike on the mainland to explore Victoria in the jungles and some of the Sanctuary. It is an unusual opportunity to observe the rare and endangered species of plants and animals. The jungle is dense and the trails difficult to find and follow.

Jaguars

In spite of the noisy growling jaguars hidden in the jungle and the various stinging, itching insects, the Victoria expedition has been enthralling. Not only have the jaguars been protected and "conserved" but the area is full of other rare animals, plants, and particularly birds. Since the forest is thick and dark, we were not aware how very late it was … past time for us to return to camp. It is a long way back, but luckily the moon is coming up. That's when it happened.

The trail from Sacred Mount Victoria peters out swallowed by the thick jungle. But in a clearing, we could see the sky. We become aware it was not very long until dusk and then dark. More importantly, we are reminded how hungry and

We need a Miracle

thirsty we'd become; but the water in the jungle seems stagnant and polluted, and we already ate all of our food in the pack! I detect rising panic. We need a miracle! We look around our open spot in the jungle and sat on a log to strategize our route back to camp.

While we're sitting there, I see on a tree stump behind us the miracle we need — four fresh coconuts that will give us coconut milk and coconut meat, all we can eat and drink. The coconut discovery is a divine intervention that even Mary Baker Eddy, the founder of the Christian Science Religion, would consider our experience a "natural phenomenon experience humanly in fulfilment of a spiritual law."

The Coconut Discovery

Thanks to the coconuts we get back to camp although it was around 3am. I probably should have given credit for a third miracle to the bright moon to be able to find our way back through the jungle.

Saved by 3 miracles

We can tell by the noise ("S-C-R-O-W-L") behind us that the jaguars tracked us on the mainland almost all the way back . . . but they apparently didn't want us for their dinner!

Sacred Mount Athos

People View-Point

I am mournful.

I ache

I am bitter with pain and rejection

God puts on me.

. . . Greek Lyrics

Location:	Greece
Range:	Athos Peninsula
Elevation:	6,670 ft (2,033 m)
Prominence:	6,601 ft (2,012 m)
Coordinates:	40°09'30"N
	24°19'38"E
Spirit:	Greek Orthodox
Pilgrimage:	*A Mountain of Monks . . . Aegean Sea*

ANGEL VIEW-POINT

The Mountain of Monks... Aegean Sea

Orthodox– Christianity– Mount Athos– Aegean Sea – A Thousand Years Ago

Esoterica: Myths, Mysteries and Imaginables

"Silence!" The King speaks:

"We are in your debt, General. Your return in the name of Christ from your monastic life to destroy the infidel Saracens invading Crete gives us victory; and now, as this Court, as God, is my witness, I hereby fulfill my promise and grant to you the peninsula of Athos of Macedonia. Here you may rule and build Christ's monasteries, your home in peace and for all who seek eternity."

King grant of Athos for Monasteries

General Aphonites thanks the King, bows and retreats to his Mountain headland in the Aegean Sea. There, he began building the largest assemblage of twenty-seven monasteries the world had ever known. Twenty-seven huge separate monastic communities, fourteen subsidiary sites and innumerable hermitages still exist on Athos this very day.

Sanctified by Homer and Aeschylus

Mount Athos had long since been sanctified by Homer, Aeschylus, and by Anchorites escaping to the wilderness from the miseries of life or preparing for the Day of Judgement, the end of the world as it is predicted for the year 1000 in the religious fervor of the Middle Ages.

End of World and Athos

At its height, this thirty by ten-mile Athos cape once housed thirty thousand monks. A theocracy, it has been and is recognized and protected by emperors and international conferences as an independent state. Plundered several times in its history, left alone in World War II by both sides and only once invaded (by the Communists), it still retains a lifestyle centuries old.

Contains valuables, libraries, works of art, jewelry, silks

"The characters, manuscripts, and ornamental books in the libraries of the various monasteries are of especially incalculable value to scholars. Its churches, treasures and libraries contain priceless works of art: icons, illuminated manuscripts, book covers, extremely valuable objects of gold, precious stones and ivory, embroidery, brocades, silks, and other aspects of the finest workmanship." (Deroko, A., *Athos: The Holy Mountain* (1967)).

20 massive stone edifices

The twenty-seven monasteries (now twenty) are massive stone castle-like edifices on Mount Athos' steep cliffs, each with its own boat dock, gardens, water supply, church, and living quarters. These institutions, though a place of life-time retreat, are the preservers of civilization, the intellectual sanctuaries of their time, exclusive centers of education. For hundreds of years, the hopes of mankind for deliverance, progress and immortality are focused here. All the Orthodox Christian nations had their own separate community. Even in recent times Russia, Serbia, Romania, and Arabia are separately represented on Athos.

Life-time retreat

Christian Orthodox represented

Cenobitic and idiorrythmic monasteries

Once the iron hand of an Abbot ruled here with absolute power ("cenobitic" monasteries). Now each monk in many monasteries regulates his own life ("idiorrhythmic" monasteries). Some of the original monasteries finally deteriorated and were unable even to feed their members. Smaller skites or schists are built by a few monks working together. Although it is claimed while I was there that over three thousand monks live there, fifteen hundred is probably more accurate today. This living history is on the edge of complete disintegration.

Skites/schists

Ruling Council

Only the main monasteries now send representatives to the Central Ruling Council of Twenty. Throughout, Greece appointed Governors control all police and external affairs. An annually elected executive committee of four governs Athos. Each member of the committee has one-quarter of the official seal. No action can be taken without unanimous consent.

Executive committee governs

The entire monastic community exists in the shadow and on the lower seacoast ranges of Mount Athos, a natural symbol of Man, God and Christ.

Breaking Down the Door of History

Permits

To reach this symbol of living history is not easy. In fact, heaven may turn out to be easier to reach than the Holy Mountain.

You need several permits. American and Greek bureaucracies lie in wait to delay your visit. Though always polite, the technique of resistance consists of: the "stand-or-sit", the "go to another office", the "you're missing something", and "come back later" variety. To be specific, you need a mimeograph and personally signed greeting from the United States Embassy. This takes at least two hours. The United States of America insists that the letter be hand-carried to the Greek foreign office (forty-five minutes by taxi). While you reach the right office (thirty minutes), you may be informed that the office is not open but that you can drop by Soloniki office. This happened to be my fate. In Soloniki, I storm the foreign ministry before they open. Their red-tape defense has not yet been organized. Even so, it takes an hour and a half to deliver my mimeographed compliments to a stern blond female in this branch of the royal ministry. "This office is willing to send its greetings to the governor and central government of Mount Athos (two copies) if the special police for foreigners

Soloniki office

Greetings to Athos and governor

approves." The special police station is a new building in a poor section of the city; the atmosphere is foreboding. But three copies, twenty drachma and one hour later, I am on my way from Soloniki through villages and forests, past desert sand beaches along the Aegean Sea, to Tripiti, port of embarkation for the trip to Mount Athos.

Athos permit bureaucracy

Once aboard the boat, I need only one more permit– from the Government of Athos. To my dismay, I learn it takes a day to reach the capitol, Karyes ("Town of Walnuts"), in the center of Athos and only by the government's sole bus, on its only road. Thanks to twenty drachma and some special help, the bus driver agrees to take my passport and pick up the permit (two copies) for me. By the time he has it, I am already on the Mountain. He left the permit and passport at the post office in Daphne (Athos' port of entry) in time for me to leave. That's of course, the best way to handle bureaucracy– avoid it!

Mount Athos impression

A Call to the Cassock

With the entry ritual behind me, my first glimpse of Mount Athos from the boat is glorious. This Mountain is higher and steeper than I expected. Its sheer, white granite towers over the peninsula, over the sea, seemingly over the clouds. The words came into my mind: "You must endure and partly die to rise to my height, to stand on my peak, the unattainable Christ."

Endure and partly die to climb peak

It is late afternoon as the boat rounds the tip of Athos putting the sun behind us. The sea is changing from its light blue, a blue that matches the sky, to the darker blue that signals the hours of evening. The only people remaining on the small boat are the captain, one crewman, and me.

Sunset, the boat and me

We pass between huge cliffs on the left and rock islands

seaward. They cast long shadows onto the sea in front of us. The low sun's rays made the dusty yellow sandstone rock light up. It is like a stage setting. Our boat seems small and irrelevant to the scene. We contribute but one thin trail of white foam in our wake. Even the chug, of the boat's old engine does not interrupt the serenity. And on stage-center, Athos; majestic, calm, with its siren call to come to rest, to respond to the inner self, to become a part of God, wafts on the soft wind.

Athos majestic calm and call to rest

In the midst of all this beauty, the thought floods my consciousness that my pilgrimage might end. Why not stay here? I could feel my burdens slipping from me. I shed the problems of my city, my world, my clients, my family. If I have the courage to leave my run-down world and stay here, I could survive as a whole person. Here I could be with the monks, kindred spirits with a proper sense of proportion about life and truth and death. Their common bond is Christ, love, contemplation, compassion and cooperation. At Kafsokalyvia Monastery; I intend at last to spend the night. The tanned faces and squint lines around the eyes of the local monks attests to their outdoor life.

End of my pilgrimage

Survive as whole person with Christ

Outdoor Life

Steep climb from Kasolvia dock to monastery

With such thoughts, I come to the Kafsokalyvia Monastery dock. From this dock, I can begin the steep climb to the Monastery.

I sleep briefly in my room in Kafsokalyvia. I hear the click of the door locking from the outside to prevent me from leaving. It's a little scary but I'm exhausted from a long day. I'll escape tomorrow in the morning. . . I hope.

25+ switchblades Rock steps and water

At three in the morning, I pick the room lock successfully and escape. I begin the climb to the peak of Mount Athos. My route is to be twenty-five switchbacks straight up from the monastery, west on the main trail, until three trails meet at the place with a wooden cross nailed to a huge oak tree. Prior advice tells me to take the higher right-hand trail.

So, I start. The switchbacks (more than twenty-five) are marvels of hand-hewed rock steps, with resting benches, caves and even water on them. But the hiking is steep and difficult.

Hermitage

By eight o'clock in the morning I come to a hermitage with a vegetable garden and a fine view of the Aegean. And here is the cross and three trails that I am looking for. I proceed about a mile until blocked by a closed gate. Behind the gate is a small lodge; sitting on green meadow, with running streams, wildflowers, a garden, all in keeping with the psalmist's words, "green pastures."

Monk points up with zig zag motion

This is obviously now the wrong way. I walk around the building yelling "Athos," "top." "Athos" until a monk appears. He is a slight man with a kindly smile. He seems to understand my hand signals. He points up from his meadow with a zig-zag motion. The wave of a stick in his hand indicates that I should turn left when I got to a large trail. With the help of the walking stick he gives me, I follow his directions. I zig and zag, but finally the path fades to nothing in the brush. Small paths lead in all directions. I follow a waterline until it is impossible to break through the bushes. I am wasting my energy. I find a small animal track and take that direction. Twenty minutes later, I break through the under-brush onto the main trail. Hooray!

Path fades out in all directions

Broke through underbrush onto main trail

Another three trail crossing with large cross

Shortly afterwards, I meet another three-trail crossing with a large cross standing by. Sure that this is the right way, I climb another mile and a half and fifteen hundred feet in elevation to an open oak grove, carpeted with leaves and wildflowers. It is difficult to know which of the many donkey trails from the grove to follow, so I take them one by one. The first ends at a small reservoir. Two more just vanish into heavy vegetations. Another leads down the Mountain. They

Donkey trails vanish in dead end.

Lost again . . . 4000 feet in elevation still to go

100 degree heat

Cross country against my pact with myself? No cross country"

Only way is to start over. Cried as I lost elevation so hard to gain.

4 monks laying pipe tell me how to get back to main road

My last lemon

By chance I found a deep well

Drink canteen full, eat beef jerky, and take 15 minute nap

are all dead ends. Again, I am lost. It shakes me. My strength is dissipating, yet there are at least four thousand more feet in elevation to climb. I decide to forget trails and climb the cliff straight above me. Although out of sight, the Mountain top must be above. Such a climb will be tough-going with my heavy pack over rocks and through the tangled willows in over one hundred degree heat. The decision also violated the pact I make with myself: "Never travel cross-country" especially if I don't know the "country".

I sat down to rest and plan my ascent. Luckily, I returned to my sense. The only way was to start over and find the right trail. Tears of discouragement crept down my cheeks as I hiked back down, losing the altitude I worked so hard to gain. Then I hear men's voices in the brush. I called and found four monks laying water pipes. Their gestures, a crude map, and a few words of English seemed to mean that I should go down the main trail to the second wooden cross and then go right.

Following their directions, I found a new path heading up the Mountain. Having long since run out of water, I ate my last lemon. I knew it would be at least a four-hour hike to the water. This new path would finally lead to the main trail in a high forest. Desperately thirsty, I sat down on a rock wall to rest. The three rocks by my left foot seemed to be covering something. Moving the rocks aside, I peer down a deep well. The light reflects on water in the bottom. But it is out of reach. It is too small to climb down. There is no bucket or rope.

Remembering an unused fifteen-foot clothesline in my pack, I tie that to my canteen. It still isn't long enough. Finally, by knotting it to shoelaces and pack straps, I lower the canteen to the water. Carefully, very slowly, I bring it up. So delicious! I celebrate, and drink a canteen full, eat a piece of beef jerky and one of my precious honey bars. Then I can't resist a fifteen-minute nap.

After ditching my tent to lighten the load, I continue the climb, harder now since I'm out of strength from the morning's panic. In fact, on the last two miles, I rest every twenty minutes. My head and body ache and even shake. It is heat exhaustion but feels like a bad flu. Nevertheless, I made it to a dirty, old, abandoned monastery, Panaghia; there I again filled my water bag and canteen. I can see the granite peak of Athos topped by a chapel. Below the chapel is a series of switchbacks that thread through a profusion of boulders and yellow flowers. These flowers later prove sweet and delicious to eat.

16 hours of hiking from Kasoly

Sixteen hours after starting from Kafsokalyvia, I arrive at the uppermost ledge with an old, abandoned chapel on top. At that moment the deep red sunset in the west and a shadow of the Mount Athos in the east both reflect their grandeur in the darkening waters of the Aegean Sea.

Mount Athos Goulash

Hunger returns with a vengeance. My "Mount Athos Goulash" tastes fabulous– three dry packets of tomato bouillon, one of split pea, one of beef broth, all mixed with water and oatmeal, and brought to a boiling mush!

Cleared off rubble to lay sleeping bag on wooden shelf in Mount Athos sanctuary

There is just enough room after clearing off the rubble to put my sleeping bag on a wooden shelf in the sanctuary of this tumbled down rock chapel. It is cold outside but warm inside my bag. The only noise is the wind and the swish of night swallows swooping by. The sky turns from red to black. Venus glimmers first in the night and I fade into a deep, deep sleep, content and happy.

Deep sleep in Chapel atop Mount Athos

My own "hotel" on the highest peak of Mount Athos is well named the Church of the Transfiguration. By the next morning, I am a different person, refreshed, buoyant, painless. Sunrise floods the whole peninsula. Istanbul, Turkey seems a wisp on the horizon; the dark Aegean and the light sky are a merger of clear blues. I clean and air all my equip-

Sleep on peak

Church transfigured me

ment and clothes. I walk around that morning naked. I feel the comfort of the day's sun and the caress of a light breeze on every pore. I rejoice. I am transfigured. I pack to leave.

Hike down

The trip down surprisingly proves to be strenuous. Beyond the lifesaving well I discovered yesterday, I leave the main route to retrace my original steps and even to find my lost glasses. It is like recovering a sacred relic or a friend to find them just where I left them on a granite cliff where I rested on the way up.

Lost in the bush

Soon thereafter, I am lost and again find myself following smaller and smaller paths. Thick brush finally hems me in on all sides. Unable to see in any direction, I restrain my creeping anxiety and sit down. I don't have enough energy to climb back up. The main trail must be between me and the sea. Oblivious to the wild rose, the thorns, the holly tearing at my back and cutting my face, arms and legs, I blindly crash downhill, throwing my whole weight into the bushes. I fight the branches with my arms. With this momentum, after thirty minutes, I literally pop out onto the main trail. It is such a pleasure to find my way I don't notice the blood running from cuts in my legs. A half mile further on I discover the real Mount Athos turn-off.

Wooden crosses on intersections

There are at least five places with wooden crosses and three trails in the area. I remember them all. I must be the world's expert on "three-trail-wooden cross intersections."

St. Annis Monastery

Downhill every step ached

My legs take a beating as I descend to another monastery, St. Annis on the dusty, hot windless mule trail. Rocks turn my ankles again and again. My muscles lose their resiliency. I have to walk on my joints. Every step aches.

I am happy to get a boat ride to my destination at St. Gregoire Monastery for a few drachma from a fisherman. It suddenly occurs to me it is the Fourth of July. The liveliness

St. Gregoire Monastery at St. Gregoire is a contrast to the deserted St. Annis Monastery, with its death-like atmosphere, its few old men with mean eyes at the dock, and a monk who hides in the rundown buildings when he sees me.

The Unfrocking

Admiring Monastics I long admire monastics. I think that if like them I have but the courage to commit my life as they have, I will surely find spiritual satisfaction. This desire to be a monk is the reason I picked Mount Athos, "Mountain of the Monks," in planning this journey. I observe the monks carefully, as if I am watching myself in their future. They come from all over the world (even Chicago, Illinois), but mostly from smaller Greek villages.

Hard to get in and out of Athos For the monks who live on Mount Athos, it is difficult to get in and even harder to get out. Those with no education are prohibited from leaving Athos for fear that they might never return when exposed to the pleasures of modern life and importuning from their families. In fact, how would (or could) anyone leave once shed of the skills, the desires and the anxieties of the outside world.

Attracted to nature and withdrawal Withdrawal, retreat to nature's wilderness, attracts these men at Athos as it could me and many others. The Mountain monasteries provide a concrete opportunity to succumb to this element of character, a place for loners by nature, those unwilling to rely on others beyond the immediate "family" or to trust the world or accept its strictures. Time on this holy Mountain could answer my need to know whether I should follow such a life, literally or figuratively. Or, whether, unknowingly, I am already a monk.

Communal life dedicated to Christ The monks at Athos give up everything for a communal life dedicated to Christ. Cut off from women and civilization, they are now old men. Their faces are lined with wrinkles like sailors, red from the sun. Most are thin and bent from strenuous labor with their hands hardened by a barren soil and rough hand tools. It is impossible from their common clothing to tell which were priests and which laymen. Health is personal and religious since there are no modern clinics, hospitals or medical doctors. They have another-world look, particularly in their eyes; some looked kind or spiritual, some distinctly psychotic.

Monks discipline tough, prayerful

Completely dependent on Christ, God and each other, each is a member of this strictly disciplined, prayerful, toughening life of a Monk. Each changes his name; serves an apprenticeship to an elder monk until that Monk's death; and from six months to a year must practice renunciation and abstinence.

Renunciation

For this period of renunciation, the Monks eat once a day. Their fare is uncooked beans soaked in water. To move up the ecclesiastical ladder to higher ranks (higher schema) depends on the degrees of asceticism and devotional prayer they accomplish. They resolve the loss of their own father and even their fatherhood by accepting and creating a demanding God, God the Father.

Christian holidays

3AM

2AM

The routine life of these monastics change only on special Christian holidays. The regular mass usually begins at 3:00 a.m. and ends at 7:00 a.m. (the Great Mass is from 2:00 a.m. to 10:00 a.m.). A nap usually follows breakfast. On a typical day, the monks see people who need their presence (family, visitors, a stranger or other monks). The time for this is from ten to eleven in the morning and from four to five in the afternoon. The rest of the day is spent at their assigned duties in the buildings, gardens or kitchen. With a little time out for dinner plus six to eight hours of prayer and contemplation their day is long.

Self sufficient

These men have become almost completely self-sufficient. They build and repair their rooms and central structures and trail-ways. They grow their food and devote their intellects, spirit and creativity to Christ. They wrench their livelihood from the Mountain's stony flanks, her springs, her meadows, her forests. Weather, temperature, humidity affect the lives of these men strongly. Their food is sparse, rough and often tasteless. To visit them is a chance to observe life as it was in the Middle Ages, and the difficulties of wringing by hand one's own livelihood directly from stubborn, demanding, unmerciful Nature.

Middle Ages

Many insects

Insects are, for them and for me, a constantly annoying enemy. I am a welter of mosquito and bed-bug bites for weeks afterwards.

Hard Labor / Progress / Prisons

Practically every life necessity is hand-made work that involves hard physical effort and skill-building, gardening, clothes-making. During the dark times of the Middle Ages, monasteries sustained man's intellectual and spiritual progress, yet now seems to be only prisons for spiritual and physical anachronisms.

Monk Robes

Only twice do I ever see a monk without his full robe. Even in the choking heat of mid-July, they wear, under their black cumbersome gowns, a heavy pair of pants and thick brown suit of burlap material. Their habit, often dirty from the dust and hard work, includes black shoes, usually without socks, and the ever-present cross strung on the neck, as well as a stovepipe, flat-top hat on their heads.

Earlier I visited monks living at St. Catherine's Monastery in the Sinai Desert. Their isolated existence is even more severe than here at Athos. Many live there in tiny cells without leaving their entire lives.

My first encounter with a monk at Kafsokalyvia Monas-

Night at Kasolyvia Monastery

tery is disillusioning. Arriving there after the strenuous climb from the dock, I am met by a gnome-like man with a deeply lined, sore-pocked face and scraggly beard. He is hunchbacked, disheveled and dirty. He smells like animal excrement. As ugly a person as I could see. He directs me towards a stone stable-like building, apparently the night guest house. He limps along at my side uttering guttural sounds. He then demands my permit. Having left my papers with the bus driver at Daphne, I was an illegal alien and at that point I give him the "Greetings" from the U.S.A. and Greece. He immediately snatches them from my hand. In an intense low voice he whispers, "Drachma!" "Drachma!" It is blackmail! No money is supposedly ever charged a visitor at any monastery at Athos. I am twice his size. But I am scared! Repulsive evil glares from his eyes, his whole being, dangerous, violent, grasping. I take change from my pocket. Among it was a dollar bill. As soon as he saw it, he demands "Dollar!" "Dollar!" This makes me both reckless and furious. In spite of the consequences, I am ready to throw him down and take my papers back. But I hand him some drachma and a dollar. When he reaches for it, I snatch my papers and push him away. Thankfully, he leaves me, but I am uneasy about spending the night there knowing that this monk roams the premises.

Blackmail Money

Contrasting friendly second monk

Contrasting sharply in education, appearance and hospitality, with that first monk, my second monk is very friendly.

He points out with pride his well-built home across the valley on a cliff overlooking the sea, high above the monastery and the mosquitoes. Creative, strongly dedicated to his religious life and living naturally in an idyllic setting, he nevertheless is as anxious and disturbed as any pressured San Francisco businessman. He is convinced we all were going to perish in an atomic war soon, but not later than 2000 A.D.

Second monk anxious and disturbed

The vehemence of his tirade against short skirts amazes me. It is impossible to tell whether his feeling stems from priestly complaints about aroused desire, personal observation or magazine pictures; stoning is too good for any women, "whores" as he calls them, who wear such clothes. He is not alone in this viewpoint. Similarly, other monks condemned such "abominations."

Magazines

"Whores" an abomination

In fact, this taboo, extends to my own short pants. Though I don't know it, they are forbidden at Mount Athos. I always wear my cut-off army pants hiking and did so the day of the hike from the top to St. Gregoire. Arriving there an hour or two before sunset, hot and exhausted, I am shown to a room by a monk. I throw my pack on the iron bed and walk out on the hallway to wash the trail dirt from my face at a sink. An old monk with a big stomach rumbles out of the room next to mine. He yells at me in a language I don't understand, pointing at my bare legs. I pretend I don't know what he is talking about, throw my hands, bow, smile. This only infuriates him more and he pushes me towards the main gate. I break away to my room and put on my long pants.

Men's short pants taboo and forbidden at Athos

There was little love here for God – "Got" in the word of my monks at Kafsokalyvia. But fear of the Almighty is dramatically restated throughout our conversation; "Got will punish", "Feat Got", "Got will destroy the world".

Fear of Almighty

Humility is not one of this man's stronger characteristics. He recites at great lengths his prowess as a sculptor, "the best at Athos." In fact, he claims that whenever any one of the monasteries celebrated an important historical event, he was called on to sculpt the cake.

Cake sculpture allegedly "the best at art.

There is no hesitation on his part about deprecating the efforts of "rival cake sculptors." He invites me to the eighth centennial at St. Gregoire two days later to see one of his cre-

Deprecates other cake sculptors

ations. He tells me I should photograph it since "you aren't at Athos unless you see one of my cakes."

At least one purpose of his visit becomes clear at the end of our conversation. He wants (almost demands) new stamp issues from America, which he says are necessary to add to his valuable stamp collection. But he warns they should be wrapped and sent in a plain envelope. Otherwise, they would never arrive since, according to him, important looking packages would be opened and often subject to being stolen at Athos, especially if containing valuable stamps!

New stamps demanded

Although he shouts it perhaps too loudly with too much emotion, he certainly believes his conclusion (that's all that matters):

"We are free men here! We are liberated! It is beautiful! We are at peace!"

45 years at peace

If he thought otherwise his entire adult life for forty-five years at Kafsokalyvia is wasted.

One of the more striking things about these monasteries are the security precautions. The buildings are like fortresses. The huge iron outside gates are locked at sunset and are opened at sunrise. No one can enter or leave for any reason during the night.

Security precautions like fortress

Windows, closet doors, rooms, churches, store-rooms, everything is locked or barred with huge bolts or bars. Either I am locked in or others are locked out of my assigned cell-like rooms at both Kafsokalyvia and St. Gregoire Monasteries.

Bolts and bars

Despite the lingual differences, I still felt that so many of the monks seem locked within themselves. The few younger men I see appear depressed behind motionless faces; the older men are withdrawn and unfriendly. My "cell keeper" at Kafsokalyvia receives me, sits quietly during my long conversation with another monk, brings me my dinner of bread, olives

Monk Psychology

and boiled potatoes with olive oil and locks me in at night, all without saying a word or smiling. However, I am surprised and appreciative hearing him give me a blessing as he locks my door thinking I am asleep. Another man at St. Annis runs from me like a rabbit– psychotic, fearful or avoiding my need for help. Younger men working on the pipeline who help me find my way going up, ignore my efforts to be friendly when I see them again on the way down.

Athos welfare

Mount Athos is not without its welfare cases, outcasts that their fellow monks shun or ignore. The harshness of social disapproval and isolation is real even in a community of Christ.

No women or female animals in Athos

These monks isolate themselves totally from women. This explains much. Because she is the last woman I see for a week, before I leave for Mount Athos, I still remember her so clearly, the one who sells me an egg and a tomato. She is standing in the doorway of a Greek café, plain and quiet, yet appealing, when I run for the boat. Since 1060 A.D., no woman (other than an invading female communist guerrilla in 1948), and allegedly no female animal even, has gained admission to Athos. By ancient rule, access to the Mountain is forbidden "to any woman, to any child, to any eunuch, to any smooth visage." There is no inter-specie discrimination. The rule applies to all female animals including cows, pigs, dogs or cats, though it is relaxed as to small or wild animals beyond temptation's grasp; which, of course, may be more of a commentary on the desires and fears of the rule-makers than proof of inherent male spiritual superiority.

Nowadays, religions and cultures once historical male dominated are no longer. For me, women can be joy; they are a key part of reality and hence religion. Permanent absence from their presence or even sexual abstinence impoverishes.

They embody much of the physical beauty of the world.

Feminine attributes

Feminine softness, intuition and intelligence are distinct characteristics. Woman arouses the intense love we all seem to need, ephemeral, permanent, ideal, romantic, sexual. Their absence is at least one reason I could never be a monk. There are many beautiful people at Athos: hospitable, generous, creative, bright, sincere, kindly, true followers of Christ.

Ozo (strong alcoholic drink) to welcome me

After the incident of the monk and my short pants, another monk came to see me with a traditional welcome: a licorice liqueur, "ozo," glass of clear water and sweet jelly candy, covered with sugar. A friendly monk even though dinner is over, takes me to the dining hall of St. Gregoire Monastery for a left-over meal of coarse bread (hand-stoned flour, so the sand munched with each bite), home-grown and cured olives and rice with traces of tomato. It is a delicious meal that wipes out the unpleasantness of the anti-bare leg encounter.

Dinner supplement

On Mount Athos I also meet a modem version of the monk, another visitor like myself.

A Monk's Tax Haven

Wild man

Just as I round a rock corner about a hundred yards down from the peak of Mount Athos, I suddenly find myself face to face with a wild looking man. He is thin, heavily bearded; his unkempt hair flared and his deep-set eyes have the look of the sea and the wilderness in them. We both recover from the initial fright and as we start to talk, we know we are kindred spirits, fellow searchers. He is a French Teacher from Switzerland; his adventures have already covered the Mediterranean Middle East. He says his two children are grown; his wife no longer cared. At fifty years of age "before it is too late" he set out seven months earlier to find "a tax haven"— somewhere to retire with or without his wife that is inexpensive, by the sea, with good water and low taxes. He explores the Middle

Kindred spirits

Seven months search for tax haven

East and Israel by car; Turkey by canoe tours and completes a twenty-eight day crossing to Greece by canoe before climbing to the summit of Mount Athos which takes him fifteen hours. It is some consolation to know that he too becomes lost in the brush on the ascent.

15 hour climb to top

I tell him of my trip and that I am heading for St. Gregoire. Although I leave him still climbing, we meet again on the main trail down from the summit hours later in the afternoon. Before I could ask, he explains my weight with pack might sink his canoe, so he couldn't give me a paddle ride to St. Gregoire. Although we plan to meet there, he didn't make it when I arrive. Just as the gates close at sunset, he appears and is assigned to my room.

My pack would sink his canoe

Our room intensifies the hot July night. Vicious bed bugs and swarms of mosquitoes keep us awake. We talk all night. He is knowledgeable and interested in religion. Even though he maintains the purpose of his pilgrimage is only the "tax haven," it is clear to me his object is both simpler and more profound. He finds happiness in the search itself; each day in the Mountains or on the sea he basks in the fresh air and sunshine; he loves to meet natural people in the fresh air and sunshine; he loves to meet natural people in their own surroundings; he admires the soaring freedom of birds.

Vicious bed bugs and swarms of mosquitoes

He found happiness with people outdoors

He confesses he will quit his job when his paid sabbatical leave is over. He also confides that he found his haven on the coast of Turkey. It is a joy to know a man who lives his desires, free and satisfied with each day, its simple pleasures and hardships in complete harmony with the world and himself.

His haven on the coast of Turkey

The last morning after we attend the mass together at St. Gregoire, there is barely enough time for me to catch a fishing boat for Daphne and from there to Tripiti, Athens and the Middle East. Before I rush down the cobblestone pathway

Attended mass together At St. Gregoire and

shook hands with tears in our eyes – friends who we never see again

to the dock, we shake hands covering our hands with our left hands too. Tears well in our eyes. We know we are now fast friends but that most probably we will never see each other again. I feel very alone.

Whether a modern or Middle Ages version of monkhood, it is a way of life that some always follow. Mountains are an inherent part of their search. For religions and their leaders, Mountains are the staging ground for divine guidance, immortality and paradise.

Mountain staging ground and part of religious search

Tibetan Lamas and Hindus use Mountains as spiritual forces and still do

Tibetan Lamas (of Tantric Buddhism) even now in exile build their monasteries in Nepal on Mountain sides. The highlands of the holy are full of cave remnants of ascetics who live in the Mountain wildernesses. Most of the ministries of the great teachers of Hindu scripture follow years of Mountain retreats. The Mountains no longer play such an important role for the leaders in today's major religions nor are these religions as vital. Yet the Mountains are not changed. The same spiritual forces abide there. They can be found by any spirit traveler.

Monks lifestyle no guarantee of spiritual goals

I find monastic life does not, per se, change people individually or as a group, nor does it eliminate violence, pride, ignorance, jealousy, repression, anxiety, cupidity, thievery, parsimony, selfishness or suspicion. A lifestyle, even one as drastic as these monks assume, is no guarantee of attainment of spiritual goals.

Mount Athos Peninsula in the Aegean Sea still has no escape

It is not that I am enamored with the ways of my world. It is only that there is no escape from woman and man and their civilization because there is no escape from the self. There is no escape from the era in which you are born or from the fellow travelers on this planet and their problems. Even in an isolated, hallowed peninsula in the Aegean Sea, there is no escape.

Decide not to be a monk

And so, I decide not to be a monk in the shadow of a

thousand years of history or anywhere else. But, like the monk, I must ask the questions: What do I need; To withdraw forever for a long time? To lock out other behind gates, wildernesses or temperament? To be left alone to contemplate? To ritualize? To climb? To pray? To meditate? To face or better, to embrace the beauty and the torment of Nature in all her moods? To rely on my own body, my own pack? To seek enlightenment in exertion, repetition, exhaustion? To experience love and confirmation from those who believe like me or from ideals and imagined forces, Gods or philosophies? To find self in singleness of purpose-to rise to a greater height? To ponder such questions is to prove we are all monks in hiker's clothes.

Singleness of purpose

Monks and pilgrims, climbers and seekers, have much in common. They find peace, beauty, solace in their own essence, in their liberation on the Sacred Mountain. Monks and pilgrims are lean. They are alone but not lonely. They know real hunger, cold, heat, fear. They breathe clear air and drink cold water. They are one with the dirt, the sun, the wind and weather and the earth itself. They must climb the Mountain as I must. We must rise to the best and the more important in ourselves.

Needs Monks, pilgrims, climbers

A seeker isw alone but not lonely

To be where men live a thousand years before now is an important experience. To be with men who are living as they live a thousand years ago is a revelation. It all comes together on my last night at St. Gregoire. Just as I was finally dozing off to sleep about 3 a.m., there was a loud clap-clap clap from the rhythmic whack of wood on wood and iron on iron. The noise was coming from the inner courtyard. This sound signals the morning mass. I decide to attend.

St. Gregoire

3AM

Morning Mass

I pretend that I don't know I am supposed to sit in the main church, so I kneel in the straight-backed stalls inside the holy sanctuary. For four hours, on my knees, I gape at the

Holy Sanctuary

ritual proceeding in this monastery as it was each day for over eight hundred years. Though unintelligible, it moves me.

Unintelligible but moving

My every sense is aroused, saturated, cleansed and stimulated again. Three times I am bathed in clouds of incense. The bells of the mass and chanting priests blow my mind with sounds of another era, another spiritual plane. The icons, rich robes, tapestries, all in candlelight, lit and relit, hypnotize me. I no longer doubt the healing power of this rite and the holy relics here. I feel myself clean.

Cleansed and able to move on

I stagger out, tired, yet sad the service is over. The early morning light seems dull, lifeless, a hangover from this religious orgy, this catharsis at Mount Athos.

Tired and sad service was over

I feel confident that I have the power of my Mountain guru and can continue my pilgrimage.

PART VI

The Americas

The power, the inspiration of Sacred Mountains usually influences more prominently local peoples more than far distant people. That is s certainly true with the "Americas," North and South.

The variety is astounding, the differences, the religions that are involved and the pilgrimages are astounding experiences. Each one. There is no claim that North and South Americas have more Sacred Mountains than any other area of the world. Only Europe, Asia, Central America, China, India, Africa, all have fairly prominent Sacred Mountain histories and spiritual experiences no matter what the current situation is politically, commercially, militarily, literaly, artistically, or other civilization values.

Sacred Mount Denali

People View-Point

Only in stillness and in movement,
Only in spirit can the Mountain speak.
On earth and in heaven.
The person who knows does not speak.
And those who speak do not know.
Only the Spirit and the Sacred Mountain
Are Real.

Location:	Alaska, U.S.A.
Range:	Alaska
Elevation:	20,310 ft (6,190 m)
Prominence:	20,157 ft (6,144 m)
Coordinates:	63°04'10"N
	151°00'27"W
Spirit:	Native American (Athabascan), Christian
Pilgrimage:	*Yahoo and His New Wife . . . From The Great White . . . Sacred Mount Denali*

Angel View-Point

Yahoo and His New Wife Form The Great White . . . Sacred Mount Denali

Esoterica: Myths, Mysteries and Imaginables

Long ago, far in the north, lived a powerful warrior named Yahoo, strong and blessed with great medicine, but he was lonely and sad. He had no wife, so Yahoo made a canoe and traveled west across the sea in hopes of finding a bride in Raven Chief's village. Raven Chief hated Yahoo, but Yahoo respected Raven Chief's power and medicine and Yahoo hoped to find a suitable wife from his rival's bloodline. As Yahoo approached Raven Chief's village, he sang a mournful song of love and desire for a wife he would cherish for all their days. Raven Chief's second wife heard the song and motioned Yahoo to come closer.

"My husband hates you," she whispered, "but everyone respects you. You are a great hunter and I trust you to be a good husband and father. Marry this young woman, my daughter. She will bear you children and you will be happy together."

The daughter was gorgeous and kind. Yahoo knew theirs would be a great marriage. He swore to always protect her and to make a happy life for them. Yahoo thanked Raven Chief's wife.

"Take care of her. That will be thanks enough," she said. "But you must leave! My husband comes, he will try to kill you if he sees you in his domain. Now, flee!"

Yahoo and his bride climbed into the canoe and paddled east. From behind them came the flap of mighty wings; Raven Chief! His howl – a wind that churned the waters and battered the canoe as black clouds and black crows filled the sky. Raven chief got into his own canoe, gave chase, his face stormy as the sea.

Yahoo calmed the storm with his medicine, but the ocean was choppy still. Cascading walls of sea rushed towards Yahoo's canoe, and Raven Chief paddled all the faster to end his foe and reclaim his daughter. Raven Chief held one of his war spears ready as Yahoo paddles up a mountainous wave.

"Now you die!" Raven Chief launched his spear. Yahoo crested the wave and used his medicine to transform water into stone. The spear clipped the top of the mountain and sailed harmlessly into the distance. The effort made Yahoo weak, but he had to keep paddling to keep him and his bride safe. But Raven Chief would not be easily deterred. He paddled around the Mountain in pursuit, noting Yahoo's waning strength. Raven Chief doubled his efforts and watched another wave of water, even greater than the first, dominate the horizon in front of Yahoo's canoe.

The wave grew higher and higher, and Yahoo paddled harder and harder. Never in all his life had his muscles ached so much; never before had he so struggled to breathe. Yahoo's shoulders ached; his head was light, but his wife gave him strength. They were nearly out of Raven Chief's domain! Soon they would be safe, but Yahoo had to keep going!

Raven Chief watched Yahoo's canoe near the top of the wave and he grabbed another war spear, waiting for the perfect moment. His rival crested the wave, and Raven Chief hurled his weapon with a mighty cry. The yell jolted Yahoo to his senses and he used the last bit of his medicine to once more turn water to stone. The spear struck the top of the mountain with a thunderous crack and that shook the land and calmed the seas. The spear sailed off into the sky, never to be seen again.

Raven Chief barely had time to react. He turned himself into a raven just as his canoe splintered against the great mountain. He flew away with an indignant "caw"!

With his medicine spent and energy depleted, Yahoo passed out. He woke in his own village, his smiling bride at his side. He looked west, to the mountains he'd created.

The smaller one called Mount Foraker

The large one, the Great One, we call Denali.

. . . .

Formerly recognized and officially once known as Mount McKinley, Mount Denali, in Alaska, is the highest Mountain in America. Indigenous people for centuries refer to the peak as Denali. In 1897, a gold prospector in support of William McKinley for President, names it Mount McKinley, which became the official name from 1917 until 2015, when it was renamed by the Federal Government, "Mount Denali", an original indigenous name.

My own last pilgrimage to Denali is only two days of special inspiration because of the gorgeous viewpoints along with recognition that the Mountain is beyond my skill climbing levels. However, the beauty and attraction of Denali is so great that I miss the last bus from the Mountain to my car at the park lodge. Then all I can do is to camp in the wilderness overnight and return to the lodge when the first early morning bus arrives. In retrospect, I was fortunate to survive the snow and the inability to sleep, thanks to a young woman who also missed the bus. We keep each other warm and alive with our hugs.

In the end, I never return since I feel so fortunate to survive. This experience proves one of my spiritual absolutes – whenever I have some kind of extreme need for help, someone "coincidentally" appears to provide it.

Note:
(See also Sacred Mount of Olives, Sacred Mount Tabor, Sacred Mount Sinai and Sacred Mount Monadnock in this book for other examples.)

Sacred Mount Whitney

People View-Point

Sacred Mountain pilgrims on this Holey Height,

Some bad, most good,

All feel the magic bliss

Of our Western Sacred Mountain's loving kiss.

        . . . THE MOUNTAIN PATH

Mount Whitney

Location:	California, U.S.A.
Range:	Sierra Nevada
Elevation:	14,505 ft (4,421 m)
Prominence:	10,079 ft (3,072 m)
Coordinates:	36°34'43"N
	118°17'31"W
Spirit:	Native American (Miwok, Paiute), Christian
Pilgrimage:	*Home of the Great Spirit of the Sierra*
	Sacred Mount Whitney

Angel View-Point

Home of the Great Spirit of The Sierra Sacred Mount Whitney

Esoterica: Myths, Mysteries and Imaginables

Although, we are not exactly sure when, the "Great Spirit" of the Northern Paiute was watching over the people from his home inside Sacred Mount Whitney.

The story is that the Northern Paiute Indians began as a "Sagehen" (bird). The bird survived a massive flood; it made the fire grow larger and bigger so the water from the flood dried up and Numuzoho, a man, "happened". But he was a cannibal and killed all the native people except for one woman who was able to escape. She kept herself alive by traveling from place to place in the region, staying and meeting with others. She later found a man living in the mountains. She married him, they had four children: Two Paiutes (brother, sister) and two Pit Rivers (brother, sister); these two sets often fought because they were from different tribes. Their father, whom some say was a Wolf, threw them in different waters, so they left and continued to fight and quarrel whenever they came in contact.

And thus, the Paiutes were created and their homes established in Nevada, California, and Oregon.

Another story claims, a man and a woman, claims they heard a voice from in a bottle. When they dumped the bottle, two boys and two girls came out. The good Paiutes were protected and cared for by the woman, while the two bad people were subject to the man.

The good Paiutes made a fire with almost no smoke; the two others made their fire with thick smoke and they thus became enemies. War and strife continued on ever since.

"Highest" Mt. Whitney

Mount Whitney is the highest Mountain in the contiguous Sierra Nevada Mountains. It is on the boundary between California's Inyo and Tulare counties 84.6 miles (136.2km)

John Muir Trail

West-northwest of North America's lowest point, Badwater Basin in Death Valley National Park, 282ft (86m) below sea level. Mount Whitney's western slope is in Sequoia National Park and Whitney's summit is in the southern terminus of the John Muir Trail. Spiritual recognition is provided by indigenous American Indians of Sacred Mount Whitney, particularly the Paiute Tribe.

Home Ground

Since Mount Whitney in California and the Sierra Nevada Mountain Range has been home ground to me, I have climbed to the summit and explored Mount Whitney often. Most Hikers spend a couple nights on the trail from the closest trailhead.

There is a small rock shack at the summit of the Mountain in case the weather is exceptionally bad. The first summit climb of the east face was by the famous "mountain man" John Muir.

While there are several trail approaches, the Eastern side involves technical free-climbing and is considered the most challenging "big-wall". Most of the climbers love the Mountain and use the regular main trail. In fact, I've slept on the trail a couple of times when I started too late and didn't have time to reach the top… and to sleep in the stone summit house when the weather was rainy, snowy and/or too windy.

Returning to the summit of Sacred Mount Whitney is a home-country for me as well as the Mountain's guru and spirit.

Sacred Mount
Junipero Serra

People View-Point

Close my eyes, feel the Mountain breeze,
Smell the truly salty sea.
And replace our burden from you and me
With friendship, love, peace, glee,
And with a Holy warming glow.

... T<small>HE</small> M<small>OUNTAIN</small> P<small>ATH</small>

Location:	California, U.S.A.
Range:	Santa Lucia
Elevation:	5857 ft (1,785 m)
Prominence:	4447 ft (1,355m)
Coordinates:	36°08'44"N
	121°25'08"W
Spirit:	(current) Christian, Roman Catholic
	(historic) Native American, Indigenous Mexican
Pilgrimage:	*To Be A Saint . . . Sacred Mount Junipero Serra*

ANGEL VIEW-POINT

To Be A Saint . . . Sacred Mount Junipero Serra

Esoterica: Myths, Mysteries and Imaginables

We humans are used to myths that are thousands of years old and represent thoughts and concepts of our ancient relatives. To support our understanding and even credibility, ancient myths seem to be easier to believe and if for no other reason than our faith. If it happened long enough ago, many homo sapiens suspend our view of reality overwhelmed by the wisdom of such stories if not the literal truth. Our acceptance of these stories may be critical to our self-credibility and readiness to believe or at least understand a human's rise from the dead, produce virgin births, hold actual human conversations with God or dead relatives, Jesus, and other Gods or immortals, supreme or otherwise.

Without relying on a claimed demonstrated miracle, how do we learn faith or come to understand heavens or hells or other situations that might otherwise be considered untenable, or just live up to the truths of our human existence. For example, is "true love" a human condition or an impossible myth?

For Millennia, "Saint" however defined, this myth is a story of a man who wanted from boyhood to be a Saint, at least as defined by the Sacred Mountain Guru, various religions and each of us. Webster considers a saint in this context as, "One officially recognized through canonization as preeminent for holiness; and one of God's chosen, and usually, Christian people".

. . . .

Serra Birth

Once upon a time, not so long ago as usual, a man was born in a small village on the island of Majorca (aka Mallorca), off the coast of Spain. This child, even at 7 years old, helped his parents cultivate wheat and beans and tended to their cows. His parents were uneducated and poor but devoted.

This young boy soon showed a special interest in a church within a block away from his home run by a group of priests. He attended that church's primary school to learn to read, write, mathematize, and especially learn Latin, religion, and liturgical songs. He had a good voice and took to vocal music so he was sometimes allowed to join the choir at special church feasts.

Church and Order

By age 16, his parents enrolled him in a school where he studied philosophy and a year later, he became a novice in an Ecclesiastical Order. He began his novitiate, a hard year of preparation, to become an accepted member of the Order. He was given a name by the Order to honor Brother Juniper, one of the first members. He vowed to scorn property and comfort, and to remain celibate. But it took him 7 years to become an ordained priest and to complete strenuous logic, metaphysics, cosmology and theology courses. In a daily routine, including a rigid schedule of prayers, meditation, choir singing, physical chores, spiritual readings and instructions, all the brothers would awaken every midnight for a round of chants. Letters and visitors were discouraged.

Soul Prayer

Of special importance, when he had time, he read about other members of his Order all over the world so as to know more souls, often suffering martyrdom. By 1737, he became a priest and in three years earned a church license to teach philosophy. Junipero Serra told his students, "I desire nothing more from you than this... when you hear of my death, please say a prayer for my soul: "may he rest in peace." I shall do the same for you so we all obtain the goal for which we have been created".

Theology Doctorate

Philosophy Chair

Considered intellectually brilliant by his peers, Junipero received a doctorate in theology and occupied a chair of philosophy until he left to join a missionary college in Mexico in 1749. At age 35, he left his fine career and his education. He wrote a letter to advise not to fret about life but to give one's life to God. In the same letter he asked his college friend to read it to his parents, who never attended school!

Refuses Horseback

For a rugged tropic high plateau and volcanic mountains in Mexico up to 7,400 feet (2,300 meters) royal officials provided horses for the 20 members of his Order for travel. All the members of the Order agreed to accept the ride, except for Junipero and a friend who refused to agree because of their patron-saint's admonition, to remember to "not ride horseback unless compelled by obvious necessity". On his walk over these mountains, he was bitten by mosquitoes that created injuries that became raw and bleeding, causing him pain for the rest of his life.

Lifetime Pain

Junipero was extremely humble and he took less so others could have more: he even served tables when needed in spite of his high stature. After a new series of studies, he was appointed as a "Lector in Philosophy". He was also honored for his activities and when 35 years old "the voice of God" called him to be a "teacher of nations". He then realized that he had "no other motive but to revive in my soul and my intense longing which I had since my novitiate when I read "Lives of the Saints". "My longings died because of my academic preoccupations."

Parent's Goodbye Letter

When he first left to sail to Mexico, he told no one, including his parents, of his secret plans, but on leaving his Order, he kissed the feet of all of the other members, down to the lowest novice. He asked another member to let his parents know of his journey saying, "I wish I could give them some of the happiness that is mine and I feel as if they would urge me ahead and never turn back. They will see that their lives are short compared with eternity… According to God's plan, they should pay no store by the little help that I may be to them if I stay, so they will earn merit from God, our Lord… If we are to do no more than see each other in this world, we will be united together in eternal glory… What they consider and endure as a great sacrifice will turn into everlasting joy… Nothing in this life should cause us sadness; our duty is to conform all things in the will of God and to prepare to die well… nothing else matters, may the Lord bring us all together in eternal glory…that is my prayer."

His Mission

He never saw his parents again.

His fame and extraordinary accomplishments enabled him to create missions for others where they could experience the joy and knowledge of having a happy and productive life just as he had. Junipero has been confirmed as the founder of many missions in California.

Serve God

He often said that his most important dream was to serve God and to set up many Missions in California, throughout the world, and especially for particular indigenous people of California. He saw this necessary work as serving God. Junipero became known as the "explorer", the "colonist" of California, the "founder of missions of California", the "Apostle of California" and the "Father of California Missions".

Demonized

Although he was demonized, and still is, for his alleged mistreatment of California Indians; he always disputed arguments that prolonged the debate.

Beatified and Canonized

Pope Saint John Paul II beatified him in 1988 and Junipero was canonized as a Saint by Pope Francis on Sept. 23, 2015 on the Basilica of the National Shrine of the Immaculate Conception in Washington D.C.

Pope Francis said, "He left his way of life as a sign for a blazing trail going forth for many people, learning to value their particular customs and ways of life and rebirthing caused light in all the faces in all of the lives". He is now called "Father Serra". The model that inspired his life and work was "keep moving forward" which to him meant "continue to experience the joy of the Gospel, keep your heart from growing numb because the Lord is waiting". His brothers and sisters were waiting, he kept going to the end.

Like him, we all should be able to say:

"Forward! Let's keep moving forward."

Sacred Mount Rainier

People View-Point

Once an earthly
Fire-full volcano force,
Spreading fear, distraction, destruction
Sacred Mount Tahoma collapses
to create Mount Rainier.

. . . The Mountain Path

Location:	Washington, USA
Range:	Cascade Mountain Range
Elevation:	14,417 ft (4,394 m)
Prominence:	13,212 ft (4027 m)
Coordinates:	46°51'11"N
	121°45'38"W
Spirit:	Native American
Pilgrimage:	*From Tahoma's Destructiveness*
	Comes Mount Rainier's Sacredness

Angel View-Point

From Destruction Comes Sacred Mount Rainier

*Northwest Indians generally worship Tahoma from a distance. They feared the Mountain and rarely climbed to its highest slope.
One of the myths of the Pacific Northwest: Why there are no snakes on Tahoma*

Esoterica: Myths, Mysteries and Imaginables

A long, long time ago, Tyhee Sahale became angry with the people. Sahale directed the medicine man to take his arrow and shoot into the cloud which hung low over Mount Tahoma. He shot the arrow. It struck fast in the cloud. Then he shot another into the lower end of the first. He shot arrows until he had made a chain which reached from the cloud to the earth. The medicine man told his children to climb up the arrow trail. And he told the good animals to climb up the arrow trail, all before the medicine man climbed up himself. Just as he was climbing up into the cloud, he looked back, and saw a long line of bad animals and snakes also climbing up the trail of arrows. The medicine man then broke the chain of arrows. So, the snakes and bad animals fell down on the mountain side. Then, it rained until all the land was flooded. Water even reached the snow line of Tahoma. When all the bad animals and snakes drowned, it stopped raining. After a while the waters sank again. Then the medicine man and the children climbed out of the cloud and came down the mountain side. The good animals also climbed out of the cloud.

This is why there are now no snakes or bad animals on Tahoma.

Mount Tahoma, said to have been a huge, active stratovolcano in the Cascade Range of the Pacific Northwest of the United States that created Mount Rainier only about 59 miles from Seattle, Washington. Mount Rainier's summit elevation of 14,411 feet (4,392 meters), is the highest Mountain in Washington State and considered the most topographically prominent mountain in the contiguous United States as well as the highest elevation of the Cascade Volcanic Arc. The experts estimate any eruption in the near future close to a major urban area, is perilous. By that standard, Mount Rainier is one of the most dangerous volcanoes in the world. That is also why Mount Rainier is on the "Decade Volcano List". Rainier can also produce huge lahars (flowing masses of mixed volcanic debris and water). Glacial ice threatens the entire Puyallup River Valley and other valleys draining Mount Rainier. The United States Geographical Survey concludes that "about 80,000 people and their homes are at risk from Mount Rainier's lahars".

Most Dangerous

Between 1950 and 2018, 439,460 people climbed Mount Rainier. About 84 people died in mountaineering mishaps from 1947-2018.

Climbers Deaths

The Mountain's long history has resulted in many peoples with their own names for the mountain (translated): "Sky Wiper", "One Who Touches The Sky" and "Snow-Covered Mountain". Anglicized names include Tacoma, Tahoma, and Tacobet. Sashaptins call the Mountain "Taxuma" (anglicized "Pooskaus"). George Vancouver actually named Mount Rainier in honor of his friend, Rear Admiral Peter Rainier. The United States Board on Geographic Names proclaimed that the Mountain would be known as "Mount Rainier". In 1987, the Pacific Forest Preserve became the Mount Rainier Forest

Mountain Names

Reserve. Even though the National Park was established three years later, there was, and still is a movement to change the Mountain's name to Tahoma. Congress is still considering that change. Mount Rainier is the most heavily glaciated peak in the lower 48 states with 26 major glaciers. The summit has two volcanic craters, more than 1000 feet (300 meters) in diameter. Geothermal heat from the volcano keeps the rims of summit craters free of snow and ice and has formed the world's largest volcanic glacier ice network with nearly two miles (3.2 kilometers) of passages.

There are three Mount Rainier summits, Columbus Crest, Point Success and Sunset Cap.

Stratovolcano

As a stratovolcano, the volcanic deposits are estimated to be more than 840,000 years old, while the present cone is more than 500,000 years old.

Mudflows

Mount Rainier has large debris avalanches and has produced enormous mudflows that have reached all the way to Puget Sound more than 30 miles (48 kilometers) away. When a large portion of the volcano slid away, it produced the Osceola Mudflow that once flowed all the way to Tacoma and South Seattle and reduced the elevation of Mount Rainier to 14,100 feet (4300 meters).

Ash Blasts

Many recorded volcanic activities were reported from 1820 to 1850 and eyewitness accounts of eruptions have been made of activity in 1858, 1870, 1879, 1882, and 1894. The massive amounts of ash blasting out of the volcano have been observed from Vancouver, British Columbia, Canada, and from San Francisco, California.

Dormant Volcanoes

Many of the volcanoes in the northwest of the United States are "dormant" but could return to activity anytime. In fact, several of them have erupted in modern times including Mount Lassen in 1950 and Mount St Helens in 1980 and 2004, which produced the largest eruption in the United States at the time.

The United States Geographical Survey advises that about 150,000 people live atop old flowing masses of mixed volcanic debris and water deposits from Mount Rainier. It is also claimed that these mud flows from the Mountain could destroy parts of downtown Seattle and cause tsunamis in Puget Sound, Washington. The Washington State Department of Natural Resources concludes a significant lahar could cause up to 40 billion dollars in damages.

The more populous King County in this area, as of a recent report, has no zoning restrictions for a volcanic hazard. During the Little Ice Age, ice and debris moved down the valley from the glacier to Tahoma.

Glacier Retreats

Since the early 1980s many glaciers have been thinning and retreating and some advances even slowed. Using satellite data, researchers at Nichols College noted that some glaciers have ceased with only fragments of ice remaining, especially between 2015 and 2022.

Tribal / Used 8,500 years

Descendants of Indian tribes surrounding the mountain include the Nisqually, the Cowlitz, the Confederated and bands of Yakama Nation. Human use of the Mountain dates at least to 8,500 years ago.

In 1899 President William McKinley established America's 5th National Park, the Mount Rainier National Park.

U.S. Largest Glaciers

Climbing Mount Rainier is difficult including crossing the largest glaciers in the United States South of Alaska; Generally, climbers take two or three days to reach the summit with a success rate of about 50%, weather and physical conditions being the most common reasons for failure. Climbing routes are graded in the NCCS Alpine Climbing Format and include the Disappointment Cleaver Route, Ingraham Glacier direct route and the Emmons Glacier Route (grade 2) and the Liberty ridge route (grade 4). This route accounts for almost 2% of the total climbers but about 25% of the deaths on the Mountain.

The Mountain, the summit, and the incredible viewpoints provide a pure Sacred Mountain experience.

Sacred Mount Shasta

People View-Point

Consciousness is Self, we're all aware:
Self never leaves
How glorious, we are all
"Self Realized".
          . . . THE MOUNTAIN PATH

Mount Shasta

Location:	Siskiyou County, California
Range:	Cascade Range
Elevation:	14,179 feet (4,322 m)
Prominence:	9,772 feet (2979 m)
Parent peak:	North Palisade
Parnt range:	Cascade Range
Isolation	335 mi (539 km)
Coordinates:	41°24'33"N
	122°11'42"W
Last Eruption:	1250 CE
Native Name:	Waka-nunee-Tuki-wuki (Shasta)
	Uytaakhoo (Karok)
Mountain type:	Stratovolcano
Spirit:	American Indian
Pilgrimage:	*Success Brings Joy, Failure Brings Wisdom*
	Sacred Mount Shasta

ANGEL VIEW-POINT

Success Brings Joy; Failure Brings Wisdom . . . Sacred Mount Shasta

Esoterica: Myths, Mysteries and Imaginables

The Klamath Tribes postulated that Mount Shasta is inhabited by the Spirit of the Above-World, called "Skell", who descended from Heaven to Shasta's summit, as requested by a Klamath tribal chief. Skell then fought with the Spirit of the Below-World, "Lao", who was throwing hot rocks and lava at Shasta and Lao's own home mountain (this probably was the volcanic eruption on both mountains).

Many spiritual faiths have been attracted to Mount Shasta, probably more than any other mountain in the Cascade Mountain Range.

Shasta has also been the location and concentration of many non-native American Legends based on stories of beings from the lost continent of Lemuria.*

By 1987, believers in the Spirit of Harmonic Convergence described Mount Shasta as one of a small number of global power centers and still remains a point of concentration and a center of attention, including for example, the place of origin of an earthquake.

Joaquin Miller, a prominent author, lived for a time in the late1800s with the Shasta Indians and recorded several of their myths on how Shasta was created and the beginnings of the Indian race in his writings about Indian legends of Mount Shasta. The Great Spirit is alleged to have made Mount Shasta, first by pushing down the snow and ice from the skies through a hole created in the blue heavens and by turning a stone round and round until the Mountain was complete.

The Great Spirit then walked out of the clouds to Mount Shasta's summit and descended the Mountain while planting trees everywhere with his fingers. The sun melted the snow so the water nurtured the trees and made rivers and afterwards fish for the rivers, birds by blowing leaves which he took from the ground among the trees, beasts from his stick. He designated the Grizzly Bear master over everything else. Finally, the Great Spirit decided to remain on earth, make the sea, and more land so he could convert Mount Shasta into a wigwam with a fire in the center. After all that creation, his family came down to the mountain and lived there ever since. Before the White Man came, the Indians could see fire ascending from the Mountain at night and smoke by day.

Indians thereafter would not climb Mount Shasta for fear of the Great Spirit and their profound worship of the Great Spirit dwelling on the mountain with his people and the respect of their privacy.

The first Indians were created from the unique children born from unions with the Great Spirit and the Grizzly Bear. The Grizzlies also built, for a "lovely red princess", a wigwam now called "Little Mount Shasta" or "Black Butte".

The Great Spirit became angry at the Grizzlies who without the Great Spirit's permission betrayed the Great Spirit by creating a new race. The Great Spirit, with a dreadful howl, put his daughter on his shoulders, turned to all the Grizzlies, telling them to hold their tongue, get down on their hands and knees and stay that way until he returned. Thereafter, he closed the wigwam, drove all of the children out of the world and went up to the Sacred Mountain, never returning to the timber forest again. Since then, just like the other beasts (animals), the Grizzlies could no longer rise up and use their clubs; they had to remain on all fours, except when fighting for their lives. With this, the Great Spirit allowed the Grizzlies to stand up and fight with their fists, like men.

To this day, the Indians around Shasta will never kill or interfere in any way with the Grizzlies. As Joaquin Miller mentions, this is the Indian Legend of a creation and as a matter of principle, legends must tell the truth, the whole truth and nothing but the truth. Who can tell?

. . .

Shasta Volcano

Sacred Mount Shasta is a potentially active stratovolcano in the Cascade Mountain Range, Siskiyou County near Shasta California. The last eruption in 1250 CE or (AD 1250), according to Native myths, is also a difficult climb to the summit. As one of the more significant spiritual sites in the world, "Pilgrims" ("Climbers") come for healing, soul connection, self-discovery, and to enjoy the spiritual energy this Mountain exudes. These climbers, in some part, climb themselves to eliminate negative energy to leave room for the "positive".

Tribes on Mount Shasta

Sacred Mount Shasta was once a part of the areas occupied by Wintu, Achomawi, Atsugewi and Modac California tribes. There are also many spiritual "hot spots" and "hot streams" on Mount Shasta.

Success/Failure Summitting

In spite of several efforts to summit Mount Shasta, I have never succeeded, even though it is not difficult. I have tried the Western, the Eastern, Red Banks, and many other routes towards the top until forced to be turned down, mostly by weather and minor personal injuries. By coincidence, my attempts were rained out, snowed out, or blown out making it impossible to reach the summit. Although probably one of the more disappointing things that can happen to a man who spent a whole lifetime climbing and summiting mountains, including Sacred Mountains that were much more difficult and dangerous than Mount Shasta. But, as usual, I also received the benefits of my failures and the Mountain became a source of several spiritual events for me.

Wisdom

Who knows? Maybe I will have a last chance to summit Sacred Mount Shasta. Or if I don't, the wisdom of joy will give a special happiness.

Religions

It is claimed, over 200 religious/spiritual organizations do obeisance to their own spiritual experience and many have placed their headquarters in the adjoining town of Shasta due to the Spiritual implications and importance.

---

* Even before Mt Lassan became "sacred", Mount Shasta was said to hold a crystal city inside. The people there were considered to be a higher-dimensional people than the Lemuria in the North Pacific Ocean, even before "Atlantis" was inhabited.

Thermonuclear war between Lemuria and Atlantis is said to have caused their respective continents to sink. The seven foot high Lemurians escaped into Mount Shasta. In fact, they were supposedly seen walking in town in their white robes to buy supplies.

Some local Shastan's even believed the smooth, saucer-shaped clouds that often come together at the summit of Mt Shasta were engineered by the Lemurians in order to camouflage their cargo ships bringing supplies to them inside Mount Shasta

Sacred Mount Haleakala

People View-Point

How can a bowl in the sand

be a sacred mountain?

Anon

Mount Haleakala

Location:	Maui, Hawaii, U.S.A.
Range:	West Maui Mountains
Elevation:	10,023 ft (3,055 m)
Prominence:	10,023 ft (3,055 m)
Coordinates:	20°42'35"N
	156°15' 12" W
Spirit:	Native Hawaiian
Pilgrimage:	*Under One Sun . . . Sacred Mount Haleakala*

Angel View-Point

Under One Sun . . . Sacred Mount Haleakala

Esoterica: Myths, Mysteries and Imaginables

The Seven Great Deeds

As the sun drops below the Pacific, I find I can't leave until I fully understand what this Mountain of the Sun means to the Polynesian. It all begins with the wonderfully alive myths of the seven great deeds of Island Maui's God.

Maui is set adrift in a canoe to die (like Moses, Romulus, Oedipus, Junti of the Ramayama in India, and innumerable other religious heroes), but jelly-fish save Maui and he returns to his birthplace to knock down the short post and the long post, to kill his uncles and break down the door to his mother's house. That is his first great deed.

He lifts the sky so the earth will stop burning from the sun and the clouds wouldn't smother the world in darkness (but he forgets to unflatten the leaves of the trees).

He fishes up the islands from the sea with a magic hook of the jawbones of his ancestors.

He takes fire from his great-grandmother in hell, loses it, forces the Alae 'Ula birds to return it, and he then gives it to man.

To save his mother, he cut up the sea monster, Kunaloa, into pieces that become the ocean's eels.

But he is never able to find his brother and sister on the island of paradise, Moana-lika-i koa-wao-ki-li.

Because the seagulls can't keep quiet, he dies in the horrible jaws of the golden Goddess of Death while trying to bring immortal life to man.

Though not great deeds, he did many other things for mankind like making the birds visible and their songs audible and darkening the clouds to warn of rain and trouble.

And this is his fourth great deed:

Because the sun moved too fast in the sky, Maui felt sorry for every one and especially his mother. It took her all year to dry out her tapa[1] sheets for her cloth and the farmers couldn't grow their crops. Maui began watching the sun closely. He observed its path as it came over the Mountain Haleakala, then called "House of the Rays of the Sun," through a chasm in its side.

After a fierce battle and thanks to his magic ax, Maui wins. Finally, the sun begs for his freedom and promises to travel more slowly across the sky if Maui gives him his life. So, they make an agreement: The sun was to take longer to go through the sky for six months; it can go fast as in the old days for the other six months.

Then Maui let the sun go but he leaves the ropes and the noose on the side of the Mountain to remind the sun every day of his agreement as he comes across the crater rim. And from that day to this, the name of the great Mountain changes from "Rays of the Sun" to "House of the Sun" and even now the people say, "Long shall be the daily journey of the sun and he shall give light for all the people's toil." And so, Maui's mother pounds the tapa board until she is tired.*[1] The farmers plant and take care of their crops. The fishermen go out to the deep sea and come back before nightfall, and the fruits and plants get heat, enough to ripen in their season.

. . . .

I rise to the heights of Arunachala... been above the ancient mysteries of Mount Lassen and Mount Olympus... beyond the Mountain inspirations of Buddha, Moses, Christ

Now need to go down to the beginning... into the crater of Haleakala

Jet to Hawaii

Maui

"House of the Sun"

Mount Haleakala

Last eruption 1750

Hawaii Islands Not Island

and Muhammad... and even Shugendo death. I now need to go down into the beginning, down into the crater of Haleakala.

All night, from Japan to Hawaii, my plane screams at the silent blackness of the Pacific Ocean. The fiery blast of its engines hurtles me against the light of the sun rising somewhere beyond the blackness. One half hour from touchdown (Honolulu Airport), the powers of man and the universe meet in a crescendo of the red light of dawn.

After a plane change and a short flight, I arrive at the airport on the island of Maui, a place far below the peak of Haleakala. The huge Sacred Mountain summit is covered in fog, green fog jungles on one side, of light gray deserts on the other. This part of the Mountain is surrounded by the deep blue swells of the ocean. They pound themselves on the coastline into a white froth.

Mount Haleakala, in a simple translation from the Polynesian, means "House of the Sun". In truth, I am coming back to the sun– a source of power– to a Mountain sacred to prehistoric generations of Polynesians.

From the airport to the parking lot below "Red Hill", the 10,230-foot top of Mount Haleakala is over an hour drive. Dormant now, Haleakala is thirty-three miles long, the last active high point in the Hana series of volcanic eruptions in 1750. Except where a patch of jungle touches one corner, a patch of jungle that receives over three hundred inches of rain a year, the crater is an open moon-scape desert of ashes. Its innards are a nineteen square mile giant furnace with inside dimensions over seven miles long and almost three miles wide. Only the sun, or a wilderness wanderer like me, could be at home in such a valley.

This "Home of the Sun" is the Mountain of the demigod

Maui, the trickster, man's benefactor, like the Loki of Norse myth, the Paul Bunyan of the Pacific. Maui is part of the history of all Polynesia. And from the heights on Red Hill where I stand, Maui oversees all of his great works, particularly the chain of Hawaiian Islands (Oahu, Molokai, Hawaii, Lanai, Kahoolawe, and Molokini) that he fishes from the sea. According to legends, if his uncles obey his orders and do not watch what Maui is doing, Hawaii would be one island instead of several.

From this lookout, Maui could even observe Pele, the Goddess of the volcano, who moved from Mount Haleakala to her new home on the summits of the snow-capped volcanoes of Mauna Kea and Mauna Loa, also part of the Islands of Maui. As I look at them, the peaks of the two volcanic Mountains are so far away, they seem to float on the billowy clouds surrounding them, high over the "big island" of Hawaii.

Mauna Kea
Mauna Loa
Volcanoes

Across the wide valley in the opposite direction, the six-thousand-foot high, west Maui Mountains show themselves soaked in dark clouds. I was in these Mountains several years before and tried to find the lost Missionary Trail, formerly the King's Highway from Wailuku to Lahaina (the only route up the Mountain from that side). I find maps over seventy years old, including the U.S. Geodetic Survey Map of Maui that shows parts of the trail. I read histories of Hawaii and the stories of missionaries who describe this route over the Mountains.

King's Highway

In a small house in the trees of Lao Valley, I find a pure Hawaiian who knows the ancient oral history of Maui. He is a small man, very old and friendly, with a twinkle in his eye. He confirms that there was such a pathway but that the jungle and heavy rains destroyed most of it. His grandfather who gathered ferns in those Mountains, told stories of this trail to

Lahaina on the coast.

Olawalu Rive

For twenty-four hours, without ropes or a machete, I struggle alone. I wade the Olawalu River, find my way through forests and scramble up steep jungle cliffs, all the while unable to see where I am going because of the mist and fog, brush and trees. Even though I am very tired, I find the lost trail and even its stone steps where they are supposed to be– "fifty paces back from the huge Hawaiian tree on the second tributary, across the sandbar– and straight up the ridge."

Sacred Mount Haleakala

I now realize that all my study and exploration is but a prelude for now. Here I am, back on Maui to "climb" down into the guts of Sacred Mountain Haleakala. Previously, I camped inside the small (relatively) craters on the peaks of Mount Lassen and Fuji-san. I know what this means. Here is the chance to venture into the Mountain itself. I wonder if I will receive any hint of the spiritual civilizations which primitive native Hawaiians think were inside their Sacred Mountains. Many claim, even now, that such a community exists inside Mount Kailash in Tibet, Arunachala in India, Mount Shasta in California or many find new strength by thinking they are not alone when on these Mountains, but that they are close to a perfect God-governed society, mystical and untouched by the cold and desolation of the outer shell of the Mountain or by the heated terror of volcanic eruptions boiling inside.

6 mile "Sliding Sands" trail

The six mile long "Sliding Sands" trail to the crater floor, which the U.S. Civilian Conservation Corps built in the 1930s, is disarmingly easy. It lures many tourists beyond their ability to hike the four-thousand-foot rise back up. The guidebook warns: "This trail is not recommended for the return from the crater."

Ascent

An ascent is a struggle to win, to reach the peak, to soar.

Descent

A descent is more thoughtful, relaxed, quiet, less concentrated. You see the Mountain and shelf as they are, from a man's eye point of view, not as you imagine they will be from the broader, higher vantage point of a God's eye view.

On the way down the trail, the magnificence of the view diminishes. The details of the crater become more evident. This is really an ancient valley*2 of ashes and volcanic residue. It is born from the earth's inner explosive power.

Kapalooa Cabin

By the time I descend to Kapalaoa, a rustic ranger cabin at the bottom of the crater, it is early afternoon. The rest of the daylight is spent exploring the south end of the valley. This valley has few trails, more jungles and their vegetation. A sudden whir of pheasants taking flight surprises me. A hard-to-follow path ascends the east rum up to a forest cliff to a small lake. Here, I hear wild boars rooting. Beyond the east rim, is thick steep green wilderness, opened only by streams and waterfalls that stretch to the sea. Another trail was a long route following a flow of lava from the last eruption that went through Kaupo Gap, out of the crater to the south desert side of Maui. It's the wrong way to leave the crater unless someone is going to pick you up, since there are very few people, no towns and only a dirt road on that part of the island. As usual, I want to go further and further along these trails, but the sun drops below the west rim. The long shadows make me uneasy and remind me to head back to Kapalaoa.

Unfortunately, I leave my pack on the other side so that I couldn't stay at the ranger cabin at this end of the crater. The cabin here is in a flower meadow against the jungle cliffs of Paliku. Behind it, I find some Akala (large wild raspberries) that make a luscious though somewhat bitter dessert before dinner.

It is dark by the time I reach Kapalaoa. I stoke up a wood fire in the potbelly stove, eat some nuts and fruit and go to sleep. The stiffness of the cabin makes me uncomfortable and wakes me up. Though there is no moon, the room is lit with starlight. I go outside. The rim of the crater is a tremendous black shadow, a fortress against the real world. But the desert crater itself is a ghostly star-scape-of whites and grays. Vibrations of mystery, the superstitions that affect natives and visitors alike in Hawaii, permeates the whole scene. It is cold. Nothing stirs. There is no wind.

Bottomless Pit

Yet I hear a whisper or a moan. Less than half a mile away is the "Bottomless Pit". It is a blowhole to the subterranean world. For centuries fathers threw the umbilical cords of their newborn babies into it.*3 Was I hearing the hum of the underworld or something else? I thought of the thousands of babies' umbilical cords now in caves and on rock platforms in this valley of the dead and of the victims of human sacrifice, their smashed skulls symbols of man's fear of the unknown.

Fear

The darkness enhances the Sacred Mountain's mystical aura. The night sky is more vivid than I have ever seen it. The crater is a telescopic lens, so powerful that it scans among the stars, among the suns of other worlds. In the vastness of this cosmos, I feel man's primitive fear creep over me. Fears of my insignificance, my helplessness, my weakness. I need an ally. It must be greater than all the universe. It must be greater than the Mountains. It must be God.

Move Outside

I bring my sleeping bag outside. In this mysterious night sky, I doze off until the cold, predawn awakens me. The dawn is important for I am here to see this home of the sun. I know the significance of each ray of rising sun as it comes over the east walls of the rim, one by one… just as the Polynesian God Maui sees it.

Maui Defeats the Sun

According to Hawaiian legend, Maui defeats the sun. But not here in this crater. Inside Haleakala, the sun rises without the influence of water, trees or shade. It takes revenge on Maui's human progeny. Those who venture into this House of the Sun respect its ruler or suffer the reported pains of hell: burns, blisters… prostration, and heat exhaustion.

Early in the morning, the heat is already uncomfortable as I hike through the cinder cones and poke around the caves and caverns of the north end of Haleakala. Many of the rock platforms and altars, even piles of stone called "Ahus" (like "ducks") still mark the trails and sacred places of ancient Hawaii. On the trail, there is a pathway of smooth water-worn rocks of a type not found elsewhere on Haleakala. The great public works king of the Hawaiian Islands, Kihapiilani, builds this trail with a chain of men who pass rocks from hand to hand thirty-one miles long from the sea to the crater. The rocks fit together and the cracks fill with sand and gravel. I am careful not to disturb even a grain of sand or a small spatter cone, "pa puaa o Pele", since to do so, is tapu (taboo) and according to tradition, brings fog, rain and even death. The valley is an incision in the stomach of the earth, one that the Master Surgeon forgets to sew-up. I feel I am walking on the open innards and not the skin of this planet. The colors, especially at "Pele's Paint Pot" pass, are pale and sickly reds or maroons, off-whites, grays, browns, dusty yellows and even dull pinks. The surface seems alert, waiting in caves and pits for the next eruption.

Pele's Paint Pot

The molten violence below had blown volcanic bombs "helter skelter" over the rock plateaus and sculpted many odd shaped formations including "bubble cave", a rock house completed with a smoke hole in the top rock.

Even the plant kingdom was wary of these sun bleached, scarred, inhospitable entrails of the earth. By looking closely, you could see a pale gray dust that is actually lichen growing in combination with algae and fungus, the advance scouts for true plants. On the fringes of the crater, especially to the south and east, there are splashes of contrasting color from tall grasses, silver geraniums, butter cups, violets, sandalwood, even green orchids but neither they nor any tree or shrub ventures onto the crater desert itself. That is left to plants that are freaks of nature — massive, rare sunflowers called "Silverswords". When in blossom, they are barrels (some over six feet high) of ghostly stems topped with a disk of hundreds of yellow flowers bordered by purple blossoms. These plant apparitions face extinction from insect parasites and marauding goats and tourists. This fantasy color and construction is too much to do more than once. After seven to twenty years of preparation, the Silverswords blossom only once and then die.

Silverswords

At noon, I begin the hike out of the crater from Holua, directly below the west rim, up the Hale Mauu Trail (a fifteen-hundred-foot climb). I struggle against the steep trail and the sun's furnace. The distance is four miles to the road. A park ranger tells me, "You can easily catch a ride at the trailhead at the top." But after trying to hitch a ride for an hour while busses and cars pass by without even slowing down, I decide to stagger the six miles up to my car; and I do.

Hale Mauu Trail

The reflection of the sun off the road makes this last 2,500-foot climb torturous. The sun grinds me to nothing. I am only a speck of sweat and dirt, oven-baked in the exposed rocks under the midday sun. The sun gives life; it also recreates the souls of the dead. I believe it.

Torture Climb

I feel my own rejuvenation. On my way driving down the Mountain in the late afternoon, I stop at Leleiwi (Lay-Lay-e-v-e), a lookout on the crater rim about nine thousand feet in altitude. I watch the clouds below roll into Koolau (Kn-n-lou as in "loud") Gap. The sun behind me creates a

Created Again

gigantic shadowy specter of my body against the cloud banks within a circular rainbow. I see myself fleetingly but surely, enlarged and enshrined by the Mountain, the rays of the sun and the clouds. Here are the cosmos of the sun; I am created again, forever. I am.

Sun Stoppers

Myths

Maui is a Polynesian God of a separate people in the isolated islands of the Pacific. This God-conflict with the sun, like all myths of Polynesia, is part of the oral tradition in detail from generation to generation. Is it really only a primitive fantasy? Does the sun really stop in the sky in its battle with Maui? What happens to the rest of the world when Maui fights with the sun? The answers are in our world history:

Sun Travel

Long before we come to America (the second time):

In eastern America, the Algonquin tribe relates that the sun is caught in its path by a boy with a noose and almost chokes the sun to death, an act that plunges the world into darkness.

Algonquin Tribe

In our earliest beginnings, in East Africa, Kyazamba of the Wachage tribe, seeks the land where the sun rises, with the help of an old woman and her magic garment. Instead of being taken to the land of the sun, he flies to zenith of the sun in the middle of the day "where the sun pauses and entertains him."*4

Sun Stands Still

While in the Middle East, Isaiah predicted that "The sun will be dark in his going forth" and that "Sennacharib's army will die before Jerusalem in a single night." The sign unto thee from the Lord will be the sun standing still.*5

Sun Goes Backwards

Even as we, the rational people, report in Ancient Greece: "Atreus stipulates with Thyestes that Atreus is to be king if the sun goes backward; and when Thyestes agrees, the sun sets in the east." And "in the time of the Argive tyrants the sun goes "speedily to its setting and evening comes before its proper time."*6

Did Phaeton delay the beginning of the day with his entreaties to his father, Helios, the sun God, to allow him to drive the chariot of the sun on what proves to be a disastrous course?

Daylight Drives Parvati Blind

Before we were conscious, in India Parvati plunged the world into darkness by mischievously closing Shiva's eyes.

In China, Huai-nan-tse reports that the Duke of Ly-yang in his historic battle against Ham, "Swings his spear, beckons to the sun, whereupon the sun, for his sake, comes back and passes through three solar mansions."*7

Sun Battle

And in Japan, the sunlight returns to the world when the Sun Goddess Amaterasu, tricked out of hiding on account of her vanity, is prevented by strong rope from retreating permanently back to the darkness of her "heavenly rock dwelling" cave.

Goddess Leaves Cave

Days Too Short

Eons ago, in our backyard, the West, the Ute Indians tell us that because the days are too short, Cottontail hides waiting for the sun to rise, with the intention of breaking the sun in pieces. "The sun begins to rise but, seeing Cottontail, it goes down again." After a battle, "the days become longer.

Myth Pool

Demigod Changes Sun

In every mythology; there are stories of a man-like demigod influencing and changing the progress of the sun (Phaeton and Helios of Greece, Maui of Polynesia, Yahweh of Sinai, Odin of the Norseland, Surya of India, Ra of Egypt). And in all these traditions either a frightening darkness without the sun, or a devastating conflagration of fire, bursting rocks and drying up waters are reported. Likewise, many mythologies tell of a great flood with only a few surviving animals and men*8, of creation from the dirt of man and woman*9 and the creation of all things in the same order: earth, moon, sun, planets, animals, man, and woman. A trinity of Gods appears in so many religions that it cannot be coincidental: the holy trinity of Christians; Vishnu, Shiva and Brahma of Hinduism; Kane, Kuu and Lao of Polynesia.

And religions also talk of promises of God and their own exclusivity. The Polynesians, before there is any contact with Judaism or any other alien culture, tell a story almost identical to that of the Garden of Eden*10, as in the Old Testament, with only the type of fruit, the names of man and woman, and the place changed. The universality of myths may be a reflection of actual similar events. For example, in Hawaiian mythology, the Mountain volcano Goddess, Pele, moves from island to island in the same order as current scientific studies have established the actual times of volcanic activity: from Kaui in the beginning to Hawaii presently. The Sacred Mountains raise those myths to truth within.

Man Built Mountains

Man has always felt the spiritual power of Mountains and worships them. Where Mountains don't exist from the earliest times, he builds them, whether they are towers, pyramids, churches, Temples or Tibetan rock piles. After all, man and Mountain are (in the beginning) both said to have come from the sea.

Life Patterns

At least people think such myths true or need to think they are true to survive. They reflect fears and dreams.

Such stories survive because they enable people to pattern their lives on a common basis.

"Us"?

The conclusion is obvious. We are made the same by ourselves. For example, in Genesis, God says, "Let us make men in our image after our likeness." Where did it get "us"?

Creation

Whether creation occurs in a way as Adam and Eve by God from the dust or from people from outer space or from a sudden chemical (organic nitrogen compound with amino acids) and electrical (from lightning) mutations, or a process of

We Are One

evolution beginning from a spontaneous primordial virus, the human race differentiates by family, tribe, country, race, religion and nation due to differences that arise from the weather, climate, happenstance, social organization and geography or some other common source. But now we come in full circle to our common creation.

In this world of inter-dependence, instant communication, space travel and progress from the physical and mental man to the emotional, spiritual man, the differentiations mean nothing. We are One again as all the world's myths tell us we began. We must recognize this universality or perish as a person, a nation, a race and mankind.

To be consistent with our Self, one first needs to know, then accept our Oneness, our universal heritage, individually (parentage) or socially (history). Otherwise, we are in conflict with our own essence and hence neurotic, destructive and likely to destroy ourselves and our species in disunity and conflict. Our ultimate reality, the boundary of our potential, the source of our power, is the gene pool from whence we all come. For no one can be my enemy or I am destroyed.

One Sun

The spirit of Maui lights my own horizons
to free me from the tyranny of hate.
On the winds, From the cliffs,
In the echoes of the great volcanoes,
On the rays of the morning sun floats the
song of Maui:

The sun is One
That all men need identically
For heat and life and catalyst of change
And hence the object proves the subject,
Universal is our core.

We began in our beginnings all the same.

Haleakala is a massive shield volcano of the Pleistocene epoch rock and part of the Hawaiian-emperor seamount chain which includes more than 75% of the Hawaiian Island of Maui. The west Maui Mountains on the same island include 25% of the island and another volcano, Mauna Kahalawai. Haleakala is the 18th most prominent peak of these ocean islands and the 10th most prominent peak in America.

It last erupted between 1480 to 1600. Haleakala means "house of the sun". Its original name is Pu'u 'Ula'ula. There is a huge depression in the surface, 7 miles (11.25 km) across, 2 miles (3.2 km) wide and almost 2,600 feet (800 m) deep. The surrounding walls are precipitous, barren and scattered with volcanic cones. The Hawaiian goose "nene" is endemic to the wild islands and exclusively found in the wild on Oahu, Maui, Kaua'i, Molokai and Hawaii.

An Exclusive Goose

The "Islands" have long been for me a favorite physically, mentally, emotionally, and spiritually since much of my life has been lived relatively close to San Francisco, an easy journey by plane of approximately five hours.

Favorite Hawaii

The Islands of Hawaii have been an inspiration after all these years of exploring; clearly one of my favorite places to be.

Footnotes:
1. This was to assure their children grew up strong and honest. Cloth made by pounding fibers of the mulberry tree.
2. 'There has been considerable debate as to whether the crater of Haleakala was the remains of a single volcano that collapsed into itself or an eroded valley in which several volcanoes had erupted. The latter is a better, more recent view. Stearns, H.T., Origin of Haleakala Crater, Maui, Hawaii, Geological Society.
3. American Bulletin, Vol. 53, pp. 1-14 (1942).
4. Bruno Guttman, Volksbuth Der Wadschagga (Leipzig 1914) p144; Campbell, *The Hero with a Thousand Faces* (Meridian Books 1960), p.69.

5. "Kings 19 and following; Worlds in Collision, pp 226-336.
6. "Ibid., p. 236.
7. *Worlds in Collision*, p. 236. Forke, World Conception of the Chinese, p. 86.
8. "For example, in the epic of Gilgamesh, as in the story of Noah, the end of the deluge is signaled by a bird with a branch; only in this myth it is a raven rather than a dove
9. "Women are, in fact, universally regarded as having brought death into the world and all our woes." Lederer, *Fear of Women* (Harcourt Brace 1968); Brifault, *The Mothers* Vol. II, p. 571.
10. Even like the story of Pandora's Box in Greek mythology.

Sacred Mount Wai'ale'ale

People View-Point

Where have our feeling waters flown?
Like the Big Springs of Yellowstone.
To honor God's springs so we can live
An extended livelihood along the Ides of time.
　　　　　　　　　　. . . THE MOUNTAIN PATH

Mount Wai'ale'ale

Location:	Island of Kauai, Hawaii, U.S.A.
Range:	Kauai
Elevation:	5148 ft (1,569 m)
Prominence:	5,148 ft (1,569 m)
Coordinates:	22°4'26"N
	159°29'55"W
Spirit:	Native Hawaiian
Pilgrimage	*Water, Water, Everywhere . . .*
	On Sacred Mount Wai'ale'ale

Angel View-Point

Water, Water, Everywhere . . . On Sacred Mount Wai'ale'ale

Esoterica: Myths, Mysteries and Imaginables

Water then becomes a strong symbol even at the spiritual level of profound depth from the changing feelings, sadness and many other human emotions. Water, of course, is a sine qua non of life, plants, and all animals including humans. We can't live without it. Water is and always has been an important symbol of sacredness and life in religious and individual concepts of purification, rejuvenation and transformation.

By way of example:

Psychology: water rites are found in elusive ideas. Waters depth symbolizes emotionalness, humanness, and endlessness

Astrology: the water signs, Cancer and Scorpio, are said to be the most emotional of all signs.

Movement: water is almost never completely still but it is continually heaving and flowing.

Sadness: sadness, sorrow, and even depression often cause water symptoms in the form of tears. In addition, bad weather causes rain, sorrow, and often remorse.

Life: water is of course critical to maintain life, growth and vitality. In ancient Egyptian culture and life, water was represented by an Egyptian symbol for water.

Water Flow: water continually moves and often becomes a symbol of moving emotions or feelings in literature.

Purification: water is critical to the idea of purity and holiness and used to cleanse people of sin, baptism, and washing away imperfections to communicate with the Spirit of God.

Rebirth: water reminds us of the continuing cycle of earth, life, and death and the symbol of renewal, rebirth and enlightenment. For example, washing away the sins of the earth is a Biblical renewal. Water has a symbol of healing, new beginnings, health, life, energy, and invigoration.

Self-Reflection: water reflectiveness is continually used in literary and popular culture. Especially to show superficiality, deception, or a person's ability to change.

Rejuvenation: water is often involved with healing, new beginnings, and the ancient claim of water's magical properties to heal.

Subconscious Metaphor: The subconscious mind is mysterious, like deep water, unpredictable, vast, ever changing. Subconscious thought comes without direction, like undersurface waves.

Transformation: water makes possibility the ability to change and transform with adequate motivation.

Wisdom: water is often considered a symbol of truthful knowledge, particularly in pathology.

Strength and Determination: water can be gentle and soft, yet one of its strongest, and most determined elements: Water follows its own path and goals and shows us the way to its goals.

Whether or not there are any specific mythical, historical references about Sacred Mount Wai'ale'ale, or any miraculous event leading specifically to this Sacred Mountain, it is a perfect Mountain to contain spirit and the Sacred Mountain

Guru in terms of psychology, emotion, sadness, life, movement, purification, rebirth, rejuvenation, self-reflection, wisdom, transformation.

. . . .

The Wettest Sacred Muntain

Sacred Mount Wai'ale'ale, in Kauai, Hawaii, until recently, was the wettest place on earth which has resulted of course, in scientific and other notoriety. After a review of many sources, the spirituality of this Mountain is directly related to its water content. It was the wettest place on earth when I explored the Mountain a few years ago. It is now, based on both research and weather changes, the second wettest place on this planet. The spiritual lessons relate directly to its world fame (even as the second wettest place).

Sacred Wai'ale'ale Mountain averages more than 373 inches of rain a year, since 1912 and is one of the greenest places on earth and of course, one of the wettest places in Hawaii.

For many reasons, I return many times with my family or with friends to the Hawaiian Islands and the islands of Kauai. The weather is usually outstanding, the hiking and biking superb, the natives of Kauai, naked or not, are a lovely people.

One of my best friends was Darwin Gross, who was the leader, spiritually, philosophically, and businesswise, of a spiritual entity named Eckankar. His effort, organization, philosophy, energy and spirit organized and developed Eckankar from a $75,000 net worth to $25 million. He inspired and gave all he could to the thousands of members and new members worldwide.

I was the attorney for Eckankar for many years and a member of their Board of Trustees. It was a joy and opportunity for me professionally and personally. Darwin often called our Board Meetings to be held in Hawaii on the island of

Kauai. During one of those trips, I had one of my first and last two explorations of Sacred Mount Wai'ale'ale.

I owe and thank Darwin, now deceased, for the opportunity and for the pleasures individually and professionally of our years together supporting Eckankar.

Sacred Mount San Jacinto

People View-Point

Gold and silver,

most durable and most sought;

Spirit lasts longer

and is worth more.

Mount San Jacinto

Location:	California, USA
Range:	San Jacinto Mountains
Elevation:	10,834 ft (3,302m)
Prominence:	8,319 ft (2,536 m)
Coordinates:	33°48'53"N
	116°40'45"W
Spirit:	Christian
Pilgrimage:	Mother Nature's Walking Range . . . Sacred Mount San Jacinto

ANGEL'S VIEW

Mother Nature's Walking Range... Sacred Mount San Jacinto

Science Confirms the "miracles" and secrets of the "Walking" Sacred Mountain

Esoterica: Myths, Mysteries and Imaginables

The following thoughts relating directly and straightforwardly to Sacred Mountains are instructive and provoking. They are all from Sacred Places by Sarah Osmen.

"Mankind could see with his eyes, hear, touch, smell, taste, all objects within his surroundings …even though these are merely pointers indicating the presence of the divine so that mystery was that which he could not sense in those certain organisms in his possession. But it was also that which he worships in the broadest sense of the word. It is his religion. Everything in his environment is sacred because everything points towards divinity." (Osmen, page 4)

"Mankind cannot live without the holy, even in his everyday life. Home is where the heart is." (Osmen, page 7)

"Each Mountain has its own exact sign." (Osmen, page 37)

"We are becoming rapidly aware that the existence of religion and Godliness rests with our own personal experience." (Osmen, page 50)

"However much we might attempt to duplicate the fate and lives of Stone Age men and women, we cannot quite feel their oneness with Nature, their close awareness of the sounds, smells, and movements of life. Or their natural meditations and religious awareness out of which comes the Sacred Monuments (or Mountains) that we now find fascinating." (Osmen, page 60)

"The meeting place between heaven and earth– here the divine enters the human world. This is often labeled Sacred Mount Meru." (Osmen, page 113)

"We build our sacred places upon the energy sources of mother earth... hundreds, even thousands of years of devotion and determination in one place may be enough to change that place and create the sacred that we now wish to understand." (Osmen, page 159)

"Mountain scenes are traditionally places where silence and peace can be achieved away from the madness and thought patterns of cities and where we can also take it easy." (Osmen, page 232)

. . . .

Sacred Mountain

After a lifetime of Sacred Mountain explorations, interest, and study, I now realize that all Mountains are not sacred or holy, but a large number likely carry a spiritual aspect whether or not their title includes some special denomination like "Sacred", "Holy", or "Spiritual", as part of their accepted and regular name.

I spend a lot of time on Mount San Jacinto in Southern California about 100 miles southeast of Los Angeles and 450 miles from my home in San Francisco. That is a long way to

Visit to son, Shan

drive, but I do it practically every weekend in order to visit my son, Shan, who was attending a high school, the Webb school, in Claremont, California, adjoining Los Angeles. Shan enjoys football, basketball, baseball and other high school sports and on weekends, played in the various student sport leagues. The school is a boarding school and has a lot of weekend curriculum presentations and academic demonstrations for parents. This gives me a good reason for visiting and provides a chance for me to participate in his education. My presence is a special encouragement to Shan and a very interesting and important opportunity for me.

San Jacinto

His high school is about half the distance from my home in San Francisco to Sacred Mount Jacinto in Palm Springs, California. After my weekend visits to my son Shan, I continue what I call my "Pilgrimage" to one of my very special Sacred Mountains, San Jacinto. Why would this Mountain be so emphasized in *Boy From Pocatello*? Because in my opinion San Jacinto is a good illustration of the ways and whys of the creation and existence of a "Sacred" Mountain recognized by humans.

These Southern California trips provide me opportunities to practice law, mostly real estate and municipal water issues, in Los Angeles County and San Bernardino County in Southern California, especially the Palm Springs and Twentynine Palms municipal areas.

Palm Springs Trail

When I arrive in Palm Springs, San Jacinto is adjoining. In fact, one of the main trails to the over 10,000-foot summit of San Jacinto, actually begins in the town of Palm Springs. When I am in a hurry or have some special project planned for the higher reaches of Mount San Jacinto, I find what I considered to be a miraculous approach to Mountain summiting– by the gondola units the voters created. Here, a political and engineering virtual miracle. The citizens of Palm

Springs, Twentynine Palms, Riverside and other communities supported and successfully passed a bond issue to finance and construct an unusual tramway from Palm Springs at the bottom of Sacred Mount San Jacinto to the summit.

The tram up the Mountain is a thrilling ride over steep cliffs and rocks. The bottom of Mount San Jacinto is a desert which as you go higher, becomes rivers, streams, forests of the Mountain and a tram station at 11,600 feet in altitude.

For some reason, probably my spiritual interest in Sacred Mountains, leads me to appreciate San Jacinto. I explore extensively Sacred San Jacinto and the San Jacinto Range. From this combining experience of my explorations and my continuing law business primarily doing legal work on California special assessment finance, I acquire by purchase and as a credit for services, over 20 parcels of desert land, all about two or three acres each except for one 30-acre parcel. Many of these parcels adjoin the Twentynine Palms Marine Base. Someday I hope to make one of these lots my home.

Personal, Spiritual Business Experiences

My own personal interest and business, whether spiritual, intellectual, or even emotional, may be an explanation for my attraction to San Jacinto. But a single person's interest and even inspiration for a Mountain, doesn't make it a Sacred Mountain. It takes religion, a special spirit, a history, a significant following anywhere in the world to become a "Sacred Mountain".

Sacred

The more I know about this Holy Mountain, I understand personally why it is "sacred". They include but are not limited to, extraordinary magical, miraculous, natural activities and events, geologically, vegetatively, aboriginally, and humanly.

"Magic" Photosynthesis

In many areas in the world, the process of photosynthesis that plants use to develop their own food is striking. In the deserts around San Jacinto, there is little, if any, surface water. Most of the process by which plants are able to feed themselves aren't effective; they have to find an alternate way to accomplish this step without water. Maybe the scientists don't consider that magical, and study will reveal that this is a logical way to describe some of these processes of survival for plants, animals, and even humans, including photosynthesis. What makes them magical, is that while scientists may advise us as to the process, none of us can do it ourselves as naturally as Nature.

Nature's Power

In fact, the analysis, study, and awareness of Nature's power and processes confirms that the trees, the rocks, the wild animals, are magical especially on a Mountain like San Jacinto and the San Jacinto Range.

Walking Mountains

Even more striking to me is that scientists confirm retroactively that the entire Mountain of San Jacinto, as well as the whole San Jacinto Mountain Range, actually began significantly south in what is now Mexico. The Mountain and its "San Jacinto" range, by natural, secret, unrepeatable processes, moved some 100 miles north. Other geologists claim the whole range and Mount Jacinto moved more like 1,000 miles, not 100 miles.

Wild Animals

Similarly, many of the wild "animals" of the Mountain, like the aboriginal human inhabitants, survive because of processes and miracles that are unrepeatable except by Nature. All this and much more has been going on for thousands and millions of years here at San Jacinto and the adjoining areas. This leads me to try to better define the entire situation as a Spiritual Mountain. Many scholars try.

Spirituality of Mountains

I then try to apply my relationship over the years with this amazing Mountain to understand the "Sacredness". I am unable to do it because the geological, biological and even human processes are, in my opinion, beyond human capability. It's a spiritual and an amazing opportunity to be a part of the spiritual, whatever that may be. I personally cannot duplicate this process alone.

I spend many days and nights appreciating and participating in life on Mount San Jacinto. I study extensively this Mountain including the history of human occupation which creates a recognition of the spiritual life of people on San Jacinto, particularly the aboriginal native Californian Indians, the Cahuilla Tribes.

Spirituality of Mountains

The Cahuilla are the dominant indigenous Indian occupants of these Mountains and the area. From my reading, they have always been repressed by their "white" brothers. But their strong spirituality and recognition that even modern-day perceptions of these holy forces on San Jacinto spurs a powerful interest in our human relationships with Sacred San Jacinto. It is gorgeous and accessible with many trails estimated to cover in total about 1,000 miles. There is also the Tramway, a human accomplishment of a political and almost impossible human effort. The San Jacinto Arial Tramway for many reasons, is initially rejected by the necessary forces, financial, engineering, etc., but manages to succeed.

Cahuilla Indians

Tramway

Even when time is short for me, I enjoy climbing and exploring the Mountains. It provides important personal and what I consider, spiritual experiences. A lot of modern commercial and residential development, besides the tram and other buildings relating to the ski lift, are impressive. A whole community, Idyllwild, exists today.

"Spiritual" Climbing

A man named Emerson came to the Mountain to develop the resorts, particularly in and around Idyllwild on the east side of the Mountain. He later gifted his property for YMCA camps, religions and other charitable activities. His secondhand development of the infrastructure is a permanent contribution to the ability of this particular area and San Jacinto to be used and enjoyed by us all as the public.

Development

Although it is difficult to transfer my own feelings and

spiritual attraction of San Jacinto to others, the Mountain inspires a lot of wisdom and understanding of what makes a Sacred Mountain and keep it Holy.

I find most interesting, instructive and true relating to the Sacredness of Mountains, three worlds that provide a quick visit through the experience of sacred places:

Sacred Places

SACRED PLACES: *A Journey into the Holiest Lands*
by Sarah Ann Osmen
[St. Martin's Press; 1ST Edition (January 1, 1990)]

SACRED PLACES: *How the Living Earth Seeks Our Friendship*
by James A. Swan
[Bear & Company; Original edition (April 1, 1990)]

CUCHAMA AND SACRED MOUNTAINS
by W.Y. Evans Wentz
[Swallow Press (July 1, 1981)]

"Travel" Love

My pilgrimage to Sacred Mount San Jacinto involved long, tedious drives from my home in San Francisco (over 500 miles). But this transformed itself into Sacredness beyond explanation– for example, my love for my son.

"Hooked" by This Pilgrimage

My own Sacred journeys…my merged self with Nature… my lifetime understanding… my appreciation of the outdoors, the many adventures I have experienced there and my sense of community with other Pilgrims, Nature, love, and inspiration. I've been hooked by this Pilgrimage and powerful Sacred Mountain for many years and still smile with my remembrances of San Jacinto.

Sacred Mount Davidson

People View-Point

Don't judge a Sacred Mountain
Whether enormous, in between, or minuscule
... Easter Spirit on a small hill
Is no less than the mighty world
of Mount Everest.

... THE MOUNTAIN PATH

Location:	San Francisco, California, USA
Range:	Seven Hills
Elevation:	928 ft (283 m)
Prominence:	628 ft (191 m)
Coordinates	37°44'18"N
	122°27'17"W
Spirit:	(current) Christian
	(historic) Native American (Ohlone, Miwok)
Pilgrimage:	A Small Hill With A Big Heart ... Sacred Mount Davidson

Angel View-Point

A Small Hill with A Big Heart... Sacred Mount Davidson

Esoterica: Myths, Mysteries and Imaginables

Sometimes the fates closely related to legends may be considered and analyzed as "esoterica".

A journeyman immigrant, Adolph Sutra, was mining another "Mount Davidson" in Alaska. Two men were a part of the thousands of immigrants who came to California in the 1850s to participate in the Gold Rush there. These two men had discovered silver in their "Mount Davidson" . . . but, without explanation, both of them died shortly after their discovery. In general, it was considered by the Mountain community that the deaths were a curse on all who worked this mine…

Later Sutro himself solved the issues of ventilation and drainage problems in the 5-mile tunnel into the Comstock Lode, an exceptional silver discovery. All the participants became mostly millionaires by 1878. Sutro returned to Europe to obtain investors and investments that enabled the silver development at Mount Davidson.

By this time, a very rich and famous person, Davidson became Mayor of San Francisco and owner of one tenth of the city and over 12,000 acres, from Baker Beach to Lincoln Park to the shores of Lake Merced. Then at the suggestion of a poet of Nature, Joaquin Miller, he changed the city by creating a Mountain-forest that still remains on San Francisco's Sacred Mount Davidson. In the long run, although he willed an original 1,400 acres to his heirs in trust for education in San Francisco, his heirs obtained a judgement from the California Supreme Court as to the "Will of Adolph Sutro". His heirs convinced the California Supreme Court to invalidate the Sutro will. Since they were more interested in economics than forests, they sold their inherited land to their treasurer, S. Baldwin.

The Sierra Club hiked into the wilderness of the Sutro Forest and in a ceremony, named the peak in honor of their Charter member and President, George Davidson.

No one, as far as I know, has reported whether all the constitutional law, legal and political effort and activity made Adolph Sutro, the original "founder", roll over in his grave from all the problems with the controversial lighted concrete cross on the summit of Sacred Mount Davidson.

. . . .

Concrete Cross atop the Mountain

Mount Davidson is the highest natural point in San Francisco... in a few cases significantly lower than the buildings. It is located near the geographical center of the city, south of Twin Peaks and Portola Drive and to the west of Diamond Heights and Glen Park. It is recognized as one of the Seven Hills of San Francisco. Open all year, night and day, a major annual event celebrates Easter under a large lighted concrete cross which was built on the top of the Mountain.

Site of Easter Prayer Service

This has been the site of yearly Easter Prayer services since the 1920s and also a yearly recognition of the Armenian genocide which occurred on April 24. The lighting of the cross is a recognition of the Armenian Genocide.

Forest Hill Family Home

A prominent citizen of San Francisco purchased the land in 1881 along with several other properties in the surrounding areas including present day St. Francis Wood, Westwood Highlands and Forest Hills. I and my family lived in Forest

Hills for years. My daughter, Sharon, and my son, Alan Jr., also attended an elementary school nearby.

Family Eastert Celebration

My whole family occasionally walked, along with a few hundred others, to the Easter sunrise service from our home in Forest Hills to the service, but my daughter Sharon and I made it a yearly ritual to celebrate Christ's Ascension. We often talked about this experience together. She died a few years ago — God rest her soul!

Years of Litigation Regarding Small Cross

Some local San Franciscans objected to the cross and the annual services as a violation of their constitutional rights. Litigation on the issue continued for many years. A final compromise was reached: An Armenian organization bought the land underneath the cross, which apparently solved the issue. The park and the yearly Easter services provide pleasure and inspiration to those who used it, particularly at the Easter Day Sunrise Service.

Daughter Sharon and Author Site

Both I and my daughter, Sharon, loved to be there before sunrise to attend the informal Sacred Mountain Easter every year! It is a confirmation of our family love for tradition!

Sacred Mount Monadnock

People View-Point

Only God knows why
My Sacred Mount Monadnock is
The last of our Spirit summits today.
She is a Sacred Hill compared to the other peaks.
The Spirits here, sacred, calm
And harboring unity, knowing ecstasy
Two aspects of the holy.

. . . Anon

Location:	New Hampshire, U.S.A.
Range:	Wapack
Elevation:	3,170 ft (966m)
Prominence:	2,149 ft (665 m)
Coordinates	42°51'41"N
	72° 06'29"W
Spirit:	Native American — Aberaki (Mountain that stands alone)
Pilgrimage:	*Nature's Sacred Mountain "Beauty" The Mountain That Stands Alone . . . Sacred Mount Monadnock*

Angel View-Point

Sacred Mountain Beauty . . . The Mountain That Stands Alone . . . Sacred Mount Monadnock

"Beauty" Pleasure

Nature seems to work with time, change and the eternal to provide beauty to us humans. "Webster tells us beauty is the quality or aggregate of qualities in a person or thing that gives pleasure to the senses or pleasurably exalts the mind or spirit". For our purposes here in "Boy From Pocatello", Beauty is a usual inherent concept of our human relationship with Sacred Mountains.

People of the Dawn Land

"Monadnock" is an Abenaki Tribe name. It translates to "Mountain Which Stands Alone". Since these Indians call New England Wabanahkik, "Dawn Land", in fact the tribe is referred to as "The People of The Dawn Land". As far as we know these were the original inhabitants of this Sacred Mountain.

"Sacred Mountain" and "Beauty"

About this time when I was on Sacred Mount Monadnock, the last Sacred Mountain featured in this book, coincidentally, I received a nonconfidential, private memo from an Idaho State University photographer about the very subject and content I was writing about – Sacred Mountain Monadnock and Beauty.

Attachment to Emotion

The subject is our human emotional attachment to mountains and mountain ranges driven by:

Awesome — Our appreciation and recognition of The Sacred Mountain's awe-inspiring Beauty.

Humbling — Humbling acceptance of the Mountain's larger and longer existence compared to our own lives.

Joy, Challenge — The joy of our physical adventure and challenge on The Sacred Mountain. Sacred Mountain encouragement and companionship with Nature so prominently involved and physically, mentally and emotionally important to us.

Encouragement, Companionship

Appreciation of Nature — A deeper appreciation of our world connected to our inner spiritual self and Nature's Beauty.

Esoterica, Myths, Mysteries and Imaginables

Ghosts — Mount Monadnock has created a lot of ghost stories in the minds of its admirers. But one devil day a group found a beautiful clearing in the woods and reported it might have been a "fairy dell". Jim Price spent the rest of the day searching for the fairies but never found them. He reported, "I know they were there…."

Emerson's "Monadnock" — Ralph Waldo Emerson titled one of his most famous poems "Monadnock":

> "…. I scowl on him with my cloud,
> With my north-wind, chill his blood;
> I lame him, clattering down the rocks;
> And to live he is in fear.
> Then, at last, I let him down
> Once more into his dapper town,
> To chatter, frightened, to his clan,
> And forget me if he can."
> (*Excerpt from Emerson's "Monadnock"*)

Thoreau's Journal — David Henry Thoreau also spent much time at Monadnock between 1844 and 1866 and celebrated his creative use of "Monadnock" in his journal writings from his June 4, 1858, descent from Mount Monadnock (his 4th journey to Monadnock).

Both famous writers can be reminded of their appreciation of the spirit of Sacred Mount Monadnock by designation in their names of special trails and lookouts....

National Landmarks

Mount Monadnock is a United States National landmark. It is in the state of New Hampshire and the highest point in Cheshire County, 38 miles (61 km) southwest of Concord and 1000 feet (305m) higher than the surrounding area. It features in the famous writings of both Emerson and Thoreau. Persons who know claim that Monadnock is one of the most often climbed mountains in the world. The barren peak is devoid of plant life because of early settlers' fires. The surface includes 400-million-year-old rock.

Special Trails / Lookouts

This Sacred Mountain is one of America's more beautiful and earlier holy places. It is no coincidence that love of Nature at Monadnock stimulates our own loves.

Nature / Love / Ourselves

Monadnock is not so dramatic physically as it is outstanding spiritually and aesthetically. Our human love of Nature stimulates anyone's reaction to this powerful and ancient part of human memory and the admiration of the Beauty of Sacred Mount Monadnock.

Human Memories

Right now, Monadnock's Beauty shines in my own personal and human memories of this Holy Mountain.

Songs and Psalms

Years ago, when beginning this book incuding the chapter "Songs and Psalms of The Mountain Guru", "Purges and Paradise" I wrote: This Mountain proves not so much the beauty of holiness but the holiness of beauty.

Whole Life Appreciation

My appreciation of beauty was and still is my special gift from the Sacred Mountains I have lived with my whole life.

End Notes

AFTERWARD: THE PAINTER PEI DU
FROM IMAGINATION COMES REALITY
THE SEVENTH AVENUE GANG
THANK YOU
BIBLIOGRAPHY
ALAN NICHOLS PUBLICATIONS & EXPLORATIONS
"THE JAILHOUSE LAWYER WAS A GRAND JUROR"
SILK WEB GENES
CYCLING THE SILK WEB
CLIMBERS

AFTERWORD
The Painter Pei Du

Out of the Streams of Sacred Mountain
Imaginables Come the Realities of Wisdom

In very ancient times lived a great painter, Pei Du. Even as a child by the age of 10, he had learned all he could from the great art masters of China. He set out to paint all over the country. Now, in those days, China was flat. Pei Du painted mythical mountains and sharp rocks and cliffs, swirling mists, a bird here and there, sometimes a solitary person or a lone mountain bridge or hut, a "wistful" wilderness. . .Those scenes were only seen in his imagination and in his dreams. He sought perfection in each stroke of his brush as he continued day by day and year after year to paint over and over each element of his landscapes.

Many people flocked to catch a glimpse of his painting just before he had finished them because as soon as they were completed, he would destroy them the next morning as too imperfect to be preserved. Pei Du continued to paint until he was an old man. When he was nearly ninety-five years old, his work had come to the attention of the God of Beauty, Huang Shu, who one night appeared to him in a dream.

The God told Pei Du that he would have time to paint only one more picture before his death, and it was to be perfect. Pei Du spent the next ten years working on that single painting every day. It was finally finished on February 13th, the day before his hundred and fifth birthday. On that night, the God of Beauty again appeared in his dreams and said, "You have succeeded Pei Du. Tomorrow, you paint with us in heaven."

The next morning before dawn, Pei Du rose and sat quietly in front of his painting. Thousands of people had already gathered, waiting for the night to pass to see the finished picture. But the mist had risen in the night, and no one could see anything. When it finally began to clear, the gigantic painting appeared, part by part. Everyone gasped. Many cried. The sheer ecstasy from the gorgeous sacred beauty overwhelmed the soul of everyone present.

They had no doubt that the painting was perfect. Pei Du's eyes misted with tears. It was the most beautiful work of art that ever would be created. As dusk came, Huang Shu, appearing in the form of a white mist, resolved the painting into reality. Seventy-two peaks emerged, with strange forests, waterfalls, hot springs, trails, and bridges. A temple stood in the background, a lotus-like summit appeared on one peak.

When the people had recovered from their shock, they looked at Pei Du. His eyes were closed. There was a smile on his face.

He was dead. And there is now a place called Hua Shan, the Taoist Sacred Mountain of the West.*

Alan Nichols provided his story of Pei Du to one of his favorite photographers, Pat Fok, for her landscape photography publications "Quiet Beauty of China" (page 193, Rizzoli Media).

FROM IMAGINATION COMES REALITY

From Imagination comes Reality.
From Reality comes Truth.
From Truth comes the Sacred Mountain.
From your Mother comes your Father.
From all these comes your Spirit.
— Sacred Mountain Guru

THE SEVENTH AVENUE GANG*

Jack

Durward

Alan
("Boy From Pocatello")

Tom and Don
(Two brothers — slightly older, advisors to the gang)

Toby and Bob

Byron

Bill

Anyone who buys this book, man or woman, is eligible to become an honorary member of the Seventh Avenue Gang. Please note: no dues, no offices, no articles, no by-laws, no obligations except $7.50 for your membership card. Write:

Alan Nichols
975 East Fremont • Pocatello, Idaho 832001
415-640-6914 • nicholsalan9@gmail.com

or contact the publisher
Regent Press
www.regentpress.net
regentpress@mindspring.cvom

Thanks to the reader for being with our Sacred Mountains and Sacred Gurus.

Bibliography

A.C. Bhaktivedanta, Swami, Prabhupada. *Bhagavas-Gita As It Is.* The Bhaktivedanta Book Trust, 1984.

Adele, Deborah. *The Yamas & Niyamas: Exploring Yoga's Ethical Practice.* Duluth, MN: On-World Bound Books, LLC, 2009.

(The) American Biographical Institute. *The Directory of Distinguished Americans.* P-153. "Boy From Pocatello".

Anati, Emmanuel. *The Mountain of God: Har Karkom.* New York: Rizzoli, 1987.

Bahar, SH. (TR.) Dar Rahe Haqq Institute, *The Truth About Christianity.* 2001

Baker, Patricia L. *Iran: The Bradt Travel Guide.* Guiford, CN: Globed Pequot Press Inc., 2001.

Bakhtiari, Saeed. *Iran Today.* 2nd ed. Tehran, Iran: Gita Shenasi Cartographic & Geographic Organization, 1995.

Baynes/ Wilhelm. *The Ching…Or Book of Changes.* Princeton University Press, 1967.

Bernbaum, Edwin. *Sacred Mountains of the World.* San Francisco, California: Sierra Club Books, 1990.

Boardman, Peter. *Sacred Summits: A Climber's Year.* Seattle, WA: The Mountaineers, 1982.

Bonavia, Judy. *The Silk Road Xi'an to Kashgar.* Hong Kong. Twin Age Ltd.

Boulnois, Lucette, Amar Grover, Adam Woolfitt, Angela Sheng, Bradley Mayhew, Helen Loveday, and Howman Wong. *Silk Road: Monks, Warriors & Merchants on the Silk Road.* Hong Kong: Odyssey, 2008.

Brifault, Robert. *The Mothers Volume II.* New York, The MacMillan Company, 1927.

Burland, Cottie. *North American Indian Mythology.* Czechoslovakia, Drury House, 1965.

Butler, Alban. *Lives of the Saints.* London. 1756.

Campbell, Joseph. *The Hero's Journey.* San Francisco, California, Harper & Row, 2014.

_____ *The Hero with a Thousand Faces.* California, Patheon Books. 1949

Carus, Paul. *The Gospels of Buddha… Compiled From Ancient Records.* La Salle, Illinois. The Open Court Publishing CO, 1943.

_____ *China's Splendors.* Beijing: China Travel & Tourism Press, 2001.

Cameron, Ian. *Mountains of the Gods: The Himalaya and the Mountains of Central Asia.* New York City: Facts on File, 1984.

Chong, Ling-Ling, and Shusun Cheung. *The Celestial Realm.* Hong Kong, China: Artist Publishing Co., 1984.

Christie, Anthony. *Chinese Mythology.* Verona, Italy. The Hamlyn Publishing Group Limited, 1968.

Coburn, Broughton. *Himalaya: Personal Stories of Grandeur, Challenge and Hope.* Washington D.C.: National Geographic Society, 2006.

Dar Rah Haqq's Board of Writers. *A Glance At The Life of The Holy Prophet of Islam.*

Dawkins, Richard. *The God Delusion.* Boston. Houghton Mifflin Company, 2008 (Mariner Books).

Dorje, Gyurme. *Bhutan Handbook.* Bath, UK: Footprint, 2010

Dr. Berg, Phillip S. *Kabbalah for The Layman… A Guide to Cosmic Consciousness.* Jerusalem, Israel. Press of the Research Centre of Kabbalah, 1981.

Dr. Brunton, Paul. *A Message From Arunachala.* London. Rider & Company, 1969.

Dr. Stone, *Randolph. Mystic Bible.* Shri S. L. Sondhi Secretary, Punjab (India). 1956.

Eddy, Mary Baker. *Science and Health with Key to the Scriptures.* Boston, U.S.A. The Christian Science Publishing Society. 1875

_____ Unity of Good. Trustees Under Will of Eddy. Boston, 1887.

Few, Roger. *The Atlas of Wild Places: In Search of the Earth's Last Wildernesses.* Washington, D.C.: Smithsonian Books, 1994.

Elverskog, Johan. *Buddhism and Islam On The Silk Road.* Philadelphia, Pennsylvania. University of Pennsylvania Press, 2010.

Esposito, John L. *Islam The Straight Path.* New York, NY, Oxford University Press, 1991.

Evans-Wentz, W.Y. *Cuchama and Sacred Mountains.* Swallow Press, 1981.

Feirler, Bruce. *Walking The Bible A Journey by Land Through the Five Books of the Torah.* New York, NY. HarperCollins Publishers, 2001.

Fiske, John. *The Idea Of God.* Boston and New York. The Riverside Press, Cambridge, 1886.

Fok, Pat and Ross Terrill. *Faces of China: Tomorrow, Today, and Yesterday.* London, England: Michael Joseph Limited, 1974.

Fok, Pat. *Quiet Beauty of China.* New York, NY: Rizzoli International Publications, Inc, 1987.

Forke, Alfred. *The World-Conception of the Chinese.* Great Britain, The Eastern Press, LTD., Reading, 1925

Forsyth, George. "Island of Faith in the Sinai Wilderness." National Geographic 125, no 1, January 1964.

Franck, Harry A. *Wandering in Northern China.* London. The Century Co., 1923.

Freud, Sigmund. *Moses and Monotheism.* Canada. Alfred A Knopf, Inc. 1957.

Fromm, Erich. *The Art of Loving.* New York City. Harper and Brothers Publishers, 1956.

Gardeshgary. *Persia Tourism Magazine.* March, 2003.

Gaster, Theodor, H. *The Dead Sea Scriptures.* Garden City, New York. Doubleday & Company, Inc., 1956.

Gibran, Kahlil. *The Prophet.* New York. Alfred, A. Knopf, 1991.

Ghosh, Oroon. *The Dance of Shiva and Other Tales from India.* New York, NY: New American Library of World Literature Inc. "Signet Classic," 1965.

Gross, Sri Darwin. *From Heaven to the Prairie.* Eckankar, 1980.

Gurnee, Jeanne. *The Explorers Journal.* New York, NY. The Explorers Club, 1988.

(The) Gov't of India, Ministry of Transport & Communication on Behalf of the Dept. of Tourism. *India/ Madras and Andhra Pradesh.* New Delhi: Director, Publications Division, Delhi-6, 1961.

Halper, Lezlee and Stephan. *Tibet… An Unfinished Story.* New York, Oxford University Press, 2014.

Handbook For Today's Catholic Beliefs… Practices… Prayers. Liguori Publications, 2004.

Harpur, James. *The Atlas of Sacred Places: Meeting Points of Heaven and Earth.* New York, NY: Henry Holt and Company, 1994.

Hedin, Sven. *Trans-Himalaya: Discoveries & Adventures in Tibet.* Vol. 1, 2, 3. London: McMillan & Co., Limited, 1909, 1913.

Hesse, Herman, and Hilda Rosner. *Siddhartha; translated by Hilda Rosner.* Toronto, Canada: Bantam Books, 1971.

Hirooka, Kosaku. *The Latest Guide-Book for Travelers in Japan: Including Formosa, Chosen (Korea) and Manchuria.* Tokyo: Seiko Sha, 1914.

Hoekema, Anthony, A. *Mormonism.* Grand Rapids, Michigan. William B. Eerdmans Publishing Co., 1975.

Hoekema, Anthony, A. *Jehovah's Witnesses.* Grand Rapids, Michigan. Willian B. Eerdmans Publishing Co., 1975.

Hollenweger, Walter J. *The Pentecostals.* Minneapolis, Minnesota. Augsburg Publishing House, 1977.

Hopkirk, Kathleen. Central Asia *A Traveller's Companion.* London, w1x 4bd, John Murray Publishers, 1993.

Hunt, Thomas H. *Ghost Trails to California: With selected excerpts from Emigrant Journals/by Thomas H. Hunt*; photos by Thomas H. Hunt and Robert V. H. Adams. Palo Alto, CA: American West Publishing, 1974.

Jigmei, Ngapoi Ngawang, and et al. *Tibet.* New York, NY: McGraw-Hill Book Company, Beograd, 1981

Johnson, Russell, and Kerry Moran. T*he Sacred Mountains of Tibet: On Pilgrimage to Kailas.* Rochester, VT: Park Street Press, 1989.

Kaidantzis, Janet. F*allen Leaf: A Lake and It's People 1850-1950.* Lafyette, CA: Janet Kaidantzis in ass'n with the Tahoe Historical Society, 2011.

Kalelkar, Kakasaheb. *Stray Glimpse of Bapu.* Jivanji Dahyabhair Desai, 1950.

Kingdom of Morocco. *Tan-Tan: Land of Memory and Future… A Federating Space.* Tan-Tan, Morocco: Kingdom of Morocco, n.d.

Kaptchuk, Ted J. *The Web That Has No Weaver… Understanding Chinese Medicine.* 1947.

Keyes, Frances Parkinson, *The Explorer.* Doubleday & Company, Inc. 1964.

Kroeber, Theodora. *Ishi in Two Worlds: A Biography of the Last Wild Indian in North America.* Berkeley, CA: University of California Press, 1976.

Lawrence, T.E. *Revolt In The Desert.* New York. George H. Doran Co, 1927.

Lefort, Rafael. *The Teachers of Gurdjieff.* New York. Samuel Weiser Inc. 1973.

LeMee, Jean Marie-Alexandra, and Ingbert Gruttner. *Hymns from the Rig-Veda.* New York, NY: Knopf Inc, 1975.

Lhasa: Inmersion Media. Beijing: China Tibetology Publishing House, 2007.

Lukan, Karl. *Mountain Adventures.* New York. Franklin Watts, Inc. 1972.

Manchao, Cheng. *The Origin of Chinese Deities.* China. Foreign Languages Press, 2004.

Matheson, Sylvia A. *Persia: An Archeological Guide.* London. Faber and Faber Limited, 1972.

McCoy, Doris Lee Ph.D. *The Magic of Gross National Happiness.* La Jolla, CA. American Spirit Publishing.

Melton, Gordon, J. *The Encyclopedia of American Religions.* Vol.1 & Vol. 2. Wilmington, North Carolina. McGrath Publishing Company.

Menghe, Ge. *A Study of Genghis Khan's Philosophy.* American Academic Express.

Ming-Dao, Deng. T*he Wandering Taoist.* San Francisco, CA: Harper & Row Publishers, 1993.

Moore, Thomas. *Soul Mates…Honoring the Mysteries of Love and Relationship.* Harper Perennial. A Division of Harper Collins Publisher, 1994.

Morgado, Martin J. *Junipero Serra, A Pictorial Biography.* Monterey, California: Siempre Adelante Publishing, 1991.

Morgan, Joyce, and Walters, Conrad. *Journey on the Silk Road: A desert explorer, Buddha's Secret Library, and the unearthing of the world's oldest printing book.* Guilford, CN: Lyons Press, 2012.

Muller, Max F. *The Upanisads… Part 1.* New York. Dover Publications Inc. First published in 1879. Part 2. First published in 1884.

Mullikin, Mary Agusta, and Hotchkis, Anna M. *The Nine Sacred Mountains of China: An Illustrated Record of Pilgrimages Made in the Years 1935-1936.* Hong Kong: Vetch and Lee Limited, 1973.

Nagel, *Encyclopedia-Guide, China. Switzerland.* Nagel Publishers Geneva, 1982.

Nasr, Seyyed H. *The Naqshbandi Sufi Way History and Guidebook of the Saints of the Golden Chains.* Chicago, IL. KAZI Publications, Inc.

Nebenzahl. *Mapping the Silk Road and Beyond: 2000 Years of Exploring the East.* London: Phaidon, 2004.

Needleman, Jacob. *The New Religions.* Garden City, New York. Doubleday & Company, Inc., 1970.

Nelson, Thomas. T*he Holy Bible… Old and New Testaments… King James Version.* Thomas Nelson & Sons. New York. (Including Index, Biblical Names and Maps.)

Nianpei, Li. *The Summer Palace Long Corridor Pictures.* China Travel & Tourism Press.

Nichols, Alan. *Brothers at War: Two American Brothers in WWI as Volunteers in the French Army.* Berkley, CA: Regent Press, 2021.

_____ *A Song From the Master…*

_____ *The Ewald Foundation Awards 2018,* Regent Press, 2019.

Nichols, Nancy Ann, James Delahunty, and Alan Hammond Nichols. *San Quentin Inside the Walls.* San Quentin, CA: San Quentin Museum Press, 1991.

Nichols, Walter H. *The Measure of a Boy.* New York, The MacMillan Company, 1925.

_____ *A Morgan Rifleman.* New York, The Century Co., 1928.

_____ *Trust A Boy,* New York, Ferris Printing Company, 1923.

_____ *Cowboy Hugh,* NY, The MacMillan Company, 1937.

Osborne, Arthur. *The Collected Works of Ramana Maharshi.* South India. T.N. Venkataraman, 1968.

The Teachings of Bhagavan Sri Ramana Maharshi In His Own Words. South India. T.N. Venkataraman, 1965.

Osmen, Sarah Ann. *Sacred Places: A Journey into the Holiest Lands.* New York: St. Martin's Press, 1990.

Phillips, Wayne H. *Plants of The Lewis and Clark Expedition.* Missoula, Montana. Mountain Press Publishing Company.

Pickthall, Marmaduke. *The Glorious Qur'an.* London. Cagri Yayinlari, 1930.

(The) Pocatellian. Published by the students of Pocatello High School, 1947.

Pucci, Juan Jose. *Chirripo… A Journey to the Magical Mountain.* Translated by Christopher Montero, Heliconia Press, Neotropica Foundation, 2001.

Puri, L., R. *Mysticism… The Spiritual Path Vol. 1 India.* Shri, K.L., Khanna, 1964-1974.

Pustak, Ratna. *"Bibliotheca Himalayica".* Story. In The Gazetteer of Sikkim 8, Vol 8.

Rajabi, Mohammad Reza. Gardeshgary Persia Tourism Magazine. Vol 4, No 14. Tehran, Iran. Zolal, H.R. Rezaei, 2003.

Reader, John. *Kilimanjaro. London:* Elm Tree Books, 1985.

Reed, A.W. *Aboriginal Fables and Legendary Tales.* Hong Kong, Shanghai Printing Press Ltd., 1965.

Rhie, Marylin M. Robert A.F. Thurman, and John Bigelow Taylor. *Wisdom and Compassion: The Sacred Art of Tibet.* San Francisco: Asian Art Museum of San Francisco, 1991.

Robertson, George Scott, and Louis Dupree. *The Kafirs of the Hindukush.* Karachi London New York: Oxford University Press/ Lawrence & Bullen, LTD, 1974.

Robinson, John W., Risher, Bruce D., *The San Jacintos. Arcadia, CA.* Big Santa Anita Historical Society, 1993.

(The) Roots of Religion. Mashhad Islamic Republic of Iran.

Rowell, Galen A. *Mountains of the Middle Kingdom: Exploring the High Peaks of China and Tibet.* San Francisco, CA: Sierra Club Books in association with the American Alpine Club, 1948.

Rutland, James R. *Old Testament Stories.* Boston. Silver, Burdett & Company

Sarf, Hal, Ph.D. *Masters & Disciplines.* Oakland, California. Center For Humanities and Contemporary Culture & Regent Press.

Satprem. *Sri Aurobindo Or The Adventure Of Consciousness.* Pondicherry, India. Sri Aurobindo Society, 1970.

Shaw, Robert B. V*isits to High Tartary: Yarkand and Kashgar.* Hong Kong: Oxford University Press, 1984.

Shor, Thomas K. *A Step Away From Paradise: The True Story of a Tibetan Lama's Journey to a Land of Immortality.* City Lion Press, 2017.

Singh Ji, Hazur Maharaj Sawan. *Tales of the Mystic East.* New Delhi, Rekha Printers Pvt. Ltd, 1961.

Smith, Joseph Jun. *The Book of Mormon…Another Testament of Jesus Christ.* Salt Lake City, Utah. The Church of Jesus Christ Latter Day Saints, 1982.

Snelling, John. *The Sacred Mountain: Travelers and Pilgrims at Mount Kailash in Western Tibet, and the Great Universal Symbol of the Sacred Mountain.* London: East West Publications, 1983.

Spalding, Baird T. *India Tour Lessons on Life & Teaching of The Masters of the Far East... Vol. 1-5* Marina Del Rey, California. Devorss & Co.
Volume 1-*Master Emil-Visit and "Temple of Silence"*...
Volume 2- *Great Tau Cross Temple... Jesus; "Nature of Hell."*
Volume 3- *Christ Consciousness*
Volume 4- *"The India Tour Lessons."*
Volume 5- *Mastery Over Death*

Speeth, Kathleen R. *The Gurdieff Work.* Berkeley, CA. And/or Press, 1976.

Steele, C. Williams "Bill" Dr. Baumer, Christopher. Phalsen, Frederick Ph.D., *The Explorers Log*, New York, NY, 2018.

Stoddard, John L. Lectures.
Vol. 1 *Athens, Switzerland, Venice, Norway, Athens*
Vol. 2, *Constantinople, Egypt, Jerusalem*
Vol. 3, *China, Japan*
Vol. 4, *India*
Vol. 5, *France, Italy, Spain*
Vol. 6, *Berlin, Moscow, St. Petersburg, Vienna*
Vol. 7, *Belgium, Holland, Mexico*
Vol. 8, *Florence, Naples, Rome*
Vol. 9, *England, London, Scotland*
Vol. 10, *Grand Canon, S. California, Yellowstone National Park.* Balch Brothers Co. (Boston). George L. Shuman & Co. (Chicago), 1897, 1901.

Swan, James A. *Sacred Places: How the Living Earth Seeks Our Friendship.* Rochester, VT: Bear & Company, 1990.

Taylor-Butler, Christine. *Sacred Mount Everest.* New York, NY. Lee & Low Books Inc. 2009.

The Explorers Club, *Through Hell and High Water.* New York, Robert M. McBride & Company, 1941.

The Explorers Journal. Winter 2003/2004

The Explorers Log. Summer 2018, Summer 2020.

Tucker, Jonathan, and Antonia Tozer. *The Silk Road: Art and History.* Chicago, IL: Art Media Resources LTD, 2003.

Twitchell, Paul. *An Introduction To Eckankar.* Las Vegas, Nevada. The Illuminated Way Press, 1966.

Vespe, Raymond B. *Lao Tzu's Tao Te Ching… Psychotherapeutic Commentaries*. Regent Press, 2016.

Walter, Robert. *Mythology An Illustrated Guide*. Director of the Joseph Campbell Foundation.

Walton, Bruce. *Mount Shasta Home of the Ancients*. U.S.A., Health Research, 1985.

Wangchuck, Ashi, Dorji Wangmo. *Treasures of the Thunder Dragon: A Portrait of Bhutan*. Haryana, India: Penguin, 2012.

Ward, Fred. "In Long-Forbidden Tibet." National Geographic 157, no. 2, 1980.

Waterman, Jonathan. "Tibet: Flames on the Roof of the World." Summit: The Mountain Journal Summer, no. 1990, June 1990.

Weatherford, Jack. *The Secret History of the Mongol Queens*. Random House Inc., New York. 2010.

Weitzmann, Kurt. "Mount Sinai's Holy Treasures." National Geographic 125, no. 1, January 1964.

Wenbin, Zhang. *Dunhuang: A Centennial Commemoration of the Discovery of the Cave Library*. Beijing: Morning Glory Publishers, 2002.

Wong, Eva. *The Shambhala Guide To Taoism*. Boston & London. Shambhala Publications Inc. 1997.

Yule, Henry. *The Travels of Marco Polo: The Complete Yule-Cordier Edition*. Mineola, New York. Dover Publications, Inc.

Zheng, Shifeng, Massimo Vignelli, Chaotien Lo, and Fuli Chen. *China*. New York, NY: Gallery Books, 1989.

Zurick, David, Eric Valli, and Holly Troyer. *Land of Pure Vision: The Sacred Geography of Tibet and the Himalaya*. Lexington, KY: University Press of Kentucky, 2014.

Zurick, David. *The Himalaya: Encounters with the Roof of the World*. Center for American Places at Columbia: College, Chicago, IL, 2011.

ALAN NICHOLS
PUBLICATIONS & EXPLORATIONS

PERSONAL EDUCATION

B.A., L.L.B., & J.D., Stanford University, Graduated Magna Cum Laude; Phi Beta Kappa; Stanford Law Review, Board of Editors.

Doctor of Science (D.S.), California College of Podiatric Medicine (Honorary).

Attended schools in Seattle, Washington; Redwood City, California; Pocatello, Idaho; New York City, New York; Falls Church, Virginia; Princeton, New Jersey; Idaho State University.

SACRED MOUNTAINS, CYCLING THE SILK WEB, AND EXPLORATION

Appointed as goodwill Ambassador to several countries in connection with a round-the-world Sacred Mountain journey by the Board of Supervisors of the City and County of San Francisco and the Board of Directors of the San Francisco Council of Churches

First westerner to circumambulate Mount Kailash in Southwestern Tibet (after Chinese occupation)

First person (with Keith Brown) to bicycle 3300 miles through Central Asia (from Urumchi, Xinjiang to Lhassa, Tibet) in the Pamir, Kunlun, Korakorum, Trans-Himalayan and Himalayan Mountains and across Tibet

First person (with Shan Nichols) to bicycle 2300 miles on the Silk Road from Ashkabad, Turkmenistan by way of Bohhara, Khiva, Samarkand, Tashikent, Bishtek, and Torugunt Pass in Uzbekistan, Tajikistan, Kyrgz Republic to Alma Ata, Kazahkistan.

First person to bicycle 10,300 miles on entire Silk Web from Istanbul, Turkey to Xian, China.

Visited, studied, climbed, wrote, and lectured on scores of sacred Mountains and ranges throughout the world including:

United States: Mount Washington, N.H.; San Francisco and Sedona Peaks, Arizona; Tetons and Rocky Mountains in Idaho, Wyoming, and Colorado; Mount Denali, Alaska; Cascades in California, Oregon, and Washington; Sierra Nevada in California; Peninsular Range in California and Mexico; Moana Loa, Moana Kai, Waimea in Hawaii

Sacred Mountains of California (Mount Shasta, Kings Mountain, Squaw Peak, Mount Diablo, Mount Whitney, Junipero Serra, Mount Pinos, Mount Baldy, San Jacinto and Tarquiz, Mount Cuchama, Mount Davidson, and others.

Sacred Mountains of China: Heng Shan (North), Heng Shan (South), Tai Shan, Hua Shan, and Sung Shan

Sacred Shugendo and Shinto Mountains of Japan, Fuji San, Omine Shan, Gassan and Yoduno Shan and Takachiho

Sacred Mountains of the Himalayas in India, Sikkim, Ladak, Kashmir, and Tibet Sacred Mountains of the World Journey: Mount Lassen, California; Olympus, Greece; Mount Athos, Aegean Sea; Mount Tabor, Israel; Mount Sinai, Sinai; Mount Arunchala, India; Japanese Alps and Haleakala, Hawaii

Sacred Mountains and Places of Peru including Inca Trail, Machu Pichu, Isle of the Sun at Lake Titicaca, and Nazca Lines

Sacred Mountains of Africa: Kilimanjaro, Mount Meru

Others: Mount Subasio and Mount Vesuvius, Italy; Swiss Alps and Ben Nevis, Scotland

Explorers Club Expedition Awards to "Advance the World's Knowledge" as to sacred Mountains, the Silk Web history, travel, medicine (lipids and stamina), ethnology and spiritual architecture in Xingjiang, Tibet, Central Asia, Iran/Turkey, China, Mongolia, and Bhutan.

PUBLISHED BOOKS

The Historical & Technical Sciences for Discovery of the Secret Tomb of Emperor Chinggis Qa'an Founder of the Mongol Empire (Regent Press 2022)

*The Hunted & The Hunter: The Search for the Secret Tomb of Chinggis Qa'a*n (Regent Press, 2021)

Brothers at War: Two American Brothers in World War I as Volunteers in the French Army (Regent Press 2021)

To Climb a Sacred Mountain. A book about an around-the-world-in-40-days pilgrimage to climb Sacred Mountains to experience the religions of those Mountains and understand the universal role of sacred Mountains in personal spiritual experiences and in the metamorphosis of all religions (IWP Press 1976) The first book on this subject.

A Gift From The Master. Photography and Commentary in a book resulting from the author's journey with a modern day guru, Sri Darwin Gross

Water for California. A two volume legal reference book for water development, water rights, and water finance in California (with Harold Rogers; Bancroft-Whitney 1965)

Faces of China. A coffee table Book of Photography by Pat Fok with text by Alan Nichols as to the Sacred Mountains of China

San Quentin — Inside the Walls. Stories, history, and pictures of San Quentin Prison with photography and partial text by Alan Nichols (San Quentin Museum Association 1991)

San Francisco Commuter. Book of Poems written while commuting (Pendragon Press 1962)

Journey — A Bicycle Odyssey Through Central Asia. A story of a 3000 mile bicycle trip by the author and Keith Brown from Urumchi, Xingjiang on the western border of China, along the Silk Web, south across the Kun Lun and Karakoram Mountains and finally across Tibet to Lhassa via Kang Rimpoche [the world's most revered (in numbers at least) Sacred Mountain] (J.D. Huff 1991)

Adventures in Time. A book of poems written between 1952 and 2000 (Rygh Publishing 2000)

Travels with Annie. Short stories (Pendragon Press 2005

Curriculum Guide for the Arts, Master Plan for Curriculum… San Francisco Public Schools

OTHER PUBLICATIONS

Annual Awards Publication, Ewald Foundation.

Higher Ground: A Sacred Mountain Primer. San Francisco: J.D. Huff and Co, 1992.

Holy Chirripo…And The Can of Noodle Soup. Eldorado, Colo.: Sacred Mountain Press, 2005.

The Long Trek ... Yosemite to Tahoe. San Francisco: Pendragon Press, 1944. (Contributor).

Adventurous Dreams, Adventurous Lives. Rocky Mountain Books, 2007.

(Contributor). *Quiet Beauty of China by Pat Pok.* Rizzoli International Publications, 1987.

San Quentin — Inside the Walls. San Quentin Museum Press, 1991.

Making Dreams Come True. Detroit Mich.: The Ewald Foundation, 1994. (Editor).

Our Children are Winners. Detroit Mich.: The Ewald Foundation, 1993. (Editor).

Welcome to the United Nations, Detroit Mich.: The Ewald Foundation, 1995. (Editor).

Who Am I? Detroit Mich.: The Ewald Foundation, 1997.

(Contributor) "Centennial Photography Competition," Explorers Journal, Fall 2003.

"Comment: How Not to Contest Special Assessments, or, You Can't Beat City Hall," Stanford Law Review 17, No. 2 (January 1965): 247-256.

Plays Authored and Produced

Siddartha. 1977 Grove Play. The life of Buddha (Bob Minser, Director)

Executive Christmas. Produced privately as the Christmas Play in 1980 and 1994

Executive Guru. Experimental play produced at private camp (Summer 1996. Bruce Bolt, Director)

Articles

"The Public Interest," The American Bar Journal

"You Can't Fight City Hall," Stanford Law Review

"Constitutional Law Problems of Water Fluoridation," University of Southern California Law Review

"Constitutional Law and Rights," Stanford Law Review

"Mount Subasio," "Mount Takachiho," "Machu Pichu," "Letters Home" and other articles and poetry in *Library Notes* of the Private Club

New York Explorers Club Articles on Silk Web Cycling and other expeditions (Bhutan, Journey I (Tibet), Journey II (Central Asia), Journey III (Turkey/Iran), Journey IV (China)

"The Return of the Dove…Tibet's Last Chance." *Tibetan World* 2008

"The Risky Road to Freedom...in the footsteps of the Dalai Lama" Explorers Journal

"Dead Men Tell Tales… Cinggis Qa'an Explorers Club Journal (scheduled for Fall 2011)

Several other legal, cycling, adventure, and Sacred Mountain articles

Major Unpublished Monograms and Works

Peaks of Gold. Photography and text about the Sacred Mountains of California

A Seven Day Spiritual Diet. A distillation of universal esoteric mystical practices for seven days to discover one's natural spiritual inclination.

Darwin. A two volume biography of an American spiritual leader of a once powerful sect in California and worldwide.

A Gift to the Master. Photography and Commentary of a journey with a religious leader in Australia and South Asia.

Ishi. A play about America's last "wild" American Indian.

The Messenger. A play about the life of Muhammad.

The Toilet Papers. A book of poetry from the authors' experience as an undercover agent in San Francisco's prison (partially published in the San Francisco Examiner)

Hello Dalai. A story of an audience in 1972 with the Dalai Lama in Dharmsala, India

Letters Home. A play about a Stanford student who joins the French Army before the United States enters World War I, becomes a fighter pilot, is wounded in a dog fight and later dies in a French front line hospital

The Art of Loving...or Making it with Microna. A book of Sufi type poetry on love--human, technological, and spiritual.

The Night Life of a School Board Member. A play about a single school board meeting about alleged pornography in school books.

Lama Krespi...Lessons from Yosemite to Tahoe. Lhamas on the Pacific Creek Trail. Movie script "The Return of the Dove." A story of the Dalai Lama's return to Tibet. *The Rise and Fall of Tibet...The Dalai Lama, Inc.*

Sacred Mountains of China. A description with pictures of the Sacred Five plus Omei Shan.

Mount Kailash. A manuscript about Kang Rimpoche, in several respects the most important sacred Mountain on the planet in Southwestern Tibet.

Honey Lake Reader. Short stories from the cattle country on the eastern slopes of the Sierras.

The Laughing Buddha. Short stories from Tibet and especially Mount Kailash.

Others too many to mention.

EDUCATIONAL EXPERIENCES

Member, San Francisco Board of Education (President 1970-71)

Authored and coordinated Master Plan and Guidelines for Schools in San Francisco

Member, Board of Trustees, San Francisco City College (President 1971-72)

Member, Board of Trustees, Cathedral School for Boys (5 terms)

Board of Trustees, California College of Podiatric Medicine (associated with University of California San Francisco) San Francisco, California

Member, Board of Trustees, Prescott College, Sedona, Arizona

Member, Board of Governors, Webb Schools of California and Vivian Webb School, Claremont, California

Member of Special Finance Committee of California State Board of Education

United States Army Instructor

University of California Extension, Real Estate Lecturer

Adjunct Professor of Forensic Medicine, California College of Podiatric Medicine

Tibetologist

CIVIC EXPERIENCES

Member, San Francisco Library Commission

Director, Officer, San Francisco Junior Chamber of Commerce

Member, Advisory Committee to Committee on Deferred Cost of

Education, sponsored by the U.S. Department of Health, Education and Welfare Member and President, Associates of Stanford University Libraries

Member and Chairman, William Saroyan Organizing Board and Advisory Board of Stanford University and the Saroyan Foundation

Member, San Francisco Special Civil Grand Jury to investigate City government

Active in the past with many community organizations and activities for which Nichols was given the Distinguished Service Award (selected by the three San Francisco newspapers as the "Young Man of the Year")

LAW

President, The Nichols Professional Law Corporation (Attorneys at Law), specializing in municipal bonds and corporate finance, non-profit institutions, business and international banking

Former President, Nichols, Doi and Rappaport, Nichols and Rogers, and Nichols, Rogers, Shreiner and Sperry

Arbitrator, American Arbitration Association

Admitted to practice before United States Supreme Court

Admitted to practice before all California Courts

Admitted to practice before several Districts of United States Federal Courts

Member, San Francisco, California, and American Bar Associations

A Rated attorney in Martindale Hubbel Bar Register of Preeminent Lawyers

LECTURER & PRODUCTIONS

Special Presentations

Dr. Buddy Rose; on the psychology of roses

Press Conference with Ishi as last wild "Indian" in America

Lecturer on law, Sacred Mountains, travel, cycling the Silk Web, politics, Tibet, China, Bhutan, Sikim, Nepal, Central Asia (Turkmenistan, Uzbekistan, Tajikistan, Kyrgyzstan, Kazakhstan), Iran, Turkey, Mongolia

Expedition photographs and movies

Photography: Photographer for Lectures, books (see below), articles, and presentations. Finalist, Centennial Photo Contest of the Explorers Club of New York and exhibition for 25 years at private San Francisco art galleries, several individual photography exhibits. Originator of Philo-Photography (aka Photo-Philosophy).

BIOGRAPHICAL LISTINGS

Who's Who in the World; Who's Who in the America; Who's Who in California; Who's Who in the West; Who's Who in the American Law; International Who's Who in Community Service

Two Thousand Men of Achievement, 1972 Dictionary of International Biography

The Directory of Distinguished Americans.

Notable Americans, American Biographical Institute "Men of Achievement"

Bar Register of Preeminent Lawyers, Martindale-Hubbell

ORGANIZATIONS

Private Club

San Francisco Stock Exchange Club

Faculty Club, Stanford University

Fellow, Vice Chair and Chair (San Francisco/Northern Califoprnia/Hawaii) Explorers Club

Ombudsman, and President, the Worldwide Explorers Club headquartered in New York City

Fellow, Royal Geographic Society, London

Alpine Club member

Delegate, United Nations NGO Committee

Several terms on the Board of Directors, Burke's Tennis Club

President, IIR (Institute of International Relations)

FLAG EXPEDITIONS

XINGGIANG / TIBET MOUNTAIN BIKE EXPEDITION ... *May-July 1986* (56 YEARS OLD)

CENTRAL ASIA BIKE EXPEDITION ... Turkmenistan / Uzbekistan / Tajikistan / Turkestan / Kazakhstan ... *June-July 1993* (63 YEARS OLD)*

JOURNEY II CYCLING THE SILK WEB ... *July 1998* (68 YEARS OLD)

GANGKHAR PUENSUM II ... Bhutan's Sacred Mountain ... *September 2001* (72 YEARS OLD)

CYCLING THE SILK WEB ... Iran / Turkey ... *March 25 - June 2, 2004* (74 YEARS OLD)

CYCLING THE SILK WEB ... Zian / China / Kashgar / Xingiang ... *April 10 - May 25, 2005* (75 YEARS OLD)

KANG RINPOCHE / LAKE MANASARAOVAR / PILGRIMAGES EXPEDITION ... *Sept 28 - November 2, 2007* (77 YEARS OLD)

PILGRIMAGE TO MONGOLIA ... Sacred Mountains, Chinggis Qa'an, Roy Chapman Andrews – all God's of their Times ... *May 22 - July 1, 2010* (80 YEARS OLD)

DEAD MEN TELL TALES: THE TOMB OF CHINGGIS QA'AN ... Inner Mongolia, Ninjsia ... *September 15 - October 12, 2012* (82 YEARS OLD)

SURVIVAL AND DEATH ... Prairie Flora on the Missouri Riveri ... *July 26–August 2, 2013* (83 YEARS OLD)

CARDIAC ARRHYTHMIA AT ALTITUDE ... *2018* (88 YEARS OLD)

*Plaque for this las been lost.

Courtesy San Francisco Examiner / Tuesday, March 9, 1976

The Jailhouse Lawyer Was a Grand Juror

by Ernest Lenn

What was Alan Nichols prominent attorney and former school board member *doing in a place like this."*

For many days and nights, he was living a prisoner's life in San Francisco's county jail system.

Wearing an inmate's faded green coveralls he sweated out the lockup, ate the jail food, endured the jail regimen, and was even imprisoned for a while in the isolation "hole." It was a fact-finding mission. As chairman of the civil watchdog grand jury's committee on the sheriff's department, Nichols wanted to learn first hand about Sheriff Richard Hongisto's jails.

Nichols, 46, is the first grand juror here to do his investigating the hard way, as a prisoner.

By arrangement with Hongisto, he entered under a fictitious "contempt of court" charge — non-payment of "alimony."

He was released yesterday morning bringing out with him a sheaf of notes for a forthcoming grand jury report on the jails.

While behind bars, Nichols surreptitiously jotted down his findings with a contraband pencil on the only "writing" paper he could find — a roll of jail toilet paper.

Nichols described it as "a powerful experience, like visiting another planet, finding a level of consciousness you don't believe exists."

Nichols was booked into the Hall of Justice county jail last Friday. He was just another "fish" — new arrival.

They fingerprinted him, made him shower, skin-searched him for contraband, sprayed him with a stinging delousing disinfectant.

That afternoon Nichols was taken from his cell and lodged in a dark, bare isolation cell for hours. The only facility was the toilet — a hole in the floor.

He was returned to his regular cell to spend the night. The next morning, he and several other prisoners were handcuffed and transported in a sheriff's station wagon to the main jail near San Bruno, California.

Saturday afternoon, he and other inmates from his cell block were allowed to go out to the recreation yard. Nichols jogged, then played goalie on an improvised soccer team.

The next day, when the walls and the bars and the gray monotony began closing in and the noise from a blaring TV, the noise of images, got too much, Nichols found a form of escape. He sat on his bed doing Yoga breathing exercises.

Nichols, after his release yesterday, said the jails appeared to be well-run. The food? It was adequate "but heavy on the starches." He said he believed the jails appeared to be short-staffed and could use more deputy sheriff jailers.

The attorney records his experiences behind bars.
(Examiner photo by Judy Calson)

SILK WEB GENES

We dawned at Olduvai
And travel, you and I
To our world of dreams
Many Peoples, one being
follow the Road's adventure,
Evolve our common genes.

Journeys, always Journeys,
Riding ancient ways
To see ourselves in other's eyes
To better judge our days.

Homeward, even homeward,
Our ways are all the same,
Whether east or westward,
Risking death, seeking fame,
Seeing inward, flowing outward,
Mountain ice, fumes, and flame,
Stir gently, harshly, starward,
Pleasures, angers, pain.

The magic way still beckons
From Turkey to Xian
Where all those nation's peoples
Live, die, and get along.

Millenia of mixing
History's siren songs,
Of ideas, spirits, treasures,
Kingdoms, warriors, vict'ries, wrongs.

Judgment Day's approaching,
The mystery knot's undone
Mazda, God and Allah rule
"On the Silk Web you're all one."

— Alan H. Nichols
The Silk Web Cyclist

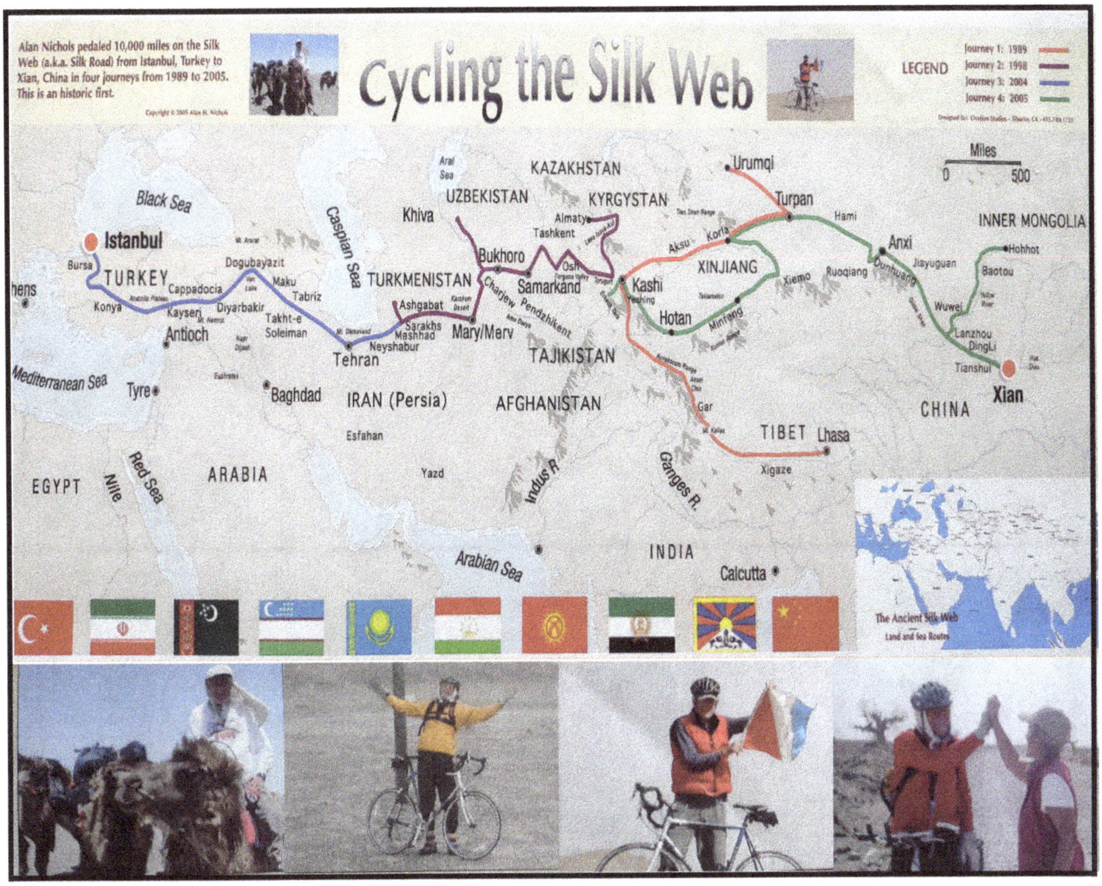
Alan Nichols pedaled 10,000 miles on the Silk Web (a.k.a. Silk Road) from Istanbul, Turkey to Xian, China in four journeys from 1989 to 2005. This is an historic first.
Cycling the Silk Web
LEGEND
Journey 1: 1989
Journey 2: 1998
Journey 3: 2004
Journey 4: 2005
Miles
0
500
Black Sea
Istanbul
Bursa
TURKEY
Konya
Cappadocia
Kayseri
Dogubayazit
Maku
Tabriz
Diyarbakir
Takht-e Soleiman
Antioch
Caspian Sea
TURKMENISTAN
Ashgabat
Sarakhs
Mashhad
Neyshabur
Tehran
Aral Sea
KAZAKHSTAN
UZBEKISTAN
KYRGYSTAN
Khiva
Bukhoro
Samarkand
Tashkent
Almaty
Osh
Mary/Merv
Charjew
Pendzhikent
TAJIKISTAN
AFGHANISTAN
IRAN (Persia)
Esfahan
Yazd
Baghdad
Tyre
Mediterranean Sea
EGYPT
Nile
Red Sea
ARABIA
Arabian Sea
Indus R.
INDIA
Ganges R.
Calcutta
Urumqi
Turpan
Hami
Aksu
Korla
Kashi
XINJIANG
Hotan
Minfeng
Xiemo
Ruoqiang
Anxi
Dunhuang
Jiayuguan
INNER MONGOLIA
Hohhot
Baotou
Wuwei
Lanzhou
DingLi
Tianshui
Xian
CHINA
Gar
TIBET
Lhasa
Xigaze
The Ancient Silk Web
Land and Sea Routes

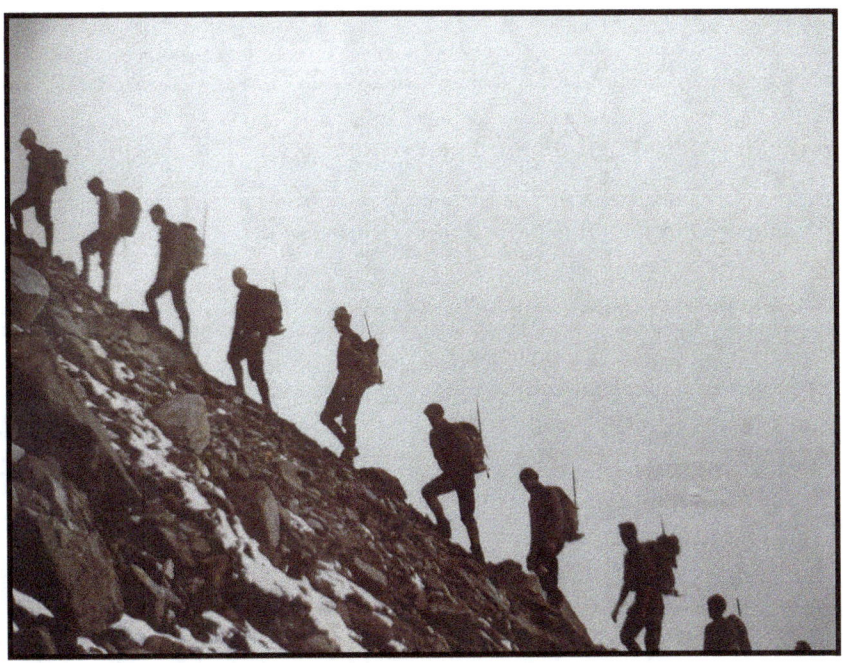

www.ingramcontent.com/pod-product-compliance
Lightning Source LLC
Chambersburg PA
CBHW081426070526
44586CB00020B/2502